The Down Syndrome Nutrition Handbook

A Guide to Promoting Healthy Lifestyles

Joan E. Guthrie Medlen, R.D., L.D.

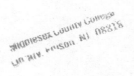

Middlesex County College
Edison, NJ 08818

Woodbine House ◆ 2002

© 2002 Woodbine House

All rights reserved under International and Pan-American copyright conventions. Published in the United States of America by Woodbine House, Inc., 6510 Bells Mill Road, Bethesda, MD 20817. 800-843-7323.
www.woodbinehouse.com

The Picture Communication Symbols © 1981-2002 Mayer-Johnson, Inc., Solana Beach, CA. Used with permission.

Photos of water bottles on inside front cover and of food items in Activity 3, Section 4, are from the *Picture This* CD-Rom and used by permission of Silver Lining Multimedia, Inc., Poughkeepsie, NY.

Library of Congress Cataloging-in-Publication Data

Medlen, Joan E. Guthrie
   The Down syndrome nutrition handbook : a guide to promoting healthy lifestyles / by Joan E. Guthrie Medlen. – 1st ed.
      p. cm.
   Includes biographical references and index.
   ISBN 1-890627-23-2
   1. Down syndrome—Nutritional aspects. 2. Down syndrome—Patients—Care. 3. Quality of life.   I. Title.
RC571.M43 2002
616.85'8842—dc21

                                                      2002010584

Manufactured in the United States of America
First Edition

10 9 8 7 6 5 4 3 2 1

To families of children with Down syndrome:
May your lives be full, happy, and healthy.

Table of Contents

SECTION FOUR: Learning Activities

APPENDICES

Acknowledgements

I used to wonder why authors thanked so many people in the acknowledgement section. Now I know why: writing a book is an enormous, collaborative task that is truly underestimated. It is impossible for me to thank everyone who has made a contribution. There are countless people who have touched my life and shaped my convictions about advocacy, nutrition education, and healthy lifestyles for people with Down syndrome. The following are only a few.

I would like to thank my parents, Curtis and Sharon Guthrie, for their unwavering support, patience, and childcare over the years. Most of all, thank you for ensuring my college education and giving me the opportunity to explore one of my childhood passions: food.

My gratitude for completing my college education at Kansas State University lies squarely on the shoulders of three women: Deborah Canter, Karen Greathouse, and Pat Freund. I enjoyed most of my instructors in the program, but the three of you kept me going and refused to let me give up when I was overwhelmed. Your friendship and love for my first son made all the difference in the world.

There are many educators and medical professionals who have been instrumental in my learning how to be a supportive, yet challenging dietitian and advocate for people with and without Down syndrome. Their contribution is priceless. They include: Doris Pavlukovich, Dennis McGuire, Brian Chicoine, Pat Winders, Patti McVay, Heidi Wilson, Luci Chiotti, Sheila Hebein, Patty Hall, George Capone, and the Down Syndrome Medical Interest Group. In addition, I would like to thank Kimberly Voss for her invaluable and effective coaching regarding communication and modifications. Without you, I would not be able to hear what my son and many other children and adults with Down syndrome have to say.

It is impossible to count the number of parents, families, and people with Down syndrome who have shaped my life as a parent and professional. Collectively, you have taught me the importance of honoring family values that make each family unique. In addition, families have solidified my belief that *everything* must be child-centered. When we focus on our children with and without Down syndrome, they will tell us what works and what doesn't. It saves a lot of time that way! Among those who deserve special attention are Donna and Joe Duffey, Jamie Todd, Greg Richards, Len Leshin, Nancy Scherbert, Mary Beth Paul, Mia Peterson,

Essie Pederson, Gretchen Koetters, John Manley, Kathy Becht, Susan Stokes, Howard Evans, and the families on the Down syndrome-autism listerv. In addition, I cannot forget the people who have given their time so I can have some time, especially Maria Baker.

The staff at Woodbine House has always had a special spot in my heart from the moment I realized they were responsible for publishing *Babies with Down Syndrome*—the first book I read after Andy was born. You all have put up with me for a very long time in a gracious, accepting, and enjoyable way. Your expertise and commitment to families is appreciated very much and your support of this project has been invaluable.

Last, and most important, I am indebted to my men: my husband, Rex, and my two boys, Ryan and Andy, for graciously sharing me with so many all these years. You are my heart and soul; without your support, nothing works.

Foreword

TIMOTHY P. SHRIVER, Ph.D.
President and Chief Executive Officer
Special Olympics International

Progress in the health, well-being, and success of people with mental retardation has, in many ways, resulted from the inquiry, dedication, and love of mothers and family members. When my mother, the sister of a woman with mental retardation, proposed the concept of competition and sports for children in the 1960s, expert opinion was not supportive. Pessimism, discouragement, and fatalistic foregone conclusions were what she encountered; passive existence in an institution was state-of-the art treatment for children with mental retardation at the time. In the subsequent thirty-five years, Special Olympics has shown that people with mental retardation can perform, excel, and thrive. Today, people with Down syndrome, mental retardation, and other developmental disabilities are contributing members of our workplaces and communities. More and more, this has become the expectation rather than the exception.

Breathtaking as the changes have been, progress has been incomplete. This is largely because so much remains either unknown or not compiled. Special Olympics sought the answer to a simple question—what is the overall health status of people with mental retardation in the United States? The data were difficult to find. Special Olympics commissioned researchers at Yale University to undertake a study to get the answers. Findings showed that people with mental retardation, including those with Down syndrome, have strikingly high rates of obesity, diabetes, and osteoporosis, leading to more frequent heart disease and shorter life expectancies.

The same gaps in awareness have existed in the areas of vision, auditory, and oral health. Until volunteers went and looked, it was generally unknown that 20-40 percent of children with mental retardation have unidentified (but correctable) eye, ear, and oral health problems. As a result, our organization has added vision, hearing, and dental programs to our sports events and is now focusing on ways to offer ongoing educational and practical opportunities to improve eating habits and physical fitness among the athletes.

Developing healthier habits and lifestyles is a challenge for the vast majority of us. People with Down syndrome often have the added obstacles of digestive systems with lower muscle tone and metabolisms that predispose to weight gain.

Nonetheless, better nutrition and fitness are the linchpins to any and all efforts to reverse the epidemic of obesity and its attendant diseases that afflict our population as a whole and people with mental retardation in particular. This is why this guide to better nutrition and healthier lifestyles—the first of its kind in the field of Down syndrome and mental retardation—is of pivotal importance.

Progress for people with mental retardation and developmental disabilities tends to follow a path that starts with necessity, travels through inquiry and discovery, and leads to knowledge and its applications. Typically, the pathfinders have been moms and dads. Joan Medlen is one such trailblazer. A registered dietitian by profession and the mother of a son with Down syndrome by happenstance, Joan has assembled what is known and what works best to optimize nutrition across a lifetime for people with Down syndrome. Drawing upon her experiences as a mother, a registered dietitian, and an editor of a publication for families interested in Down syndrome, her book combines science with good sense, facts with wisdom, and reality with hope. It is as indispensable a guide for parents who are raising a child with Down syndrome as it is for professionals who seek to lessen the health risks associated with Down syndrome. For the estimated 7.5 million people with mental retardation in the United States, Ms. Medlen has brought light and direction to a critical aspect of their health and well-being.

Introduction

*"The Troops and rangers along this side of the water call me Pathfinder
in as much as I have never been known to miss one end
of the trail when there was a friend who stood
in need of me at the other."*

—James Fenimore Cooper, *from* THE PATHFINDER

When my son with Down syndrome was born, there was so much to think about. My husband and I voraciously read the books given to us in those first weeks. Many of our questions were answered, yet for each one answered, a new one emerged. Over time, our concerns moved away from immediate medical issues to the everyday ones: feeding, constipation, introducing baby foods, our family meals, and so on. We participated in early intervention, which was a good experience for all of us. Yet I found that I still needed to read about Down syndrome to ensure we were using the most up-to-date methods and approaches to supporting our son.

I found information about how to use sign language to promote speech, methods for teaching reading, general medical information, information about inclusion, and information regarding the laws pertaining to special education services. There was, however, almost no information that was easy to access, understand, and apply to daily life about feeding, nutrition-related concerns, nutrition education, or building a healthy lifestyle for children, teens, or adults with Down syndrome. Some of the best information written about feeding children and the interactions between parents and children at mealtime exempted children with disabilities as a group. As a registered dietitian, I felt even more isolated without this much-needed information.

And so I realized that my role as a parent, for both of my boys, and with my fellow professionals was similar to *the Pathfinder's*. Parents and professionals stand in need at one end of the trail, seeking proactive information, education, and discovery about food, feeding, and family in a way that includes the twists and turns, as well as the fun of raising a child with Down syndrome. In this book you will find everything I have learned, experienced, and used to guide people with Down syndrome and their families on the various trails toward a healthier lifestyle that fits each person's needs, interests, and abilities. Use these tools as you begin or adjust your journey on your own path to a healthy lifestyle and to prepare or coach your child with Down syndrome on this.

Throughout each section I have embedded the strategies I have learned the last thirteen years to promote communication, choice making, and participation, and to understand and manage some of the common struggles families of children and adults with Down syndrome and those who work with them experience every day.

All of these strategies are founded on four basic assumptions:

TRUST

Any positive experience related to learning, whether it is learning how to eat, how to read, or how to make healthier choices, begins with trust. Your child needs the security of knowing you are not only listening to what he is saying, but also to what he isn't saying as he learns. He needs to know you will make the modifications and accommodations he needs to be successful. Last, he needs to be able to trust that you believe in him. Your child wants your unconditional support in learning, regardless of the topic. Try to avoid being judgmental or over-controlling in your child's experiences with food and activity.

Trust yourself. You have been in this relationship with your child longer than anyone. You know what motivates him, what annoys him, and how he will respond to different situations. Use that knowledge to your advantage. If something suggested in this book doesn't quite fit, alter it so it does. Trust your instinct about your child.

Last, these tenets regarding trust also apply to the people who work with your child. Professionals have an obligation to trust not only you, but your child as well. While professionals can provide guidance, support, and assistance, it must be applied within the values of the family, not the values of the professional. If you or your child do not trust that your uniqueness is valued, any advice, strategies, or suggestions offered will not be heard, nor should they be.

In short, experiences with food, feeding, and family are based on trusting each other to listen with the intent to hear and understand. Create an enriching, nurturing environment around your family's lifestyle while encouraging healthful choices.

CHOICE AND CONTROL

If there's one thing I've learned as a parent of a child with Down syndrome, it is the power of choice and the control that making those choices brings to a situation. Ensuring your child has choices about his food does not mean he is allowed *free* choice. It means creating situations in which your child makes choices within certain parameters and you follow through with them, *no matter what* he chooses. For example, when my son makes breakfast choices, he is only given choices that I am willing and able to make that day. Sometimes his options are diverse, while other times they are very discrete. As he takes on the chore of preparing his own breakfast, his choices will be limited in the same way mine are: "Do I have the food I need?" "How much time do I have?" "Do I have time to clean up?" "What do I feel like eating?"

We make choices all day long; it is a freedom we take for granted and view as an individual right. Many children, teens, and adults with Down syndrome do not have the same freedom to assume they will be "allowed" to choose even their own meals or mealtimes. So much of the day is controlled by others and often hinges on behavioral expectations. You have the opportunity to show your child from the moment he is born that his choice about food and feeding matters greatly. Learning to listen to your child's choices the same way you listen to the choices his siblings make is the first step to a healthy lifestyle for both of you.

The most difficult lesson for both you and your child is learning to accept "no" as his choice. It is, however, the most powerful choice you can teach your child: that you will accept "no thank you" without trying to change his mind. There will be times when your child says "no thank you" to everything you have cooked for no apparent reason. You must trust that he knows what he's doing (or teach about it later), and respect that clear answer. It's hard, but it is a powerful lesson. As he becomes confident with saying "no" to you, he will exert that power in other situations that involve food rather than learning to eat because he is expected to eat when he is offered food.

When our children, teens, and adults with Down syndrome learn that they can make healthy choices—and not so healthy choices—they experience control of their life. With control comes a sense of self-confidence and pride. As your child grows, try to provide choices that are diverse, challenging, and appropriate. Begin to broaden his choices in a way that nurtures responsibility. If you control your child's food and activity choices too tightly, even with the best of intentions, then expect him to take great pleasure, and even pride, in making choices you would not approve of whenever he can. It's human nature.

LIVING A HEALTHY LIFESTYLE IS A *CHOICE*

Changing well-worn habits and living a healthy lifestyle is also a choice. When your child is young, you influence that choice greatly. As he grows older and becomes more independent, only your child can choose to make changes, to learn to make balanced meals, or commit to regular exercise. You can encourage, teach, and model a healthy lifestyle, even sign him up for exercise class, but the choice to take action is his alone.

MODEL THE EXPECTED BEHAVIOR

It is well known that most children with Down syndrome are great imitators. One of the many benefits of an inclusive education and community is being around people of the same age, living a typical life, and modeling the expected behavior for our children to learn. Guess what? It's true at home too. In order for your child to choose to be healthy, you must choose to be healthy too. For parents of teens and adults, this is a great opportunity. If you would like to improve on some things in your lifestyle, do it with your child. There are many ways to do this: join a health club together, take up a new sport together, keep a food record together, learn to cook together. While you may need to do some things on your own, doing them together is very powerful.

The book is divided into four sections:
- Section One: Building Healthy Attitudes
- Section Two: Nutrition-Related Concerns for People with Down Syndrome

Much more work remains to be done to promote healthy living for children, teens, and adults with Down syndrome. This book is a step in that direction. There are many other people working to bring health information and healthy living up to a level families and adults with Down syndrome seek. As you discover helpful resources, programs, or strategies, share them with others. It is much easier to navigate the path to healthy, fulfilling lives together than to do it alone.

What lies at the end of the path you create with your child is unknown. Some adults with Down syndrome will be independent. Others will live with their parents or other family members all their lives. Some will be able to write prolifically; others will not. Some will be able to ride a bike; others will struggle to walk down the block. Regardless, your child with Down syndrome can choose to live life healthily. Let him define what that means by nurturing the areas he is most interested in. After all, a healthy lifestyle is merely a lifestyle that brings a sense of fulfillment and self-confidence, and promotes health rather than illness. It looks different for everyone, but everyone is included.

Section One:
Building Healthy Attitudes

CHAPTER 1

Successful Eating

The table is set, the food is in dishes to be served, and everyone is coming into the kitchen filled with their stories of the day. Each family member picks up a plate and begins to serve himself. Your oldest child stops for a minute to help your younger child, who has Down syndrome, fill a glass of milk. Your children, your spouse, and you have filled your plates—but not too full—and everyone seems happy with the food available to eat. As you all eat, everyone uses a fork or spoon, carries on a lively conversation, and eats most—if not all—of what is on their plate. No one chokes, spits, throws food across the room, or sits in a huff because they can't find anything they like. No one is being cajoled into eating something or asked to eat "just one bite" even though their face is green with the thought of it. In fact, the only time food enters the conversation is when someone comments on a new dish that has been prepared. As each person finishes their meal, they take their plate to the sink, scrape it, and put it in the dishwasher.

This is successful eating. It has a comfort to it similar to an old shoe. Everyone at the table knows what is expected of them. They know how to behave and use the utensils, and are comfortable with the setting and people around them.

Many of us take successful eating for granted, but it is one of the most complex things we do. We think of it as something everyone is born knowing how to do, but it is actually the culmination of dozens of developmental stages, experiences, and sensory skills. It is a process that takes years or decades to master. It's an awesome accomplishment, though we give it little thought. For children with Down syndrome, successful eating happens, but not without some bumps in the road along the way.

Essentially, there are three prongs to successful eating:

1. **Physical**—getting the food to your mouth, moving it around in your mouth, swallowing it;
2. **Sensory**—managing the smell, taste, feel, sight, and sound of food;
3. **Emotional**—managing how you feel about eating.

Each area is separately complex, with seemingly little in common, and yet they are inextricably linked to each other. There is no way to predict which areas your child will find easy and which will be difficult, either alone or in interaction with the other areas. As with other skills, each child with Down syndrome develops eating skills on his own timetable. Watch your child as he experiences the process of learning to eat and experience the process together.

The Physical Process (Oral-Motor Development)

Learning to eat foods, from the first bites of baby cereal to regular table foods, is a long process for any child. For children with Down syndrome, learning to coordinate tongue and mouth movements often takes longer and can cause parents concern. Your child might choke and gag frequently when you feed him. You might think your child is deliberately being a a picky eater or that he is going through a never-ending food jag. (A food jag occurs when a child relentlessly eats the same food, such as peanut butter and jelly sandwiches, sometimes for every meal.) Food jags are usually short-lived, but can seem like an eternity. Often, what the child needs at this stage is a little extra attention to his feeding skills to promote the tongue movements and muscles he needs to move on in the food continuum. That is, he may need help promoting the *oral-motor development* needed for eating. This is the process of developing the muscles and coordination to move foods around in your mouth, chew them, and swallow them.

It helps to understand the developmental stages and skills children must go through in learning to chew. This section discusses what chewing skills to look for before changing the texture of food and how to encourage and teach your child with Down syndrome to chew different foods. With this information you can sit back and enjoy the fun and messiness of discovering foods together with your child.

There is little information available to parents explaining what to look for when introducing new food textures to children with Down syndrome. Most information is written for children without disabilities and presents the introduction of different food textures as an age-related table. The ages recommended for different types of foods (strained baby food, pureed, ground, chopped foods) reflect the typical age that certain tongue and jaw movements develop. Some children with Down syndrome will follow the progression in these tables and experience little or no trouble with the introduction of foods or with chewing. Others will experience delays because of lower muscle tone, difficulties learning to coordinate their tongue movements, apraxia, or a smaller mouth cavity.

Understanding chewing development and the key tongue and jaw movements that signal readiness for a new food texture such as going from strained, pureed foods to thickened, pureed foods is essential to the process. (See table on next page.) Rather than using your child's age to decide when to introduce a new texture, I suggest you watch your child eat and look for the emerging skills that signal he is ready to progress.

MAKING THE
TRANSITION
FROM MILK TO
TABLE FOODS

SUCKLING AND EARLY SUCKING

Before your baby is offered his first bite from a spoon, he is getting his food through breast- or bottle feeding. (See Chapter 2 for more information.) The mechanism for swallowing during that time is called *suckling*. Suckling is accomplished by thrusting the tongue out and pulling it back, making forward and backward jaw movements, and loosely closing the lips around the nipple. This movement is a reflex that most children are born with. Your baby learns to eat voluntarily through the reflexive movement of suckling.

Developmental Progression of Oral Motor Skills and Food Textures

Food Type	Pre Food	Puree	Thick Puree	Ground	Choppped Foods	Table Foods
Chewing Stages	Suckling	Sucking	Strong Sucking Early Munching	Munching	Beginning movement of tongue to follow foods. Chew is more rotary than up-and-down.	Mature, rotary chew
Feeding Skills to Note	Rooting	Attempts to hold bottle. Decrease in gag reflex.	Shows interest in "guiding" spoon.	Decrease in gag reflex. Increased use of cup. Grasps spoon to play with.	Assists with feeding and drinking with increasing independence.	Messy self-feeder, switching back-and-forth between utensils and fingers.
Types of foods to offer	Breast milk or formula	Infant cereals should resemble a "heavy thick liquid" or applesauce. Other foods include blended, strained, baby foods (jar or home made).	Gradually increase the thickness of pureed foods with baby cereal, wheat germ, or potato flakes. Introduce hard munchables.	Mashed, cooked vegetables, scrambled egg, mashed soft-boiled egg, cottage cheese. Introduce meltable hard solids.	Chop regular table foods in small, fine pieces. Introduce finger foods that are easily chewed. Introduce soft cubed foods (cheeses).	Monitor easy-choke foods for safety. Modify list as appropriate. Introduce crunchy and chewy foods to build jaw strength.
Indications for next step	The beginning of a sucking motion.	Strong, well-developed sucking motion.	Emergence of up-and-down chewing motions.	Side-to-side movement of food with tongue.	Individualize for preferences and abilities.	
Cautions			Heed choking precautions. Always hold on to one end of edible hard muchables.	Do NOT mix textures (such as spaghetti with meat sauce or meatballs, peas in mashed potatoes, etc).		

© 2000
Joan E. Guthrie Medlen, R.D.

Throughout those first months of breast- or bottle feeding, your baby builds strength in his tongue and mouth and a new swallowing pattern called *sucking* begins to emerge. Sucking includes a more rhythmic up-and-down jaw movement, an elevation of the tip of the tongue, and a firm closure of the lips around the nipple, which creates a negative pressure in your baby's mouth. In typically developing children, this sucking period usually begins between four and six months of age and is when the first bites of baby food, usually very thin rice cereal, are introduced.

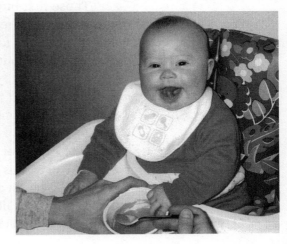

If your baby is drinking well from the breast or bottle at four to six months of age, there is no reason not to introduce him to cereal at this age.

Introducing Foods to Your Baby

Rice cereal is the most commonly used first food for babies because it will take on the flavor of the milk you mix it with and it is the cereal least likely to cause an allergic reaction. You want these first bites of cereal to be more liquid than cereal. They should be only slightly thicker than milk. Use a very small, flat bowled spoon that allows your child to suck the food off the spoon.

There's no hurry to introduce new foods. Your child is getting most of his calories and nutrition from breast milk or formula at this stage. The purpose of introducing new foods is to add variety to your child's eating, promote eating skills, and enjoy the experience of eating together.

Once your child is eating food from a spoon, it is important to introduce new foods in a systematic manner. Make an effort to introduce one new food at a time and wait three to five days before introducing another new food. The reason for waiting a few days in between new foods is to help identify any food intolerances your child may have. If you have just introduced wheat cereal and your baby develops a rash, it makes it easy to know which food may have been the culprit. Stop feeding your baby that food, wait five days to make sure the rash has cleared, and try the same food again. If he develops a rash again, stop feeding the food and consult your pediatrician.

There are a number of different opinions about the best order for introducing food groups. I like the following progression: cereals, vegetables, fruit, and meat. I like this progression because it does not promote the sweeter foods first. Meat is usually introduced last due to the grainy texture.

Remember, the main goal of feeding your child baby food at this stage is to help him learn to enjoy food and the experience of eating. Nutrition is secondary for quite a while yet.

Those first bites of baby cereal are very messy. Generally, babies lose a certain amount of the cereal as they try to coordinate their tongue and jaw movements to handle this new, foreign food. Babies with Down syndrome often lose more food than those without Down syndrome as they coordinate these movements. If too much food is lost, your baby's jaw movements may still be more of a *suckling* pattern—tongue and jaw thrusts resulting in loss of food—than a *sucking* pattern. A good rule of thumb is if your baby with Down syndrome seems to be losing 75 percent or more of the food from each bite, it might be best to wait a few days and try a bite of cereal again. It may be hard to tell what 75 percent of a spoonful of food is. Use this as a guide: if more comes out than stays in or your baby seems to be struggling with more than just the surprise of a new substance in his mouth, you might want to wait a few days. If you need to wait, don't panic. Try to keep the experience fun each time you introduce your baby to baby cereal.

Your baby's first bite of baby cereal is a big event for everyone. Not only is it a new developmental stage, it is a change in the relationship between your baby and everyone around him. Eating from a spoon requires more participation and interaction from you and your baby. Those who feed him will learn to listen to his cues regarding how fast or slow to present each bite. In these early interactions the groundwork is laid for other give-and-take situations. It is a natural time for parent and child to develop an awareness of overall body tone and stamina, and to develop a feeling of mutual trust and respect.

Once your child is eating baby cereal successfully, follow the typical pattern for introducing first baby foods. This category of foods is called strained, pureed foods, and includes baby cereals; jarred, strained baby foods; and homemade, pureed, strained foods.

Give yourself and your baby some time together at this stage. It takes practice to develop a rhythm you are both comfortable with. If mealtimes seem to be stressful for you or your baby, consider what is going on around you.

- Is the television on?
- Are people running in and out asking questions?
- Are you constantly interrupted?
- Is the sun shining in your baby's eyes?

It is important to keep these early exposures to food pleasant for your baby. You want him to associate eating with good feelings and positive interactions with those around him. If he is overwhelmed by noise or activity, he may be too distracted to focus on the experience of learning to eat.

At this stage, some children with Down syndrome have tongue thrusting movements. When a child has a tongue thrust, his tongue moves in and out of his mouth, and he loses some food as he eats. If your baby is eating without coughing or gagging, then he has most likely found a way to use his tongue movements in a safe way. If he is coughing, gasping, gulping, or gagging after most bites of food, check with your doctor or speech-language pathologist to make sure he is swallowing safely.

TIPS AND TRICKS FOR EARLY FEEDING

If your baby continues to lose a lot of food with each bite due to jaw and tongue thrusts, there are some things you can do to help him learn to control his mouth and tongue while eating:

- **Check your child's positioning.** The best position is as near a sitting position as possible, with his legs, head, back, and feet supported as needed. Talk about seating with your child's early intervention provider or occupational therapist about your child's positioning. He may benefit from some additional support in the seat or a different type of seat (infant seat, highchair, and so on) for better positioning. Do not spoon feed your child in an infant walker. A walker promotes a different posture and may make it more difficult for your child to manage food in his mouth or swallow safely.
- **Your baby should be able to look straight ahead at the person feeding him.** Looking up to see the person feeding him causes him to lift his head back and makes swallowing more difficult.

- **For the very first bites of food, use an infant-sized spoon with a shallow bowl to feed your child.** As he grows, you may want to consider a coated spoon to protect his gums if he decides to bite down hard on the edge of the spoon. Avoid using spoons that are designed primarily to entertain the feeder—such as this spoon shaped like an airplane.

- As your child begins to hold the spoon, even if only to play the drums on his highchair tray or table, **give him a spoon with a thick, easy-to-hold handle.**

- **Food should be warm, like breast milk or formula, for the first feedings.**

- **Spoonsful of food should be small.** Too much food makes the process more tiring and frustrating for both of you. It's easier for your baby to move a small amount of food around in his mouth than a large one. It's less messy, too.

- **Present the spoon from slightly below your baby's mouth.** As he accepts the spoon, place the bowl of the spoon firmly (but do not push hard) on the center-front of his tongue. This helps him keep his jaw and tongue from thrusting forward.

- **Remove the spoon straight out of his mouth (do not lift the spoon to scrape food off).** This will encourage him to use his lips to close around the spoon to get the food.

- **Watch your baby's cues.** Learning to handle food is not easy. Wait for him to completely finish his bite before offering him another. It may take him extra time to coordinate his movements between bites. Watch for his receptiveness for each bite rather than providing the next spoonful of food before he is ready.

- **Watch for signs of fatigue.** Tiring early in a meal is very common for children with Down syndrome, particularly in the beginning stages of eating. Try not to push your baby past his limit to frustration. If he tires too early to get enough calories, consider more frequent meals for him (six to eight times in a day). Focus on increasing the length of each meal until one or more can be eliminated from the daily schedule without sacrificing calories. Babies begin by eating only one to two tablespoons of food at a time. By the time they are a year old, serving sizes are about one-fourth cup of each entrée. While they seem to eat all the time, babies need very little volume of food at this time. A good resource for learning about amounts of food to feed babies is: *Child of Mine, Feeding with Love and Good Sense* by Ellyn Satter.

- As your child begins to scoop foods on his own, **use a bowl with a straight side so he can push the spoon up against it to gather the food.**

PROGRESSING TO THICKENED FOODS

PROFICIENT SUCKING

As your baby gets accustomed to strained, pureed foods, he will begin to develop a strong *sucking* action. With time, he will develop a stronger sucking action, which is a sign to begin thickening his foods. While eating these thickened, pureed foods, your child learns to use his tongue to move food from side-to-side in his mouth. Moving food from side-to-side is one of the skills he will need to be able to move foods in his mouth to his molars to be chewed. This same movement develops strength in his tongue, which is also important for developing speech.

To thicken foods, add instant potato flakes, wheat germ, bread crumbs, or dry baby cereals. Using wheat germ to thicken foods is also an excellent way to increase fiber, which is especially important if your child is having trouble with constipation (see Chapter 5). When you thicken strained, pureed foods, there are a few things to remember:

- Foods will continue to thicken after you are done mixing. Check the consistency of the food every three bites or so. You may need to add some liquid so it doesn't become too pasty.
- Use a thickener (baby cereal, potato flakes, and so on) that makes sense for the food you are thickening. Strained pears with baby oatmeal have a funny flavor. Rice cereal might be a better choice because it has a less distinctive flavor.

PHASIC BITE REFLEX

As he becomes proficient with thickened, pureed foods, your child will develop what is called a *phasic bite reflex*. This is a rhythmic bite-and-release pattern that looks like he is opening and closing his mouth when something touches his gums (a toy, a spoon, some baby food, or your finger). This is a good time to let him explore chewing on different things. This exploration has a purpose with two basic goals: to help develop his chew, and to expose his mouth to a variety of textures. If your child doesn't explore chewing on his own, you will want to introduce a category of foods and toys called *hard munchables*. Hard munchables are for oral exploration only. Your child should not be able to get a piece of them in his mouth by biting on them. Hard munchables are most often toys: Duplos, rubber figures, spoons from the kitchen, and so forth. Foods that are considered hard munchables include bagel strips, raw carrot sticks, frozen waffles, jicama, baby pretzels, and maybe jerky.

Letting your child explore a hard munchable food is a supervised, two-person activity. Place a hard munchable food such as a bagel strip on the molar area of your child's gums on one side of his mouth. Hold on to one end of the bagel strip while your child chews on the other end. When it gets mushy or looks like it might break off, remove the strip for a new one. If this seems too complicated, nonfood hard munchables will do the trick as long as they are safe and age-appropriate.

What IS a "Hard Munchable?"

"Hard munchables" are things that are acceptable for a child to chew on and too tough for him to bite off a piece to actually eat. Anytime your child is chewing on a hard munchable food item he must be supervised.

Hard munchables include:

- Spoons, toys, teething items
- Strips of buttered bagel
- Raw carrot sticks
- Large pretzels
- Jicama sticks

They are NOT for eating! If a food hard munchable such as a raw carrot stick is used, you must monitor carefully. If your child breaks off a piece, be ready to swish your finger through his mouth and remove it.

ADDING MORE TEXTURE TO FOODS

MUNCHING

The next chewing stage to look for is *munching,* which occurs when your child moves food in his mouth by flattening and spreading his tongue while moving his jaw up and down. Some children with Down syndrome may initially munch by flattening food with the tongue on the roof of the mouth and then pushing outward with the tongue to move the food while opening the mouth.

When you see your child is beginning to *munch,* it is time to introduce some finely ground foods, such as cooked, mashed vegetables; scrambled eggs; or cottage cheese. This is your child's first experience with texture in his food. He may be surprised or react strongly. Be prepared for a lot of messes. If he rejects a food (throws it, spits it out, smears it all over), don't take it personally. Offer a small amount again in a few days. Eventually the food will make it to his mouth.

It is not uncommon for children with Down syndrome to continue to struggle with oral motor development at this stage. You may see your child moving food from side to side with his tongue, but his tongue may come out of his mouth in the process. Or he may seem confused about which way he wants his mouth to go as he starts to use the up-and-down motion of munching. It's all a part of the process of learning how to manage food in his mouth. Some children may find ways to move foods with their tongue that is slightly different from what is considered "typical." Again, if your child is choking, gasping, or gagging a lot, ask for help from your doctor or speech-language pathologist. If, however, he is handling foods without choking or gagging, but is having trouble coordinating his chewing or tongue, here are some things you can do to help encourage his eating skills:

- **During a meal, sit directly in front of your child.** Place your thumb in the middle of his chin just below his lower lip. Extend your index finger so it follows his jawbone back to the joint of his jawbone. Curve your middle finger so it rests under his jaw on his chin. Gently encourage his jaw movements in an up-and-down action. Do not force this movement. If he protests and asks you to remove your hand, it's best to respect his wishes.
- **Place food (scrambled eggs and small graham cracker pieces work well) between his gums or molars on one side of his mouth.** This encourages him to move his tongue to get the food.
- **If your child seems to prefer to chew on one side of his mouth, place food on the other side.** This works especially well if it is a favorite food.
- **Offer toasted bread strips, strips of soft cheese, and other appropriate finger foods.** It is safest to hold on to one end of the food as he chews so he doesn't get too much at once.
- **Do not mix food textures!** Foods that have more than one type of texture, such as Spagettio's® , most junior foods (spaghetti with meatballs), or lumpy ground foods, require different chewing movements. It is confusing to your child to have more than one texture to deal with in a bite of food.
- **To encourage him to move his tongue from side-to-side (a skill needed for rotary chewing), offer an ice**

What Is That Noise?

Children with Down syndrome may be more likely to choke, gag, or aspirate foods than other children. There are a number of reasons for this, including: sensitive gag reflex, difficulty coordinating mouth movements for swallowing, or being distracted. Usually your child will make some great noises and let you know that he is having trouble. Remember, this is a sign that your child is not physically ready for the type of food you are giving him.

Another type of swallowing concern that is more difficult to detect is called silent aspiration. This typically happens when your child is drinking. You may hear him make little chirpy noises, as if he is swallowing air, after taking a drink or while drinking from his bottle or cup. This means that some of that liquid was going down his throat before he was ready—and perhaps into his lungs.

If your child chokes or gags frequently or seems to take three or four swallows for a swig of milk, visit a speech-language pathologist for a swallowing evaluation. He may need to drink thickened liquids for a while as he learns to swallow more safely or practice specific mouth movements to develop different muscles and skills.

cream cone to lick and try to vary the position he licks it from, or place small dabs of smooth peanut butter or another sticky food in the corners of his mouth to lick off.

As your child develops his munching skills, it is time to introduce foods called *meltable hard solids*. These are foods that dissolve in the mouth with saliva only and require little or no pressure from a chewing motion to eat. They include Cheerios, graham crackers, and baby crackers. If your child is older at this stage, include more age-appropriate foods such as Cheetos, chocolate (no nuts), Pringles, and Jello.

Remember, it is very important not to introduce your child to mixed textures yet. As he becomes more proficient with mashed table foods and meltable hard solids separately, he will begin to develop the necessary movements and sensory-related skills to effectively manage different textures together in his mouth.

What Is a "Meltable Hard Solid?"

A meltable hard solid food is a food that is hard, but will melt as your child gums it. Unlike a munchable hard solid, these foods are generally safe for your child to gnaw on without your direct involvement. Some meltable hard solids include:

- Zwieback toast
- Teething cookies
- Soft cheese
- Graham crackers

This is a good time to begin watching for the side-to-side movement of your child's tongue while he eats, which signals he is ready for the next stage of chewing. This is the same type of reflexive movement you may have experienced when you visit the dentist. Whenever something is put in your mouth, your tongue tends to follow it around and get in the way. This is what you are looking for in your child. One way to check for this reflex is to hold on to a baby biscuit or strip of toast as he begins to chew on it. If you see his tongue come naturally to the center of his mouth and try to push the food over to the side or if he moves his tongue to meet the strip of toast you placed on his molars (or gums), he is probably ready.

HINT: Some children do better moving foods around with their tongue if they have a strong or spicy flavor. For hard munchables, food such as spiced jerky or a big mustard-flavored pretzel will work. Some people add a small amount of tabasco or red pepper spice to eggs, spaghetti sauce, and other foods. The extra bite to the flavor raises the child's awareness of where foods are in his mouth. Using very cold foods such as ice cream or popsicles is also effective for some children. Don't be afraid of letting your child try a bite of spicy or cold food; he may surprise you.

MOVING FOODS SIDE-TO-SIDE

When your child is able to move foods from side-to-side with his tongue, it is time to introduce *finely chopped foods*. Use foods from the family meal that you chop very small. It's best to begin with foods that are easy to chew, such as chopped pasta, cooked vegetables, cooked potatoes (without the skin), or canned or very ripe fruits. Let him watch you remove his food from serving dishes so he sees it is the same as what the rest of the family is eating. This usually makes these new foods particularly interesting to experiment with and eventually eat. As he becomes comfortable with finely chopped foods, gradually increase the size of his foods to bite-sized pieces.

It is at this point, when your child is comfortable with soft mashed table foods, thick purees, and finely chopped foods *separately*, that you can introduce foods with mixed textures. As with all the stages, if he chokes, gags, or coughs repeatedly, wait a few days and try again. If he seems to get stuck at this spot, consult your physician or speech-language pathologist for possible medical reasons he may be having trouble. Some of the things they will consider include:

- Your child's swallowing mechanism. Some children swallow in a way that causes them to aspirate or send food down their esophagus to their lungs rather than to their stomach.
- Your child's gag reflex. Sometimes children will have an extra sensitive gag reflex. If so, a speech-language pathologist can work with your child to make him less sensitive to the feeling of foods too early in the swallowing process.
- If your child is swallowing safely, an occupational therapist may want to determine if he is sensitive to certain types of textures.

During this time, your child will slowly work toward a *mature rotary chew*, using the tongue to move food from side-to-side in the mouth along with a coordinated movement of the jaw in vertical, lateral (side-to-side), and diagonal movements. A mature rotary chew looks like a smooth, circular motion while the jaw opens and closes to chew. For many children, with and without Down syndrome, this is easy to observe because it is difficult to do with the lips together, eliciting the familiar comment, "chew with your mouth closed!"

In elementary school, a new tooth-related concern may begin to emerge. Children with Down syndrome do not always lose their baby teeth and when they do, they are not always replaced with permanent teeth. You can find this out by asking your dentist to take x-rays when your child is young. If x-rays show there are some permanent teeth missing, you may want to pay close attention to your child's dental hygiene habits. For instance, is he brushing his teeth at least two times a day? Do you avoid sticky sweet candy such as gummy bears?

Our son has lost all the baby teeth that will have permanent teeth come in after them. X-rays show that he does not have adult teeth for his bottom four front teeth. This affects his ability to bite things off using the front of his mouth. He avoids biting off sandwiches by taking them apart and eating them one component at a time (bread, pickles, meat, cheese, lettuce and so on). One day I watched him eating and realized he tends to introduce foods that need to be chewed on the sides of his mouth on his molars right away. It is interesting to see how children adapt their eating styles appropriately.

The delayed eruption of teeth in the beginning of life may continue through middle school. One mother shared with me her frustration in understanding her

Promoting Dental Health

There are some basic rules to promoting healthy teeth that begin when your child is an infant:

- Find a pediatric dentist who is familiar with children who have Down syndrome and visit regularly.
- Avoid nursing bottle syndrome. Don't let your baby or toddler fall asleep with a bottle in his mouth.
- Limit foods that are high in sugar and sticky, such as raisins and gummy-type treats.
- Choose snacks that are crunchy and do not stick to your child's teeth, whenever possible.
- Brush and floss teeth at least once a day. Brushing after each meal and snack is the best approach, but may not always be practical.
- If your local water does not contain fluoride, use a toothpaste that does or ask your child's physician or dentist for a prescription flouride supplement.

Remember, good dental health and good nutrition are partners in your child's overall health. A well-balanced diet is one of the primary defenses against gum disease and problems with tooth development.

eleven-year-old son's moods. When they went to the dentist, she learned that his six-year *and* his twelve-year molars were erupting at the same time. How painful that must have been some days. Obviously, tooth eruption will affect food choices. When teeth are erupting, it is likely your child will choose softer foods to avoid aggravating the gums.

Last, some children with Down syndrome grind their teeth. Over time, this grinding may flatten the shape of molars, making it difficult to chew some foods. While I'm not sure what the solution is, it is something to consider if your child is avoiding foods that are hard to chew, crunchy, or chewy. It is a good idea to consult with a dentist who has experience with people who have Down syndrome or other disabilities about tooth-related concerns. The more you know about any problem, the easier it is to have realistic expectations.

Sensory Stages of Learning to Eat

Everyone has a picture of their child gleefully covered in food or diving hands first into their birthday cake. For every child, the process of learning to eat includes this kind of serious sensory play and exploration. Children with Down syndrome are no different. In fact, they may have a greater need to explore and understand food before they decide it's safe to eat.

Eating is one of the few things we do that uses all of our senses:

- We smell the food while it's cooking and when it's on our plate.

- We hear it being prepared. We hear it when we chew it too.
- We see the food when it is presented to us. We also see it while it's being prepared.
- We feel it either when we pick it up in our hands or in our mouth. If we're lucky we feel it both ways.
- We taste it if we put it in our mouth.
- We need to be able to balance ourselves to coordinate the movements required to pick it up and eat it.
- We need to have an understanding of our body. Once we eat the food, we need to know where it went and how to follow it in our mouth with our tongue and not lose it.
- And last, we need to agree to swallow it. Swallowing a food is a commitment to allowing it to become a part of us.

When you look at it this way, it is easy to see that eating a food is far more than learning to chew or picking it up and putting it in our mouth. It's a big commitment for your child to agree to put that foreign object in his mouth, and swallowing is an entirely different decision. This decision-making process is more obvious if your child has sensory-related concerns (from a delayed introduction to eating, sensory integration disorders, or autistic spectrum disorder). For instance, some children cannot stand the smell of a particular food, such as Brussels sprouts. Every time they smell Brussels sprouts cooking they head for the hills, screaming. Put one on his plate and he'll send it careening across the room. Ask him to eat one bite? Not likely. And yet, your child has never even tasted a Brussels sprout.

For children with sensory issues related to food, *anything* out of the normal routine causes an extreme reaction. A new food on your child's plate causes mayhem to break loose. Sometimes children won't eat foods if they are touching each other. Sometimes children avoid a particular texture or color of food. Regardless of the rate they pass through the sensory stages to eating, every child goes through a similar process before eating a new food.

Some children with Down syndrome struggle with food acceptance; others do not. For those who do, a small portion struggle with the oral motor demands of learning to eat. Some may have had a delayed introduction to foods because of tube feedings or other medical procedures, while others may have trouble learning to safely swallow. Eating becomes a fretful event that is a lot of hard work. Other children with Down syndrome have sensory barriers to food progression along with emotional barriers (see the next section on Emotional Stages to Eating).

You should not worry a lot about whether or not your child is going to have these difficulties. Instead, try to be sensitive to the complexity of the process of learning to eat new foods for every child from a sensory point of view. As you consider these concepts, you will begin to understand your child's individual preferences and how to successfully introduce new foods to him.

THE SENSORY STAGES OF EATING

In her work as a feeding therapist, Kay Toomey, Ph.D., suggests that the stages to eating as they relate to sensory systems can be thought of as a staircase. (See the table on the next page.) Each forward movement leads to another, which eventually leads to eating the food. For some children this may take five steps. For others it may take thirty or even seventy. As you listen to your child and watch how he responds at each stage, you will begin to understand the pattern that works best for him.

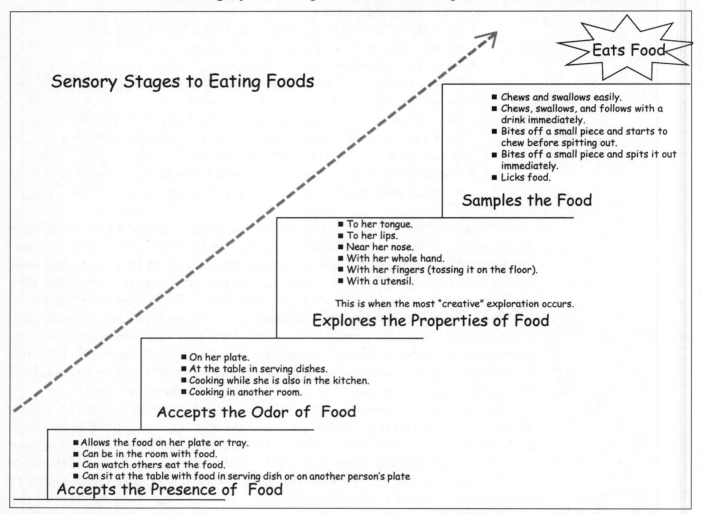

Sensory Stages to Eating Foods

Eats Food

■ Chews and swallows easily.
■ Chews, swallows, and follows with a drink immediately.
■ Bites off a small piece and starts to chew before spitting out.
■ Bites off a small piece and spits it out immediately.
■ Licks food.

Samples the Food

■ To her tongue.
■ To her lips.
■ Near her nose.
■ With her whole hand.
■ With her fingers (tossing it on the floor).
■ With a utensil.

This is when the most "creative" exploration occurs.

Explores the Properties of Food

■ On her plate.
■ At the table in serving dishes.
■ Cooking while she is also in the kitchen.
■ Cooking in another room.

Accepts the Odor of Food

■ Allows the food on her plate or tray.
■ Can be in the room with food.
■ Can watch others eat the food.
■ Can sit at the table with food in serving dish or on another person's plate

Accepts the Presence of Food

Adapted from "Steps to Eating" by Kay A. Toomey, Ph.D., Denver, CO
J.E. G. Medlen, R.D., 2000.

The process is something like a task analysis: you must break the process of eating a food into the smallest steps needed by your child.

Step 1: Tolerating the Food. The first step is to *tolerate* the food. To tolerate a food means your child will tolerate the existence of the food in the same space (house, room, table, plate). For most children this step involves the introduction of a new food to the family table. They are not required to do anything but allow it to be on the table. Some things that might happen during this stage include:

■ Discussing the name of the food and how it is prepared.
■ Showing your child the food while you are preparing it.
■ Letting him help with the preparation if he wants.
■ If your meal is served "family style," passing the serving dish around the table.
■ After a time, putting the food on the child's plate with no other conditions.

In most situations, you will present this new food as a side dish or extra choice at the family table. It is important that you and others at the meal eat the food (unless it's something really esoteric like escargot). Your child's goal is to merely allow the food to be there without making a fuss. If your child chooses to do more, then go with it. For some kids and with some foods, this will be all they are willing to do the first few times they are introduced to a food. Don't take it personally. Be unemotional about the situation. You will try again another day.

Step 2: Smelling the Food. It is difficult to see how smelling the food is different from tolerating a food since many foods have an odor when they are prepared. However, some foods do not have an obvious odor when they are placed at the table or the odor becomes more intense when right under your nose. In this case, your child might:

- Lean down to smell the food on his plate.
- Get close to the food preparation area to see how it smells.
- Watch you smell the food in a dramatic way.
- Talk about how the food smells.
- Talk about how the smell of the food changes as it is prepared.

Step 3: Handling the Food. Handling the food means your child touches the food in some way, including mashing, twirling, poking, tossing, and wearing it. This is when kids learn what food is made of. The goal of this stage is to be able to experience food in so many ways that it is no longer foreign and less challenging to your child to put in his mouth. If your child seems cautious about touching foods, you can help him by using food in a playful way in an activity. You might:

- Let him help prepare the food using his hands. Make a mess of it.
- Let him help serve the food to others, as well as himself.
- Serve foods with your hands.
- Eat with your hands.
- Put sauces on the food with your fingers.
- Make "art" with the food rather than eating it.
- Lick the food—or serve it on a stick to encourage that.

When you do these things, encourage your child to join in without being pushy. Sometimes all it takes is for your child to see that food can be fun without eating it to make him curious enough to try it. As he plays with the food, he will eventually get it all over himself and even into his mouth. He may not even know that he did it.

Step 4: Tasting the Food. *Tasting* food comes next. Although this means your child will get it to his mouth, it doesn't always mean he will chew and swallow it. Most parents have memories of putting something in their mouth and being so overwhelmed by the taste or how it felt in their mouth (too spicy, too slimy, and so forth) that they spit it out before realizing what they had done. When your child spits something out, it's no different. The food didn't taste or feel the way he thought it would. This does not necessarily mean that he doesn't like it. You won't know until he tries again and again—it may take many more exposures to the food.

For parents, the hardest part about this stage is not insisting that everyone "just try one bite." Try to encourage your child to taste new foods (by licking or being allowed to spit the food out if he doesn't like it), but don't push him. If you push too hard each time, your child may feel forced into tasting new foods. Sometimes this leads to refusal of all new foods because new foods are associated with negative emotions. Take your time. Watch him subtly toy with the idea. Some ways you can encourage him without pressure include:

- Talk about how the food tastes as *you* eat it.
- Ask others at the table how they like the food.
- Make sure your child has something to drink to "wash the food down" after his first taste.
- If your child tries a bite, do not praise him. Ask him what he thought of the food, whether he swallows it or not.
- If your child is not yet talking and tries a bite, comment on the face he makes and validate what he is communicating. ("Oh, you scrunched your nose up! Does it feel funny?")
- When the meal is over, tell him how much you enjoyed his presence at the meal.

Step 5: Eating the Food. The last stage is actually *eating* the food. Your child is comfortable with it, picks it up, and chews and swallows comfortably. Each time your child successfully reaches this last stage, his repertoire of foods increases a little more. He won't require the same amount of time to accept every food. The more foods he adds, the easier it will be for him to add other new foods.

As you can see, the sensory stages of eating go hand-in-hand with the physical stages of learning to eat. Most children with Down syndrome will progress through the stages seamlessly. A small number of children with Down syndrome will develop oral motor skills and yet eat only a very limited number of foods. Even though they can chew and swallow well, they choose to eat a limited selection of foods with a variety of textures. For these children, paying attention to the sensory stages to eating is more important. Every child, however, will dislike certain foods and may never eat them just like everyone else.

TIPS FOR INTRODUCING NEW FOODS

- **Review the "Sensory Stages to Eating Foods."** Many children with Down syndrome will combine the first two stages. However, the overall process is the same for everyone in your family.
- **Remember the "Rule of Ten." (It takes ten exposures to a new food before a person is ready to try it.)** Be prepared for something more like the "rule of 50" or perhaps 500.
- **When planning the meal, make certain there is at least one food each person likes offered as well as**

Picky Eating, Oral-Motor Concerns, or Food Jag! Which *IS* it?

Dietary Cues to Low Oral-Motor Tone:
- Prolonged bottle use or breastfeeding
- Desires sweets and other low nutrient foods (fries, chips...)
- Slow to progress through food textures
- May not enjoy eating in general

Dietary Cues to Picky Eating:
- Skipping food groups
- Over-use of supplements to fill in dietary gaps
- Variable eating: What he will eat changes with the environment
- Seeks attention or control during mealtimes

Dietary Cues to Food Jags:
- Requesting the same one or two items every day, for every meal, if given the option.
- Will accept other foods if not given a choice or given structured choices ("Do you want an apple or an orange?" instead of, "What do you want to eat?").
- Food selected lasts for a period of time, then is replaced by another absolute favorite

the new food. This reduces the unspoken pressure to try a foreign-looking entrée to satisfy hunger.
- **Introduce new foods as a side dish**—an option—the first few times rather than as the main dish.
- **Talk about the new food.** Share with others why you chose it, what it tastes like, how you prepared it, what foods it is similar to that they already eat.
- **Avoid commenting when your child—or anyone—decides to put the food on his plate or in his mouth.**
- **Avoid pressure tactics for trying new foods.** Do not use the "just one bite" rule.
- **Let your child help prepare the new dish.** Talk about what you are putting in it as you make it together.
- **Let your child choose which new food to try** from a group of three or four new foods or recipes.

Emotional Stages to Eating

Generally, eating and learning to eat are pleasant experiences. When your child is an infant, you focus on creating a nurturing bond between you and your baby while you feed him. As he grows, it is important to have a positive feeding

> *Many children have a past history that has given feeding a bad rap. Our son had a long history of aspiration (getting milk in his lungs while drinking a bottle), reflux, and a slow-to-empty stomach. All these things contributed to him not feeling hungry. Because of his low muscle tone, he had trouble swallowing and moving the food around in his mouth. For him, eating was painful and frustrating. All babies have a natural instinct to avoid doing painful things. And if eating hurts, then eating is something to avoid. We had to take away the pain of eating before Zac could overcome his fear of the pain he had always known from eating.*

relationship for your child to feel comfortable with eating and choosing foods. (For more information about the feeding relationship, see Chapter 3.)

However, sometimes, children learn that eating is not a pleasant experience. This usually is the result of a medical trauma that is unavoidable, but leaves a child fearful of eating and the process of eating. For instance, children who have multiple surgeries with ventilation or prolonged tube feeding may be anxious about having things near their mouth. Children who experience chronic reflux may also associate eating with a negative consequence: the pain of reflux or vomiting. (See Chapter 5 for more information on reflux disease.)

If your child dislikes eating due to medical problems, you should be connected with a feeding specialist or team. (See "When to Ask for Help," below, to get the process started.) They will work with your child to reduce the anxiety he feels about the process of eating. For instance, they may begin by letting him play with a spoon. Or they may hold a spoon in the same hand that holds his bottle when he is fed. Your feeding specialist or team will coach you through the process of creating a positive feeding environment for your child.

For most children, emotional concerns about food are limited to a single incident. For instance, your child may associate a particular meal or food with an experience with vomiting from the flu. Or, if your child experienced a choking episode that frightened him, he may decide not to eat that food again. These aren't conscious decisions, nor are they unreasonable. If you want to encourage him to try these foods again, use the suggestions for sensory eating to help introduce that food to him again. Keep in mind that it may take a long time. As long as his food choices do not significantly limit the variety of his eating, it is normal, if not expected, for there to be some foods he simply does not like.

Sometimes children enjoy eating food too much. This is true for children who have Down syndrome and those who do not. It is important to tease out *why* your child enjoys eating to understand if he is eating because he doesn't want a good thing to end, to fill the time, or to curb strong emotions, or because he doesn't know how to tell whether or not he is full. Overeating is discussed in more detail in Chapter 13 (Weight Management) but is something you may begin to see signs of very early in life. If your child absolutely loves the process of eating and all that goes along with it, you may want to keep a watchful eye on his rate of growth, eating patterns, and activity level.

Another food-related sensory concern is food stuffing. This is when a child puts a large amount of food in his mouth with every bite. Basically, food stuffing is a sensory-related concern. If your child stuffs large amounts of food in his mouth, it is likely he cannot *feel* the food in his mouth until there is too much to manage. Some things you can do to help reduce food stuffing include:

- Try the strategies above for moving foods from side-to-side.

However, talk about the food and having your child find it

and follow it in his mouth with his tongue and as he chews and swallows.

- Try having your child eat a snow cone or iced drink with a spoon. Again, have your child practice feeling the food in his mouth.
- Check with a speech-language pathologist with a specialty in oral motor techniques about other ways to help your child be more aware of the food in his mouth.

Food jags are another very common food-related behavior in children, with or without Down syndrome. A food jag is when a child has an intense preference for one or two foods, preferring them over all others. If the latest food jag is for a peanut butter and jelly sandwich, whenever your child is given a choice about what to eat, he chooses a peanut butter and jelly sandwich. Use the responsibilities of the feeding relationship (Chapter 3) to your advantage. Plan your menu and provide options within that menu selection rather than giving your child open-ended choices. This will reduce the number of battles with regard to his food jag. When he does get the opportunity to choose his favorite food, use common sense. Is there a good reason why a peanut butter and jelly sandwich is not appropriate for breakfast, lunch, and dinner? No. It may be boring, but it's a perfectly healthy entrée. Choose your battles wisely.

Setting the Stage

Successfully navigating through these stages of eating is a lot of work for everyone. It is essential to set the stage for success by remembering your role in the feeding relationship (Chapter 3): you are responsible for what, where, when, and how food is presented.

Keeping the physical, sensory, and emotional stages of eating in mind as you choose *what* your child will eat is no small task. Add to that taking responsibility for *where* and *how* foods are presented to your child, and your portion of the feeding relationship begins to take shape. It's not always easy.

It isn't easy for your child to fulfill his side of the equation either. Learning to eat foods and progress through textures is more than developing chewing and swallowing skills. Creating a positive environment for him to practice with and experience different foods will help him focus on his food. As with most things, there will be times of frustration along with joy in accomplishments for both of you. Sometimes, in the middle of the frustrations and the stress of day-to-day living, it is hard to remain positive. When you are feeling frustrated, here are some things to remember that may be helpful:

- **Learning to eat is a messy, messy process.** This can be the hardest thing to remember. A lot of learning happens in the midst of the mess. While exploring food, children learn about the feel, smell, temperature, and aerodynamics of foods (and sometimes the sound as they plunge to the floor).

- **Children with Down syndrome often take longer to progress from baby food to regular table foods.** However, that doesn't mean you have to forfeit table manners. Your child is learning about table manners from everyone around him. It's a great time to remind others to eat politely and model successful eating for your child with Down syndrome.

- **Make mealtime pleasant.** Learning to eat, use utensils, and try new foods is a lot to do. Your child may become overwhelmed if too much is going on around him during mealtime. Try to limit the amount of extra activity at your family table by turning off the television, radio, video games, and so on.

- **Remember, your child is always growing.** The seating position that is best for your child will change as he grows. It is most important to provide upper body support and a place to rest his feet so his knees are at a 90-degree angle. This may be a concern even when your child is in middle school or high school, depending on his height. These two things will affect his ability to feed himself as well as his ability to chew and swallow safely. If he has to add the work of supporting his upper body or legs while eating, he will not want to also work on using his spoon or fork.

- **Eating takes time for children and adults with Down syndrome.** It is worthwhile to allow for extra time, if needed.

- **Offer new foods one at a time.** As your child grows, continue to introduce new foods along with old favorites. This is good for all family members. Do not force him to try "just a bite." Instead, offer a small amount over the course of many meals. Consider it a side dish. Eventually he'll give it a try.

- **Establish a family mealtime.** It is important for your child to be a part of the family meal. Whenever possible, even as a baby, include him in the family mealtime so he can see how others eat and talk with each other. Try to serve foods that are as similar to what the rest of the family is eating (either in color or type of food) as possible.

Learning to eat is a delightful time for parents and children. It's a time full of new experiences and creative ways to explore foods, utensils, and the reactions of others. Understanding when and why to introduce new foods to children with Down syndrome makes it possible to move forward while you relax and enjoy the messes together.

When to Ask for Help

Yesterday Zac's occupational therapist was at our house watching me feed him. She said, "I can really tell you're more relaxed and confident about what you're doing." Zac ate a whole bowl of cereal during her visit. One of the main things I have learned from all this is to make eating more enjoyable. It has to start with me being more relaxed and having realistic expectations of Zac at mealtime. It may take six months or a year before Zac enjoys eating, but I need to be patient with him.

There are times when, despite your best effort, your child with Down syndrome may have trouble with the physical, sensory, or emotional aspects of eating. You may benefit from assistance from professionals who work in this area to encourage your child to eat a variety of foods safely and without trauma.

If your child is under the age of three, you can ask early intervention team members questions about feeding your child. Each EI team usually has a speech-language pathologist and an occupational therapist, and some have registered dietitians—all of whom should be familiar with feeding concerns. If your child has graduated from early intervention, ask your educational team's speech-language pathologist or occupational therapist for assistance.

In some cases, it may be necessary to consult a group of professionals who specialize in feeding concerns called a feeding team. If you are unsure whether to consult a feeding team, guidelines are available to help you, your educational team members, or your pediatrician decide. One tool is called the Parent Eating and Nutrition Assessment for Children with Special Health Needs (PEACH) survey (see Appendix). The PEACH survey was written for parents to complete at the request of their pediatrician or other health care provider to help identify children who need feeding assistance.

You do not have to use the PEACH survey to decide if your child needs assistance from a feeding team, however. If you answer "yes" to two or more of the following questions, you may want to discuss a referral to a feeding team with your physician.

- Are you talking to more than one or two professionals about feeding your child? For instance, are you getting advice from more than one professional regarding oral motor skills, exercises, or ways to promote his feeding skills?
- Are more than one or two professionals giving you advice about feeding that is difficult to put together? Sometimes when more than one person is giving suggestions, the suggestions seem to work against each other or are difficult to manage. If you're overwhelmed, confused, or stressed about feeding your child, he will feel the same way about eating.
- Is feeding your child taking a lot of time and therefore taking time away from other family members and responsibilities?
- Are you worried about your child's eating to the extent that it interferes with your family life, free time, or work?
- Are you unable to describe the feeding plan you are following for your child?

Answering yes to any one of these questions suggests that you are struggling with your child's eating. Sometimes you will need to point out your concerns to education team members or health care providers.

WHAT IS A FEEDING TEAM?

A feeding team is a group of professionals trained to:

- evaluate feeding skills,
- provide intervention for problem eating, including motor and behavioral concerns,
- monitor growth and nutrition status, and
- develop plans for families to implement and improve feeding skills.

Feeding teams can be found in many places depending on your community's services, including in children therapy centers, children's hospitals or medical clinics, early intervention programs, school-based special education programs, the local health department, neurodevelopmental centers, or a WIC (women, infants, and children) Program.

Usually a team includes: a behavior therapist, nurse, registered dietitian (nutritionist), occupational therapist, speech therapist, and a consulting physician. Others may include a dental hygienist, physical therapist, or social worker. Of course, the most important members of the feeding team are the child and his parents.

Information about your child's feeding can be gathered in a number of ways: through individual assessment by team members, family questionnaire, family observations, and videotaped observations of your child feeding. Team members will review all the information and meet with you to identify, prioritize, and address feeding concerns for your child. Success is measured by your child's improved nutritional status, feeding skills, and a strengthened relationship between you and your child at feeding time.

WHEN PROBLEMS WITH TEXTURES PERSIST

While most children with Down syndrome eventually eat all textures, if your child is five or older and still requires finely chopped and soft foods, it is a good idea to seek help if you have not already. It isn't the end of the world if he still has trouble with textures. However, it is definitely time to examine the reasons behind limited food choices. There are number of reasons an assertive approach to texture progression and food acceptance is important.

- **A delayed introduction to a variety of food textures may have an impact on speech development.** Appropriate intervention for oral motor skills not only assists with texture progression, but development of muscles and skills needed for speech.
- **A child who begins school unable to manage crunchy or chewy textures may need to be watched more carefully for choking than his peers.** While on the surface this does not seem detrimental, it can lead to differences in seating arrangements in the lunch room or other situations that separate him from his same-age, nondisabled peers.
- **If a child begins school with a need for texture modifications, it impedes his ability to participate in**

the regular lunchtime routine. Foods provided by the school will need to be modified separately, or the student will need to bring food from home. This child may also be separated from his peers secondary to choking precautions.

You don't have to accept that your child's eating problems are "just the Down syndrome." There is help available, though it may take a bit of explanation and tenacity on your part to get it. This may be due to insurance limitations or a mistaken belief that children with Down syndrome do fine without assistance. Although the latter may be true in many situations, it is not always the case. Be careful to accurately describe your child's eating difficulties and your frustrations. Also come armed with information such as the *Health Care Guidelines for Individuals with Down Syndrome* to assist your child's medical team. (The *Guidelines* are available on the Internet at www.Denison.edu/dsq/health99.shtml or from the National Down Syndrome Society.)

If you have trouble obtaining a referral for a feeding team, call the children's hospital closest to you. Ask for the nutrition department and begin by asking if they have a feeding team associated with the hospital. Every community is different, so the feeding team may or may not be on the hospital campus. Be persistent in your inquiry; you will find someone who can help you. In addition, some early intervention teams have extensive feeding teams. If your child is still receiving early intervention or early childhood services (Part C), ask if they have this type of consultation available.

Struggling with "picky eating" is common, if not a rite of passage for all children. Yet if it persists for a long period of time, it may be more than a food jag. When it is, parents must receive the support and coaching needed to overcome issues related to sensory, oral motor, and mealtime dynamics to build the foundation of a healthy adulthood.

CHAPTER 2

Breast or Bottle Feeding

All mothers make plans while they're pregnant regarding how they will feed their baby once she is born. Some decide to breastfeed, some to bottle feed, and others deliberately choose to combine the two. It is a personal choice made for emotional and practical reasons, some of which are out of your control.

When your baby is born with Down syndrome, you may encounter unexpected issues, such as feeding difficulties or the need for immediate surgery, that change your original feeding plan. This chapter covers the common feeding difficulties for babies with Down syndrome. It also presents information about breastfeeding and bottle feeding, but is not meant to be an explicit guide. Work with your pediatrician, nurses, and support team to provide your child with the nutrition she needs in these first months of life.

Breastfeeding

Breast milk is the natural first food for babies because it is made specifically for that purpose. Breast milk, including colostrum, which is the first milk, is filled with antibodies that help babies fight off germs and bacteria that can lead to diarrhea, respiratory infections, or urinary tract infections.

Babies with Down syndrome are presumed to have a weaker immune system than other babies, which makes the allure of providing antibodies through breast milk compelling for many mothers. Babies who are breastfed for six months or

more tend to have fewer allergic responses (food allergy, dermatitis, and asthma) throughout childhood, as well. In addition, studies suggest that babies who are below six pounds at birth (low birth weight babies) may experience a positive cognitive benefit from being fed breast milk by bottle, breast, or tube. Breastfeeding may also improve oral motor tone, leading to speech benefits, since a baby uses more muscles for breastfeeding. (This is one reason breastfeeding is more difficult for some babies.) Last, breastfeeding is presumed to be less expensive than bottle feeding. The cost involved is centered on feeding yourself and the value of your time.

I have always wanted to be a mother and nurse my children. I read all I could on the topic and determined to breastfeed my babies. I knew it was best for them nutritionally and I wanted the bonding experience. When the nurse at the hospital asked me if I were going to be breastfeeding my baby, I responded with a resounding "YES" each time. However, with my first four, success was not to be mine. I tried, but always ended up stopping.

Madison is our fifth child. We learned within minutes of her birth that she had Down syndrome. We were shocked and terrified, like so many parents when they learn this news. How would we manage? What was her future going to be like? How would this affect our other children? Our hearts were filled with questions. But the one question I knew the answer to was the familiar one the nurse asked yet again: "Would I be a nursing Mom?" Yes, of course I would try again.

Maddie proved to be a voracious nurser and gained weight at a healthy rate her first year. I received exceptional support from my husband and other family members to ensure success. I knew when I started I was doing the very best for my baby that I knew how. I believed that by nursing Maddie, I was giving her a most precious gift. The truth is, this precious gift was for me. Those first few months after her birth were so uncertain as we adjusted to how our life would be different. Nursing Maddie was my one touchstone to reality, filling me with immense peace and joy during a time when my life seemed so unstable. When she weaned herself at the age of fifteen months, I was not ready. I still relish every moment and I am grateful to Maddie for the time we shared.

It is easy to see the benefits to breast feeding, but it is equally important to recognize that it can also be difficult. When using breast milk to feed a baby with Down syndrome, the greatest barriers are often time and stress. It may take your baby a long time to feed, which is time you may not have if you need to return to work. If your baby cannot latch on to breast feed, then you will need to spend time pumping your breast milk as well as feeding it to her by bottle. If she is in the hospital for a prolonged period, this may mean pumping your breast milk, storing it in the refrigerator, and taking it to the hospital for you and the nurses to feed her. These demands on time, particularly for mothers who return to work or have other young children, can be hard. They require patience and support of your family, friends, and employer.

Breastfeeding a baby with Down syndrome can be easy and smooth or fraught with challenges. Some of the more common difficulties include:

- Your baby becomes tired early during feeding.
- You have trouble getting your baby to "latch on."
- Your baby has a weak suck, making the process of getting the milk from your breast harder.
- Hospital staff may misguidedly try to discourage your efforts if your baby has a heart defect or if they are not aware of the great successes many mothers of children with Down syndrome experience when breastfeeding their child.

Many of these obstacles have easy solutions. They may take time, dedication, and persistence to accomplish, but it is worth the effort.

To be successful, it is important for you to have the support of a lactation consultant or other feeding specialist during this time. A lactation consultant can help with strategies to breastfeed and help you investigate different methods of breastfeeding or bottle feeding if needed. If possible, try to get in touch with someone who has knowledge and experience with breastfeeding a baby with Down syndrome before you leave the hospital. Ask the nursing staff, lactation consultant, or social worker to call the local parent support group or La Leche League for some names of mothers who have breastfed their baby with Down syndrome.

Lactation consultants have practical and educational experience with breastfeeding in all sorts of situations. Lactation consultants or lactation nurses are usually on the hospital staff. In some cases, this may be a nurse who is experienced in lactation but does not have the actual credential. In areas where a lactation consultant or a nurse who is skilled in teaching breastfeeding is not available, contact the La Leche League for assistance (see Resources). Reading about different strategies to support a variety of breastfeeding concerns cannot replace the effectiveness of individualized instruction and support.

Sheila was a very reluctant nurser and slept through the second day of her life. Having nursed her older sister, I thought I could handle the problem. But she was having nothing to do with waking to nurse. Eventually I called a friend who was also a La Leche League Leader. She came over and spent half a day with me. Together we discovered Sheila needed to be stripped so that she was cool and to be held in a "football" hold. She needed to have her lower jaw supported while I "milked" her throat at the same time [dancer hand]. By doing this I was teaching her how to nurse.

PUMPING BREAST MILK

Sometimes babies with Down syndrome have trouble with the mechanics of breastfeeding. Some babies have medical concerns that get in the way of breastfeeding. Some mothers have to spend hours away from their baby while at work. And sometimes, it just doesn't seem to work early on. If you want your baby to have breast milk, it is still possible in these situations. Even if your baby is receiving her milk by tube feeding, you can provide breast milk for part or all of her feedings. Mothers who want their baby to have breast milk can pump their milk for supplemental feedings. There are many types of breast pumps, from battery-operated to electric. Ask your lactation consultant to help you locate one that meets your individual needs for portability and ease of use.

If your main goal is to give your baby the nutrition and other benefits of breast milk, but for some reason nursing is not working out, consider long-term pumping as an alternative. It *is* a lot of work, but is an option that buys time until, hopefully, your baby catches on.

If you are pumping your milk to be fed to your child later, be sure to investigate how to properly store your breast milk. If you are transporting it to the hospital or a childcare provider, you will need to use an insulated bag to transport your milk from home. The La Leche League or a lactation consultant can guide you in creating a method that works well for you and your baby. They will help you find any specialized equipment you need such as larger breast pumps than the ones commonly sold or any special storage or transport equipment.

Even after many months of pumping breast milk for your baby to be fed through a feeding tube or bottle, it is still possible to establish a more traditional breastfeeding mechanism. Let your pediatrician or lactation specialist know if you are ready to give it a try again. They will support you as you attempt to transition from bottle to breast. Remember, even if your baby does not receive your breast milk directly from your breast, she will still reap all the same health benefits from pumped milk as she would from breastfeeding.

Feeding Techniques

Although breastfeeding and bottle feeding are quite different, there are some common concerns in feeding babies with Down syndrome that crop up with both feeding methods. Additionally, many mothers do both breast- and bottle feeding in some combination. The techniques and strategies for successful feeding—with breast or bottle—are included in this section together. Please use what is appropriate for you and your baby. When you are having trouble with feeding by either method, please seek help from a lactation consultant, neonatal nurse, or your pediatrician. There is no need to try to work through troubles alone.

The most important point in feeding your baby is for *you* and your baby to be comfortable. Regardless of feeding method, if one of you is in an uncomfortable position, the feeding will not go well. It often takes babies with Down syndrome longer to complete a feeding than new mothers expect, so taking precautions to be comfortable will pay off almost immediately.

You may want to begin your feeding experiences with more frequent, short sessions. This allows for some feeding and learning time without frustration for either mother or baby. As you become more comfortable with the feeding routine, sessions will become longer and less frequent.

With all that is going on in these first months, a common concern for mothers is whether or not their baby is getting enough nourishment. Generally, you will be able to determine this by her weight gain and her diapers. Your pediatrician will be keeping a close eye on your baby's weight. If there are problems, you may be asked to weigh your baby's diapers and keep track of the number of ounces she eats at each feeding. If this happens, remember that folks are only looking to see if she is gaining weight and how to promote that. It does not mean that you are not doing a good job with your baby.

Opinions differ as to the best feeding schedule to use for babies with Down syndrome. The first choice is usually to use a feeding on demand schedule in the beginning. Your baby's request for food is her first communication to you and your first opportunity to show her she can trust you to listen to her. However, some babies with Down syndrome are very sleepy and will not necessarily wake up on their own to feed or cry to be fed. Our son with Down syndrome was one of these babies. He was a good sleeper from the moment we brought him home, rarely awakened to eat, and tired easily. In this situation, it is important to keep track of when your baby is eating and wake her to be fed on a regular schedule. However, try not to be too rigid in this schedule. As her alertness and stamina grows, she will start to wake on her own and ask to be fed by crying. When she does, respond to her requests and modify your schedule and technique. For a while, it can feel like a delicate balance between the two methods. Soon, however, you will find a routine that works for the two of you and that promotes the trust babies need when learning to feed.

HELPING YOUR BABY LATCH ON

A common obstacle in feeding babies with Down syndrome is low muscle tone in the mouth and tongue. This affects the way a baby can "attach" to the nipple of a breast or bottle. With successful attachment, there is a strong suction between the nipple and the baby's mouth. In breastfeeding, this means that she has taken in the nipple and some of the areola (the colored part around the nipple). The nipple of the breast will extend to the back of her mouth. With both bottle and breastfeeding, if attachment is good, the suction must first be broken (by sliding a finger in the side of the baby's mouth) before the nipple can be removed.

Because attachment requires work from the mouth and tongue, your baby may have trouble learning how it is done. As she grows, this will become easier, as will feeding her. Some mothers are able to encourage good attachment by doing some exercises to stimulate the mouth and tongue. Try these stroking exercises about fifteen minutes before feeding:

- With your index finger, stroke around the corners of your baby's mouth starting at the center top and moving around one side in an arc to the middle bottom. Repeat on the other side. Do this once just before introducing her to your breast.
- Stroke upward from her mouth to her cheeks.
- Gently stroke in a downward motion on the outside of the throat to encourage the swallowing reflex.
- Put your finger in your baby's mouth and rub the gums (upper and lower and on both sides) gently from the front to the back of the mouth, and the roof of her mouth from front to back. Remember to wash your hands and make sure your nails are short before doing this exercise.

If you do not have time for all of these exercises prior to feeding, there are some other things you can do that take less time immediately before feeding:

- Stroke around her mouth with ice or a wet cloth two times: once to each side and then repeat.
- Just before offering your baby a nipple, put your clean finger in her mouth. With the pad side of your finger on the top of her tongue, push her tongue down from the roof of her mouth and wait until you feel her tongue begin to cup your finger to suck. Quickly and smoothly remove your finger and introduce the nipple. This is difficult to do and may not be effective with your baby.

Many mothers who breastfeed their babies with Down syndrome find the *Dancer Hand Position* helpful in early feedings. To use the Dancer Hand Position, use the hand on the same side as the breast you will feed from. Your other hand will support the baby's head and neck. Support your breast with your thumb on top, four fingers underneath. Slide the hand supporting your breast forward, so that you are supporting it with three rather than four fingers. Your index finger and thumb are now free and in front of the nipple. Bend your index finger slightly so it gently holds your baby's cheek on one side while the thumb holds the other cheek. If needed, you can slide your index finger under her chin to encourage your baby to suck, moving her jaw a little. Using the Dancer Hand Position keeps the weight of the breast off her chin while providing her head some support, so she can concentrate on feeding.

HOLDING YOUR BABY

There are a variety of different ways you can try holding your baby when feeding. Most babies with Down syndrome feed best if their body is well supported from head to toe in positions such as the football hold or the straddle hold. You can also try having your baby lie next to you, but make sure her body is well supported, either by a free arm or pillows. Each baby will respond differently to feeding positions, so be open to trying different positions and techniques until you find a couple that fit you both. A lactation consultant is a good resource for holds and other methods to improve feeding sessions, whether you are breastfeeding or bottle feeding.

If your baby spits up a lot or is experiencing reflux, it is important to feed her in a more upright position rather than lying down. It is also a good idea to have her sit up in an infant seat for ten to fifteen minutes after a feeding to help keep her reflux or spitting up to a minimum. For more information on reflux, see Chapter 5.

SLEEPINESS

Babies with Down syndrome tend to be very sleepy in the first weeks of life. This can be troublesome for feeding because it is unsafe to feed a baby when she is asleep. If you have a sleepy baby, wake her every three hours or so to feed her. Some suggestions for waking your baby, raising her alertness for feeding, and keeping her awake include:

- Undress your baby down to her diaper while talking to her gently before feeding.
- Change her diaper just before you feed her.
- Massage her feet and legs.
- Feed her in the bath or give her a bath before feeding her.
- Make sure the room is not so bright that she needs to close her eyes.
- Wipe her face, legs, or arms with a damp cloth.
- Take short breaks in feeding, using this time to talk to her and reawaken her.

> *Heather's suck was so weak she seemed to fall asleep when she tried to nurse. A mother at the Down syndrome support group told me to try feeding her using the football hold, which worked better. I wish I had known about the La Leche League then. It would have been helpful to have someone to talk to with experience.*

Bottle Feeding

> *I tried to breastfeed Emily for the first six weeks of her life. She did suckle and latch on well, but her suck was just too weak. She wasn't gaining weight at all. It took her seven weeks to regain her birth weight. My pediatrician wanted to give us time to work it out, so she didn't intervene for six weeks. At that point I started pumping my milk and feeding her with a bottle. Another problem was that Emily would fall asleep while nursing. With the bottle, I could see how much she was getting with each feeding. Once I started pumping, she gained an ounce a day!*

Some mothers decide they want to bottle feed their child long before she is born. Some attempt to breastfeed and switch to bottle feeding later. Others have trouble producing enough milk to breastfeed. And some mothers will choose bottle feeding

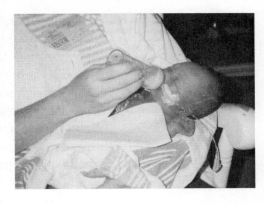

for their baby for other reasons. Whatever the reason, using a bottle to feed your baby formula or breast milk is a great experience for you and your baby. If attempting to breastfeed was very stressful, you may be able to feed your baby without feeling pressure. Your baby will appreciate your calmer demeanor as well.

As discussed above, pumping breast milk and then bottle feeding it to your baby is a good option for many mothers. However, if the logistics of pumping breast milk are too difficult for you, bottle feeding your baby with formula is an equally good method of providing nourishment. While formulas do not provide the antibodies of breast milk, they provide good nutrition and are improved on a regular basis. Using formula to feed your baby is often helpful to others who care for your child, as they are able to provide as much as your baby wants and needs. It is also easier to store. In addition, most formulas come in a powder that is less expensive than canned formula, and is easy to customize for your child's needs, should she need a high calorie formula to gain weight. Bottle feeding also offers many different nipples and approaches to feeding to accommodate for your baby's individual needs.

Remember, there is not a single "right" food to feed your baby with Down syndrome. Work with your pediatrician, registered dietitian, and lactation consultant to create a plan that works best for you.

Dental Health and Bottle Feeding

A leading cause of long-term dental problems is a condition called "bottle mouth" or baby bottle tooth decay. Bottle mouth is a condition seen generally in kids under three years old and is characterized by cavities in the front portion of the mouth. These cavities are caused when children's teeth are exposed to liquids other than water for a continuous or extended period of time. Even if your child does not yet have teeth, lengthy exposure to milk or juice can be detrimental to the health of her gums. To prevent bottle mouth:

- If your child wants a bottle between regular feedings or during naps, comfort her with a bottle filled with cool water.
- Always make sure your child's pacifier is clean and never dip a pacifier in a sweet liquid.
- Don't allow your child to fall asleep with a bottle containing milk, formula, fruit juices, or other sweet liquids. Never let your child walk with a bottle in her mouth.
- Promote cup drinking when she is ready. When she is physically able to use a cup for her drinking, begin to reduce her use of a bottle.
- If you see any unusual red or swollen areas in your child's mouth or a dark spot on any of her teeth, consult your child's pediatric dentist.

CHOOSING A NIPPLE

At some point, most babies are introduced to bottle feeding. Choosing a nipple to use on a bottle is an important decision, whether you are feeding breast milk or baby formula. If you are using a bottle to supplement breastfeeding, choose a nipple that is as soft, round, and long as you can find (not one of the orthodontic nipples). Mothers who are feeding breast milk by bottle may be able to reintroduce breastfeeding with success at a later date. To introduce the bottle nipple to your baby, first touch her lips with the nipple at the center of her mouth and wait for her to open her mouth. Slide the nipple into her mouth as far back as it can go comfortably. If she gags, remove the nipple and try again. If you consistently hear gulping, gasping, or coughing during feeding, call your pediatrician or lactation consultant.

Others who are eager to help you may make suggestions such as enlarging the hole in the nipple to make it easier for your baby to get milk from her bottle. Always consult with your pediatrician, nurse, or speech-language pathologist (SLP) before making any changes to a nipple. Although your baby may be able to suck the milk out of the bottle more easily, the milk may come through the nipple faster than she can swallow, which could result in her aspirating.

For the same reasons, do not add any thickener, such as baby cereal, to the milk or formula in your baby's bottle without consulting the SLP or pediatrician. Baby cereal adds few calories and thickens the milk or formula in the bottle. For babies who are having trouble coordinating their swallow, this may be a good thing because it helps them feel the milk and swallow safely. For others, it means having to work so hard they tire more easily. Sometimes babies work so hard to get the thickened milk or formula out of the nipple, it then flies through their mouth too quickly, causing them to aspirate a portion of it. Your baby's SLP or pediatrician will help you with these decisions. In addition, the speech-language pathologist or feeding specialist may recommend a special nipple to help your baby swallow more safely.

> *After a couple of months of not even attempting to nurse, I thought I would try one last time. At this point, Erin was six months old and had been bottle fed breast milk exclusively for over five months. Well, wouldn't you know—Erin took to it like a pro! Three weeks later, Erin was almost exclusively breastfed. I still pump once a day to give my husband a chance to feed Erin.*

CHOOSING A BABY FORMULA

Sometimes commercial or specialized formulas are used for feedings. There is nothing wrong with using formula to feed a baby. Sometimes it is the best option for both you and your baby.

There are as many different types of baby formulas as there are babies. Generally, parents and physicians choose cow's milk formulas, which are the most common, followed closely by soy-based formulas. However, there are many other types

> *When I left the hospital, Tommy was nursing, but not nearly enough. He lost a lot of weight the first week, so I started pumping and giving him breast milk and formula in a bottle. I pumped for six weeks and tried to nurse, but it was exhausting. It took him so long to even drink from a bottle that I was spending my days pumping and feeding; pumping and feeding. It never ended.*
>
> *My Mom finally said, "It's not a sin to formula feed your baby." I had tremendous guilt about not being able to breastfeed, since everyone said it would be best for him. Yes, maybe I could have breastfed with more support, but I also needed someone to say that it would be okay to formula feed from a bottle, too.*

of formula for different situations: for premature babies, babies with allergies, and babies who need more calories. In addition, if your baby is not tolerating her formula, is losing weight, or is in some complicated medical situation, your doctor, registered dietitian, or lactation consultant may recommend some individualized changes to her formula to increase tolerance or improve weight gain.

All manufacturers of baby formula are regulated by the Food and Drug Administration, which enforces manufacturing regulations, quality control, and recall procedures as well as nutrient content and labeling. All baby formulas are stamped with a "use before" date to ensure freshness and quality. The Committee on Nutrition of the American Academy of Pediatrics provides nutrient composition guidelines, which allow for some individualization by individual manufacturers, yet sets parameters that are designed to promote good health and optimal growth for babies.

These guidelines are based not only on nutrient needs (caloric composition, vitamins, and minerals) of infants, but also on the body's ability to tolerate the formula overall. For instance, two lesser-known factors to consider when selecting or modifying baby formulas are *osmolality* and the *renal solute load*.

The *osmolality* of a formula is the amount of pressure that the feeding exerts on the membranes of the gastrointestinal tract as the intestine absorbs the nutrients it needs. Human milk has the same osmolality as our blood, making it easy for babies to digest and for the nutrients to pass from the gut to the blood. When the osmolality of a baby formula is too high, your baby may be uncomfortable and have loose stools, diarrhea, or bloating, which is a sign of intolerance to a formula.

The *renal solute load* is the amount of electrolytes and metabolic waste that must be filtered through the kidneys and expelled in urine after all the nutrients are digested and used. In other words, it's the amount of work the kidneys have to do to get rid of the extra vitamins, minerals, and other compounds not used from the feeding. If a formula has a heavy renal solute load, the kidneys must work harder than they are intended to work.

For these reasons, whenever you decide to alter your baby's formula—in any way—it is important to discuss it with your pediatrician or dietitian before you do. Some alterations may change the osmolality or the renal solute load of the formula. For instance, if you add a supplement of any kind to your baby's formula or breast milk, your baby's kidneys will have more nutrients to send to her urine to remove from the body. It's important not to work her kidneys too hard at too early an age as they are not fully developed for the first year of her life.

INTRODUCING MILK

The guidelines for switching your baby with Down syndrome from breast milk or formula to cow's milk or soy milk are the same as for children without Down syndrome. Generally, when your baby is taking more than 50 percent of her calories from table food or baby food, you may begin to reduce your use of breast milk or formula and use milk or soy milk instead. The age when this occurs is different for every child and depends on your baby's chewing skills and interest in table food.

CHAPTER 3

The Feeding Relationship

While your child is a baby, you are his entire world. Whether you feed him by breast, bottle, or with a tube, feeding time is an opportunity for bonding and learning about each other. It is during this time that he will learn how well you are listening to his cues. There is a natural turn-taking involved in feeding a baby that builds mutual respect between the two of you. It is also a time you see hints of his personality and can guess what is in store in the years to come. In these early months, it is important to consider the feeding environment and the interaction between you and your baby during feeding. As often as you can, make it a time when you can focus primarily on your child with Down syndrome. When you do this, you learn to listen to the subtle cues he provides about being full and he learns to associate feeding with warm feelings.

Even if your baby with Down syndrome is in the hospital during his first months, or is being tube fed at home, you can establish this relationship with him. It takes more thought, but it is well worth it. If he is in the hospital, ask the nursing staff how you can spend some time with your baby. The nurses will do whatever they can to help you find a quiet time to bond with him despite the environment. If your baby is at home with you on a tube feeding, consider the time that you administer the tube feeding (breast milk or formula) the same as nursing your baby. Touch him, talk to him, and hold him if possible while he is receiving the tube feeding. Your touch, voice, and care will help your child associate a positive feeling with being fed rather than regarding it as just another procedure that happens frequently throughout the day.

The time that you spend with your child during these months creates an un-questionable bond and relationship between you. It will grow with the ebb and flow of life as your child grows. This relationship centered on feeding, or eating, is lifelong and essential to understanding your child's food-related behaviors. Remember, the way you engage with your child from the moment he is born sets the stage for how he experiences food.

The Feeding Relationship

Ellyn Satter, R.D., CICSW, has observed and studied food-related behaviors in children for a number of years. In her work, she learned that the feeding rela-

tionship revolves around trust. Children must trust parents and parents must trust children. She further defined the essential components to trust by defining the role of the child and the parent in the feeding relationship (see adult/child responsibilities below).

In contrast to typical children, however, children and adults with Down syndrome generally are influenced by many people (therapists, teachers, etc.) outside of the home, beginning at an early age. Additionally, some adults with Down syndrome live in situations in which support people have more control over the foods available than they do. These support people can be as influential in our child's life as we are, and must be included in the feeding relationship for it to be effective.

- ■ *Adults:* Parents and extended family members. Adults are responsible for *what, where, when,* and *how* food is presented to your child. It is up to those in the role of "adult" to thoughtfully provide attractive, safely prepared, balanced, and tasty foods at appropriate times, and that's it. The person in the adult role is not responsible for whether or not the person with Down syndrome, regardless of age, chooses to eat that food.
- ■ *Your Child:* The person with Down syndrome, regardless of age. Your child is responsible for *how much* and even *whether* the food is eaten. In other words, your child is responsible for making the choice of whether or not to eat the food provided by adults and support persons.
- ■ *Support Persons:* Babysitters, speech-language pathologists, physical therapists, occupational therapists, teachers, educational assistants. These individuals are responsible for *what, where, when,* and *how* food is presented within the known parameters of your family values, as long as it does no harm to your child. For instance, if your family does not use food rewards, everyone working with your child should follow that rule also. If you are a vegetarian or follow a casein-free diet, food choices offered by support people should respect that lifestyle. Of course, in some instances, you may need to provide food to caregivers to accomplish your goals. Those in a support role must not arbitrarily change or ignore food-related decisions made by your family without discussing it with you first.

These roles give everyone a structure to work within that is respectful. This division of responsibility is key for promoting healthy lives from the first feeding onward. The feeding relationship is also an important component in working through food-related issues such as weight management or picky eating for people with Down syndrome.

It sounds simple and, in many ways, it is. However, each child and family has a distinct personality, values, and issues that challenge the simplicity of the feeding relationship. When mealtime or food choices are a battlefield, it is difficult to envision peaceful solutions to the situation. Use these roles as a road map to promoting healthy attitudes about food and healthy food choices.

Your Role in the Feeding Relationship

Filling the role of "adult" in the feeding relationship is a great responsibility. When you first look at the definition of the adult role in feeding it creates an image of someone putting food on the table, a child choosing not to eat any, and the adult saying, "too bad, that's it for now." That is not exactly what I have in mind, however. The adults in your child's life must take their job seriously. The division of responsibility encourages meals to be battle free, creative, communicative, and interactive. This division also provides natural teaching moments and a gradual shift of responsibility as your child becomes more independent. Most importantly, it limits each person's control in a way that is appropriate for the situation and individual.

As explained above, your responsibilities include choosing what, where, when, and how to present food. Some of the considerations to bear in mind when carrying out these responsibilities are explored below.

YOUR ATTITUDE ("HOW")

Mealtimes and food preparation time are opportunities to communicate your thoughts and feelings about food choices, exercise, health, and body image. Those in the adult and support person roles of the feeding relationship are responsible for modeling a healthy attitude regarding food, as well as their own and others' food choices.

From an early age, your child with Down syndrome will be quite savvy at reading your attitude about any situation, including mealtimes. This makes it important to consider the messages you are sending him regarding his food choices. Take a moment to think about how you respond to your children and spouse when they make food choices that you disagree with, such as drinking regular soda rather than juice or water or taking what you think is an excessive second serving.

To teach your child a positive attitude about food, you must consider and shape your own attitude about others inside and outside your family. Your goal is for your attitude and actions to show your child that eating is a normal and enjoyable activity. Embedded in that goal is the need for your child to realize that everyone is different in size and shape and everyone has their own unique combinations of favorite foods and foods they do not like. In doing so, you let him know that all these things are part of each person's individuality. Some ways to reach this goal include:

- **Communicate an attitude of acceptance of your own and others' body image.** Say positive things about the way you look in front of your children and others. Avoid negative comments about specific body parts or lack of exercise. Avoid comparing yourself to others. Focus on your own choices about healthy eating and exercise.

- **Do the same for everyone in your family.** View each child as a unique individual and resist comparisons between siblings or friends. What your child hears you say about him, or how you respond to him when he makes choices that you do not accept, will affect his attitude about himself as an adult.
- **Be positive about the process of making food for your family.** Try not to grumble about foods you are preparing or the chore of creating a meal for your family. As your children get older, ask them to help lighten the load.
- **Avoid excruciating analysis of family members' eating habits.** The less attention you give to unwanted behaviors, the more likely your child will not continue them.
- **Compliment your child on what he does well.** If he has been helpful with meal preparation, tell him. If he is sitting nicely at the table or has been fun to talk to during the meal, tell him.

It can be hard to be positive all the time about the chore of getting everyone fed. Your child needs to hear that you sometimes get tired of shopping, cooking, and cleanup, but he needs to hear it in a way that tells him it isn't his fault. Your child feels your stress or resentment when you let it overwhelm you, which in turn affects his eating patterns.

Of course, it can be difficult at times to suppress your reaction to the foods someone else chooses to eat. An occasional comment such as, "That's a lot of food," or "Do you really like that?" is natural. However, constant monitoring of family members' food choices and amounts is outside of the parent and support person role. Your child needs the freedom to experiment with food combinations, even when you think them a bit odd. His choices are not "odd" to him; they are his experiment. In this way he learns how to combine foods that complement each other. He also needs to learn about the sensations of being full, hungry, too full, and too hungry. This may take some time, but it is an important part of successful eating.

THE ENVIRONMENT ("WHERE" AND "HOW")

Consider the environment where meals will be served. Mealtimes are wonderful opportunities for encouraging communication and developing relationships between family members. As the adult in the feeding relationship, your goal is to offer food in a positive environment where your child can learn and experience food and eating in a developmentally appropriate way.

Limit eating to specific areas of your home. There are myriad reasons why this is a great idea—for *everyone,* not just your child with Down syndrome. If the rules are different for different people in the house, it will be more difficult for your child to understand what he can and cannot do. Some practical reasons to limit eating to specific areas include:

- If eating is only allowed in a couple rooms, there is less food to clean up.
- If eating is restricted from the room with the family TV, the habit of eating while watching television is less likely to develop.

- Learning to pair other activities with eating is less likely if the areas where eating occurs are restricted.
- Your child with Down syndrome (and other family members) will be less likely to develop unconscious eating habits (eating when not aware of what they are doing).

It's a good idea to keep the focus on the meal and the people at the meal rather than on other distracting activities (television, games, or reading). You want everyone's attention to be on each other. When your child is very young, scoot his highchair over to the table where the family is eating. He should be a part of the group from the very beginning. Long before he eats the same food textures as the rest of the family, he needs to see how others interact with foods. He will become comfortable with the way food is served, what to do if he dislikes a food, and other techniques specific to your family.

If your child is not eating at this time, still bring him to the table in his highchair or infant seat so he can interact with those around the table. Give him a spoon, a plastic cup, or some foods he can chew on to play with and explore during the meal. All of this sets the stage for family meals later on.

USE APPROPRIATE TOOLS ("HOW")

It is very important to consider physical adaptations to the environment and tools your child may need to be successful during mealtime. Consider the chair, the table, the silverware, the cup, the method of distributing food, and other things that may need to be modified so your child is comfortable. Some of these are discussed below or in Chapter 1.

- Use appropriate utensils. (Consult with your OT for advice.)
- Use dycem (or nonskid shelf liner) to hold bowls and plates in place when your child is learning to scoop.
- Roll towels to use as bolsters to help him stay upright in his highchair.
- Once your child outgrows his highchair, use a footstool under his chair so his feet are supported.
- Use serving utensils that are easy to manage.
- Use serving bowls and casserole dishes with easy-to-use handles.
- Provide visual cues to help your child set the table. (See below.)

PRESENT FOOD IN A DEVELOPMENTALLY APPROPRIATE MANNER ("HOW")

Every family has a different idea of what mealtime should look like. There is no right or wrong way to engineer family meals, as long as you *have* family meals (see "Family Mealtime"). Each method has good and not so good points:

Restaurant Style Service. Some families put everyone's meals on their plates in the kitchen before serving them. This is called restaurant style service. With this style of service, serving sizes and combinations of food served is decided by someone else before it is delivered to the table. Restaurant style service is a good option when your dinner table is too small for serving dishes or when you want to control serving sizes. It is important, however, that serving sizes are appropriate and do not feel discriminatory. If your child thinks you are depriving him by giving him miniscule amounts of food, he may binge on other foods later. Restaurant style service provides the least amount of choice for people at the family table.

Family Style Service. Some families prefer a family style meal. With this style of service, foods are passed around the table, allowing each person to serve themselves at their place setting. Family style service gives the responsibility of what and how much food is served to the individual. The challenges to this style are:

- For younger children, managing casserole dishes or large bowls of salad can be difficult. You can help by using light-weight dishes and dishes with easy-to-grasp handles.
- Serving yourself can be messy. Anytime someone is transferring food from one dish to another there is a potential for spilling. Remember, no one is doing it on purpose. As children get older, they can clean up their mess.
- It is difficult to discourage multiple or grandiose servings. With family style service, there is no built-in mechanism to confine the amount of food a person takes. Whether it's taking an amount of food that could feed four people or taking seconds, thirds, and fourths, the only way to reduce the amount is by making a comment that everyone will hear.

Buffet Style Service. Another method of serving meals is buffet style. In this style, entrées are put in serving dishes in an area separate from the table. Family members go to the area to serve themselves. Each person has control of how much and which foods are on their plate. Buffet style service is a common way for large families to handle mealtimes to keep the dinner table from becoming cluttered. There are basically two differences between buffet style service and family style service for your family:

- You don't have to worry about passing the dishes, and
- You have an opportunity to discuss the pros and cons of taking second helpings of a favorite food individually with your child, instead of making it a topic of conversation at the family table. Rather than making this judgment for another person, quietly talk about how you decide whether or not to take a second helping. Are you still hungry? Why not wait fifteen minutes and see if you're still hungry? Do you want the food because it was exceptionally good? Or take half the amount you really want to try and cut back on how much you are eating.

CHOOSING THE RIGHT STYLE FOR YOUR FAMILY ("HOW")

Understanding your family's strengths and weaknesses will help you choose which style works best. Often the style of service changes as the needs of the family change. Regardless of what method you choose for serving foods, there are activities for your child with Down syndrome that provide multiple learning opportunities. For example:

- ***Holding and passing bowls and pitchers successfully.*** Granted, there is some risk for messiness here, but these are important skills to learn. In fact, they are important motor

Family Mealtime

Some professionals have looked at the importance of family mealtime and the effect of the busy American lifestyle on children's eating habits. They found that having a family mealtime is a great way to reserve time to connect with each other. The establishment of a regular family mealtime often serves as a touchstone for children (and parents) during stressful times. Although a daily family meal—usually breakfast or dinner—is recommended, it isn't always possible. Rather than worrying about it, some families establish a weekly family meal where attendance is expected on the weekend.

For your child with Down syndrome, there are many benefits of regular family mealtimes, such as:

- Time to practice new communication skills such as telling jokes, asking questions, and so on.
- Sharing events of the day.
- Practicing meal-related skills that are important when visiting family and friends or going to a restaurant. It's doubtful that your child's friends at school are worried about asking for foods to be passed appropriately.
- A safe and quiet environment to try new foods or practice various eating skills.

skills that you may find on your child's IEP or IFSP. Being able to pick up and pass the bowl or pitcher encourages upper body strength, bilateral skills, and weight shifting.

- **Waiting for a turn to serve yourself.** This is a great social skill. Not only is your child learning to wait his turn to serve herself, he is also learning not to impulsively leap across the table and grab the food he wants. Self-control is a very important skill. If introduced early, you have the opportunity to teach your child not to take others' food or more than his share. This is a frequent issue at IEP meetings.
- **Balancing serving containers while serving from them.** This is another skill that is important for different activities, such as handwriting, drawing, and so on. It's a bilateral skill: learning to hold something still with one hand while doing something different with the other.
- **Learning the give-and-take of conversation.** Mealtime is a wonderful time for modeling conversation skills. There are opportunities to make requests ("May I have the vegetables please?"), to practice waiting to speak in a conversation, and to learn to look at the person with whom you are speaking. Rarely do we have the opportunity to keep everyone sitting basically face-to-face without it feeling contrived. Sometimes the conversation needs to be controlled or shaped to get everyone involved. Here are some ideas to help:

Setting the Table

While setting the table seems like an obvious lesson, it is still something your child needs to learn and may need assistance with for a while. There are some things you can do to help your child master this skill more quickly:

- Make placemats with outlines or small pictures to cue where utensils go, as in the photo below.
- Use lightweight dishes that are easier for your child to carry.
- Give your child a list of what plates, cups, bowls, and utensils are needed to set the table.

- ❑ Encourage everyone to make requests.
- ❑ Have each person at the meal share something good from their day. Ask questions about their stories to show interest.
- ❑ Appoint an "interviewer" to ask questions about each person's day.

MAKE TIME FOR SUCCESS ("HOW")

Parents of children with Down syndrome learn very early that everything, *everything,* takes a little longer for their child. This doesn't change at mealtime or snack time. Unfortunately, Americans are among the speediest eaters in the world. The average amount of time spent on a meal is less than twenty minutes in America. By contrast, the French spend forty-five minutes or more at meals. Many countries close stores for the mid-day meal and a nap.

There are some common behaviors that are the result of being rushed through meals, including:

- not thoroughly chewing foods,
- gulping,
- taking large bites at one time,
- not using utensils because it is too hard,
- eating more than necessary to meet hunger,
- feeling angry or frustrated at not being able to finish,
- wanting more snacks to quench a desire to eat that wasn't met during a rushed meal,
- not being able to appreciate the social aspects of eating.

Some of these behaviors can result in aspirating foods into the lungs, which is very serious.

Whenever possible, build extra time into mealtimes so your child doesn't feel pressured to finish. This isn't easy, but there are some things you can do that will help.

- **At school, ask if your child can leave for lunch a few minutes early.** This gives him time to wash his hands and get to the lunchroom before other children arrive. He will be able to finish the necessary tasks leading up to lunch (washing hands, getting money, etc.), as well as choose his food and find a seat without the chaos and time constraints of going with his classmates. This does *not* mean that he should eat separately from his peers! All you want is for your child to arrive between groups of children or before other students arrive to promote his success. In time, it may not be necessary at all.
- **When traveling, allow extra time for meals.** If you cannot allow extra time to eat, take extra snacks along or be willing to take the food from unfinished meals with you. This will discourage unwelcome behaviors at other times. Knowing that your eating needs will be met is important in order to relax about food.
- **At home, try to make sure someone stays at the table to talk with your child while he finishes his meal.** If it takes him longer to get through the process of eating, he still needs and wants the company of others. In addition, try to ensure there is enough food for him if he takes longer. If he's worried that the strawberry shortcake will be all gone by the time he finishes dinner or that all the food will be gone if he needs more, he will be frustrated, eat too fast, or eat too little of one thing in favor of another.

Making time for success is really a component of positive behavior support. Supporting your child's need for time encourages a positive outcome, which is something everyone needs.

> When our son was younger, we often did not build in the extra time he needed to finish a meal. This was especially true when we were traveling to visit relatives. We planned our trips to eat at a fast food restaurant an hour or so into the drive to break it up. We would finish our food long before Joe was done. When he paused to join in the conversation or look at something interesting to him, we assumed he was finished because that was what we wanted to be true. Inevitably, Joe would be grumpy and stubborn during the visit. It wasn't until he was older and able to tell us with words that we realized he was hungry during these times. When we asked him why he didn't eat more at lunch, he replied, "You took my food away!"

TAKE CARE IN MENU PLANNING ("WHAT")

In the role of "adult," you also have the responsibility of choosing to offer appropriate foods. Things to consider include:

- age appropriateness of food,
- food preferences of family members,
- appropriate foods for chewing ability,
- appearance of food,
- skills with utensils,

- temperature of food, and
- nutritional quality of the meal.

The good news is that meal planning does save time and money. The bad news is, it can feel like a chore. However, it can also help you avoid unnecessary food battles, introduce new foods, and teach others about shopping and menu planning.

It is easier to provide meals that are as satisfying to make as they are to eat if you have an idea of everyone's preferences and abilities. A detailed description of one method for doing this is "Family Food Favorites" and "The Art of Menu Planning" in Chapter 16.

MEALTIMES ("WHEN")

Everyone likes to know what time they will eat. It is helpful to establish a routine, but not a rigid schedule, for the timing of meals. If meals are provided at what seem to be inconsistent times, your child may be anxious that he will be too hungry before he eats again, which sometimes leads to overeating or hoarding food to compensate. Menu planning and attention to basic nutrition principles are helpful guides.

Generally, we need to eat every three to five hours for our bodies to function without complaint. When more than five hours pass between eating opportunities (this means nothing with calories at all), you may experience a blood sugar drop, intense hunger, headache, and general malaise. If you know it will be more than five hours before you eat again, planning for a snack of appropriate size between meals is a good idea.

Children and adults with Down syndrome have the same snacking needs as everyone else. However, the way they express the need for a snack may not effectively convey that message. Common behaviors include the "stop, drop, and flop," angry outbursts, grumpiness, and other "noncompliant" behaviors.

SNACKS ("WHEN" AND "WHAT")

Take time to plan for snacks. If there is a long time between meals, plan for a snack on a regular basis. Careful planning for snacks will encourage your child to focus on things other than food throughout the day. The role of snacks is to shorten the amount of time between meals so your child does not become overly hungry. Choose snack foods for their convenience as well as their nutritional value. If snack choices are always from the "sometimes" category of the food pyramid (such as chips, candy, or ice cream), your child will learn that "snack" means "free for all."

It is also important to work with support people to encourage them not to offer snacks just because it's part of the classroom routine. For instance, one mother told me about her son going to school each day after eating a good breakfast at home, only to be expected to participate in another breakfast at school. He was eating two breakfasts an hour apart from each other. The school personnel saw it as a way to teach social and communication skills, but hadn't taken into account the family culture of eating a good-sized breakfast. Sometimes activities that seem good from one perspective are not as good when other perspectives are added.

Snacks often come during a transition time of the day. Transition times are often times of the day that are unstructured or open ended for kids. This makes them a good time for teaching about making choices, how to determine hunger, basic nutrition principles, and including activity to be healthy.

For most people, planned snacks are not common as we age. However, many teens and adults with disabilities have specific, planned snack times that may or may not be appropriate. For example adults with Down syndrome may have down times during work when they routinely eat, whether or not they are hungry, to pass the time. This is a good opportunity to offer a choice between a snack or going for a walk during break. It is also an opportunity to socialize. Learning to socialize without eating is an important skill for weight management. Accomplishing this requires the support of the job coach or other staff.

USE FOOD APPROPRIATELY ("HOW")

Use food for the purpose it was designed: to fuel your child's body. Using food as a reward or as a way to nurture a child in a tough situation (a skinned knee or hurt feelings) teaches something completely different. As a general rule of thumb, use other things your child finds motivating as a reward. Comfort him through tough moments with your time and affection rather than a candy bar.

In our culture it is easy for food and eating to become much more than fuel for our bodies. Some people eat when they are angry or upset. Others eat when they are happy. Food is often the focus of our attention when we are bored or doing relatively inactive things such as watching a movie. This is true for persons with Down syndrome, too—perhaps more so. It is also reinforced by media images and others who are involved in our lives. However, if we heed our own body's signals and teach our children to do the same, they will be less likely to succumb to suggestive advertising or false impressions regarding how much other people eat. Chapters 11 and 12 discuss the use and misuse of food rewards in more detail.

Communicating Your Values to Support People

Throughout your child's life, it is important to communicate your values and priorities related to food choices to others who care for or work with your child. Share your feelings regarding use of food as a reward, food preparation activities, and developmentally appropriate food choices for your child. As your child becomes an adult, choose secondary programs, camps, and living situations that fit the values you and your child have developed together over the years.

USING FOOD AS A REWARD ("WHEN" AND "HOW")

Communicating your values about using food rewards, snacks, or any other food-related topic is difficult to do at times. Everyone has an opinion about what is reasonable, best, or what your child wants. Some teachers and therapists routinely use food rewards with all the students in class—such as having them count colors of candy, make a graph, and then eat the candy afterwards. Some teachers use specific teaching strategies that seem to promote using food rewards, but other

> *When my son was two years old, he had little speech. He worked with a speech-language patholo-gist every week in his early intervention program. Toward the end of the year, I was excited because he had really started talking. I asked if I could videotape a session. We agreed to have the educational assistant do the taping so I would not distract him. When I viewed the tape I was very upset. Every time Stephen made a request such as saying "book" and signing "please," they would give him a piece of candy. Of course he was very motivated with this strategy. Was he really learning to ask for the book? No. He was learning to perform to earn candy. When I discussed this with the therapist, he was upset by my reaction. Of course, at the time Stephen was still underweight from his heart surgery. At our IEP meeting later I asked for something to be written into his IEP to ensure food was not used as a reward. The team did not want to do that. Instead they included wording about using positive reinforcement.*
>
> *The most frustrating part of this experience was that for months afterward, every time we told Stephen "good job" for something he replied with, "mum mum?" (his version of M&M). He associated any kind of praise with candy. Each year I make a point to tell his IEP team that food is not to be used as a reward. While it seems common sense to me, it is necessary to remind everyone each year.*

"motivating rewards" could work just as well. Many students are motivated by things other than food such as stickers, "high-fives," and recess time.

Sometimes your message about avoiding food rewards is not shared with the entire team or is misinterpreted by someone.

> *When my son was in the first grade, I went to a meeting with his classroom staff. They were sharing his "present levels of performance" as we prepared for writing IEP goals. Because my son is nonverbal, we were discussing his ability to make appropriate choices using a symbol system. The teacher gently explained to me that he could not make a choice. This seemed odd to me, because he was making choices in a variety of ways at home. When I asked him to explain, he told me: "For ex-ample, when I hold up the symbol for snack or writing, I expect Scott to choose "snack" because he loves his snack and he despises writing. However, he just sits and stares."*
>
> *I asked him if it was time for snack when he offered the choice. He said, "no." I burst into tears and said, "My son is not one of Pavlov's dogs. He only chooses food options when he is hungry. It is one of his strengths. Given that people with Down syndrome often have significant weight problems, I expect you to use other means of determining choice than food—unless it is an appropriate time for him to eat." Although my reaction was extreme for the situation, it is frustrating to me as a parent that food choices are used so often as a test or reward.*

Here are some strategies for communicating with school staff about the use of food as a reward:

- **Include a sentence regarding food rewards in the accommodations and modifications section of the IEP or IFSP: "Team members will not use food re-wards."** If the team balks at including this, calmly explain that children with Down syndrome are prone to obesity in adulthood because they use fewer calories than other children. Why use food to reward him when other things will do the job? Your goal is to promote a healthy weight and you feel that not using food rewards is one way to do that. If you still feel some resistance, ask them to defend their desire to use food rewards instead of other things your child finds equally rewarding.

- **Keep a list of the things that motivate your child. Update it frequently.** One way to do this is to ask each person on the IEP team to come prepared with a list of things your child finds motivating. Add their suggestions to the list. Distribute a copy of this list to all of your child's teachers and therapists at the beginning of the year and each time you update it as a way to remind them that food is not to be used as a reward.

DEVISE DEVELOPMENTALLY APPROPRIATE MEALS ("HOW")

Parents of children with Down syndrome often work very hard to promote inclusion of their children at school and in the community. The concept of inclusion is introduced to families when children are in early intervention. Mealtimes are another area where we need to work toward inclusion—with proper supports—for our kids. At school, children with Down syndrome may be in the same lunchroom, but separated from their nondisabled peers. How can we expect them to learn appropriate mealtime behavior?

There are many seemingly practical reasons why children with disabilities might eat in a separate area. They include the need for special diets, modified textures, and learning to eat appropriately. However, all of these things can be provided through accommodations and modifications without separation. (See Chapter 12.) If your child is learning how to eat appropriately (using spoon and fork), he may need to eat with a smaller group for a while. The end goal, however, should include eating with friends.

Here are some strategies for communicating your values regarding developmentally appropriate food and eating with those who are involved with your child. Please individualize these for your situation.

- **If your child's IEP has goals related to eating, include phrases mentioning "with nondisabled peers."** For instance, "Given a spork with an adapted handle, Sarah will use her spork to eat appropriate foods with nondisabled peers in the lunchroom."
- **Use lunch buddies to teach routines related to lunchtime:** "Given natural, environmental, and visual cues, Sam will empty his lunch tray and follow recycle procedures with a lunch buddy." Using a lunch buddy promotes a natural inclusion in lunchroom conversation.
- **If your child's IEP/IFSP does not include any eating-related goals, write fine motor, communication, and**

socialization related goals to encourage lunchtime inclusion. For instance, "Holly will set up her lunch independently, including opening her milk carton daily." Or "given visual cues for making conversation, Holly will ask a buddy from her circle of friends about her weekend." Or "Holly will approach a peer at her table and use picture exchange communication symbols to request assistance in opening food items in her lunch." Or "When purchasing lunch, Holly will follow a buddy's cues to use complete sentences to verbalize her food choices to the cafeteria workers."

Implementing the Feeding Relationship: Tips for Different Ages and Stages

Here is a summary of ideas and tips for promoting a healthy feeding relationship between you and your child depending on your child's age.

INFANT AND TODDLER YEARS

- **Develop trust.** As you feed your child, he will learn to trust that food will be there for him. Your goal is to let him know there is no reason to worry about whether or not he will be fed.
- **Create an environment conducive to eating.** Remember to focus on your child during feeding times. The communication between you is important. When possible, try to create an environment that is soothing during feeding times so you and your baby can focus on each other.
- **Learn your child's cues.** Early communication begins during feeding time as you discover how your child lets you know he is ready for another bite, full, or hungry.
- **Provide appropriate support.** Providing physical support such as a rolled towel on each side of the highchair or special positioning and adaptations for success such as tube feeding or a cut-out cup is an important part of learning to eat. A more detailed description of these supports is available in Chapters 1 and 2.

TODDLER TO PRESCHOOL YEARS

- **Provide choices carefully.** The process of making choices about food is very important at this stage. Being able to choose the vegetable for dinner or what to eat for snack this afternoon will give your child a feeling of power. However, it is important to be thoughtful about the choices you are providing. For instance, don't give him a choice that you can't or don't want to follow-through with. You don't want the message to be "you chose, but you can't have." You want him to believe in the process of making a choice. Do your best to make sure his options are available and appropriate for his eating skills.
- **Respect his choice.** The purpose of providing children choices (within an array you select) is for them to experience that power. If

your child chooses a very odd combination or a food you're pretty sure he won't like, you are not allowed to amend the choice. You *are* allowed to decide if you will allow him to choose again if he hates it. Again, you don't want the message to be, "I know you made a choice that I provided, but you didn't choose right."

Sometimes your child will choose *not* to eat when it seems like he should be hungry. Again, you must respect that choice. See Chapter 9 for more on choice making.

- **Decide when to serve meals and snacks.** As the adult in the feeding relationship, this is your area of responsibility. You must first and foremost take care to provide meals and the options for snacks reliably and appropriately. If your child chooses not to eat, you are also responsible for deciding whether you will give him another opportunity to eat before the next meal and what the choices might be. You don't want to abuse this power and be too restrictive, but you also don't want to become a short order cook. Use care in deciding what's appropriate. By limiting the options within the snacks and meals, you can control the amount of cooking and cleanup to accommodate your child.

- **Permit sensory experiences with food.** Learning to eat is a messy, messy process. This is especially true during this stage of life. For each new food, your child will need to discover its physical properties. How does it feel when I squish it between my fingers? How does it smell when it's hot or cold? What does it do when I drop it on the floor? Will the dog eat it? And finally, what does it taste like? Be a prepared parent and allow this sensory exploration within limits. Bring a sheet to put under your child's chair in a friend's home and travel with lots of cleaning supplies. If he's interested, allow your child to "help" during the meal preparation process.

- **Keep serving sizes small.** Young children do not need adult-sized servings of food. Check the Food Guide Pyramid for Young Children (ages 2-6) in the Appendix.

- **Establish the rules of eating in the house.** As your child becomes more mobile and independent, it's important to establish some household rules about food and eating. It will be easier for your child to learn these rules if they are in place from the start. Consider setting rules for the entire family related to these topics:
    - ❑ Which rooms are appropriate for eating.
    - ❑ Not eating while watching TV, playing computer or other games, reading, or doing homework.
    - ❑ Sitting down at a table with food rather than roaming about the room or eating over the sink.

EARLY CHILDHOOD OR PRESCHOOL TO KINDERGARTEN

- **Be prepared to change the number or timing of snacks** if your child begins going to a preschool or education program outside your home.
- **Share your values** about food, eating, and activities with your child's education team.

- **Let your child exercise his independence with food choices.** Occasionally agree to buy foods you don't ordinarily buy, or to let your child make his own combinations. Respect your child's opinion regarding the acceptability of a new food.
- **Present food in a way he can serve himself when appropriate.**
- **Treat spills as a mundane occurrence.** They are part of the learning process. Avoid chastising him if he is messy or sloppy.
- **Use child-size utensils** that are not overly heavy or long.
- **Confine your disappointment if your child decides your great new recipe tastes like bird feed.**
- **Present child-sized portions of food.** Try not to overwhelm him with large servings.

ELEMENTARY SCHOOL (GRADES 1-5)

Continue to allow him to make choices. How do you respond when your child wants to have pizza for breakfast? These are impressionable years for your child. He is looking to see how you will react to odd food choices to see if you really trust him to make choices for himself.

- **Make sure the team of professionals at school allows him to make choices.**
- **Make sure school staff is using rewards other than food.**
- **Make sure he is getting the support he needs to eat successfully at school** (built-up handle, a footstool at the lunch table).

MIDDLE SCHOOL AND JUNIOR HIGH

- **Give your child increasing responsibility for choices:** Let him occasionally choose the menu for a family meal or choose his own snacks from a "Snack Budget" (see Chapter 9).
- **Choose your battles over food wisely.** Sometimes it is OK to let your child eat the same things peers are eating, even if they are not the most nutritious.
- **Talk with your child about your own choices related to healthy eating**—for instance, explain why you decided to eat or not eat that second serving of lasagna.
- **Think about allowing your child to have more responsibility for food with friends and at school,** while retaining more control at home.

Conclusion

As you can see, the adult and support person roles in the feeding relationship are complicated. To develop a relationship between you and your child that encourages healthy food choices, you need to do much more than provide food. Use these guidelines to influence the atmosphere and attitudes you want to surround eating for your child. Remember that you know your child best, so do what makes sense for him and your family. As you think about your family's meal- and snack times, ask yourself if they are more often stress-filled and difficult or if your family is at ease. Although "the family meal" may have been redefined in the last fifty years, it is still one of the most valuable opportunities for bonding, developing positive relationships between each other, and shaping our attitudes regarding eating.

Section Two:
Nutrition-Related Concerns for People with Down Syndrome

CHAPTER 4

Nutrition 101

Promoting a healthy lifestyle for your child with Down syndrome and the rest of your family is an important job. But where do you start? As with most things, it's best if you begin at the beginning, which is with basic nutrition concepts. This chapter is designed to provide the most basic nutrition primer to assist you as you wade through all the nutrition hype and conflicting information in the media. After reading through it, you will know why peanut butter has always been "cholesterol free," and whether or not there are known complications from exceeding the DRI for a particular vitamin or mineral. With this knowledge base, you will better understand how food and exercise choices are different for your child with Down syndrome as you read further in the book.

What Is Nutrition?

You've heard about nutrition all your life, but what is it? Simply put, nutrition is the process of nourishing, or fueling, your body. In other words, eating is nutrition. The study of nutrition focuses on what is in the food we eat and its role in our body. To do this, scientists study the effect of the nutrients in food, which are substances that our body needs, but cannot produce on its own. In other words, for your body to function, you not only need to eat for energy, but to obtain specific nutrients (amino acids, vitamins, minerals, sugars, and so on) that allow your organs to work.

Nutrients are grouped into six categories: carbohydrate, protein, fat, vitamins, minerals, and water. The purpose of eating a balanced diet is to include adequate amounts of each of these six categories to promote health and fitness. Each of the six nutrient categories is further classified as either a macronutrient or a micronutrient, and are discussed in detail below.

Macronutrients

Three of the six categories of nutrients are classified as macronutrients. The macronutrients are the only nutrients that provide *calories,* or energy for your body. The macronutrients are: carbohydrate, protein, and fat. Each one plays an important and unique role in fueling your body.

CARBOHYDRATES

Carbohydrates are the primary and preferred source of energy that our body gets from food. When we eat foods that contain carbohydrates, they are broken down to a form called glucose, which is the source of energy for every cell in the human body. You probably don't remember eating a "glucose bar" recently, though. This is because foods provide glucose in combination with other sugars such as fructose, the smallest sugar derived from fruit, or galactose, a sugar derived from milk. These sugars are considered *simple carbohydrates* because they are quickly

broken down through digestion to the smallest chemical form and therefore easy for your body to use for energy. Other carbohydrates, such as those in whole wheat bread and other grain products, are combined in long chains of these simple sugars to form starches and fibrous carbohydrates. These are called *complex carbohydrates*. The more fiber a food has, the longer the chain of simple carbohydrates is. Your body takes more time to break these longer chains apart to simple sugars that are used for energy.

When you eat carbohydrates, whether in a piece of bread, rice, or an apple, enzymes break them down during digestion to the simplest form of sugar and other molecules possible, such as vitamins and waste products. (Enzymes are protein molecules that act as catalysts to change the rate of a reaction in your body.) Once the glucose molecules have been separated, they pass through the walls of your intestine to the blood. Your blood carries the glucose through your body to participate in millions of reactions that require energy to occur.

Most complex carbohydrates also contain fiber, an indigestible carbohydrate that plays an important role in moving foods through our digestive system. (See Chapter 5 for more information on the importance of fiber for children with Down

Words to Know: Carbohydrates

- **Primary role:** to provide energy.
- **Complex carbohydrates:** starches and foods that are high in fiber.
- **Simple carbohydrates:** sugars such as fructose, galactose, and sucrose found naturally in foods.
- **Soluble fiber:** fiber found in food sources such as oat bran and pectin that dissolves to become a gummy or thick substance.
- **Insoluble fiber:** fiber in food sources such as wheat bran, which does not dissolve during digestion, but holds on to water to provide bulk to food passing through the gut.
- **Calories per gram of carbohydrate:** 4 calories per gram of carbohydrate.

syndrome.) This is why a diet full of complex carbohydrates or high fiber foods is recommended: for regularity and for adequate energy to fuel the body throughout the day and night.

All carbohydrates provide 4 calories per gram. Thirty grams of apple provides the same number of calories as 30 grams of table sugar: 120. However, it will take longer for your body to digest the 120 calories in the apple for energy than the 120 calories in table sugar. This is because an apple is a complex carbohydrate made up of fructose molecules combined with indigestible fibrous material that must be digested, filtered, and separated, while table sugar is a simpler carbohydrate, made up of two glucose molecules and no fibrous material. Because carbohydrates are the main energy source for the human body, it is recommended that 55 to 65 percent of the total number of calories eaten in a day come from carbohydrate sources.

PROTEIN Think back to the last time you or your child skinned a knee. When the bleeding stopped, the blood was clotting. After the scab had been there a while, it began to gloss over with a gooey substance and then underneath all that, suddenly there was new skin. This entire process is dependent on amino acids. Amino acids are found in protein in our food. The main role of the protein we eat is growth, maintenance, and repair of body tissues, including our organ tissues. Some amino acids in protein work as enzymes in reactions necessary to growth, maintenance, and repair. There are twenty-two types of amino acids, including nine that are essential. The essential amino acids are the building blocks needed to create body tissue. The other thirteen are considered nonessential amino acids, primarily because they can be created with the essential ones. You do not need to consume foods with all twenty-two amino acids to be healthy, but you do need to consume a variety of foods that, in combination, will provide the nine essential amino acids.

Many different foods contain protein. In fact, the only food groups with no protein at all are fruit and fat. But not all proteins are "complete." A complete

Words to Know: Protein

- **Primary role:** growth, maintenance, and repair.
- **Amino acids:** There are twenty-two different amino acids found in food. Amino acids are small parts of protein.
- **Essential amino acids:** the nine amino acids needed to build a complete protein.
- **Complete protein:** a food or combination of foods that have at least the nine essential amino acids required to generate tissue for growth maintenance and repair. Examples include meat, dairy, and soy products.
- **Complementing proteins:** combining specific foods considered incomplete proteins to combine the essential amino acids (typically done with vegetarian diets).
- **Incomplete proteins:** foods such as bread, nuts, and vegetables that contain protein in the form of amino acids but not all of the essential proteins.
- **Calories per gram:** 4 calories per gram of protein.

protein is one that includes all nine essential amino acids. Foods containing all the essential amino acids are from animal sources, with one exception: soy. All other sources of protein must be "complemented," or combined, to provide these essential building blocks for our body. For example, a peanut butter and jelly sandwich provides a complete protein by combining bread and peanuts, while a jelly sandwich does not. Combining proteins is only a concern if you choose to be vegetarian. Even then, it is not a great concern for adults if you eat a wide variety of foods or include soy products in your diet. However, if you are raising your children as vegetarians, you must plan meals and snacks carefully to insure that an adequate amount of the essential amino acids are available for growing children. This is why some families following vegetarian diets include cow's milk or egg products in their diets when their children are young.

When the protein we eat in food is digested, it is immediately put to use for tissue generation and repair. To protect the ability to maintain and repair body tissues, protein is used to produce energy only as a last resort. When looking for energy, our body's first choice is to derive it from carbohydrates and fats we have eaten, second, to pull energy from glycogen and fat stores, and last, to create energy from dietary protein. This means that if you have not eaten in a long time and are experiencing low blood sugar, eating a piece of meat will do little to help you recover, while drinking a glass of juice will have an immediate effect.

Each gram of protein provides 4 calories, regardless of its source. The difference in calories between one ounce of chicken breast and one ounce of prime rib is in the fat content. Each of these, for instance, contains 7 grams of protein, which is 28 calories. But the chicken is a lean meat, providing approximately 3 grams of fat per ounce, while the prime rib is a high fat meat with around 8 grams of fat per ounce, making the difference in their total calories.

FAT

Fat is the nutrient that is constantly struggling with an identity crisis. For years, fat has taken the rap for heart disease, cancer, and other calamities. However, as new categories of fat are discovered and researched, we are learning that some types of fat are more helpful than others.

Chemically, fat is a long chain of molecules with hydrogen atoms surrounding them. A **saturated fat** is a long chain of molecules making up a fatty acid that is completely surrounded by, or saturated with, hydrogen molecules. Saturated fats are solid at room temperature. This makes it very difficult for the body to break it apart in the process of digestion. Most saturated fats contribute to the production of cholesterol in the liver and fatty plaques or groups of fat molecules in the bloodstream. They contribute to your very low density lipoprotein (LDL) levels, which is known as the "bad cholesterol," your physician tests each year. **Trans fatty** acids are relatively new to the mix. They are the fats that are created when polyunsaturated fat goes through a process called hydrogenation. This process turns a liquid fat or oil into one that is more solid at room temperature. Trans fatty acids are the most dangerous of fats with regard to heart disease.

A **monounsaturated fat** is a chain of molecules making up a fatty acid with one unfilled carbon molecule on the chain, which is how it was named. Studies have

Words to Know: Fat

- **Primary role:** Energy, transport of fat soluble vitamins, flavor, and satiety (a feeling of satisfaction contributing to feeling full).
- **Essential fatty acids:** linoleic acid and linolenic acid.
- **Lipid:** a term for all dietary and body fats.
- **Lipoprotein:** Protein-coated fat.
- **Cholesterol:** a waxy, fat-like substance found in foods of animal origin.
- **Serum cholesterol:** cholesterol that is made as a waste product by our liver. A small amount of serum cholesterol is from the food you eat.
- **Saturated fat:** fats that are solid at room temperature, such as shortening, beef fat, and butter.
- **Polyunsaturated fat:** fats that are soft, yet have body at room temperature, such as tub margarine or canola oil.
- **Monounsaturated fat:** fats that are liquid at room temperature, including peanut, olive, and canola oil.
- **Omega three fatty acids:** polyunsaturated fats found in fish oils.
- **Trans fatty acids:** polyunsaturated fats that have been hydrogenated to increase their saturation. For example, shortening is a vegetable oil that has been processed (hydrogenated) to become a fully saturated fat, solid at room temperature.
- **Calories per gram:** 9 calories per gram of fat.

been changing our view of the role of monounsaturated fats in the diet. It is now believed that monounsaturated fats such as olive oil play a role in lowering LDL cholesterol (the bad guys) and preserving the HDL cholesterol (the good guys) in our blood.

Polyunsaturated fats are chains of molecules making up a fatty acid that have more than one unfilled carbon molecule throughout the chain. This makes them easier for the body to break down into smaller and individual fatty acids. Omega three fatty acids, or fish oil, are included in the polyunsaturated fat category and are believed to play a role in reducing the risk of heart disease.

The recommendations for heart health are described in a publication called the *Therapeutic Lifestyle Change Diet,* by the National Cholesterol Education Program. The recommendations for fat are:

- Less than 7 percent of total calories each day from saturated fat,
- Up to 10 percent of total calories each day from polyunsaturated fats (this includes the trans fatty acids such as shortening or vegetable oil with hydrogenated fats),
- Up to 20 percent of total calories each day from monounsaturated fats,
- Total fat intake should be between 25 to 35 percent of total calories each day.

Cholesterol is a waxy, fat-like substance that is found in animal fats and oils. It is found throughout our body but is produced primarily by the liver. Cholesterol circulates in the blood, commonly in association with other saturated and unsaturated fats, and can be either beneficial or harmful. For instance, it is necessary for making cell membranes and many important hormones. However, cholesterol may also form gallstones and harmful deposits in blood vessels.

Foods that contain cholesterol either come from animal sources or include a source of animal fat. An easy rule of thumb is this: If the food did not have a liver before it was packaged, it does not have nor did it ever have cholesterol in it. This means all brands of peanut butter have always been and always will be "cholesterol-free" despite what the label implies. What you really need to look for in peanut butter is the amount of hydrogenation.

The amount of cholesterol your body produces is primarily determined by family history. What you eat and how you live your life helps reduce the total amount of cholesterol in your bloodstream, but does not reduce the amount your body creates. In some cases, changing diet and lifestyle are not enough to lower the risk of heart disease.

Now that all the different types of fat have been defined, we can look at the role that fat plays in our diet. Fat is a rich source of calories and energy for our body. However, because it takes longer for the body to digest fat and pull energy from it, carbohydrates from food are burned first and fat is burned later. This means there is a ready source of energy for muscles and other cells after the energy from recently eaten meals has been used. Eating a small, but adequate amount of fat with a meal keeps us from being hungry too soon afterward.

The role of fat in the diet is different for infants. Healthy babies up to two years of age should consume a diet that is generous in fat compared to everyone else. Approximately 50 percent of the calories in breast milk, formula, and tube feeding products for infants come from fat. For infants and toddlers who are struggling to gain weight due to medical complications (such as preparing for and recovering from heart surgery) a diet that is liberal in fat is also desirable. The reasons for a high-fat diet for babies include:

- It is very hard to provide enough calories to promote the rapid growth rate of infants without fat.
- An infant's brain and other organs are still developing and maturing in the first two years.
- The preferred energy source for the infant brain is fat.

As your child grows, the rate she is growing will slow down. Around one year of age, if she is growing well, recovered from any early surgeries, eating a variety of table foods, and getting over 60 percent of her total calories from table foods, you can move away from formula and breast milk by introducing whole cow's milk or high-fat soy milk. At age two, if she is growing well, recovered from surgeries, and eating a variety of foods, it is suitable to switch to 2% milk—either cow or soy. You may be able to consider milk that is even lower in fat at this time. It is best to discuss this decision with your child's pediatrician. Because children are still grow-

Cholesterol and Cardiovascular Disease in People with Down Syndrome

There are very few studies regarding blood lipids (cholesterol, LDL, HDL) in people with Down syndrome. The research that does exist, however, suggests that regardless of blood lipid levels, the incidence of coronary artery disease is very low in people with Down syndrome. While it is "good news" that people with Down syndrome appear to be less likely to develop this type of heart disease, it is prudent to follow the recommendations for the general population for blood fat testing and dietary goals. These are:

Children: Check blood fat levels in children at age five and every five years after that. More frequent testing may be indicated if a sibling or parent has a total cholesterol of 240mg/dl or more before the age of fifty-five.

Adults: Check blood fat levels every five years unless there is a history of heart disease in a sibling, mother, or father.

ing at a relatively rapid rate, you may want to wait until she is a little older. (See Chapter 1 for more information about transitioning to table foods.)

Another essential role of fat is to carry the fat soluble vitamins to the body. These are vitamins A, D, E, and K. Fat molecules encapsulate these vitamins to carry them into our digestive system and on to our cells. Without fat, these important vitamins would not have a pathway into our bloodstream. Children under five years of age who eat a very low fat diet may develop a fatty acid or fat soluble vitamin deficiency due to their rapid growth rate. However, in most cases, children and adults are not at risk for developing a deficiency when eating a low fat diet.

Fat also provides us with two essential fatty acids: linoleic and linolenic acid. These essential fatty acids are the building blocks to fat storage (see below). They also play a role in preventing dry skin and other body functions.

Stored fat, or *adipose tissue,* helps insulate the body both from cold and injury. All of our organs and spine are surrounded by a layer of fat that acts like bubble wrap or a shock absorber to protect them during everyday movement. Adipose tissue also helps with temperature regulation of the body by insulating us from cold temperatures. However, when there is too much fat, this insulating effect can prevent the body from cooling effectively and restrict movement.

Probably the most overlooked quality to the fat in food is that it provides flavor and a sense of fullness. Fat absorbs the flavor of the foods it is cooked with and enhances them in a way that no other food can. That is why foods high in fat, such as chocolate delicacies, have a rich flavor that is satisfying and desirable to most people.

Of the three nutrients that provide calories, fat provides the most calories per gram: 9 calories per gram of fat. The type of fat is inconsequential. One teaspoon (or 5 grams) of shortening will have the same number of calories as 1 teaspoon (5 grams) of olive oil: 45 calories. Along with concern about its role in heart disease and cancer, this is a good reason to limit the total amount of calories from dietary fat to 30 percent or less for children five years of age and older. Keeping the total amount of fat in your child's diet reasonable will help keep the caloric intake down and reduce the chances of a battle with weight. (See Chapter 13 for more on weight management.)

Micronutrients: Vitamins and Minerals

Vitamins and minerals are the micronutrients of the diet because it takes very little of them to do their job. Although they are called the micronutrients, they are in no way less important. In fact, research and study of vitamins and minerals are among the more exciting areas of nutrition research today. The discovery of vitamins and minerals is relatively new, from the scientific point of view. Vitamins were first discovered as an essential part of the diet in the early twentieth century. Scientists continue to discover new roles and interactions of vitamins and minerals all the time and will likely continue to do so for the rest of this century and more.

VITAMINS

Vitamins are key compounds found in foods that are required for fundamental functions of the body such as energy, growth, and maintenance of health. They act as partners with enzymes, another type of compound, to cause needed reactions to take place within cells. There are two categories of vitamins: water soluble and fat soluble.

What Happened to the RDAs?

The first Recommended Dietary Allowances (RDA) were established in the 1940s. They were designed to provide information about known nutrient needs for "practically all healthy persons." The RDAs for different vitamins and minerals reflected the amount of each nutrient that scientists believed was needed to prevent deficiency.

As scientists have discovered, and continue to discover, more nutrients, the role of the RDAs is changing. We now need information not only about how to prevent deficiencies, but also about how much of a nutrient is too much. We are learning about the medicinal nature of different nutrients such as the role of antioxidants in cancer. Therefore, with the expansion of knowledge, the National Academy of Sciences created *Dietary Reference Intakes (DRI)* for vitamins and minerals.

Like the old RDAs, the DRIs are designed to be applicable to practically all healthy persons. Unlike the old RDAs, the DRIs are a compilation of different values: 1) the RDA, 2) Adequate Intakes, and 3) the tolerable Upper Limits of each nutrient. The RDAs serve the same purpose they always have. They reflect the amount needed of a nutrient to prevent deficiency or disease in a group of "apparently healthy" people. A new value, *Adequate Intakes (AI)*, is used when there is not adequate research to determine an RDA for a nutrient. It is used as a goal for nutrient intake in individuals. At the upper end of the range are *Tolerable Upper Limits (UL)*—the highest level of daily nutrient intake that poses no adverse health effects to the general population. The work to create the DRIs, AIs, and ULs began in 1997 and in 2002. The new DRIs have been released for all the nutrient categories except the electrolytes, which include sodium, potassium, and chloride, among others. Supplement labeling will begin to change to include these values over the next few years.

Because our knowledge of vitamins is always growing and because the regulations regarding claims that can or cannot be made are vague, it is sometimes difficult to know what to believe about the properties or potential harm of large doses of one or more vitamins. A general understanding of each vitamin's purpose and any potential side effects from getting too little or too much will help you understand how to evaluate claims that are made.

WATER SOLUBLE VITAMINS

The water soluble vitamins include Vitamin C and the B-complex vitamins. Water soluble means these vitamins dissolve easily in water or liquid. This make it easy for them to be transported through your body in your blood. If you eat too much of a water soluble vitamin, through food or supplement, the excess amount is filtered through your kidneys and comes out in your urine. Recommended daily allowance and benefits are described in the table on pages 66-68.

FAT SOLUBLE VITAMINS

The fat soluble vitamins are vitamins A, D, E, and K. As the name of this category implies, the fat soluble vitamins are found only in foods that contain fat. In order to be passed through the digestive system and into the bloodstream, fat soluble vitamins are encapsulated by fat molecules. Each of the fat soluble vitamins is essential to our body, though we know more about some than others. All of the fat soluble vitamins are antioxidants, which have been found to be helpful in preventing disease such as cancer and heart disease.

Because they are encapsulated in molecules of fat, these vitamins do not leave our body as readily as the water soluble vitamins. Excesses are filtered primarily through the liver and some are stored along with fat in adipose tissues. For this reason, dosages at or above the UL for a fat soluble vitamin should be handled with care. This is especially true for children under two years old, especially if they are still drinking infant formula, which is laden with vitamins. Consult with your pediatrician before adding a supplement to your infant's diet to ensure you are not reaching the UL for any one vitamin. Over-supplementation can have negative or even harmful effects, as described in the table on pages 71-72.

Words to Know: Vitamins

- **Enzyme:** protein molecules that act as a catalyst to change the rate of a reaction in your body. Substances that are enzymes usually have names that end in "ase," such as lactase or lipase.
- **Coenzyme:** a complex organic molecule, often a vitamin, needed by some enzymes to perform as a catalyst.
- **Antioxidant:** A substance, such as vitamin E or vitamin C, that protects cells from the damage due to oxidation or peroxidation.
- **Oxidation:** The removal of electrons and hydrogen ions from a molecule.
- **Peroxidation:** The process of oxidation; usually triggered by an enzyme.

Dietary Reference Intakes (DRI): Water Soluble Vitamins

Vitamin	Function	Age group	RDA/AI*,		UL	Excess	Deficiency
Ascorbic Acid (Vitamin C) Measured in milligrams per day (mg/d) Food sources for Vitamin C: Citrus fruits, tomatoes, tomato juice, potatoes, Brussels sprouts, cauliflower, broccoli, strawberries, cabbage, and spinach	An antioxidant. Maintains the structure of cartilage, bone, and dentine. Important for collagen synthesis (precursor to new skin). Also a protective antioxidant.		(m)	(f)		Relatively non-toxic. Extremely high doses may contribute to the formation of kidney stones, GI discomfort, or excess iron absorption.	Scurvy: first visible signs of scurvy, raised red spots appear on the skin around the hair follicles of the legs, buttocks, arms, and back. When the tiny capillaries of the hair follicles hemorrhage, the hair-producing cells do not receive the nourishment needed for the hairs to grow normally. Consequently, the skin becomes flecked with small lesions that begin to appear on the body after about five months on a diet deficient in vitamin C. Gums hemorrhage and their tissue becomes weak and spongy. Dentin, which lies below the enamel and is part of the root of teeth, breaks down. Teeth loosen and eating becomes difficult and painful.
		0-6 mo	40*	40*	ND		
		7-12 mo	50*	50*	ND		
		1-3 year	**15**	**15**	400		
		4-8 year	**25**	**25**	650		
		9-13 year	**45**	**45**	1200		
		14-18 year	**90**	**65**	1800		
		19-70 year	**90**	**75**	2000		
		70+ year	**90**	**75**	2000		
Thiamin (Vitamin B-1) Measured in mg/day Food sources for thiamin: Enriched, fortified, or whole grain products; bread and bread products; mixed foods whose main ingredients are grain and ready-to-eat cereals	Acts as a coenzyme in reactions that remove CO_2		(m)	(f)		No adverse effects associated with thiamin from food or supplements. This does not mean there is no potential for adverse effects from high intakes (200% or more of the DRI).	Beriberi: Early symptoms of beriberi are nonspecific and include fatigue, irritability, restlessness, loss of appetite, and vague abdominal discomfort. While rarely seen, beriberi is most common in people who are alcoholics.
		0-6 mo	0.2*	0.2*	ND		
		7-12 mo	0.3*	0.3*	ND		
		1-3 year	**0.5**	**0.5**	ND		
		4-8 year	**0.6**	**0.6**	ND		
		9-13 year	**0.9**	**0.9**	ND		
		14-18 year	**1.2**	**1.0**	ND		
		19-30 year	**1.2**	**1.1**	ND		
		31-50 year	**1.2**	**1.1**	ND		
		51-70 year	**1.2**	**1.1**	ND		
		70+ year	**1.2**	**1.1**	ND		

Vitamin	Function	Age group	RDA/AI*,		UL	Excess	Deficiency
Riboflavin (Vitamin B-2) Measured in mg/day Food sources of riboflavin: Organ meats, milk, bread products, and fortified cereals	Involved in coenzyme actions to produce energy	0-6 mo 7-12 mo 1-3 year 4-8 year 9-13 year 14-18 year 19-30 year 31-50 year 51-70 year 70+ year	(m) 0.3* 0.4* **0.5** **0.6** **0.9** **1.3** **1.3** **1.3** **1.3** **1.3**	(f) 0.3* 0.4* **0.5** **0.6** **0.9** **1.0** **1.1** **1.1** **1.1** **1.1**	ND ND ND ND ND ND ND ND ND ND	No reported health problems with very high intakes (200% or more of the DRI).	Red lips, eye lesions, cracks at the corner of the mouth
Niacin (Vitamin B-3, nicotinic acid, nicotinamide) Measured in mg/day Food sources of Niacin: Meat, fish, poultry, enriched and whole grain breads and bread products, fortified ready-to-eat cereals	Involved in reactions related to oxidation	0-6 mo 7-12 mo 1-3 year 4-8 year 9-13 year 14-18 year 19-30 year 31-50 year 51-70 year 70+ year	(m) 2* 4* **6** **8** **12** **16** **16** **16** **16** **16**	(f) 2* 4* **6** **8** **12** **14** **14** **14** **14** **14**	ND ND 10 15 20 30 35 35 35 35	No adverse effects from consumption of niacin in food. Adverse effects from niacin-containing supplements may include: flushing, burning, and tingling around face, neck, and hands, and GI distress.	Pellagra: Symptoms include: weight loss, diarrhea, depression, and dementia.
Pantothenic Acid Measured in mg/ day Food sources include: Chicken, beef, potatoes, oats, cereals, tomato products, liver, kidney, yeast, egg yolk, broccoli, and whole grains	Part of coenzyme A, which is essential to energy metabolism	0-6 mo 7-12 mo 1-3 year 4-8 year 9-13 year 14-18 year 19-30 year 31-50 year 51-70 year 70+ year	(m) 1.7* 1.8* 2* 3* 4* 5* 5* 5* 5* 5*	(f) 1.7* 1.8* 2* 3* 4* 5* 5* 5* 5* 5*	ND ND ND ND ND ND ND ND ND ND	No reported health-related problems from very high (200% or more of the DRI) amounts from either food or supplements.	Fatigue, sleeplessness, lack of coordination
Pyridoxine (Vitamin B-6) Measured in mg/day Food sources include: Fortified cereals, organ meats, fortified soy-based meat substitutes	Involved in amino acid and glucose metabolism	0-6 mo 7-12 mo 1-3 year 4-8 year 9-13 year 14-18 year 19-30 year 31-50 year 51-70 year 70+ year	(m) 0.1* 0.3* **0.5** **0.6** **1.0** **1.3** **1.3** **1.3** **1.7** **1.7**	(f) 0.1* 0.3* **0.5** **0.6** **1.0** **1.2** **1.3** **1.3** **1.5** **1.5**	ND ND 30 40 60 80 100 100 100 100	No reported health-related problems from very high (200% or more of the DRI) amounts from either food or supplements.	Irritability, muscle twitching, dermatitis near the eyes, and kidney stones

Vitamin	Function	Age group	RDA/AI*,	UL	Excess	Deficiency
Folic Acid (Folicin) Measured in micrograms/day (mcg/d) Food sources include: Enriched cereal, grains, dark leafy vegetables, enriched and whole-grain breads and bread products, fortified ready-to-eat cereals	A coenzyme involved in transferring carbons within cells and in amino acid metabolism.	0-6 mo 7-12 mo 1-3 year 4-8 year 9-13 year 14-18 year 19-30 year 31-50 year 51-70 year 70+ year	65* 80* **150** **200** **300** **400** **400** **400** **400** **400**	ND ND 300 400 600 800 1000 1000 1000 1000	If also deficient in vitamin B_{12}, neurological disorders will be difficult to detect. No reported health-related problems from very high (200% or more of the DRI) amounts from either food or supplements.	Anemia, GI disturbances, red tongue, diarrhea
Cobalamin (Vitamin B_{12}) Measured in micrograms per day (mcg/d) Food sources include: Fortified cereals, meat, fish, and poultry	Coenzyme involved in transfer of carbon molecules in cells.	0-6 mo 7-12 mo 1-3 year 4-8 year 9-13 year 14-18 year 19-30 year 31-50 year 51-70 year 70+ year	0.4* 0.5* **0.9** **1.2** **1.8** **2.4** **2.4** **2.4** **2.4** **2.4**	ND ND ND ND ND ND ND ND ND ND	No reported health-related problems from very high (200% or more of the DRI) amounts from either food or supplements.	Pernicious anemia and neurologic disorders. Because 10-30% of older people may malabsorb food-bound vitamin B_{12}, it is advisable for people over 50 years to consider supplementing vitamin B_{12}.
Biotin Measured in micrograms per day (mcg/d) Food sources include: Liver and smaller amounts in fruits and meats	Works with coenzymes required for fat synthesis, amino acid metabolism, and glucogen formation.	0-6 mo 7-12 mo 1-3 year 4-8 year 9-13 year 14-18 year 19-30 year 31-50 year 51-70 year 70+ year	5* 6* 8* 12* 20* 25* 30* 30* 30* 30*	ND ND ND ND ND ND ND ND ND ND	No reported health-related problems from very high (200% or more of the DRI) amounts from either food or supplements.	Fatigue, depression, dermatitis, muscle pain
Choline Measured in milligrams per day (mg/d) Food sources include: Milk, liver, eggs, and peanuts	Precursor for acetylcholine, which is necessary for energy production.	(m) (f) 0-6 mo 7-12 mo 1-3 year 4-8 year 9-13 year 14-18 year 19-30 year 31-50 year 51-70 year 70+ year	(m) (f) 125* 125* 150* 150* 200* 200* 250* 250* 375* 375* 550* 400* 550* 425* 550* 425* 550* 425* 550* 425*	ND ND 1000 1000 2000 3000 3500 3500 3500 3500	Fishy body odor, sweating, increase in salivation, low blood pressure, toxicity in liver.	Deficiency may result in fatty liver. Although AIs have been set for choline, a dietary supply of choline may not be needed at all stages of life. It is possible choline requirement can be met by outside synthesis at some stages of life.

NOTE: This table is adapted from the DRI reports. The Recommended Dietary Allowances (RDAs) are in bold type; Adequate Intake (AIs) are in plain type followed by an asterisk. RDAs and AIs may both be used as goals for individual intake. ND is used to note that an Upper Limit (UL) for a vitamin is undetermined.

Dietary Reference Intakes (DRI): Fat Soluble Vitamins

Vitamin	Function	Age group	RDA/AI*,		UL	Excess	Deficiency
Vitamin A Measured in micrograms per day (mcg/d)*** Food sources include: Liver, dairy products, and fish.	An antioxidant. Plays a role in vision and maintaining the body's skin and linings of parts of the body such as the lungs, eyes, and intestine. Vitamin A is also important for bone growth and reproduction.	0-6 mo 7-12 mo 1-3 year 4-8 year 9-13 year 14-18 year 19-30 year 31-50 year 51-70 year 70+ year	(m) 400* 500* **300** **400** **600** **900** **900** **900** **900** **900**	(f) 400* 500* **300** **400** **600** **700** **700** **700** **700** **700**	600 600 600 900+ 1700 2800 3000 3000 3000 3000	Adults: headache; dry, scaly skin; liver damage, bone and joint pain; vomiting; or appetite loss. Children: irritability, swelling bones, weight loss, dry skin, abnormal bone growth, loss of calcium in the bones. Excess vitamin A is almost always secondary to large amounts of vitamin A supplements over a period of time. Megadoses of beta carotene (the form of vitamin A in food sources) rarely occur.	Night blindness resulting in permanent blindness if left untreated for a period of time (xerophthalmia).
Vitamin D Measured in micrograms per day (mcg/d) Food sources include: Fish liver oils, flesh of fatty fish, liver and fat from seals and polar bears, eggs from hens that have been fed vitamin D-fortified milk products, and fortified cereals.	Promotes absorption of calcium and phosphorous, which are important in bone growth and maintenance.	0-6 mo 7-12 mo 1-3 year 4-8 year 9-13 year 14-18 year 19-30 year 30-50 year 51-70 year 70+ year	5* 5* 5* 5* 5* 5* 5* 5* 10* 15*		25 25 50 50 50 50 50 50 50 50	Kidney stones or kidney damage, diarrhea, weak muscles, weak bones, excessive bleeding, and weight loss. Calcium deposits in other organs of the body. Excesses usually due to supplementation over twice the DRI.	Rickets in children. Rickets is characterized by a softening of bones that can lead to malformation as the child grows. Symptoms include: tenderness and pain in the bones– especially those of the arms, legs, pelvis, and spine, along with a growing sense of overall weakness. Osteomalacia (i.e., softening of bones) in adults. Symptoms are similar to those listed above for rickets.

Vitamin	Function	Age group	RDA/AI*,		UL	Excess	Deficiency
Vitamin E Measured as alpha-tocopherol in mg/d. Food sources include: Vegetable oils, unprocessed cereal grains, nuts, fruits, vegetables, meats	An antioxidant. It has been found to be helpful in reducing the risk of heart disease and cancer, and may play a role in preventing memory loss.	0-6 mo 7-12 mo 1-3 year 4-8 year 9-13 year 14-18 year 19-30 year 31-50 year 51-70 year 70+ year	4* 5* 6 7 11 15 15 15 15 15		ND ND 200 300 6y00 800 1000 1000	No reported health-related problems from very high (200% or more of the DRI) amounts from either food or supplements. Large doses of synthetic forms of vitamin E may cause jaundice.	No known deficiency syndrome.
Vitamin K Measured in micrograms per day (mcg/d) Food sources include: Green vegetables (collards, spinach, salad greens, broccoli), Brussels sprouts, cabbage, plant oils, and margarine	Involved in making proteins that are involved in blood clotting and coagulation.	0-6 mo 7-12 mo 1-3 year 4-8 year 9-13 year 14-18 year 19-30 year 31-50 year 51-70 year 70+ year	(m) 2.0* 2.5* 55* 60* 75* 120* 120* 120* 120* 120*	(f) 2.0* 2.5* 55* 60* 75* 90* 90* 90* 90* 90*	ND ND ND ND ND ND ND ND ND ND	No reported health-related problems from very high (200% or more of the DRI) amounts from either food or supplements, unless taking a blood thinner or clotting agent such as coumadin.	Inability for blood to clot.

* NOTE: This table is adapted from the DRI reports. The Recommended Dietary Allowances (RDAs) are in bold type; Adequate Intake (AIs) are in plain type followed by an asterisk. RDAs and AIs may both be used as goals for individual intake. ND is used to note that an Upper Limit (UL) for a vitamin is undetermined.

****Given as retinol activity equivalents (RAE). 1 RAE = 1 mcg retinol, 12 mcg beta-carotene, 24 mcg alpha-carotene. For preformed vitamin A in foods or supplements and for provitamin A carotenoids in supplements, 1 RE = 1 RAE*

MINERALS

Minerals make up the fifth nutrient category essential for our bodies. Minerals are naturally occurring elements found in foods and often other items that are necessary for body functions. Minerals are an even more recent discovery to the science of nutrition than vitamins. Each year, we are learning more about the importance of minerals to our body functions, as well as discovering new roles for minerals we did not previously believe were essential. This is especially true for the trace minerals because they are needed in miniscule amounts.

Minerals, like vitamins, are involved in the reactions that take place in our cells. Some are needed to convert carbohydrate, fat, and protein to storage products (glycogen and adipose tissue), some are involved in converting glucose, fatty acids, and amino acids to energy, some help convert amino acids to protein tissues, and others are important in the fluid or electrolyte balance in our body. We may not need great quantities of minerals in our diet, but they are very important. See the table on pages 73-77 for guidelines.

Words to Know: Minerals

- **Minerals:** essential, natural minerals found in food that are required for various body functions such as the balance of body fluids and bone health.
- **Major minerals:** also referred to as macrominerals, and are more prevalent in the body than trace minerals.
- **Trace minerals:** also referred to as microminerals, and are found in very small amounts in the body, but are necessary for health.
- **Electrolytes:** minerals that have a positive or negative chemical charge. The balance of these electrolytes promotes water and other fluids passing through different membranes during digestion.
- **Acid-base balance:** also known as pH balance, is regulated by the kidneys. Minerals play a role in keeping the pH balance to promote absorption of necessary minerals.

Dietary Reference Intakes (DRI): Minerals

Vitamin	Function	Age group	RDA/AI*	UL	Excess	Deficiency
Calcium Measured in milligrams per day (mg/d) Food sources include: Milk, yogurt, corn tortillas, calcium-set tofu, Chinese cabbage, kale, broccoli.	Involved in bone and tooth formation and blood clotting.	0-6 mo 7-12 mo 1-3 yr 4-8 yr 9-13 yr 14-18 yr 19-30 yr 30-50 yr 51-70 yr 70+ yr	210* 270* 500* 800* 1300* 1300* 1000* 1000* 1200* 1200*	ND ND 2500 2500 2500 2500 2500 2500 2500 2500	No reported health-related problems from very high (200% or more of the DRI) amounts from either food or supplements.	Stunted growth, rickets, and osteomalacia. Rickets in children. Rickets is characterized by a softening of bones that can lead to malformation as the child grows. Symptoms include: tenderness and pain in the bones— especially those of the arms, legs, pelvis, and spine, along with a growing sense of overall weakness. Osteomalacia (i.e., softening of bones) in adults. Symptoms are similar to those listed above for rickets.
Phosphorus Measured in milligrams per day (mg/d) Food sources include: Milk, yogurt, ice cream, cheese, peas, meat, eggs, some cereals, and breads.	Involved in bone and tooth formation. Involved in pH balance of the body fluids and transfer of energy.	0-6 mo 7-12 mo 1-3 yr 4-8 yr 9-13 yr 14-18 yr 19-30 yr 30-50 yr 51-70 yr 70+ yr	100* 275* **460** **500** **1250** **1250** **700** **700** **700** **700**	ND ND 3000 3000 4000 4000 4000 4000 4000 3000	Metatastic calcification, interference with calcium absorption. Athletes and others with high energy expenditure frequently consume amounts *from food* greater than the UL without apparent effect.	Weakness, demineralization of bones.

Vitamin	Function	Age group	RDA/AI*		UL	Excess	Deficiency
Sodium (Na+) Measured in milligrams per day (mg/d) See NOTE (2) below.	An electrolyte. Also involved in acid/base balance of body fluids.	0-6 mo 7-12 mo 1-3 yr 4-8 yr 9-13 yr 14-18 yr 19-30 yr 30-50 yr 51-70 yr 70+ yr	120 200 225 300 500 500 500 500 500 500		ND ND ND ND ND ND ND ND ND ND	Possibly high blood pressure.	Muscle cramps, decreased appetite, mental apathy.
Magnesium (Mg) Measured in milligrams per day (mg/d) Food sources include: Green leafy vegetables, unpolished grains, nuts, meat, starches, milk.	Activates enzymes in protein synthesis.	0-6 mo 7-12 mo 1-3 yr 4-8 yr 9-13 yr 14-18 yr 19-30 yr 30-50 yr 51-70 yr 70+ yr	(f) 30* 75* **80** **130** **240** **410** **400** **420** **420** **420**	(m) 60* 75* **80** **130** **240** **360** **310** **320** **320** **320**	ND ND 65 110 350 350 350 350 350 350	Diarrhea resulting in dehydration. The UL for magnesium is for intake from a supplement or other pharmacological agent (such as Milk of Magnesia) only and does not include sources of magnesium from water or food. There is no evidence of adverse effects from intake of magnesium from food.	Behavior disturbances, decrease in growth.
Iron (Fe) Measured in milligrams per day (mg/d). Nonheme food sources include: fruits, vegetables, and fortified bread products. Heme food sources include: meat and poultry.	Part of hemoglobin and works with enzymes involved with energy.	0-6 mo 7-12 mo 1-3 yr 4-8 yr 9-13 yr 14-18 yr 19-30 yr 30-50 yr 51-70 yr 70+ yr	(m) 0.27* **11** **7** **10** **8** **11** **8** **8** **8** **8**	(f) 0.27* **11** **7** **10** **8** **15** **18** **18** **18** **8**	40 40 40 40 40 45 45 45 45 45	GI discomfort.	Anemia. Iron absorption is lower for those consuming vegetarian diets than for those eating nonvegetarian diets. Therefore, some suggest that the iron requirement for people consuming a vegetarian diet is approximately double.

Recommended intake assumes 75% of iron is from animal sources.

Vitamin	Function	Age group	RDA/AI*		UL	Excess	Deficiency
Fluoride (Fl) Measured in milligrams per day (mg/d). Food sources include: fluoridated water, teas, marine fish, fluoridated dental products.	Involved in bone structure and development of dentine for teeth.	0-6 mo 7-12 mo 1-3 yr 4-8 yr 9-13 yr 14-18 yr 19-30 yr 30-50 yr 51-70 yr 70+ yr	(m) 0.01* 0.5* 0.7* 1* 2* 3* 4* 4* 4* 4*	(f) 0.01* 0.5* 0.7* 1* 2* 3* 3* 3* 3* 3*	0.7 0.9 1.3 2.2 10 10 10 10 10 10	Neurological disturbances, mottling of teeth, increase in bone density.	Increase in tooth decay.
Zinc (Zn) Measured in milligrams per day (mg/d) Food sources include: fortified cereals, red meats, some seafood.	Promotes cell reproduction, tissue growth and repair, and is involved with 70 enzymes.	0-6 mo 7-12 mo 1-3 yr 4-8 yr 9-13 yr 14-18 yr 19-30 yr 30-50 yr 51-70 yr 70+ yr	(m) 2* 3 3 5 8 11 11 11 11 11	(f) 2* 3 3 5 8 9 8 8 8 8	4 5 7 12 23 34 40 40 40 40	Fever, nausea, vomiting, diarrhea. Reduced absorption of copper.	Small sex glands, poor overall growth, susceptibility to colds and other infections possible. Zinc absorption is lower for people consuming vegetarian diets. A requirement that is double the DRI is suggested for people who are vegetarians.
Copper (Cu) Measured in micrograms per day (mcg/d) Food sources include: organ meats, seafood, nuts, seeds, wheat bran, cereals, whole grain products, cocoa products.	Involved in creating hemoglobin, helps with energy metabolism.	0-6 mo 7-12 mo 1-3 yr 4-8 yr 9-13 yr 14-18 yr 19-30 yr 30-50 yr 51-70 yr 70+ yr	200* 220* 340 440 700 890 900 900 900 900		ND ND 1000 3000 5000 8000 10,000 10,000 10,000 10,000	GI distress, liver damage. Excesses are seen in Wilson's disease, a rare metabolic condition.	Anemia and bone changes.
Selenium (Se) Measured in micrograms per day (mcg/d) Food sources include: Organ meats, seafood, plants (depending on soil content where grown).	It works in association with vitamin E as an antioxidant and aids cell growth.	0-6 mo 7-12 mo 1-3 yr 4-8 yr 9-13 yr 14-18 yr 19-30 yr 30-50 yr 51-70 yr 70+ yr	15* 20* 20 30 40 55 55 55 55 55		45 60 90 150 280 400 400 400 400 400	Hair and nail brittleness and loss.	Anemia, though rare.

Vitamin	Function	Age group	RDA/AI*		UL	Excess	Deficiency
Iodine (I) Measured in micrograms per day (mcg/d) Food sources include: seafood, processed foods, iodized salt.	Part of the thyroid hormone system.	0-6 mo 7-12 mo 1-3 yr 4-8 yr 9-13 yr 14-18 yr 19-30 yr 30-50 yr 51-70 yr 70+ yr	110* 130* **90** **90** **120** **150** **150** **150** **150** **150**		ND ND 200 300 600 900 1100 1100 1100 1100	Depresses the actions of the thyroid (may result in hypothyroid-like condition)	Goiter (an enlarged thyroid gland in the neck) and cretinism (usually due to congenital dysfunction of the thyroid gland).
Molybdenum (Mb) Measured in micrograms per day (mcg/d) Food sources include: legumes, grain products, and nuts.	Works with riboflavin to move iron into hemoglobin for red blood cells. It is also involved with many other enzyme reactions.	0-6 mo 7-12 mo 1-3 yr 4-8 yr 9-13 yr 14-18 yr 19-30 yr 30-50 yr 51-70 yr 70+ yr	2* 3* **17** **22** **34** **43** **45** **45** **45** **45**		ND ND 300 600 1100 1700 2000 2000 2000 2000	May interfere with copper, but very rare.	No reported health-related concerns.
Chromium (Cr) Measured in micrograms per day (mcg/d) Food sources include: some cereals, meats, poultry, fish, beer.	Involved in glucose metabolism (works with insulin).	0-6 mo 7-12 mo 1-3 yr 4-8 yr 9-13 yr 14-18 yr 19-30 yr 30-50 yr 51-70 yr 70+ yr	(m) 0.2* 5.5* 11* 15* 25* 35* 35* 35* 30* 30*	(f) 0.2* 5.5* 11* 15* 21* 24* 25* 25* 20* 20*	ND ND ND ND ND ND ND ND ND ND	Usually a result of an occupational exposure resulting in skin and kidney damage such as chronic kidney failure.	Decreased ability to metabolize glucose or produce insulin.
Chloride (Cl) Measured in milligrams per day (mg/d). See NOTE (2) below.	An electrolyte. Also involved with digestion and absorption of nutrients. Transmits nerve signals.	0-6 mo 7-12 mo 1-3 yr 4-8 yr 9-13 yr 14-18 yr 19-30 yr 30-50 yr 51-70 yr 70+ yr	180 300 500 600 750 750 750 750 750 750		ND ND ND ND ND ND ND ND ND ND	Possibly high blood pressure.	Muscle cramping, decreased appetite, mental apathy.

Vitamin	Function	Age group	RDA/AI*		UL	Excess	Deficiency
Potassium (K+) Measured in milligrams per day (mg/d). See NOTE (2) below. Almonds, apples, apricots, avocados, bacon, bananas, beans, beef, liver, beet greens, beets, blackberries, Brazil nuts, breads, broccoli, cabbage, caviar, celery, cheese, chicken, chocolate, clams, corn, dates, fish, garlic, green peas, macadamia nuts, milk, molasses, mushrooms, parsnips, potatoes, raisins, Swiss chard.	An electrolyte. Involved with blood pressure, muscle contraction, and nerve signals.	0-6 mo 7-12 mo 1-3 yr 4-8 yr 9-13 yr 14-18 yr 19-30 yr 30-50 yr 51-70 yr 70+ yr	500 700 1000 1400 1600 2000 2000 2000 2000 2000		ND ND ND ND ND ND ND ND ND ND	Usually excreted, but excesses may cause heart palpitations.	Deficiencies are usually seen secondary to dehydration: weak, decreased appetite, nausea, fatigue, and headache.
Manganese (Mn) Measured in milligrams per day (mg/d) Food sources include: nuts, legumes, tea, and whole grains.	Involved in bone formation and with enzymes involved in amino acid, cholesterol, and carbohydrate metabolism.	0-6 mo 7-12 mo 1-3 yr 4-8 yr 9-13 yr 14-18 yr 19-30 yr 30-50 yr 51-70 yr 70+ yr	(m) 0.0003* 0.6* 1.2* 1.5* 1.9* 2.2* 2.3* 2.3* 2.3* 2.3*	(f) 0.6* 1.2* 1.5* 1.6* 1.6* 1.8* 1.8* 1.8* 1.8*	ND ND 2 3 6 9 11 11 11 11	Elevated blood concentration and toxicity in the brain. People with liver disease may be particularly susceptible to the effects of excessive manganese.	A deficiency in manganese has not been shown conclusively to be linked to any specific set of symptoms

NOTE: This table is adapted from the DRI reports. The Recommended Dietary Allowances (RDAs) are in bold type; Adequate Intake (AIs) are in plain type followed by an asterisk. RDAs and AIs may both be used as goals for individual intake. ND is used to note that an Upper Limit (UL) for a vitamin is undetermined.

NOTE (2): The DRI report for the electrolytes sodium, chloride, and potassium has not been released at the time of publication. Values listed are the Recommended Dietary Allowances (RDA) of 1989.

Vitamin and Mineral Needs in Children with Down Syndrome

Unfortunately, there have been few definitive studies published about the effects of the extra 21st chromosome on the vitamin and mineral needs of people with Down syndrome. As the research on specific genes continues, it is likely we will know much more about the effects of trisomy 21 overall, including any differences in vitamin and mineral needs. For now, we are limited to what is known about Down syndrome and vitamins and minerals to guide our decision making.

WHAT WE DO KNOW

First, studies suggest that children and adults with Down syndrome have a lower basal metabolic rate (BMR). This means that overall, people with Down syndrome need fewer calories to maintain their body weight than someone of the same height and weight who does not have Down syndrome. The implications of this are two-fold:

1. To maintain a healthy weight, children and adults with Down syndrome must eat smaller quantities of foods and be wary of eating foods that have a lot of calories.
2. Since they require fewer total calories, it is a challenge to eat well enough to meet nutrient needs from food alone.

Even a low fat diet that is perfectly balanced may not meet the nutrient needs of someone with Down syndrome. This concern is highlighted by a study that compared food choices of children with Down syndrome with those of their nondisabled peers. The researchers discovered that children with Down syndrome compensated for the lower calorie need naturally when making food choices. However, in the process, they consumed significantly fewer micronutrients (vitamins and minerals). This means that while children with Down syndrome may choose appropriate amounts of foods for their calorie needs, they may still be at risk for vitamin and mineral deficiencies. It is important to note that sometimes the lower micronutrient intake may be the result of food choices determined by chewing concerns (eating only soft-texture foods) or another developmental eating dysfunction.

From studies done on zinc and selenium for the general population, we know that adequate amounts of these two minerals are helpful in building up immune system status. There have also been a small number of studies or articles written that have found similar results in people with Down syndrome. As a result, it is generally accepted that children and adults with Down syndrome may see an improvement in immune function with supplementation of zinc and selenium.

WHAT WE DO **NOT** KNOW

There are more questions than answers with regard to what we do *not* know about vitamins and minerals for people with Down syndrome at any age of life. As with many areas of nutrition, new theories emerge regularly. Some of these theories relate to whether vitamins and minerals might be used to improve the health, cognitive functioning, and growth of people with Down syndrome. For instance, some people wonder if supplementing vitamin E could improve mental functioning or prevent Alzheimer's disease in people with Down syndrome. Others believe that iron supplementation in children with Down syndrome should be discouraged to reduce the risk of plaque formation in the brain. Others think it may be possible to come up with a unique combination of vitamins and minerals that would boost the immune system, and maybe intelligence, of people with Down syndrome. Still others believe there are no dramatic vitamin and mineral need differences between people with Down syndrome and those without. The list is long and confusing with no clear-cut answers for parents and professionals. See Chapter 8 for a discussion of the history of vitamin supplementation in Down syndrome.

Over the past fifty years, there have been multiple studies on the effects of various supplements for people with Down syndrome. The vast majority of the studies about vitamin or mineral supplementation for people with Down syndrome were not randomized controlled studies. A randomized controlled study is the gold-standard of studies. It means that people with Down syndrome are selected randomly to receive the supplement, do not know if they are taking a supplement or a pretend one, and that the data obtained are compared to the data obtained from a group of people without Down syndrome who are also randomly receiving supplements. Without these types of studies, there will always be room for criticism and questions regarding the results from a study.

There *has* been an abundance of anecdotal stories on television and the Internet claiming improvements from the use of various supplements, but there are also anecdotal stories from families who used the same supplements and noted no effects. For more on this controversy and how to evaluate information about supplements and alternative therapies, see Chapter 8.

WHAT CONCLUSIONS CAN WE DRAW?

Unfortunately, the studies needed to corroborate specific differences in vitamin, mineral, and other micronutrient needs for children and adults with Down syndrome do not exist. Until they do, there is no definitive answer to questions about specific differences for people with Down syndrome, only speculation.

Based on this information, you may want to consider a multivitamin supplement if your child:

- is a picky eater,
- is having trouble with food textures,
- is on a calorie restricted diet for obesity, or
- complains of fatigue and appears more listless than usual.

An over-the-counter vitamin and mineral supplement will bridge whatever micronutrients your child may be missing. If you are breastfeeding your baby, an infant supplement such as PolyViSol with vitamin D or TriViSol with vitamin D may be appropriate. Check with your pediatrician. If your baby is drinking formula, you probably do not need to supplement her diet at all at this time.

If you are seriously concerned that your child may have a deficiency in one or more vitamins or minerals, discuss it with your child's doctor. It will be most helpful if you bring a list of foods and the amounts your child has eaten over a number of days (3-7) with you. This will give your doctor some good information about your child's eating habits. He will likely discuss your concerns, look for signs and symptoms classic for deficiencies, or order some blood or urine studies.

Tips for Selecting Over-the-Counter Multivitamins

Going to the store to buy a multivitamin is no longer a simple task. There are multiple versions of every brand, each claiming some specific benefit over the other (One-A-Day Maximum, One-A-Day Performance, One-A-Day for Women, and so on). Here are some general tips to help make your shopping a little easier:

- **Choose a product that provides a wide variety of vitamins and minerals in amounts anywhere from 50 to 100 percent of the RDA and less than the UL for each vitamin and mineral.** You may need to take a list of the UL's to the store with you, as they are not reflected on the label at all. The "percent daily value" listed on the label is not a lot of help.

- **Choose brands that have been tested for quality.** One way to determine this is to look for quality approval seals on the label. You can also learn about the quality of supplements sold in stores through websites such as www.Consumerlabs.com.

- **Check the expiration date.** Do not purchase supplements that are close to their expiration date, as you may not use them before they expire.

- **Be prepared to try several brands of chewables to find one with a flavor your child likes.** If your child is not ready for a chewable vitamin, crush vitamins and mix with a food such as applesauce or yogurt. Do not hide the fact that you are giving your child vitamins.

Water

The last of the six nutrient categories is no less important than the other five. Water, often called the forgotten nutrient, is an essential part of nutrition, health, and body functioning. Generally, a person needs around eight cups of water a day.

Without adequate water you become dehydrated, which can affect not only how your body works, but also how well you are thinking. Many of us tend to be around 1 percent dehydrated a lot of the time. How do I know this? Because when you feel thirsty, you are already approximately 1 percent dehydrated. At 2 percent dehydration, you experience a stronger thirst, discomfort, and a loss of appetite. You feel like you've spent a summer day in the sun without anything to drink. With a 3 percent deficit, you experience trouble with physical performance.

This is a problem for anyone involved in a sport. (See chart below.) Your game will be off if you aren't adequately hydrated. For children and adults with Down syndrome, this level of dehydration may induce the "Stop, Drop, and Flop" mechanism or an increase in other stubborn behavior. It is easy to see that water plays a dramatic role in body functioning and performance.

Having enough water in your diet does not necessarily mean drinking only water. There are a number of foods and beverages that hydrate the body along with providing calories. Hydration is very important in helping your child's body work well. Water plays a pivotal role in preventing constipation, which is a common concern for children and adults with Down syndrome. Some foods and liquids that help and hinder with hydration include:

Percent of Body Weight Lost Due to Dehydration

0	1	2	3	4	5	6	7	8	9	10	11
	Thirst	Stronger thirst, discomfort, and loss of appetite	Dry mouth; impaired physical performance	Apathy and nausea	Trouble concentrating	Dysfunctional temperature regulation during exercise		Dizziness, labored breathing, and increased weakness during exercise		Spastic muscles, delirium, wakefulness, and swollen tongue	Abnormal blood circulation, impaired kidney function

GOOD FOR HYDRATION

- water,
- fruit juices,
- sport drinks,
- herbal tea,
- milk,
- watermelon,
- orange wedges,
- Jello,
- Popsicles

BAD FOR HYDRATION

- high salt foods,
- drinks high in caffeine such as coffee, tea, and soda,
- drinks high in sugar such as some sport drinks, fruit drinks, and soda,
- alcoholic beverages.

Summary

There are six nutrient categories provided by foods we eat or drink. The macro-nutrients are those that provide calories, while the micronutrients, which are found in food sources, contain the vitamins and minerals necessary for our body to use the food we eat for its intended use. Each category depends on the

other to do its job. Too much of one or too little of another affects the millions of reactions that go on in our body's cells each day.

Scientists continue to learn more about our need for minerals, as well as to discover new purposes and actions of nutrients. The latest discovery includes a new category of minerals, the Ultra trace minerals: Vanadium, Boron, Arsenic, and more. It is important to remember this new information and the process of discovery may affect the type and depth of information available specific to Down syndrome. The next fifty years will be exciting to watch.

CHAPTER 5

Physiology 101

The previous chapter covered half the story about nourishing your body with food. The other half of the story is the physiology of feeding your body or what happens to the foods inside your body once you eat them. Once food is eaten, it must be digested, broken down into nutrients, absorbed, sent to appropriate cells for use, and disposed of. Once the nutrients are absorbed in our body they play key roles in our metabolism, energy, fat storage, and overall health. This chapter will focus on both the normal process of digesting and using food in the human body, as well as some of the most common intestine-related problems children and adults with Down syndrome encounter.

As more vitamins, minerals, and phytochemicals are discovered, our understanding of their role in body processes changes. We are far from having definitive knowledge about nutrition and how it affects the intricate details of our bodies, but this chapter reviews what we do know that is relevant to children with Down syndrome.

Digestion

The digestive system is a series of hollow organs that are joined by a long twisting tube beginning with your mouth and continuing all the way to your anus. These organs and tubes are lined with a tissue called the mucosa. Certain areas of the mucosa contain glands that produce juices or enzymes to help digest the food you eat.

The process of digestion begins the moment you put food in your mouth. As you chew foods, they begin to break into smaller pieces and molecules. In the process of chewing, your salivary glands release an enzyme called amylase, which starts the process of breaking complex carbohydrates into simple carbohydrates. For example, if you take a large piece of bread (white bread is best for this exercise) and chew without swallowing until it is merely liquid in your mouth, you will notice it becomes sweet tasting. This is because amylase breaks down the long carbohydrate chain that makes up the starch in the bread to sucrose and glucose, which are very simple sugars. In fact, any glucose that is available in your mouth at this point can be absorbed through your mouth tissues to provide some immediate fuel for your body cells.

Words to Know: Digestion

- **Mucosa:** tissue that lines the walls of the digestive system.
- **Peristalsis:** muscle contractions that help propel foods through the digestive system.
- **Enzymes:** protein molecules that act as a catalyst to change the rate of a reaction in your body. Substances that are enzymes usually have names that end in "ase," such as lactase or lipase.
- **Gastric secretions:** a combination of enzymes and acids for digestion that are released in the stomach to break foods down so they can be absorbed by the small intestine.
- **Small intestine:** the portion of the intestine attached to the stomach. The small intestine is the longest (approximately six meters) and most convoluted or twisted portion of the digestive tract.
- **Large intestine:** the portion of the intestine that continues about one and a half meters from the small intestine to the anus, where waste is excreted from the body.

Once you swallow food, it is propelled away from the mouth and down the esophagus, or "food tube," toward the stomach, where further breakdown occurs. Once in the stomach, the chewed foods are barraged by a variety of gastric secretions and acid necessary to isolate the nutrients in foods for absorption and use.

As foods are further broken apart, they move from the stomach to the small intestine. The mucosa of the small intestine has specialized cell systems, called the villi, which look like tiny fingers protruding from the intestinal wall. The villi ensure the absorption of the isolated nutrients such as carbohydrates, protein, fat, vitamins, minerals, and water. Approximately 90 percent of the nutrients from foods, including water, are absorbed in the small intestine. Once these nutrients have been absorbed by the mucosa wall, your body is able to use them for energy, to create tissue, or to transport needed vitamins and minerals through the bloodstream to other parts of the body.

As foods are absorbed in the small intestine, the remaining products are moved through by peristalsis to the colon. The colon absorbs the remaining water in the waste product (usually fiber and other indigestible components). These waste products are then expelled from the body through the anus.

When foods are digested and absorbed through the intestinal wall to the bloodstream, the molecules of carbohydrate, protein, and fat are put to work. Each of these macronutrient categories has a different primary purpose, as explained in the previous chapter. Carbohydrates provide the most efficient and pure form of energy for the body, glucose. Therefore, your body will first look for sources of carbohydrate, or glucose, when it is low on energy. If there is not enough available, it will then seek sources of dietary fat and then protein from the intestine to convert to energy in the form of glucose for the cells. This glucose that your cells find and make through conversion is what is measured in your bloodstream when someone checks your "blood sugar."

A certain amount of glucose in your blood is good (70-140 mg/dl). If you do not have enough, you will be tired, hungry, and have trouble concentrating. If your blood glucose is too high, you may have diabetes (see Chapter 7). The blood glucose is then taken up by cells and sent from your veins and arteries to organs and muscles, with the help of insulin, to be used for energy.

While carbohydrates, dietary fat, and protein can be converted to glucose, stored fat (adipose tissue) cannot. Stored fat produces an alternate source of energy called *ketones,* which is less efficient for the body. If there are no sources of carbohydrate, protein, or dietary fat readily available, your body will then convert adipose tissue to ketones and use this for energy. This is what happens when you are on a weight loss program, eating fewer calories than your body needs to maintain weight and exercising readily. This also occurs when you are very ill and unable to eat enough food to maintain your body. While it is not unhealthy for your body to use ketones for energy at times, it is not the preferred way to fuel your body for a long period of time.

When you exercise, your body will first seek to use the energy available from the foods you recently ate. In other words, it's easiest to convert foods directly to glucose for energy. Once this source of glucose is used, your body will convert stored glucose, called glycogen, to use for energy. Glycogen is stored within the muscle lining and is easily converted from its stored form to glucose. If you are exercising aerobically, it usually takes fifteen to twenty minutes to use readily available glucose and glycogen stores. Once your glycogen stores are used, your body will seek other sources of energy such as adipose tissue.

Digestion in People with Down Syndrome

The overall process of digestion works the same in children and adults with Down syndrome as it does in anyone else. Foods pass through the intestine (stomach and intestines) in the same manner, are digested in the same area of the intestine, and are excreted from the body in the same way. However, the process of passing food through the esophagus, intestine, and bowel may take longer due to lower muscle tone. In addition, people with Down syndrome may be less active overall or have diets that are relatively low in fiber. All these things combined often make it more difficult for food waste to pass through the intestine. This frequently results in constipation.

CONSTIPATION While you may have your own definition of constipation, it is technically defined as hard or thick, pasty stools that are difficult to pass. One mother described her son's diaper as being filled with "rabbit pellets." These rabbit pellets are often followed by large stools that are difficult to pass. The primary cause is from too much water being removed from the stool as it passes through the intestines or gut. In children with Down syndrome, this often happens because food takes longer to pass through the intestine, which allows it to absorb more water than usual from the stool. Chronic constipation can lead to a number of troubles including rectal pain, rectal bleeding, and sometimes stretching of the intestine wall, making it difficult to feel when you are ready for a bowel movement. This can lead to bowel accidents or behavioral issues related to toileting, and sometimes intestinal blockage.

If your baby is having trouble with constipation, it's a good idea to talk to your pediatrician. If he is bottle fed, a stool softener such as Karo syrup or lactulose is usually introduced. Your pediatrician may teach you how to do some gentle massage or movements to help stimulate the peristalsis of your baby's intestines. Sometimes a glycerin laxative will be used, either in suppository or liquid form.

If your older child is prone to bouts of constipation, the preferred treatment is to increase fiber and fluids in his diet. However, when constipation is severe, your child's appetite may decrease, making it difficult to provide adequate dietary changes.

There are two types of fiber in foods: soluble and insoluble. Soluble fiber, such as oat bran, wheat germ, and whole wheat products, absorbs water as it goes through the digestive system. It provides bulk to stool and also increases the amount of water absorbed by stool as it passes through the intestine. This is important for forming soft stools that are easy to pass.

Insoluble fiber, found in fruits, vegetables, and seeds, does not absorb extra water as it goes through the digestive system. It primarily provides bulk to the stool. This bulk gives stool form and pushes against the intestinal wall, signaling the need for the muscles to propel it onward. It is important to have a diet filled with both types of fiber.

How much fiber is enough? A good rule of thumb for children is a minimum of "age plus 5 grams of fiber" to a maximum of "age plus 10 grams of fiber." For example, the fiber recommendation for an eight-year-old child with Down syndrome would be between 13 to 18 grams of fiber a day. For adults, a diet high in fiber is between 30 and 40 grams each day. Packaged food products in the U.S. list the number of grams of dietary fiber they contain in the nutritional information panel on the box. If your child is constipated and very limited in his food selection, take note of whether or not any of his preferred foods are sources of fiber. A diet that consists primarily of white bread, bananas, white rice, and milk, while perhaps typical for young children, may contribute to constipation. Gently encourage your child to include some fruits and vegetables. See Chapter 3 for tips on introducing new foods.

In addition to fiber, it is essential to provide ample fluids throughout the day. Water is the best source of fluid, but it may be a tough sell for your child to drink adequate amounts (four to eight cups a day). There are plenty of other sources of fluid: milk, juice, fruits, vegetables, popsicles, gelatin, and other drinks. Be wary of drinks high in sugar and foods high in salt, as they may increase your child's need for fluid. Drinks high in sugar may actually draw water away from body tissues for digestion, as well as fill your child up with nutritionally empty calories.

Last, physical activity encourages the intestine to propel stool through the intestine. Going for a walk, swim, or riding a bike on a regular basis will help in overall prevention of chronic constipation.

There are many ways to increase the amount of fiber and fluid in your child's diet, as well as his level of physical activity. The real magic is finding the right combination of food, fluid, and activity that is compatible to your child's preferences and schedule.

If dietary fiber and fluid intake do not improve or prevent bouts of constipation, or if your child is fearful of having bowel movements because they often hurt, talk with your child's physician regarding medical intervention. There are a variety of methods to manage constipation. The use of laxatives, stool softeners, and mineral oil are effective, but should not be used on a long-term basis if possible or their effectiveness will be lost. If you have continued problems with constipation, you may benefit from visiting a gastroenterologist.

Dealing with Constipation

If your child is chronically constipated, here are some things you can do to try to help the situation.

Children and Adults

- *Have your child's thyroid checked.* Constipation is one of the early symptoms of hypothyroidism. If your child is having trouble with constipation for the first time in a long time, have his thyroid checked when you go to your pediatrician.
- *Encourage your child to drink fluids.* Try using sports bottles or novelty straws that are interesting shapes or change color to make drinking seem fun to young children. Let your child choose new drinks that are acceptable to you at the store.
- *Encourage your child to eat high fiber snacks* such as raisins or prunes, if possible.
- *Try some of the "magic fiber cookies"* that are made from prunes, raisins, and so forth especially for constipation (see Appendix for recipe).
- *Talk with your pediatrician or family practitioner about using stool softeners* such as miralax or lactulose, or fiber-increasing products such as Metamucil or Citracel. It is a good idea to discuss how and when to use these products to promote good bowel habits.
- *Talk with your child about how he can help prevent painful bouts of constipation.*

Infants

- For babies who are bottle fed, *stool softeners* such as Karo syrup or lactulose are often used.
- *Sometimes a type of glycerin (suppository or liquid) is used* to help with constipation.
- *Always work with your pediatrician* to resolve constipation issues for your baby.

GASTROESOPHAGEAL REFLUX DISEASE (GERD)

Adults call reflux (the movement of stomach contents back up into the esophagus) "heartburn." Most babies experience reflux or "spitting up" at least once a day during the first months of life. Babies experience different types of reflux ranging from extreme vomiting (sometimes projectile vomiting) to "silent" reflux, which has no obvious symptoms (more like constant heartburn). If your baby cries or arches his back regularly during or after feeding, or vomits after consuming about two ounces of feeding or more at a time, talk to your pediatrician about the possibility of reflux.

In older children and adults, symptoms of reflux include eating two or three bites of food and then stopping eating and fussing and whining. This behavior persists regardless of who is feeding your child, and is not the result of a change in mealtime techniques. It is also usually the only compliance problem your child routinely has—that is, it isn't that he has trouble doing as he is expected in most areas of life, including at school or when asked to do chores. Sometimes there is vomiting after a meal. If you see most of these behaviors consistently when your child eats, ask your physician about the possibility of gastroesophageal reflux disease (GERD).

In most cases, reflux resolves within the first year of life as your baby's body continues to grow and mature. However, reflux may persists longer in children with Down syndrome, due to developmental delay or other physical concerns. If your child is showing signs of aspiration or persistent and painful GERD, your physician may recommend further investigation, including an esophageal pH probe or X-rays of the upper gastrointestinal region.

The first line of defense for reflux is to consider your baby's positioning during feeding. Generally, babies do the opposite of everything recommended to adults to reduce reflux: they eat high fat diets, drink lots of liquid, and eat lying down. However, most babies go on to gain weight and do fine. For babies with persistent reflux, try the following techniques while feeding:

- Provide small, frequent feedings.
- Position your baby in an infant seat during feeding.
- Keep your baby upright in the infant seat for thirty minutes after feeding.
- Thicken the feeding when recommended by your physician or speech-language pathologist.

For older children and adults, add the following recommendations:

- Avoid snacks at bedtime.
- Avoid foods that linger near the esophagus, including: chocolate, citrus juices, meals with primarily fatty foods, carbonated beverages, and caffeine.

Some babies and children with GERD can manage reflux with a variety of medications that help foods pass through the stomach and reduce the acidity of foods as they are digested. In some cases, surgery is needed to manage GERD. If so, look for a gastroenterologist who is interested in helping to manage your child's GERD over a long period of time rather than only for the surgery.

Metabolism

Once nutrients are absorbed from the digestive system, they are sent through the bloodstream to various cells to create energy, bone mass, and muscle tissue, and contribute in countless other reactions essential to your body. One of these reactions is *metabolism,* or the process of changing food to useable energy.

Simply put, metabolism is a biochemical process that combines oxygen with nutrients to produce the energy your body needs to function. People often talk about having a fast or slow metabolism to explain their weight or eating habits. It is true that the rate your body uses energy is different from anyone else's. Some aspects of metabolism can be controlled, while others cannot. This section will cover the basic components of the process of metabolism. Once that is established, you will be better prepared to understand the effect Down syndrome has on your child's metabolism and the role lifestyle plays.

There are two phases to metabolism: *anabolic* (building) and *catabolic* (taking apart). The anabolic process of metabolism converts nutrients into substances the body can use. For instance, individual amino acids taken from food are put together in a specific manner to form a specific protein needed to rebuild the skin over a skinned knee. The catabolic process of metabolism changes nutrients by breaking them apart to produce the energy needed by cells throughout your body.

Words to Know: Metabolism

- **Basal Metabolic Rate (BMR):** the rate at which your body uses calories when completely at rest. In other words, the rate your body burns calories when you are asleep.
- **Calorie:** the unit used to measure energy provided from foods.

BEGINNING WITH THE BASICS

The rate of metabolism is measured in calories. A calorie is a unit of measure for energy expended (see next page). Basal Metabolic Rate (BMR) is the term for the number of calories used when our bodies are completely at rest, such as when we are asleep. Even sitting up awake uses slightly more calories than sleeping. The number of calories used at rest is often calculated using an equation called the Harris Benedict Equation that takes height, weight, and age into account (see Appendix). However, most people don't sleep twenty-four hours a day, so their actual rate of metabolism is different from their basal metabolic rate.

There are many factors that affect your calorie needs. Each one increases your BMR at a different rate. For instance, if you are seriously injured or have surgery, you will require more calories and more protein to heal. Most important, there is an addition to your BMR for the calories used each day based on your activity habits. If you spend most of your day sitting and do not have a regular exercise routine, you

will need fewer calories than if you exercise regularly. If you have a job that requires a lot of lifting, walking, or other physical activity, then you will need more calories in a day to maintain your weight than someone who works at a desk. Based on your daily habits, your BMR is multiplied by activity factors to provide the estimated number of calories used to maintain your weight. Once these variables are included in the equation, you can estimate calorie or activity needs to increase or decrease your weight.

Your BMR is also affected by the amount of lean muscle mass as compared to the amount of fat stores you have. For instance, the more lean muscle mass you have and the less fat, the more calories you burn each day. This is one of the reasons health professionals recommend a well-planned strength training program. By nature, men have more lean muscle mass than women, which is one reason they burn more calories and have less difficulty losing weight.

Finally, there are other factors that temporarily affect your metabolism, such as fevers or menstruation. Even digesting food uses some energy, which is called the *thermic effect*. There are also some hormonal conditions that affect metabolism, such as hypothyroidism (lowers it) and hyperthyroidism (raises it).

As you age, your BMR decreases by about 2 percent a year after about age 25. This decline is related to the typical loss of muscle mass as you age, rather than your age alone. Therefore, if you are involved in a vigorous strength-training program, you may be able to slow the rate of decline in your BMR.

CALORIES

Calories are the unit of measure for energy used by our body. Technically, one calorie is the amount of energy needed to raise one gram of water one degree Celsius. To determine how many calories particular foods provide, researchers test foods in calorimeters, which are chambers that burn foods while measuring the energy created in the process to determine the number of calories provided. This information is then disseminated in databases, allowing others to estimate the number of calories, grams of fat, protein, and carbohydrate in foods. For instance, *Bowes and Church's Food Values of Portions Commonly Used* is an extensive list of nutrient breakdown of different foods. Using this resource, you can look up individual components to a recipe to determine the nutrient content of an entrée.

Calories used by our body are measured in a similar manner. No, we don't burn folks up. Volunteers wear a piece of equipment that measures the amount of oxygen taken in and the carbon dioxide put out by our lungs. Using this device, the number of calories used doing activities such as jogging, walking, riding a bike, skiing, and sitting in a chair are determined.

Yet even with all the mathematical equations and scientific measurements involved in determining metabolic rates, food calories, and calories used during activity, there remains an element of educated guesswork. Professionals working in weight management, sports fitness, and other areas use these equations and values along with their judgment, shaped by their experiences, to create weight management and exercise plans.

METABOLISM IN DOWN SYNDROME

Studies suggest that people with Down syndrome use fewer calories when at rest than people without Down syndrome. This difference can be as much as 15 percent. This means that a person with Down syndrome burns about 15 percent fewer calories than usual when at rest. To keep from gaining weight, he needs to subtract 10-15 percent from the number of calories typically recommended for a person of his size, age, and activity level. This is the only difference in energy metabolism for healthy people with Down syndrome. All other aspects of energy used for activity, illness, and disease are the same as for people without Down syndrome.

There appears to be no difference in the rate people with Down syndrome expend calories during activity, both low intensity (walking) and high intensity (swimming or running). Therefore, the number of calories used in activities is calculated in the same way as for a person without Down syndrome. In addition, people with Down syndrome are presumed to experience the same natural decrease in metabolism as they age. The process of estimating calories for children and adults with Down syndrome is discussed in greater depth in Chapter 13; equations for estimating calorie needs are in the Appendix.

HYPOTHYROIDISM AND HYPERTHYROIDISM

People with Down syndrome have a greater risk for thyroid disorders. These disorders occur when the thyroid gland produces either too much or too little of the substances that ordinarily play a key role in metabolism and growth. If the thyroid gland produces too much of the hormone T3 (thyroxine), metabolism increases, making it difficult to use calories for growth. When there is too little T3, metabolism slows, causing weight gain.

Hypothyroidism. *Hypothyroidism*, or too little T3, is the most common thyroid dysfunction in people with Down syndrome. The *Down Syndrome Health Care Guidelines* recommend screening for it every six months the first year of life and each year thereafter for children and adults with Down syndrome. Screening is accomplished by doing a blood test to check the levels of Thyroid Stimulating Hormone, T3, and T4.

The symptoms of hypothyroidism include: decreased growth, decreased development, and enlarged tongue, decreased muscle tone, dry skin, and constipation. In older children, teens, and adults, unexplained weight gain is added to the list. Many of these symptoms can be difficult to detect in people with Down syndrome, making screening even more important. Changes in behavior, sometimes described as a regression of skills, is often one of the first tangible symptoms seen by family members of adults with Down syndrome.

If your child has hypothyroidism, the treatment is simple: a synthetic thyroid hormone called synthroid, which comes in a liquid or a pill. Once your child's thyroid levels are normalized with medication, he will grow at a normal rate for a child with Down syndrome and unexplained weight gain will decrease or stop. Unfortunately, any weight gained while untreated will likely remain.

Hyperthyroidism. *Hyperthyroidism,* also called Grave's Disease, occurs when the thyroid gland produces too much T3. It is far less common than hypothyroidism and is detected with the same blood tests. Symptoms of hyperthyroidism include: rapid heart rate, nervousness, sweating, bulging eyes, decreased attention span, flushed skin, always feeling hot, loss of hair, and unexplained weight loss. In children and adults with Down syndrome, the first signs of these changes may include unexplained changes in behavior, increased "noncompliance," or regression of skills.

There are different types of treatment for hyperthyroidism including drug therapy, surgical intervention, and use of radioactive iodine. It is important to work with your child's medical team to determine the most appropriate intervention.

Weight Management

All of these physiological factors—metabolism, activity, and calories eaten—affect your body weight. Although weight management is a complex topic, the *Energy In vs. Energy Out* equation is simple: One pound of body weight = 3500 calories. The equation is the same whether you are trying to gain or lose weight. This means that in order to gain one pound of body weight, you must consume 3500 calories more than you need to maintain your weight. If you are trying to lose a pound, you must consume 3500 calories fewer than what your body needs to maintain your weight. The type of weight you gain, muscle or fat, depends on your activity program. (Metric conversions for calories to kilojoules are provided in the Appendix.)

The "Energy In vs. Energy Out" equation is but a small part of overall weight management. Weight management for children and adults with Down syndrome is discussed more thoroughly in Chapter 13.

CHAPTER 6

Celiac Disease

If your pediatrician is very knowledgeable about Down syndrome, you probably know whether or not your child has celiac disease. Otherwise, you may not even have heard of the condition or realized that it can be a concern for children with Down syndrome. In fact, medical professionals have only recently become more aware of the incidence of celiac disease in children with Down syndrome. Celiac disease, which may also be called celiac sprue, gluten intolerance, or gluten enteropathy, is a genetic condition. The incidence of celiac disease in people with Down syndrome in the United States is estimated to be around 4 to 5 percent, which is slightly higher than for the general population.

Celiac disease is caused by a sensitivity to gluten (a protein found in wheat, barley, oats, and rye) in the lining of the intestine. In a healthy gut, the membranes lining the intestine have finger-like protrusions called villi. As food is digested, it passes over and around the villi, which absorb nutrients such as glucose, vitamins, minerals, and electrolytes. Once absorbed, these nutrients are sent through other membranes and on to the bloodstream. In a person without celiac disease, these finger-like villi are flexible and clearly separate from each other, moving about freely like a field of grass. When a person has celiac disease, exposure to gluten (a protein) causes the villi to begin to lose their flexibility. Over time, the surface of the villi flattens. This makes it difficult for them to absorb nutrients from food. Sometimes, the villi are completely flattened against the wall of the intestine. When this happens, very little energy or nutrients are absorbed from food. This process can occur quickly, or gradually over the course of years.

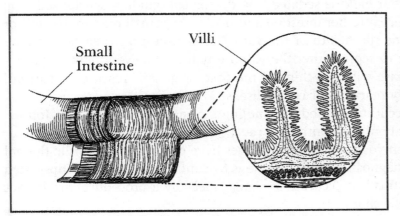

Small Intestine

Villi

Villi on the lining of the small intestine help absorb nutrients.

The symptoms of celiac disease are the result of the inability of the gut to absorb nutrients from food as it is digested. The most common include:

- frequent diarrhea,
- vomiting,

- unexpected weight loss or a reduced rate of growth for children despite good caloric intake,
- excessive gas, or
- abdominal pain.

Sometimes stools are very bad smelling, larger than usual, or float. When celiac disease goes undiagnosed for a long period of time, you may notice fingernails and toenails thickening or a yellowish tinge. Undiagnosed or untreated celiac disease also means long-term nutrient malabsorption, which may result in vitamin deficiencies or other undesirable side effects such as: dehydration, anemia, difficulty passing stools, behavior changes (irritability or inability to concentrate), and confusion.

Diagnosing Celiac Disease

It is important to obtain an accurate diagnosis if you suspect your child with Down syndrome has celiac disease. The *1999 Health Care Guidelines for Individuals with Down Syndrome* recommend screening all children with Down syndrome between ages two and three for celiac disease. Your pediatrician can do this by ordering a blood test called an antiendomysium IgA (IMA). Or he might order a test called tissue transglutaminase (IgA-tTG), a new test that is emerging as possibly an even more sensitive and equally reliable screen for celiac disease. If your child hates having blood drawn, try to arrange it so other yearly tests such as thyroid testing are all done at once, but don't put the test off for this purpose.

If the blood test shows an elevation of IgA antibodies, further investigation is needed for a definitive diagnosis, which usually means having a biopsy of the small bowel done. To get the biopsy, you will need to take your child to a doctor who specializes in illnesses and conditions related to the digestive system (a gastroenterologist). While your child is sedated, the doctor will guide a specialized scope down your child's throat to her intestine and take a very small piece of tissue from the lining to examine the health of the villi. This sample can then be examined under a microscope to see whether the villi are flattened. (Eventually, biopsies to diagnose celiac disease will be a thing of the past, as genetic research is currently underway to identify markers for celiac disease.)

Another less accurate method of handling a positive blood test is to follow a gluten-free diet for about six months and repeat the blood test. If the antibodies are lower or absent, then your child probably does have celiac disease. While the only accurate means of diagnosing celiac disease is by confirming it with a biopsy, some parents will choose this less accurate method, especially if procedures are particularly difficult for their child.

We have a ten-year-old daughter with Down syndrome who was diagnosed with celiac disease. When we realized she was not growing at the same rate she had been, the doctor suggested a blood test that came back positive for celiac disease. She then had a biopsy done that confirmed that she had celiac disease. We now realize she had also been complaining of stomach pains at bedtime and seemed very fragile emotionally. She seems much better now, though she is still very small.

We had Annie's blood work done and it showed her antibodies were elevated. Because her brother had celiac disease, the pediatric gastroenterologist suggested we do a trial of the gluten-free diet without doing a biopsy. If she responded to the diet, then we all agreed that she probably had celiac disease. For us, this felt better than taking the risk of sedating her, especially since we knew her brother has celiac disease already.

If your child has no symptoms of celiac disease, is older than three, and has not been tested, it is still a good idea to do a blood test. The observable symptoms of celiac disease sometimes take a while to develop or are subtle enough that they are not noticed. In addition, it is especially important to have your child with Down syndrome (as well as your other children) tested if parents, aunts and uncles, grandparents or other close relatives have been diagnosed with celiac disease. Celiac disease is often genetic, which means it is more likely to occur if there is a history of it in the family.

Celiac Disease in Children with Down Syndrome and Autism Spectrum Disorder

There is no evidence that children with a dual diagnosis of Down syndrome and autism are more likely to have celiac disease than any other child with Down syndrome. However, in recent years use of a gluten-free, casein-free diet for children with autism has grown in popularity. A gluten-free, casein-free diet is different than the diet prescription for celiac disease (see below), but is similar. (Casein is a protein found in other foods such as milk and cheese, which means even more foods are eliminated from the diet.)

Use of a gluten-free, casein-free diet to reduce "autistic-like behaviors," while popular, is not proven to be an effective one for children with autism. However, many times the process of following a diet such as this has a positive effect on a child's behavior. Why? No one can say for sure. There are hotly debated theories about "leaky gut syndrome" in children with autism. Regardless, following a strict diet also promotes meal planning and attention to eating habits that may not have been in place before. Is it the composition of the diet or the reliability of the structure following the diet demands? I don't know. Does it matter? I don't think so. Is it magic? I don't think so. But if your child has this dual diagnosis and you think the diet will help—or you want to find out—then research the diet and give it a try. You won't know unless you try, and the wondering isn't worth it.

A few families on the Down syndrome and autistic spectrum disorder listserv are using this type of diet for their children. In a few instances, these families found their children indeed had celiac disease *after* they had begun implementing the diet.

A carefully planned, gluten-free, casein-free diet is a nutritionally sound eating plan for anyone. While I don't recommend it unless your child has celiac disease, it will not do any harm. If you try this type of dietary intervention with your child and see a positive result, that is important. If you do not see a positive change in behavior, then reconsider whether or not the diet is worthwhile to your child and your family. Your energy may be best used in a different manner.

Treating Celiac Disease

If your child with Down syndrome is diagnosed with celiac disease, the treatment is a gluten-free diet. Gluten is a protein that is found in anything that contains wheat, rye, oats, or barley. The main purpose for gluten in baked products is to give them shape and form or to thicken sauces. A gluten-free diet removes all sources of gluten from foods eaten. It sounds simple, but it is a little complicated. Once you know what to look for, however, it becomes routine. Gluten is found in multitudes of foods: thickeners, flavorings, sweeteners; processed dairy products; and even some medications. Discovering which products contain gluten can take some detective work.

Usually when a child is diagnosed with celiac disease, the diagnosing physician will give you a referral to a registered dietitian. A registered dietitian should be able to provide you with basic information regarding which foods to look out for as well as information on celiac support groups. It is a good idea to call the dietitian prior to your visit. Share information about your child and family either on the phone or in a letter. This makes it easier for the dietitian to provide information that will be most helpful to you.

After your child with celiac disease has followed a gluten-free diet for approximately six months, the villi will appear healthy, as if nothing was ever wrong. In addition, any symptoms your child was experiencing will disappear. The treatment, a gluten-free diet, is remarkably effective.

> *"The whole idea of a gluten-free diet is overwhelming at first, but you will find that after a period of adjustment for everyone—family, friends, as well as yourself—you will be able to handle it with ease. Your child won't have to make dramatic changes in food, they just have to be made from different ingredients. There are some things your child will never have again, but he can still have M&M's, Reese's Peanut Butter Cups, and Peanut Butter!*
>
> *—Amy, Indiana*

Getting Started

Whether or not you visit a registered dietitian, the first thing you want to do is implement a "survival diet." This is a very basic meal plan designed to make the most obvious changes as quickly as possible (see below). Begin by evaluating what foods your child eats and has available to her during the course of the day. An easy way to do this is to make a chart that includes all the food groups along with a category for "combination foods" (grain, vegetable, fruit, dairy, meat, milk, sometimes foods, and combination foods). List all the foods your child eats that come to mind. Pay particular attention to foods or dishes that contain breads, pastas, flours, crackers, and cereals. Highlight the foods that are a part of her daily routine. These will be the first foods to replace. Don't forget to include snack foods.

Make a list of the foods you need right away. Take that list to a grocery store that has a nutrition health foods section or to a health food store. You should be able to find many specialty products that are gluten free to get you started. Don't overlook foods that are always gluten free, such as fresh fruits, vegetables, fruits, and unprocessed meats. Once you have enough food to get through a few days, you can begin to experiment with other foods and recipes from information you obtain in cookbooks, on web pages, or from manufacturers. For instance, the Red Star

Yeast Company has a recipe for gluten-free bread for the bread machine available. They also can help you decide which bread machine to purchase. Some machines do better with gluten-free breads than others. It is also good to find a gluten-free support group near you (see Resources at the back of this book).

Next, you can start reading labels of foods in your home. It is surprising how many foods have gluten in them. You probably won't recognize their gluten-containing ingredients at first. "Gluten" will not be listed on the label. You will need to learn what foods, ingredients, additives, and products have gluten in them and look for those foods on the ingredient label. A registered dietitian who is familiar with the practical aspect of implementing a gluten-free diet will be able to give you, or find for you, a list of thickeners, sweeteners, and other compounds that contain gluten to look for on food and product labels. If you have access to the Internet, you will be able to find information on ingredients to avoid, as well as vendors for gluten-free products. These vendors specialize in gluten-free food products, including spaghetti mixes, seasonings for ethnic foods, cookies, bread machine mixes, and many other products. A sampling of these vendors is listed in the Resources section.

Although your child may be able to eat some gluten-containing foods without showing immediate side effects, it is not advisable. Any time your child eats food with gluten in it, there is some damage to the villi in the intestine. Most parents choose to be fastidious about what their children eat.

We pack lunches and snacks for school and day care every day. We bake cupcakes (three or four dozen at a time), decorate them, and freeze them for parties. We send a packet of four cupcakes to school and the daycare where they also freeze them for special occasions so Annie isn't left out. We decorate the cupcakes so that Annie will feel like they are special too. When the container comes home empty, we send more. We have found that if we are steadfast with the diet, she is too.

Families disagree on whether or not the entire family should eat gluten-free foods or not when a child has celiac disease. It is a decision only you can make. You may want to consider, however, how difficult it will be for your child with Down syndrome if you ask her to eat completely different and separate foods from the rest of the family. Also, if you aren't eating any of the gluten-free entrées, how do you know if they are any good or not? There are many practical reasons for providing a gluten-free menu for the entire family.

For a more thorough discussion regarding parenting a child with celiac disease, look into *Kids with Celiac Disease* by Danna Korn (see References and Suggested Reading).

Staying Gluten-Free Away from Home

Staying gluten-free is sometimes hard for children when they go to school or to a friend's house after school. The best thing to do is to teach your child about the food she eats from the beginning. When you share with your child about her diet, use words such as "safe" and "not safe" foods rather than "good" and "bad" foods. Although the terms mean the same thing, the way foods are labeled makes a difference in your child's attitude about food. One approach is to teach your child that she has an "allergy" to certain foods. By eating "safe" foods she will be healthy.

Consider providing your child with a laminated card that explains her dietary restrictions (no wheat, oats, rye, and barley). Over time you can teach her to show it to others who may offer her food or to give it to a friend's parents when she is at a sleepover. If your child uses a communication book or augmentative communication device, you can include this information in her communication systems.

When sending your child to visit a friend or relative, make sure they understand the importance of your child's diet before she arrives. You may want to consider sending foods that are acceptable along for the visit. If you do, it is nice to include enough for both children when visiting a friend's house. For her friend, your child's "special" food is an adventure. Children are curious and will enjoy the opportunity to be involved.

Celiac disease is a condition that qualifies for dietary modification by your school district, if you ask for it and provide them with a note from your physician. (See Chapter 12.) If you choose to send your child's food from home, communicate clearly with your child's teacher regarding her diet and the importance of providing "safe" foods. You may want to provide the teacher and the school office with a list of "safe" and "unsafe" foods for your child.

Students with Down syndrome who also have celiac disease need both a written 504 plan (basically a food plan) and specific accommodations related to celiac disease included on their IEP. The 504 plan is required under Section 504 of the Rehabilitation Act of 1973. It should be attached to your child's IEP, as well as distributed to school personnel who work with your child.

Because your child's IFSP and IEP are individualized for her needs, you can include goals and objectives related to helping her learn to manage her food while at school. Here are a few examples for you to modify for your child:

- During a class unit on nutrition, ask the teacher to include activities for your child that illustrate where foods that contain gluten fit in the food pyramid. What foods that do not contain gluten are in the same food group?
- If your child is receiving 1:1 speech therapy, include foods from the safe food list in her vocabulary or augmentative communication training.
- If your child is older and learning some functional words for living, include foods from the safe list and ingredients to avoid on food labels.
- If your child is known for food-swapping in the lunchroom, consider creating a positive behavior support plan for this behavior.

We know that under Section 504 [of the Rehabilitation Act of 1973] we can ask the school to provide a gluten-free lunch. Since that is the least of our concerns at school, we have chosen not to pursue that.

Sample Menu

The following is a sample starting menu with modifications noted for a gluten-free diet. For more menu ideas, see the books in the References and Suggested Reading section.

BREAKFAST:
Egg (scrambled, fried, boiled, poached...)
Toast (use gluten-free bread)
Orange juice

SNACK:
Apple with peanut butter
Soda

LUNCH:
Turkey sandwich made with gluten-free bread
(lettuce, tomato, mustard, pickle)
Or
Tacos made with corn tortillas
Cranberry juice
String cheese
Fruit cup or dried fruit

SNACK:
Celery sticks
Snap peas
Apple juice

DINNER:
Spaghetti made with gluten-free noodles
Homemade spaghetti sauce
(tomato sauce, oregano, basil, pepper, mushrooms, diced stewed tomatoes, thickened with corn starch if needed)
Browned hamburger
Steamed broccoli
Gluten-free rolls with jam

BEDTIME SNACK:
popcorn

> *The Internet was one of the most helpful resources I found in the beginning. The websites and email lists have lots of good information as well as an easy way to get in touch with other people. The information I found scared me, reaassured me, answered my questions, and answered questions I hadn't thought of yet.*

Conclusion

Finding out that your child has celiac disease on top of Down syndrome certainly does not simplify your life. You need to spend some time finding gluten-free foods that your child will eat and figuring out healthy and palatable meals and snacks she can have. You may also need to buy some new cookbooks and find new places to shop for groceries. In addition, you will need to educate your family, your child, and her support people about what she can and cannot eat and think about ways to enable her to take some responsibility for her diet. But as complicated as this all sounds now, it will eventually become routine. Just as you probably already know which foods are high in fat, you will learn to automatically recognize foods that contain, or could contain, gluten. Your child, too, will learn which foods make her feel good and which foods make her feel bad. Your whole family will feel better, knowing that your child is eating a healthy diet that she can thrive on.

CHAPTER 7

Diabetes

The chances are good that someone you care about will eventually have diabetes (if they don't already). Why? For one thing, diabetes becomes increasingly common with age and weight gain, and many of us will have older aunts, uncles, parents, or grandparents who develop the condition. For another thing, people with Down syndrome appear to be at a slightly greater risk of developing diabetes. Studies cite the incidence as anywhere from 3 to 10 percent among people (mostly adults) with Down syndrome, as compared to an incidence of 5.9 percent in the general population. Since diabetes can be a serious health concern if not properly diagnosed and treated, it may be worth your while to glance over this chapter, even though you may not think that diabetes is a concern for your family at present.

What Is Diabetes?

Diabetes is a condition that affects the way your body is able to use glucose for energy. (See Chapter 5 for more information.) Ordinarily, your body converts the carbohydrates you eat into glucose, a simple sugar. Then, with the help of insulin, a hormone made in the pancreas, the glucose is absorbed into various cells to provide energy. However, if you have diabetes, your pancreas makes no insulin or not enough insulin, or for some reason your body is unable to use the insulin your pancreas does make. When this happens, the glucose converted from foods is trapped in your bloodstream and accumulates there until it is excreted in urine. Meanwhile, your body is not receiving enough energy in the muscles and cells to function properly. This leads to a number of symptoms, which include:

- increased thirst,
- unexplained weight loss,
- unexplained increase in eating,
- increasing tiredness,
- blurred vision,
- frequent urination (both day and night),
- cuts and infections that do not heal, and
- incessant hunger.

For children and adults with Down syndrome, the first noticeable signs may be behavior changes such as regression, aggression, increased stubbornness, or lack of motivation, and perhaps an increase in illnesses such as colds and flu.

Types of Diabetes

There are three types of diabetes:

Insulin Dependent Diabetes (Type 1 or IDDM). In type 1 diabetes, the pancreas can't make insulin or cannot make enough. Children who have diabetes (with or without Down syndrome) are usually in this category. People with type 1 diabetes need to get insulin by a regular injection. There are many kinds of insulin, all of which act differently. Your physician or diabetes team will work with you, your child, and any other support people to determine the right combination.

Non-insulin-Dependent Diabetes (Type 2 or NIDDM). In type 2 diabetes, the pancreas either still makes insulin or can be stimulated to produce insulin with oral hypoglycemic agents (a pill). Sometimes the body develops a resistance to the insulin made naturally (even with medication), which makes it less effective than for people without diabetes. Some people with type 2 diabetes can manage their blood glucose through diet and exercise without the addition of medication. Type two diabetes is more common in people who are significantly overweight. This type of diabetes is more prevalent than type 1 and the rate of incidence is climbing rapidly in the United States. Although typically seen in adults, particularly older adults, type 2 diabetes can develop at any time. In the United States, 90-95 percent of those with diabetes have type 2. The incidence for children in the United States is on the rise, but there is no evidence that it is increasing for children with Down syndrome at this time.

Gestational Diabetes. Gestational diabetes is a fairly common complication during pregnancy and requires careful monitoring to keep both mother and baby healthy. Gestational diabetes is usually a temporary condition, though it may signal a higher risk of developing diabetes later in life. Gestational diabetes requires specific, immediate attention and is not discussed in this book.

How Likely Is Your Child to Get Diabetes?

While people with Down syndrome appear to be at a greater risk for diabetes, it is not clear whether the proportions of people with type 1 and type 2 are different than in the general population. Studies have focused on the incidence of diabetes in general for people with Down syndrome, rather than on the type or specific risk factors (whether they are the same or different). Generally speaking, people who are more than 20 percent over their desired weight range, lead a sedentary lifestyle, and have a family history of diabetes are at greater risk of developing diabetes. In addition, simply having Down syndrome increases the risk of developing diabetes.

A common time for diabetes to emerge is after a surgical procedure or extreme illness. When your body is in physical stress, such as after a surgery or after fighting an illness or infection, blood glucose levels naturally rise. Sometimes a person's blood glucose will rise to the point of needing medication to keep it within a reasonable level. When this happens, it may not be necessary to continue with diabetes medication after the illness has resolved or the stress of the surgery has passed. If it does resolve, it is something to be mindful of because your child may be more susceptible to developing diabetes later. If his blood glucose does not go back to normal, then he will be diagnosed with diabetes.

Diagnosing Diabetes

Diabetes is diagnosed by drawing a sample of your child's blood and then analyzing it to see how many milligrams per deciliter (mg/dl) of glucose there is in his blood. What is considered a normal reading depends on what your child has eaten or drunk, and how long ago he consumed it. The box below lists the three different types of blood tests that can be done to diagnose diabetes, and under what circumstances.

Blood Tests Used to Diagnose Diabetes

Test A: Report of symptoms consistent with diabetes plus a "casual blood glucose" of =200 mg/dl.
     A casual blood glucose is a test of blood glucose at any time of the day, without fasting or other preparation.

Test B: Fasting blood glucose of =126 mg/dl.
     Fasting blood glucose is measured after not eating or drinking anything but water for at least 8 hours before the test.

Test C: Two hour plasma glucose of = 200 mg/dl during an Oral Glucose Tolerance Test.
     An Oral Glucose Tolerance Test involves drinking a flavored solution with a specific amount of sugar in it. Blood samples are obtained before drinking the solution and at one-hour intervals afterwards to determine the effect on blood sugar.

For your child to be diagnosed with diabetes, a positive result on one of these tests must be confirmed on a day following the first test. In other words, if you took your child to the doctor because he was tired, losing weight, had some behavior changes, and was going to the bathroom all the time and his blood glucose at the time of the office visit was =200 mg/dl, then your physician would suspect that your child may have diabetes. To confirm this, he would ask you to bring your child in the following week to test his blood glucose again and inquire if the other symptoms had changed. Or, if your child had a fasting blood test done for his annual checkup and the result was a blood glucose of =126 mg/dl, with or without noticeable symptoms, your physician would order another fasting blood test on another day. If the result was another blood glucose of =126 mg/dl, then he would tell you your child has diabetes and begin the education necessary.

What helped most initially was that our family doctor had recently attended a workshop on endocrine-related conditions and was able to refer us to an excellent pediatric specialist the same day our son was diagnosed. The staff there did not focus on Down syndrome. They explained to me that all seven-year-old boys and girls need total support in the months following diagnosis. They spoke directly to my son when it was appropriate and took his dad and me out of the room to discuss what was not appropriate for him to overhear.

Treating Diabetes

Your child with Down syndrome can develop diabetes at any age. If he does, it is important for you, your child, and the people who support your child to work together to create and implement the best treatment plan possible. It is important to be diligent about managing diabetes and keeping blood glucose levels low. Consistently high blood sugar results in further physical complications, such as:

- Vision problems (blurriness, spots),
- Tiredness or pale skin color,
- Obesity (more than 20 pounds overweight),
- Numbness or tingling feelings in hands or feet,
- Repeated infections or slow healing of wounds,
- Chest pain,
- Constant dry, itchy skin,
- Vaginal itching,
- Constant headaches (this may be a symptom of high blood pressure).

The treatment for diabetes is a combination of medication, weight management, exercise, and diet.

MEDICATION The type of diabetes medication your child needs is determined by his physician. People who have type 1 diabetes need to take insulin, which is delivered by injection. There are many different types of insulin available. Administering insulin shots is relatively easy. You and your child and appropriate support persons will need to learn how to do this. It is difficult, however, for many people with Down syndrome to manage the details of administering insulin, so your child will likely require good supervision. Your physician and diabetes educator will work with you and your child to determine the best combination of medications, dietary management, and overall treatment plan.

If your child has type 2 diabetes, he may need to take an oral hypoglycemic. This is a pill, or combination of pills, taken usually once or twice a day that stimulates your pancreas to make more insulin. In the last ten years, many new types of oral hypoglycemic medications have been introduced that are very effective. Again, your physician and diabetes educator will work with you and your child to determine the best combination of medications, dietary management, and overall treatment plan.

WEIGHT MANAGEMENT

Many times people who have diabetes, whether or not they have Down syndrome, are overweight. If your child is motivated to lose some of that extra weight, it will be helpful in managing his blood glucose. Sometimes it is possible to lower blood glucose by losing weight. In this situation, a person may take oral hypoglycemic medications while working on weight loss. As weight decreases, the pancreas may be able to produce enough insulin to reduce or even eliminate the need for this type of medication. It is, however, a lot of work and not always possible to achieve this. See Chapter 13 for information on weight management strategies. Do not feel as though you have failed if your child's diabetes is not controlled by weight loss.

EXERCISE

Another way to lower blood glucose is to begin a regular exercise program. Regular exercise such as walking, biking, or swimming will help your child's body work more efficiently and therefore use glucose and insulin more effectively. It is very important for you and your child to talk with your physician and diabetes educator or registered dietitian any time you are going to change an exercise routine significantly. It is important to coordinate the exercise routine with medication and eating to avoid diabetic reactions or low blood glucose. This should not dissuade you from helping your child begin an exercise program, however.

What Is a Diabetes Educator?

A Certified Diabetes Educator (CDE) is a medical professional who has taken extra coursework and passed rigorous examinations to become certified as a diabetes educator. A CDE can be a nurse, physician, or registered dietitian. While each person is trained in the other's area of expertise, most diabetes education programs include both registered nurses and registered dietitians. The Nurse CDE teaches the medical aspects of diabetes: foot care, medication management, managing sick days, and other concerns, and creates a personalized plan to manage and monitor diabetes. The Dietitian CDE teaches the food-related topics: meal management, timing of meals, effects of foods on blood sugar, as well as creating a personalized plan for participants.

Many hospitals have CDEs on staff who can help you and your child. You may also benefit from attending a diabetes education class, which is an intensive course for people with diabetes about the disease and how to develop a workable treatment plan. These programs encourage each participant to bring a support person. Whether or not your child attends, this is a good way to get a crash course in diabetes so you can best support your child.

We always carry a diabetes kit that has a can of apple juice, breakfast bars, water or diet soda, a glucagon kit, insulated insulin, a blood test meter with extra strips, and other essentials. For sporting events like Little League, martial arts, and Special Olympics, Evan packs an extra bag because he needs juice, snacks, and water during and after exercise.

DIET

Last, blood glucose is affected by food. Thankfully, the dietary intervention for diabetes is not as restrictive as it once was. In fact, there is no "diabetic diet" or "meal plan" for everyone with diabetes. Work with your registered dietitian or certified diabetes educator to develop an eating plan that works well for your child. For example, while it is not advisable to eat a handful of Jolly Rancher candies, there are ways to include *one* when others are eating them, if it is too difficult for your child to do without.

Generally the guidelines for meals and snacks for people with Down syndrome who have diabetes are the same as those that are taught throughout this book. The goal of the meal plan for your child will be the same as it is for everyone:

- Eating an appropriate number of calories for weight management,
- Eating a variety of foods,
- Planning balanced meals and snacks,
- Eating snacks at appropriate times,
- Including "sometimes" foods such as desserts and candy in the plan to avoid frustration, and
- Encouraging regular exercise.

This meal plan is your child's diabetic diet and is a healthful plan for everyone. Therefore, if you're wondering if you need to cook differently for your child with Down syndrome who has diabetes, the answer is a resounding "no." You may hit some resistance from family members who do not like the idea of eating the same healthy diet your child needs, but this is easily refuted by a case for overall good health for everyone.

If you have recently been given a diagnosis of diabetes for your child and have not yet met with a registered dietitian or diabetes educator to discuss dietary intervention, see the section called "Getting Started" on page 112. Information on planning meals is provided in Chapter 16: The Art of Menu Planning.

Monitoring Blood Glucose

Another important aspect of managing diabetes is monitoring your child's blood glucose. This is accomplished by doing a finger stick blood test (FSBS) every day using a glucose monitoring kit purchased through your pharmacy, physician's office, or diabetes education program. Performing the FSBS is a simple procedure that is easily learned, although your child with Down syndrome may need assistance doing it. Sticking your finger can feel intimidating, and some glucose monitors require good fine motor skills. In addition, for some, performing a FSBS more than once a day means waging war. They just don't like it no matter what you say.

At school, your child may need to have FSBS performed by the school nurse or other approved personnel. The procedure should be clearly outlined in the 504 Plan developed with your school (see page 110). In some adult living situations, it is difficult to find staff who are willing or able (due to regulations) to assist with FSBS and document blood glucose values. Make sure a clear plan of action is documented so you and your child knows who is responsible for what. While performing a FSBS does not require a specialized degree, in group living situations, state regulations may require that licensed staff (a nurse, CNA, or physician) perform FSBS and maintain records rather than a support person.

Monitoring blood glucose is the best way to decide about changes in eating, medication, or exercise routines. Your physician may sometimes order a blood test called a Hemoglobin A1c (HgbA1c). This test provides an idea of what your child's blood glucose has been like over a period of time. A value of 7 or lower is considered good blood glucose control. Work with your physician or diabetes educator to balance your child's comfort and the best possible diabetes care.

LOW BLOOD GLUCOSE

Next to medication timing and amount, the most important thing for your child to understand is what it feels like to "have a reaction" or low blood glucose. This is extremely important because those who do not know your child may confuse a medical need with "having Down syndrome."

Low blood glucose, or hypoglycemia, occurs when there has been too much time between eating opportunities, when extra exertion occurs without a change in food or medication, or when too much medication is taken. The signs of low blood glucose may include:

- slurred speech,
- confusion,
- anger or aggression,
- dizziness,
- a cold sweat, and
- loss of consciousness.

Unfortunately, some people may not realize there is a problem until the situation is scary for your child. Teach your child what to do when he is experiencing low blood glucose. If he needs to ask for help, teach him to use the right words to get the attention of the people he reaches out to for assistance. For instance, it may be more effective to say, "I have diabetes. I feel sick. I need help testing my blood glucose" or "I have diabetes. I need help" than to simply say, "I feel sick."

Even with the most diligent education of support staff, teachers, educational assistants, and others who work with your child, there will be times when your child may be with people who do not know he has diabetes or what to do. One thing you can do is create a special card for your child's wallet or to keep in a pocket or backpack so he can simply hand it to someone if he is feeling ill. If your child can tell people what is wrong, they are more likely to quickly seek appropriate help.

It is also very important to purchase and teach your child to wear a medical alert bracelet. These are available at most pharmacies for a low cost. If a low blood glucose reaction goes too far or too fast for your child to ask for help, emergency medical personnel know to look for a medical alert bracelet.

Your child should carry the following information at a minimum:

- diagnosis (diabetes),
- name of physician,
- medication, and
- emergency plan for hypoglycemic incident.

The information should be concise enough to be carried with him at all times, yet inclusive enough to deal with an emergency.

If your child lives in his own apartment, have him keep an old medication bottle inside the refrigerator door with medical information in it. In many cities emergency personnel (EMT, firemen, and policemen) are trained to look on the refrigerator door, near the butter compartment, for medical information about the person living there.

> *My son was seven years old when he developed juvenile diabetes. He is now in high school. He carries a card I made for him that lists ranges of blood glucose readings along one side and what he needs to do when he has those readings on the other. This is helpful for him to show adults in charge who cannot remember that he needs juice, a snack, and to retest his blood glucose when it is low, or needs water plus a bathroom break when it is high. I put all of our phone numbers on the card, in his diabetes kit, and in his binder so we can be reached in an emergency.*
>
> *We found it is important to remind teachers that it could be a medical emergency when a child with diabetes "falls asleep" in class. In addition, it is important to train teachers and other adults working with my son that not all emergency medical personnel responding to a 9-1-1 call can treat a child with diabetes on arrival. The person making the 9-1-1 call must tell the dispatcher it is a diabetic emergency so she will dispatch EMTs who have the proper tools to handle the situation (administer glucagons or start an IV).*

HIGH BLOOD GLUCOSE

It is also important for your child to understand what it feels like to have high blood glucose or hyperglycemia. High blood glucose levels happen for many reasons, such as:

- eating too much food (or bingeing on high sugar foods),
- being less active than usual (missing a day walking the dog could affect blood glucose),
- not taking medication as prescribed,
- being ill,
- feeling emotional stress (anger, worry, fear, frustration, confusion about changes in life or routine).

The symptoms of high blood glucose are the same as for the onset of diabetes. They include:

- increased thirst,
- unexplained weight loss,
- unexplained increase in eating,
- increasing tiredness,
- blurred vision,

- frequent urination (both day and night),
- cuts and infections that do not heal,
- incessant hunger,
- behavior changes,
- irritability,
- regression of skills.

If your child has high blood glucose, it may take some time to discover why. If it is related to medication, exercise, or eating, you will want to make adjustments. If he is dealing with a particularly stressful or frustrating situation, help him work through it or learn to relax. It is a good idea to consult with your diabetes team when you encounter trouble understanding the cause of high blood glucose.

ILLNESS AND HIGH BLOOD GLUCOSE

If your child has type 1 diabetes and becomes ill, he will experience a high blood glucose. This will be more dramatic if he is running a fever or vomiting, but can happen with any illness, including a common cold or bad headache. It is important to continue to give your child his medication (insulin or pill), even if he is vomiting, having diarrhea, or not eating. Discuss a "sick day plan" with your child's physician or diabetes educator and share it with your child's team at school, home, and work. It is usually important to check blood glucose levels more often and make adjustments to insulin dosage during this time. Always consult your physician before making changes in your child's insulin.

Teaching Your Child with Down Syndrome about Diabetes

To date, I've not been able to find diabetic education materials or programs designed with people with Down syndrome or related disabilities in mind. There are, however, some materials written for people with low literacy skills. These may be the easiest to adapt for your child and even for communicating with people working with your child. (See the Resources and Reading sections at the back of the book.) Key topics to discuss, teach, and continually reinforce with your child are: blood glucose testing; what to do for low blood glucose; what to do for high blood glucose; and what to do before, during, and after a physical activity.

Following the Routine. It is also important to teach your child the importance of following the routine outlined by your health care team. If your child's blood glucose is high for long periods of time over many years, it can seriously damage his nervous system, making it hard to feel things in his fingers, toes, and even legs. It can also cause damage to the blood vessels of the kidneys, eyes, heart, and feet. The great thing is that he can help to prevent all these complications by following his food plan and taking his medication. This is, of course, easier said than done.

If the food plan is frustrating to him, plan a meeting with the registered dietitian or diabetes educator so he can discuss his frustrations and make changes to the food plan that he is happy about and will follow reasonably well. Share your child's specific challenges with your diabetes care team. Discuss with them situations such as your child's difficulties in limiting himself to just one hamburger when he goes on his weekly trip to a restaurant with his friends. Planning for and finding ways to accom-

> *One day in second grade several of my son's classmates told me, in confidence, they had seen my son eat half a donut from the breakfast program treat tray that morning. None of the adults in charge had noticed. On the way home from school I asked him if he had eaten a donut. He told me, "No, Mommy." And then, "And it was sooooooo good!"*

modate "planned impulse eating" may be possible, depending on your child's medical condition. As our children's and adult's lives become more diverse with increasing opportunities for choices and food, we need to be as creative and supportive as possible.

Adults who live in a group home or other supervised situation may have fewer problems with impulse eating because they have fewer opportunities to break the routine. However, human nature suggests that when there is an opportunity for "cheating" or bingeing on favored, typically restricted foods, your child will jump at it. As group living situations become smaller (shared homes and apartments) with less onsite medical supervision, the routines may not be as limiting. For this reason, it is important to educate your child as much as possible about diabetes and what it means for him. The more your child takes responsibility for his health and diabetes care, the more likely he will be to have better control of his blood glucose levels.

Diabetes in School

Students with Down syndrome who also have diabetes need both a written 504 Plan (a diabetes care plan) and specific accommodations related to diabetes included on their IEP. This typed of plan is required under Section 504 of the Rehabilitation Act of 1973. It should be attached to your child's IEP, as well as distributed to school personnel who work with your child.

The Diabetes Care Plan (504 plan) should include information such as:
- The necessity for there to be staff members trained in testing blood glucose levels, recognizing and treating both hyper- and hypoglycemia, and the administration of appropriate medication such as insulin and glucagon.
- Blood glucose testing procedures. Some students will benefit from being able to test blood glucose in the classroom. You may need to show that other students in the school will not be endangered by in-classroom testing.
- Procedures for your child to treat hypo- or hyperglycemia, *in class* whenever possible, and in other school locations with appropriate support.
- The requirement that your child be allowed to participate in all activities. Having diabetes is not a legally acceptable reason to exclude a student from a field trip, extracurricular activity, or sport.
- A plan regarding precautionary steps to physical activity to prevent hypoglycemic attacks, such as a snack before PE class if FSBS is =120 mb/dl.
- Guidelines for class-wide snacks and special events that include food.
- Contact information in emergencies.

Typically, school personnel merely need education about diabetes and how to treat it effectively to be supportive. There will be times you will need to advocate and even negotiate for your child's health. If you need assistance in this area of advocacy, contact the American Diabetes Association (see Resources). A sample 504 Plan and diabetes care plan forms are provided in the Appendix.

Accommodations that you may need to consider including on your child's IEP include:

- Having information repeated. Sometimes if your child's blood sugar is low, he will have trouble concentrating.
- Allowing make-up tests if your child has a hypoglycemic or hyperglycemic incident during the test period.
- Allowing your child to eat whenever and wherever necessary to follow his diabetes plan for good blood glucose control. A child with diabetes should not be restricted from eating in the classroom during reading time if his blood glucose level requires a snack.
- Accommodations as needed to allow adequate time for your child to finish eating his lunch.
- Allowing your child to go to the bathroom or the drinking fountain as necessary. When his blood glucose is high, he may need to go to the bathroom more often until his medication has had an adequate effect.
- Allowing for absences without punishing for poor attendance.
- Allowing adequate time for blood glucose testing, medication administration, and unscheduled snacks, if indicated.
- Assigning an aide or peer buddy to your child if he needs a lot of help finding and using the bathroom, going to the nurse's office, fixing and eating snacks.

Diabetes in the Workplace & Living Groups

Adults with Down syndrome also need to have a concise, written diabetes care plan available to everyone who supports them on the job or in their home. If your child lives in a group home or other living arrangement with hired staff, this support may already be in place. If your child lives in an apartment, it is important for those who live with or who support him to know what to do.

This is also true for your child at work. Talk to your child's employer, supervisors, job coach, and coworkers about diabetes and create a written plan for blood glucose testing and treatment plans, if needed. Your child may not ordinarily require testing at work. However, the people who work with him should know how to identify symptoms of high or low blood glucose levels and how they may affect your child's behavior. This will ensure that coworkers know how to handle emergency situations, and also help them understand that some behavior may not be "noncompliance" or "stubbornness," but related to a medical condition. It might make the difference between having a job or not.

Getting Started

If your child has recently been diagnosed with type 2 diabetes and you want to get started on some basic eating changes, here are some first steps. Share this information with the registered dietitian or certified diabetes educator when you meet, as these steps are not individualized or meant to replace diabetes education or treatment for your child. If your child has type 1 diabetes or is using insulin, follow the instructions of your health care provider or diabetes educator.

- Using the information on "Determining Calorie Needs" in the Appendix, calculate the energy needs for your child to maintain his weight.
- If your child needs to lose some weight, create a meal plan with your diabetes educator or registered dietitian that provides no fewer than 500 calories below your child's estimated energy needs.
- Talk over exercise options with your child. Solicit his ideas regarding activities he enjoys and is willing to do more often.

Conclusion

When you have a child who has diabetes on top of Down syndrome, your child's basic nutritional needs do not change. He can follow the same guidelines for a healthy lifestyle outlined in this book. However, because of the possible health consequences that can occur if his diabetes is not managed well, it is essential that you consult a diabetes educator to develop an individualized management plan. Over time, it will become apparent how independent your child can be at managing his own special needs related to diabetes. You can do your part by modeling a healthy lifestyle and by seizing on every opportunity to educate him and those who support him about what they need to know.

CHAPTER 8

Alternative Therapies

As soon as there's a standard therapy for something, there is usually an alternative one. An alternative therapy is simply a treatment that has not been proven effective or ineffective, safe or unsafe, or is not widely accepted by professionals in that field. Many alternative therapies of the past are now proven, accepted treatment options today. Other alternative approaches have since been discarded when they were found to provide no discernible benefit or to be laden with problems.

In recent years, Americans and the rest of the world have become entranced by the possibilities of nutrition-related alternative therapies. Vitamins, minerals, amino acids, and other supplements have been touted as the cure for various diseases, as well as for improving our sex lives or athletic prowess. Now, with a few good connections, a parent's story about an alternative approach can wind up on a national news program and splattered all over the Internet. This type of attention and hype may make a treatment popular, but it does little to prove or add to our understanding of its safety and efficacy. In fact, if the attention polarizes the medical and support group community, the publicity may do more to slow the process than help it. This type of publicity has recently brought nutrition-related therapies for people with Down syndrome to the forefront once again.

Nutrition-Related Therapies in Down Syndrome

Nutrition-related alternative therapies for people with Down syndrome have existed for decades. One of the earlier well-known therapies was concocted over fifty years ago by Henry Turkel, a physician in the United States. Dr. Turkel claimed that a mixture of some forty-eight different ingredients, called the U-Series, improved the intelligence and appearance of children with Down syndrome. Dr. Turkel promoted and distributed his treatment for about forty years. However, no group of adults with Down syndrome treated with the U-series or any other nutrition-related supplement has emerged with dramatic benefit.

Currently there are three primary nutrition-related products for Down syndrome on the market: Warner's Hap Caps distributed by Warner House in California; MSB distributed by NutriChem Labs in Ontario, Canada; and the Nutrivene Family of Products distributed by International Nutrition in Maryland. There are similarities and differences among the formulas, which continue to evolve, but the makers of each make similar claims, which currently include:

- improved health,
- improved growth,
- improved immune function,
- cognitive enhancement,
- prevention or amelioration of long-term degeneration and disability.

Do Nutritional Therapies Work?

A few dozen studies are done each year on topics related to Down syndrome. Usually a handful of them look at nutrition-related topics. There is enough information to suggest that vitamin and mineral supplementation probably does play a role in improved overall health for people with Down syndrome by giving a boost to their immune system (see Chapter 4). However, there is no evidence to suggest that anything more than an over-the-counter multivitamin and mineral supplement is needed to do that. And to date, there have been no conclusive, clearly written, well-designed studies to determine whether a nutritional therapy could achieve the other goals that have been claimed by some supplements' manufacturers. In particular, there is no proof that nutritional supplementation can prevent or delay the development of Alzheimer's disease, or improve cognitive skills in general.

The best summation of the situation comes from an article published in *Developmental Medicine and Child Neurology*. In the conclusion, the authors state:

> ...We believe that to date there has been no consistent or rigorous proof that any form of nutritional supplementation improves the outcome in DS. There is, therefore, an urgent need for a well conducted clinical trial to evaluate the hypothesis that antioxidant supplementation may improve the outcome in DS.

Sorting Out Anecdotal Claims from the Evidence

I was first exposed to these nutrition-related products over the Internet in 1994. I was there participating as a parent in chats, listservs, and bulletin boards. At that time, some amazing claims were being made for a nutrition-related alternative therapy for children with Down syndrome: changes in facial structure, reduction of mental retardation, prevention of Alzheimer's disease, and, if started within the first six months, prevention of mental retardation. How could a parent not be inter-

Understanding Research

Parents of children with Down syndrome and other disabilities often spend time reading complicated research. Unfortunately, research is not easy to read. Not only do you need to understand the topic of the article, but you also need to be able to evaluate the quality and validity of study presented. Here are some of the ingredients that can help you determine whether you are reading an article about a study that reflects good research practices:

- **Publication in a Peer-reviewed Journal**—If a study has been published in a peer-reviewed journal, you know that the article has been critiqued and approved for publication by fellow researchers in the field of study. Research that is accepted for publication in peer-reviewed journals follows a similar outline: title, author list, abstract (a brief description of the entire article), introduction, methods, results, discussion, and conclusion.

- **Statistical Significance**—Research that has a statistical significance means that the hypothesis of the study is true. For example, if the hypothesis is that giving children with Down syndrome a zinc supplement decreases immune-related illnesses and it is found to be statistically significant, then it is true for this study. Statistical significance is considered to be a probability of less than .005. ($p<.05$). This means the chance of finding the result of the study to be wrong is less than 5 percent. Statistics are difficult to understand and can sometimes be influenced by other factors in a study. Therefore, statistical significance is not the only measure of a well-designed study.

- **Study Design**—There are a number of ways to set up study design that affect the outcome and reliability of the study. These include sample size (the more people involved, the more weight the results carry), the tools used to measure the outcome, and whether the outcome can be clearly measured. (For example, which of these is easier to measure: Children with Down syndrome who take zinc supplements will experience a decrease in immune-related illnesses over a three-month period, or children with Down syndrome who take zinc supplement will experience a change in immune-related illnesses. The first example is more specific and therefore easier to measure and determine the outcome of the hypothesis.)

- **Control Groups**—Generally, in medical research there are two groups. One group receives the medication or supplement being studied (the experimental group), while the other receives a placebo, which is a pretend drug or supplement (the control group). The purpose for doing this is to be able to measure the difference, if any, between the two groups at the conclusion of the study.

- **Double Blind**—When a study is double blind, it means that no one—researcher or participant—knows for sure whether they are receiving the drug or supplement or whether they are receiving the placebo. After the study is over, participants may be told whether they received the medication or the placebo. Double blind studies rule out any differences related to attitude of the participant or the researcher. This increases the credibility of the study in the eyes of other professionals.

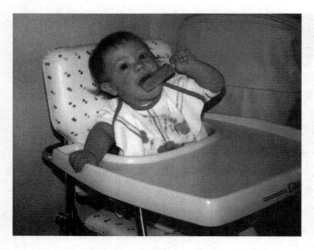

ested in those outcomes for their child? We all listened carefully. But when people asked questions, heated and often disrespectful debates ensued.

Since the late 1990s, extreme claims have not been made in literature associated with any dietary supplement for children with Down syndrome sold in the United States. I'd like to believe this change is due to new marketing staff or approaches, but it is likely due to the implementation of legislation that restricts the type of claims manufacturers of dietary supplements are allowed to make. There are, of course, no regulations on communication or claims made by parents and others that are not in print. There are many anecdotal stories on the Internet related to the use of nutrition-related alternative therapies. While the debate seems to have taken on a more respectable tone, there is still a lot of conflicting information for parents to decode. There are so many different products, it is similar to shopping for an herbal or vitamin-related weight management protocol.

Evaluating Popular Therapies

When looking for information to help your child, it is easy to be swayed by persuasive and dramatic reports of success. Parents of kids with Down syndrome or other disabilities are constantly searching for the method or therapy that will make the greatest gains for their child. The following are some questions to ask yourself and others when you begin researching a popular alternative therapy or educational strategy.

1. Where did you learn about it? Be discerning about what information you consider to be true. Sadly, therapies, articles, and research are sometimes skewed by the interests of the people involved. Regardless of where you learn about an alternative therapy, consider the reputation of the source along with the questions described in the following sections. Common sources of information include:
   - popular magazines such as *Exceptional Parent,*
   - peer-reviewed professional journals such as *Down Syndrome Quarterly,*
   - mass media such as television news magazine programs,
   - nonprofit organizations, such as the National Down Syndrome Society, or
   - professional organizations such as the American Academy of Pediatrics.

2. What type of information are you looking for? Each person has a different idea about what is important when researching therapies for their child.
   - Are you looking for research with solid, reproducible evidence?

- Do you want information that will benefit all people with Down syndrome or do you want information that is more individual, but may come with a greater personal or financial risk?
- Are research results about a therapy more important to you than anecdotal evidence?
- Is it important to you to know who is benefiting financially from this therapy?

3. Are any tactics being used to filter or skew the information you are able to obtain? Learn to spot persuasive or filtering tactics commonly used by media and scientific professionals. Some of these tactics include:
    - peer pressure,
    - underwriting,
    - gift giving,
    - creative statistics,
    - using language to evoke guilt or trust,
    - diverting attention to unrelated topics,
    - threats,
    - difficult-to-obtain references,
    - undocumented claims, and
    - delay tactics ("We need further research").

Other important tactics to watch for include:
- evidence that is not available to the public,
- data or research that is not published in a peer-reviewed journal,
- ignoring or twisting data to prove a point, and
- requiring extremely narrow and difficult to achieve parameters for proof.

Any time you are researching an alternative therapy for your child, it is important to talk to people who do and do not support the therapy, as well as to read research articles on the topic. The more information you have, the easier it is to make your decision.

This explosion of information and debate about nutrition-related alternative therapies has been interesting, to say the least. The effects on the community of people who care about individuals with Down syndrome has been unmistakable. Some of these effects are good and some are not.

Perhaps the greatest benefit has been the increasing use of the Internet first to promote alternative therapies, but second, to provide an avenue for communication, debate, and individual research. Parents are far better educated and connected—nationally and internationally—than ever before through the Internet. This connection and education is changing the way we see each other around the world and strengthening families so they can do their best for their children.

At the same time, this connection and collaboration has caused some deep divides in the Down syndrome community. At times, it has even reached the medical and educational professionals who work with our children. Mean-spirited dis-

Dietary Supplement Laws

The Dietary Supplement Health and Education Act (DSHEA) was enacted in 1994. This legislation gives the United States federal government the power to assure the safety of dietary supplements as well as the accuracy of their claims and labeling. DSHEA also gives responsibilities to the Federal Drug Administration (FDA) to regulate labeling just as it does over commonly used foods.

According to current law, makers of dietary supplements can make limited claims regarding their products. Health-related claims must be sustained by scientific literature and claims that products are designed to diagnose, treat, cure, or prevent a disease are prohibited. Additionally, manufacturers must be able to substantiate that any statement made in literature or advertising regarding the product is truthful and not misleading.

cussions, name calling, and denouncing the efforts of those who work in the medical or research field does nothing to promote our need for more research about our children. These discussions also do not promote respect among parents who choose different approaches to raising their children. Nor do they promote the inclusion of our children in community activities. We must accept and include each other first.

If you choose to use an alternative therapy of any kind, please make sure your medical team knows exactly what you are doing. Sometimes it makes a big difference. For example, during a question-and-answer period for parents with volunteers from the Down Syndrome Medical Interest Group, a physician shared concerns that parents tell their doctors and specialists if they use any herbal supplement for their child. With an increase in use of an herb called Ginkgo Biloba in children with Down syndrome, she has encountered more instances of increased bleeding during routine procedures such as the insertion of ear tubes. When she did not know the child was taking the herb, the bleeding was unexpected and alarming. Frequently, she learned that those who were bleeding more than she expected were taking Ginkgo Biloba, which can affect bleeding time.

QUESTIONS TO ASK ABOUT NUTRITION-RELATED THERAPY

There are some specific questions about nutrition-related alternative therapies that are important to consider.

1. How do I know if my child is deficient in a vitamin or mineral? Look for testing that is available at any reputable laboratory that is not associated with a product. In other words, there is always more than one laboratory that can test for a deficiency, especially in the United States. Testing should not be exclusive to one laboratory.
2. If your child is tested for deficiencies prior to starting the therapy, is a follow-up test performed after a period of time to determine the effectiveness?
3. Is this testing very expensive or is it reimbursable by insurance?

Hiding Supplements and Medications in Food

If you decide to use a nutrition-related alternative therapy such as vitamin supplements, it is important to give it to your child using a consistent approach. Generally, supplements have a strong flavor and odor that makes it difficult for a child to take them. You may want to combine the supplement or medications your child needs to take with food that she enjoys. However, *tell* your child that she is taking her vitamins or medicine. Do not pretend that nothing has been added to the food.

Your child needs to trust that the food you give her is what you say it is: applesauce, yogurt, or vitamins mixed in applesauce or yogurt. If you sneak a supplement into a food without telling her, when she chooses not to eat that food anymore, you will have to choose another food. What will you do when you've gone through all of your child's favorite foods? It is far better to be honest with your child. If you tell her it's time to take her vitamins, she knows exactly what she is being asked to consume. If there is a battle, it is about the supplement or medication rather than the food.

4. Is this testing reliable? Some tests, such as hair analysis, are not accurate for determining a nutrient deficiency. If you cannot find information you are comfortable with about the reliability of a particular test, discuss it with your physician.

5. What issues am I targeting for my child (such as cognitive changes, fewer ear infections, improved immunity, or behavior changes)? Do they match the claims of the therapy?

6. What are the positive effects of the therapy?

7. What are the side effects of the therapy? Are they short-term concerns or could they be long-term problems?

8. How much does the therapy cost? Is it a reasonable, long-term expense for your budget?

9. How much time does it take to coordinate the therapy? Will it interfere with your time with other children, your spouse, or your work?

10. Is this treatment specific for children with Down syndrome or is it beneficial to all people with or without a disability? It is unlikely that a supplement can make dramatic changes in *all* disabilities.

11. If the therapy is "individualized," how is this done? Does it cost more to do this?

12. Is the product tested for quality and purity?
13. What is my child's physician's opinion of the therapy? If he is unsupportive, am I willing to continue to work with him?

HERBAL SUPPLEMENTS

Use of herbs for a variety of reasons is increasing in popularity. As research is being conducted, some supplements are holding up to scientific scrutiny and being found to be beneficial, while others are not, or have not been tested. However, most of the research that has been conducted has been done on adults, not children, and need-less to say, little or no research has ever been conducted on the use of herbal supplements with children with Down syndrome. In addition, some herbal supplements are being found to change the effectiveness of various prescription medications. There are also some herbs that should be avoided prior to any surgery, including insertion of ear tubes or dental work, to minimize any unexpected complications for your child. As with any alternative therapy, you should consult your pediatrician before starting your child on an herbal supplement.

Conclusion

Alternative therapies are a difficult area for parents to navigate for their children. There is no dispute that *all* parents are making decisions with their child's best interests at heart, whether or not they choose to use alternative therapies. It is important to be respectful and accepting of each individual's choice. Avoid being dogmatic that your way is the only way to do something or suggesting that parents who do not agree with you are neglectful or misinformed. If you do choose to use an alternative therapy, always inform your child's physician so he can be aware of any possible side effects or drug-nutrient interactions while he is treating him. One day we may have enough information to know beyond a shadow of a doubt whether current nutrition-related alternative therapies are making a difference. By that time, however, there will undoubtedly be new therapies to investigate.

Herbal Supplements and Why They're Used

Herb	Reason
Echinacea (*Echinacea angustifolia, E. Purpurea, E. Pallida*)	May cause inflammation of the liver if used with certain other medications such as anabolic steroids, methotrexate, or others.
Goldenseal (*Hydrastis canadensis*)	May worsen swelling or increase blood pressure.
Ginseng Panax ginseng or Siberian ginseng (*Panax ginseng or Eleutherococcus senticosus*)	May decrease the effectiveness of certain anti-clotting medications. May see increase in heart rate or an increase in blood pressure. May cause bleeding in women after menopause.
Saw Palmetto (*Serenoa repens*)	May see effects with other hormone therapies.
Ephedra (also called Ma-Juang)	May interact with certain antidepressant medications or certain high blood pressure medications, causing dangerous elevations in blood pressure or heart rate. Could cause death in certain individuals.
Ginkgo (*Ginkgo biloba*)	May increase bleeding, especially in patients already taking certain anti-clotting medications.
Ginger (*Zingiber officinatle*)	May increase bleeding, especially in patients already taking certain anti-clotting medications.
St. John's Wort (*Hypericum perforatum*)	May prolong the effect of certain anesthetic agents.
Feverfew (*Tanacetum parthenium*)	May increase bleeding, especially in patients already taking certain anti-clotting medications.
Garlic (*Alium sativum*)	May increase bleeding, especially in patients already taking certain anti-clotting medications.
Natural Licorice (*Glycyrrhiza glabra*)	Certain licorice compounds may cause increases in blood pressure, swelling, or electrolyte imbalances.
Valerian (*Valeriana officinalis*)	May increase the effects of certain antiseizure medications or prolong the effects of certain anesthetic agents.

Excerpted from *What You Should Know about Your Patients' Use of Herbal Medicines*, © 1999 and *What You Should Know about Herbal Use and Anesthesia*, © 1999 of the American Society of Anesthesiologists. A copy of the full text can be obtained from ASA, 520 N. Northwest Highway, Park Ridge, IL 60068-2573 or on the web at: www.asahq.org/PublicEducation/list2.htm.

Section Three:
Teaching Healthy Choices to Encourage Healthy Lifestyles

CHAPTER 9

Teaching Your Child to Make Choices

I am often asked, "Why is it so important to allow our children to make choices?" The truth is that it is easier *not* to give children choices about food than it is to teach them how to make choices. When life gets too busy, the first thing that is left behind is offering your family a choice about what to have for dinner. You will make whatever is the easiest to keep your sanity. There's nothing wrong with this. It happens to everyone. But hopefully it doesn't happen every day. Making time to teach any child how to make choices during mealtimes and in meal preparation is an important skill that will promote his independence. It's worth the time and trouble.

For our children with Down syndrome, learning to make any kind of choice is very important. Since food is one of the earliest things most children communicate about, it's a natural subject to use in learning the art of communication. Not only must your child learn to send a message, but *you* must learn to receive that message. Here are some key lessons learned when we encourage and honor our children's choices with regard to food.

- Early choice-making has immediate feedback your child learns from. "I ask, therefore I get."
- Making choices gives your child a sense of power and control over his environment.
- This sense of control builds his self-confidence.
- If you honor his choices, he learns that you are listening to him and care about what he says, whether you agree or not.
- Giving your child controlled choices about what he eats teaches him that he is in control of what goes into his body and doesn't have to just take whatever is offered. He can choose *not* to eat something without being judged. That is a huge message.
- If your child already knows he controls his food choices, he will be less likely to engage in power struggles over food.

With these ideas in mind, it's time to take a look at how to encourage your child to make early choices as well as more complex choices as he grows.

The First Choices

The first choices your child makes need to result in immediate feedback. This immediate response teaches him he has power and control in his life. It also shows him you are listening to what he has to say rather than trying to control him unnecessarily. He will feel your trust, and in turn, he will trust you.

Your child's first choices begin in infancy. He cries when he needs more when he is breast- or bottle feeding. He turns his head away when you offer a spoonful of food and he is full. He plays in his food rather than eating it when he doesn't really want to eat. If you are sensitive to these cues, you have set the stage for him to learn the power of choice. He doesn't feel like eating is a time that is out of his control. He knows that he chooses when to begin eating the food offered and when he is done.

Over time, you will teach your child other ways to communicate. Feeding time is a natural time for this to happen. The earliest choice-making activities include communicating about:

- more,
- all done,
- no thanks.

Using natural meal and snack times to learn to communicate choices is not using food as a reward. Instead, it is teaching your child skills he needs at the time he needs them. There are many things to learn during meal and snack times. To be successful, here are some important things to consider when teaching choices:

- You will want to **make sure opportunities for making choices regarding food** during meals and snacks are available and respected at all times.
- Making a choice is a natural activity when children are learning sign language: "more" and "all done" are usually among the first signs learned. "No" is also an early lesson. **The key issue here is to respect what you are being told.** Even if you know that your child really wants more, if he signs "all done," you must follow through on that. If you offer something to eat and he says "no," you must respond to this statement also. By doing this you are teaching your child some important lessons:
  1. He has control over how much or whether he eats,
  2. You are listening. What's the point of communicating if no one is listening?
- **For some children, sign language is not a viable communication method.** Don't wait for your child to have "speech" to allow him to say he wants more, is all done, or doesn't want to eat. There are many ways to do this:
  - **Listen to his gestures.** Most children will have a natural way of telling you if they want more to eat: staying at the table, grabbing others' food, or shoving

food away to say "no" when you offer it. Validate what your child is saying to you through active listening and then follow through appropriately. For instance, if your child is grabbing the applesauce container after finishing a bowl, you might say, "Oh, you want more applesauce? OK, here you go."

❏ **Offer your child choices about what to eat by holding out two different foods.** He will point or reach for the one that is the most enticing. As he grows, show him his choices with the box rather than the actual food or teach him the sign for the foods.

❏ **Offer symbols or photographs that convey the message.** (See photo below.) Some children with Down syndrome will use different AAC systems. "More and "all done" are common early messages to provide. It's important that the method you would like your child to use is readily available. If his AAC system is on the other side of the kitchen, he will use more convenient, equally effective communication such as taking other people's food or throwing food on the floor.

When you do these activities, don't frustrate your child if he is having trouble telling you what he wants. For example, your child is eating a snack of dry cereal and banana. He has finished his first serving of banana and wants some more. You want him to learn to sign "more," but he points to the banana instead. You hesitate and ask for confirmation by saying and signing, "You want more banana?" He responds by pointing and looking a little frantic. You have two choices. You can either provide the banana while signing "more" to him, or you can hold out a little longer asking him to sign "more." Which will you choose? If your child is looking frantic—like he doesn't believe you'll give it to him—and especially if he is quite hungry, this isn't the time to hold out. You want him to know that he can count on his food being available when he needs it. As this snack time continues, and he is less frantic about his request, it is a better time to hold out for him to sign "more." Don't turn the process of communicating into a food battle.

As your child gets older, you will need to re-evaluate the process of asking for more. This is especially true in the pre-teen to adult years. Like everyone, people with Down syndrome often eat more when they are not hungry. There are a number of reasons this happens. Understanding your child, looking at the situation, and discovering what is motivating him to eat more than one serving is essential. Some ideas for handling these situations are discussed in the Chapter 13.

TEACHING ABOUT HUNGER

It is very important not to comment on the amount of food a child chooses. This is probably the hardest of all these areas. If you control the amounts your child eats, either through your comments or by what you provide for a meal, your child may decide to eat more or less as a means of protesting. Pre-teens and teenagers are more likely to modify how much they are eating as an act of rebellion, but sometimes younger children make those choices without realizing it. As a young child, your child may choose to eat something to please you. Or, he may feel so much stress about food and feeding that he eats very little or nothing at all.

You can help by teaching your child to eat when he is hungry and focus on the interactions at the meal. Some ways to do this include:

- Practice sitting at the table to talk after a meal is over. This will help your child when he is with friends. Sitting in a restaurant without having food in front of you is an important thing to experience.
- If you are eating away from home, make the focus of the social event an activity (movie, putt putt golf, bowling, dancing (rather than the type of food or restaurant).
- If the purpose of the outing is to learn how to order food independently, include a discussion about ordering the appropriate amount of food.
- Be practical. The less idle time your child spends in a restaurant or at the table around food, the better. It is very hard to resist an impulse for long. There's no sense in setting him up for frustration by expecting him to be around food that is available and not partake.

It is equally important to know how to let people know you are "all done." Use the same types of communication techniques (symbols, photographs, sign language, and example) to teach this communication skill. As your child's communication abilities increase, these options still need to be practiced by both of you. For instance, you can teach polite ways of asking for more ("May I have more cobbler, please?") or asking to leave the table ("May I be excused?") rather than grabbing or leaving the table in the midst of a conversation. If the focus at the table is on manners, then you will spend less time arguing over amounts of food.

> *One mother shared with me how she taught her daughter about hunger. When her daughter complained about being hungry and wanting a snack at an unlikely time, she put her ear on her daughter's tummy to see if it was rumbling. If quiet, she told her, "Gee, I don't hear anything. Maybe you can wait awhile." If she did hear rumbling, she agreed that her daughter was hungry and made her a snack.*

DEALING WITH TOO MANY "MORES"

Sometimes children seem to be constantly asking for "more" no matter how much they've already had to eat, whether it is a snack or a meal. When you run into this situation, it's important to first understand your child's motives for asking for more. Here are some questions to consider:

- Does it get your attention?
- Does it prolong a pleasant activity?
- Does it prolong a pleasant taste?
- Is he eating too fast for his brain to get the message he's full?

Once you have a general idea of the reason your child continually asks for more, you can take action to help change this behavior. Remember, whenever you try to change a behavior, it's important to provide another way to meet the original need for the behavior. For example, if your child is primarily gaining your attention by asking for more, give it to him before he asks. Talk to him while he is eating and offer to play a game, go for a walk, or do another favorite activity when he is done eating.

The other situations, prolonging an event or taste or eating too fast, require different types of intervention. Offering to do something with your child may be enough to encourage him to terminate eating that is pleasurable because you are offering something that is equally pleasurable. Sometimes, however, asking for more becomes a habit. One way to deal with this is to decide how many servings of a food is acceptable. Some families offer a choice of second helpings of entrées or dessert. Another way to teach older children and adults about extra servings is to have your child keep track of what he is asking for. Use a check system within a pyramid to count the number of servings eaten at a meal or each day (see Appendix). If you use this system, set a limit to servings in a day with your child that is compatible with the Food Pyramid Guidelines.

Last, use the techniques in "Teaching about Hunger" above to help your child understand he is in control of the situation.

Choosing Specific Foods

The next level of choice-making is to choose between specific foods. This is not only an important experience when it comes to eating, but a great communication opportunity as well. Begin by selecting one time during the day to give your child the opportunity to choose. A common time to do this is during the afternoon snack. If you follow the roles of responsibility in the feeding relationship, it is easy to see how this works. Parents and support people are responsible for *what food is offered.* Your child is responsible for *which food* he chooses from what you offer, *if any.*

What you are *not* doing is providing free choice of everything in the house. Give your child specific choices. Some will be more nutritious than others, which is also natural. This is not the time to teach him about nutritious snacks, but rather to practice the process of making a choice about what to eat and letting others know what he wants. If you consistently have a snack time at 3:00, offer your child a choice between two foods he likes, such as apple slices and animal cookies. Over time, you will be able to offer a wide variety of foods that are acceptable snack choices.

We began offering our son snack choices as a way to promote communication. Our first choice system was made from box tops and photographs of his favorite foods. The problem with this system was that I could not change what was on the list. Every night he had the same four choices. This didn't bother him, but when we ran out of something, I had no way to remove it from the list. After a few

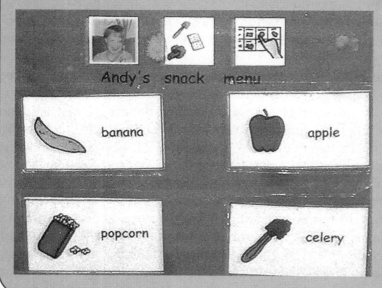

weeks of lifting him up to show him there was no ice cream, I found another way to present his choices. Instead of printing the choices on the menu board, we bought clear plastic business card pockets with adhesive on the back from an office supply store. We then made food cards from labels, photographs, and drawings that we could slip into the pockets to represent the foods available for snacks. The extra cards were kept in an envelope taped to the back. The menu board had adhesive-backed magnet strips on the back to hold it to the refrigerator so it was readily available. This worked much better, because I could change the menu to represent things I knew I had on hand.

Often when I talk to parents of younger children, they are reluctant to consider giving their children an opportunity to choose their snack. One mother told me, "If I do that, all he'll ask for is a cookie." As we talked, she told me "He thinks 'cookie' is any food. Whenever he's hungry he asks for 'cookie.' But if I give him a cracker or a piece of broccoli, he's fine with it. I don't think he knows what he wants." While we talked, her son Matt came in and said something neither of us understood. I waited while she worked this through with him. After several attempts at saying something, he finally signed and said "cookie." Later, we wondered if it was possible he was asking for a different food, but she did not understand him. Maybe he asked for a "cookie" because he knew she would understand.

Together, Matt's mother and I made a list of foods for the afternoon snack choices. Some of the foods were what she would like him to choose (and she knew he liked) and some of the foods were things that Matt liked that were clearly not "nutritious." We created a snack choice menu with four choices on the front and a slot on the back to hold the extra foods. When snack time came, Matt's mother put the menu on the refrigerator door for Matt to look at. When he came in, she read the choices to him and waited for him to touch the item he wanted for his afternoon snack. Matt was thrilled with the ability to communicate something besides "cookie" and began to look forward to the process of choosing his snack each afternoon. Matt's mother used the opportunity to find out what Matt liked and to teach him signs for the different foods on the snack menu. Even if Matt had continued to choose "cookie" for his snack in the afternoon, there would be no question about whether or not that was what he wanted.

BROADENING SNACK CHOICES

If your child is very rigid in his snack choices and chooses the same item from the menu each time, you will want to set up a time to teach your child that sometimes the preferred item isn't available. For instance, if your child only chooses a cookie each time from his snack menu, plan a day when cookies aren't available. First, make sure you don't have any cookies in the house. If you say it's not a choice, but it's clearly on the shelf, then your child will likely put on a great display of ingenuity in obtaining those cookies. Then, change the snack menu so there are choices for him to make that he likes, just not cookies. Remember, the lesson at this moment is not about the nutritional quality of foods, but learning that although there are no cookies available, there are other choices he likes available. Stay positive. Your script is something like, "I'm sorry, Matt. We don't have any cookies! But we have crackers or yogurt. Which would you like?" Prepare yourself for a potentially long day.

Another way to handle this situation is to decide how many cookies your child can have in a day. Make a snack board that represents the total number of snack options available in a day, such as 2 cookies, 2 juice boxes, 2 pre-portioned bags of pretzels, 1 pre-portioned bag of peas or baby carrots. As he makes his choices, they are removed from the board. If all the cookie options are gone, then he has to choose something else.

Yet another way to broaden your child's choices is to have two different snack choice boards: one that represents snack options that are available at any time of the day and one that has snack options for planned snack times. The choice board that is always available is filled with options that are relatively low in calories such as pretzels, celery, apple, or water. The choice board for scheduled snack times includes cookies, along with other options such as crackers and cheese or string cheese.

Remember, adults are responsible for what is offered, when it is offered, and how much is available overall. Children are responsible for whether or not they choose to eat the choice available and how much of it they eat. If Matt wants a cookie, but it's not an option on his choice board, then he either needs to choose something else or choose not to have a snack. It may be difficult for Matt to accept these options. Even though his options are limited by the choice board, there is no question about the expectations for snack time.

If your child continues to show very rigid snack choices over a period of time (such as six months), make sure there is not a physical reason for that choice such as heartburn or swallowing concerns. If he is healthy and appears to be stuck on a food, first ask yourself how important it is to change this. If he is eating a variety of foods throughout the day, it probably isn't important. If the amount of snack he is eating affects his ability to eat a well-balanced meal, try limiting the number of opportunities available for choosing that snack. You can do this by setting a specific number of servings available each day using symbols or a checklist, or you can make it unavailable by not having it in the house.

COMMUNICATING CHOICES

There are a variety of ways to give people with Down syndrome the ability to make choices regardless of their communication skills. It is important to know how best to represent things so your child will use the system. Some children prefer to point to the specific food in the cupboard or refrigerator. If so, consider grouping foods that are appropriate snack options in one section of the pantry and refrigerator. Label it in a way your child knows that is what it is for ("Joe's Snacks"). Others prefer to make selections from box tops, product labels, or photographs. Some will be able to use symbols or drawings. And some will use sign language or words to make their requests.

Regardless of the method your child uses to communicate a choice, find a way to visually represent the selections that are available and appropriate for snack time. This visual representation makes the options more concrete and decreases the chance that your child will attempt to negotiate a change. There will be times when your child wants you to expand the choices that are available. You are in charge of whether or not the selection will change. Try not to keep the choices static for too long. Evaluate the choices you are providing at least once a month to keep your child from being bored with them. Variety keeps things interesting and also gives you the opportunity to include some emerging tastes.

Using the Picture Exchange Communication System at Mealtime

The Picture Exchange Communication System (PECS) is a very useful method of teaching communication to children. It is most often used with children who have autism, but is equally valuable for children with Down syndrome or the dual diagnosis of Down syndrome and autistic spectrum disorder. PECS is an especially useful method of teaching communication if your child has difficulty with the fine motor task of making signs or pointing. The PECS system centers on the exchange of a symbol, photo, or object to communicate a message such as "I want _____ " or "I see _____."

Many of the first exchanges are easy to set up at snack or meal time. If you are considering using PECS as a communication method for your child, you can set up snack menus and other systems with this in mind.

For more information about PECS, refer to *A Picture's Worth*, listed in the References and Suggested Reading, or contact:

Pyramid Educational Consultants
226 W. Park Place, Suite 1,
Newark, DE 19713
888-732-7482 (within the U.S.); 302-368-2515
Web site: www.pecs.com

Snack Budgeting

Children in middle school and high school, as well as adults, may appreciate the independence of having a specific snack shelf, container, and section in the refrigerator. It's a good idea to put limits on the amount of food that is freely available. One way to do this is to stock a specific container with snacks you and your child choose together. This selection is for after school or work for the entire week (Monday—Friday). If he runs out before the end of the week, have some less-preferred back-up items. These are foods that he will eat if he's really hungry, but would never choose to eat if something else is available. It is especially important to have this back-up system if your child is prone to anger or problem behaviors when he is over-hungry.

If you choose this setup, be ready to coach for a while. For instance, if you see your child taking more than one serving of a favorite snack, remind him that if he eats it all in the first two days, there won't be any by the end of the week. Consider setting up a daily section on the shelf so he can move the foods around and see how much is there. Let him put three servings of his favorite in one day and try to fill out the rest of the week. If he has used up all his favorite foods by the end of the week, be sympathetic, but stick to the rules you've set up together. Food budgeting is hard for everyone. However, this is a good way for your child to begin to learn the effects of impulsive eating. (For instance, he ate all the good stuff on Monday, so there's none left for Tuesday—Friday.) The underlying message is that it's OK to eat all those foods, but it works out best if they aren't eaten all at once. This is another lesson that takes a long time. Make sure you set it up in a way that you can support your child without getting frustrated yourself.

Another method of budgeting snack foods is to keep a drawer or shelf in the refrigerator, as well as a shelf in the cupboard or pantry, that is devoted to healthful snacks for everyone. It is important to fill the snack shelves with a variety of foods that everyone enjoys; some will be healthier than others. If you have trouble keeping up with what you need to buy to replenish the shelves, ask people to make a mark on a list after the item they ate so you know how much is being eaten. Don't make the mistake of having someone write down when the last item is eaten. They might eat it all in one afternoon! If everyone makes a mark on a list when they take an item, you will be able to tell if excessive amounts are being eaten during the week. How you proceed from there is up to you. One option is to purchase only enough for the week. If the foods are eaten before the week is over, then everyone does without for the rest of the week. Be forewarned, however, that this can lead to sneaking foods from other areas of the kitchen.

Our son likes an afternoon snack. Recently he started taking some medication that makes him very hungry in the afternoon, too. There's no denying his need for an afternoon snack! We used to give him whatever was handy: chips, cookies, and other high fat foods. Once we realized there was a specific time when he was hungry, we began to plan for his snacks better. We made a relish tray with a selection of crunchy fruit and vegetables such as: pickles, baby carrots, celery, apple slices, or snap peas. He is just as happy, if not more, with the relish tray as he was with other less nutritious foods. He likes the crunchiness and he can have more to eat this way.

Household Rules for Snacks

When teaching teens and adults about snacking and snack budgeting, it's important that the rules are the same for everyone. This gets a bit tricky because the physical needs for food are different for each person in your home. If one child is an avid athlete and the other is a couch potato, the amount of food they need is obviously different. How you handle this disparity will depend on the emotional maturity of everyone involved. For some, the rules about serving sizes will need to be rigid to avoid fights and battles. For others, the rules about actual food choices will need to be the same. For example, if serving sizes are an issue, then create a structure that everyone can follow. If your child with Down syndrome is allowed one serving (1 cup) of ice cream a day, the same is true for your other children and *you*. Later, as your child with Down syndrome begins to understand the difference between his calorie needs and the calorie needs of his siblings, you can change the rules to teach other lessons.

Follow your instincts regarding your children's reactions and choose a method that is the least likely to cause undue friction.

Snacking and Impulse Control

Some children with Down syndrome have a difficult time with what I call "impulse control." The food is there, therefore it must be eaten. This needs to be handled delicately, yet decisively. For instance, you may need to lock up certain foods or the refrigerator while you work through impulsive eating with your child.

The measures you take to try to reduce access to food from impulsive behavior will depend on your child's behavior. For example, some families remove serving dishes as soon as plates on the table are filled for a meal. Others find it important to scrape dishes clean and put them in the dishwasher immediately after a meal. Even with these environmental changes, talk about the purpose of snacks and when they are needed or important. It is important for your child to understand what you are trying to teach.

Sometimes impulsive behavior becomes disruptive to the entire family. If this happens, you may benefit from consulting with someone skilled in positive behavior support.

Choosing from Categories

As your child gets older, he may be interested in choosing his foods by category such as the dinner entrée, vegetable, fruit, or dessert for a meal. As he gets older, you can expand or change the categories he chooses from to include foods that are lower in fat or high in fiber. To begin with, however, have him choose from categories that complete your menu for a meal or snack. Snack time is a natural opportunity for lessons about balancing food choices to promote health and to stay fit. In working with children, teens, and adults with Down syndrome, I've found the best lessons are those with a tangible outcome that makes sense. You will need to be the judge of how much or how little information your child is interested in hearing regarding *why* he is choosing snack foods in a particular way. The important message is:

"We eat snacks to help fuel our body so it will have enough energy to do what we want to do: skateboard, dance, be a good student, and just to feel good. You need to have a snack when you know it will be a long time between meals (breakfast, lunch, and dinner). But if you eat foods that have very little or none of the right types of fuel for your body, you still may not feel good and you won't be able to do your best at anything. That's why you need to choose snacks with foods from the bottom five food groups of the food pyramid. Let's pretend we're going to plan a lot of different snacks and try to pick some that we want to eat that are from these food groups: bread or grain, fruit, vegetables, dairy, and meat."

(The Food Guide Pyramid is a very useful teaching tool. See "Learning the Food Guide Pyramid" in Section 4 to brush up on your own knowledge of pyramid concepts. Methods for teaching your child how to use the pyramid to plan meals, keep food records, and other activities are covered in Chapter 10, as well as Section 4.)

You might want to add information to your explanation of the purpose of eating, depending on your child's interests and activities. Some variations to this description include:

- If your child is involved in a sport that is very important to him, you might want to focus the discussion on the need to fuel his body so he can be the best athlete possible or to have the energy to enjoy the game.
- If your child is concerned about his looks, focus on eating well to be healthy, because healthy people always look best.
- If your child is trying to watch his weight or lose some weight, let him know that eating snacks that do not come from the "sometimes" group of the food pyramid is a very big step in reaching that goal. Create a list of low calorie but satisfying foods for him to choose for snacks.

- If your child is having trouble with his behavior at school, focus on the way healthful eating—even at snack time—will help him handle tough situations better.

LEARNING TO GROUP FOODS Grouping things (including foods) by category is an important topic in all school curricula. Children group things by color, shape, size, weight, and so on. Older students take the things they have grouped to create graphs. All of these activities are easy to create using food, and offer some necessary early nutrition lessons as well.

- **Use the Food Guide Pyramid to learn which foods are in the same group.** The activity called "Learning to Group Foods" in Section 4 describes a system for learning to group foods using visual cues that are faded as your child's skill level increases.
- **Group foods by taste.** Teach your child the names of different tastes (sweet, sour, bitter, and salty) and group foods in these categories. You may find that your child has a different idea of what is sour or bitter than you do.
- **Group foods by preference.** The menu planning activity in Section 4 offers another way to group foods.
- **Once your child has some familiarity with these food groups, you might focus on the process of choosing snacks from two of the bottom five food groups only.** Do it as a game at first. Make it fun by choosing silly combinations such as eggplant and tortillas, or cornflakes, peanut butter, and a chocolate bar. Also include selections that don't work because they include only the "sometimes" group or only one choice from the bottom five groups (for example, soda and chips or chips and juice). It is helpful to use symbols, pictures, labels, or photographs of foods to create these first menus.
- After you have introduced the idea of choosing foods by food group, you can **encourage the skill by offering snack choices of specific foods and prompting your child to choose two items that are from the bottom five food groups.** A Snack Balance activity and worksheet is included in Section 4 to help with this lesson.

As your child becomes better at making choices and categorizing foods, begin to generalize that knowledge by having him make choices related to the following areas:

- Category of food: we need a vegetable for dinner; what should we have?
- Choices related to more than one entrée of a meal: Have him help choose two entrées for a weekly or daily menu, then three, then four.
- Choosing the entire menu: Once he is used to making three and four choices about the menu, he will be ready to begin selecting the foods for an entire menu. Remember, the combi-

nations may be odd, and that is fine. The lesson is to learn to make a nutrient-rich menu with at least one thing each person at the meal likes to eat.

CHARTING FOODS

Learning to chart groups of items is an early math skill. For younger children, it helps if charting activities have a direct application to life. The following charting activities give visual examples of "more" and "less" and one-to-one correspondence, and show the differences between family members or classmate's eating preferences. For very rigid eaters, this is yet another way to expose them to the variety of foods available and acceptable to other people.

- **Charting by preference.** After your child collects food preferences of family members, you can chart how many foods each person likes in each food group.
- **Charting food groups in a meal.** Chart the number of foods in each food group in each meal. Chart the number of servings each person ate of the foods offered.
- **Chart foods eaten each day.** The food record sheets in Section 4 are a form of charting. This form encourages charting by using checkmarks. Another way to do this is to chart the foods by adding squares to a line for the food groups. See Activity 9 in Section 4.

See Chapter 10 for more information on teaching your child about the food pyramid.

Advanced Choice Making

As your child becomes proficient with choices regarding the immediate menu, begin to involve him in longer-range decision-making about eating. This will give him the practice he will need later in life, regardless of his living situation.

One of the easiest ways to begin is to involve your child in menu planning. A variety of ways to do this are described in Chapter 16.

Examples of subcategories related to menu planning include:

- Do you have what you need to make the things on your menu?
- Can you afford to make the things on your menu?
- What activities are you involved in during the week? Will you have enough time to make the menu?
- When will you go shopping?
- How many people are you cooking for?

Other advanced choices include deciding what to do with leftovers:

- Keep them or throw them out?
- If you keep them, can you make something else out of them?
- How will you know when it's time to throw them out?

You can also involve your child in making choices about eating outside the home. For example:

- Planning for sports activities (Do you want to bring a snack or drink? What should you bring? How will you keep the drink cold?)
- Planning for special occasions (Will you eat with abandon or will you think about what you are going to eat at the party? Should you bring something for other guests to eat?)
- Planning for eating in a restaurant (What will you order off the menu at an Italian, Chinese, or grill-type restaurant?)

Conclusion

As you will see in the next chapter, choice-making is intertwined with nutrition education. As your child learns to make choices about what to eat and when, he will also be learning many skills needed to take charge of his own eating habits.

CHAPTER 10

Nutrition Education for All Ages and Stages

As your child grows, there will be many natural opportunities to teach her about how food and activity choices relate to a healthy lifestyle. The question is whether you will recognize these opportunities. Many things I have learned that are important to supporting children with Down syndrome in these areas are the outcome of hindsight: the things I wish I had known or had thought of at the time.

Generally, your child needs the same nutrition education as any other child. The long-term goal is to provide myriad learning experiences that enable your child to choose to be as independent and healthy as possible. As with everything, independence for one child with Down syndrome will be different than it is for another child with Down syndrome. The following sections regarding nutrition education are loosely arranged by age and common experiences for children, teens, and adults with Down syndrome and assumes that you deliberately chose to promote and encourage healthy lifestyles from the start. (See Chapter 11 if you are starting to do this later in life.) As you read this chapter, remember that each child learns at a different pace, has different interests, and needs different types of support. Feel free to modify activities and borrow ideas from different age groups to best fit your child and family.

Infant & Toddler Years

The first few years are filled with new experiences, growth, and changes. For children with Down syndrome, this sometimes includes valiant health-related struggles that challenge their nutrition status. It is awesome to consider all that happens developmentally and physically in these first years.

THE FEEDING RELATIONSHIP

During this time, you and your child will develop a rhythm for feeding. You develop your feeding relationship (see Chapter 3). How you interact during feeding time is your child's first "nutrition education" lesson. Some of the key topics to consider during this time include: developing your child's trust, creating an environment conducive to eating, learning your child's cues, and providing appropriate physical support.

MOTOR SKILLS

During these first years your child is learning to sit, crawl, stand, and walk. She is also learning to use her arms and hands to play with toys and feed herself, as well as to manipulate food in her mouth. While the process of learning to chew continues beyond these first years for children with Down syndrome, it is important to watch and encourage your child's progress by providing appropriate foods. This is discussed in detail in Chapter 1.

NUTRITION EDUCATION ACTIVITIES

What is there to teach at this stage? Developing a positive feeding relationship and learning to eat table foods is quite a bit. Teaching your child to make early choices about when and how much to eat, as discussed in Chapter 9, is also an important activity.

Much of the teaching you do at this stage will happen incidentally as your baby watches you and other family members at mealtime. Children with Down syndrome are wonderful imitators. They watch you and learn myriad things from you. Use this skill to your advantage. In these early years, you are your child's example. She's watching to see what goes on at mealtimes. How do people use their forks, spoons, and knives? What do they do with food on their plates? How do people talk to each other when they eat? Include your child in mealtimes whenever possible. Even as an infant, this interactive time is important.

Much of what your baby with Down syndrome learns during this time is covered in Chapters 1 and 3. Your focus is on building a trusting relationship, supporting your child as she learns how to eat, and enjoying her as she does.

Toddler to Preschool Years

As your child leaves infancy and is firmly in the throes of being a toddler, she begins to realize that she has a little to say about what goes on in her life. This is when most parents of children with Down syndrome first experience "the noodle," an amazing, yet aggravating technique of becoming almost gel-like and slipping out of any hold. You may experience a "noodle" when trying to put your child in a highchair or booster seat, usually in public. As annoying as this type of behavior is, it is a good developmental step. Your child is learning that she has some control over what happens to her.

In addition, this is also when your child learns that she is, without a doubt, the most adorable and important child on the planet. And you know what? She *is* the most adorable and important child on *her* planet. Whether or not you occupy the *same* planet is sometimes in question, however. This stage may last a while, so be prepared. The point is that she wants to be seen and heard. Your job is to teach her *how* to do that by making choices that promote overall health.

THE FEEDING RELATIONSHIP

At the beginning of this stage, your child is still learning about food and how to eat. Which foods make the best smears on the highchair tray, which foods taste the best, whether you can eat yogurt with a fork, and so on. Toward the end of this stage, your child will test what it means to be an individual. She wants to know that her communication attempts are powerful and change her environment. She wants to know that she can affect what happens in a way that is pleasing to her. She also wants to try to take over your portion of the feeding relationship and turn you into a short-order cook, if you will let her. Somewhere in this developmental phase, your child will test you and learn the most effective way to get your attention. Some examples include: picky eating, being a good eater, refusing to eat, or asking to eat often.

Some areas related to the feeding relationship your exploring child may be ready to learn include:

- learning how to choose among foods offered,
- learning that her choice matters,
- learning about the sensory properties of foods (how they look, smell, taste, feel, bounce, and so on),
- learning the family schedule for meals and snacks, and
- learning where in the house it is OK to eat.

MOTOR SKILLS

There is a lot that goes on during this time in both fine motor and gross motor skills. Your child is developing the fine motor skills in her hands and hand-eye coordination as she learns to eat with a utensil. It is important to provide supports for success. Work with the OT in your early intervention program to provide appropriate supports for success.

During this phase, your child will still be learning to develop a mature, rotary chew. It is important to pay attention to what types of food you are providing to discourage choking or eating foods that are not completely chewed. (See Chapter 1 on texture and chewing.)

Some activities to encourage motor skills include:

- **Let your child feed herself as much as possible.** This is a messy process and is a built-in part of the sensory play your child does with her food. For instance, if she can use a spoon to scoop ice cream but needs help digging out the next bite, soften the ice cream in the microwave or help her scoop the next bite, but do not feed her. If she can feed herself with just a little support at the elbow, do that rather than providing hand-over-hand support. Provide as little support as possible while enhancing success with the process of eating. Try not to wipe her face excessively or take over the process of learning in order to reduce mess.
- **Let her add ingredients when you are cooking** (bread maker, mixer, adding sprinkles or chocolate chips, etc.) Pouring encourages motor skills, hand-eye coordination, and bilateral skills.
- **Ask her to tear or break foods into smaller pieces** (fine motor skills, hand-eye coordination). Have your child tear

apart lettuce leaves, break spaghetti noodles in half, or snap peas or beans into smaller pieces.

- **Let her rinse dishes in the sink** while standing on a footstool. Be prepared for a bit of mess.
- **Let her stir** batter, pudding, or hot (lukewarm) chocolate.

Your child's interest in being active is also developing at this stage. While she learns to walk, she is also learning the joy of getting around and doing things. You can encourage her interest in being active by taking her on walks, playing games that encourage movement (chase, dancing, Simon Says, leap frog, hide and seek, freeze tag, and so on), and keeping an eye out for activities that seem interesting to her such as kickball or swimming. A list of common activities children with Down syndrome enjoy at this age is provided in the Appendix.

NUTRITION EDUCATION ACTIVITIES

At this age, nutrition education is a daily event. The activities discussed earlier related to the feeding relationship are all nutrition education activities. Probably the best lesson to begin to introduce is the concept of hungry vs. full or hungry vs. not hungry. As your child becomes more involved in making choices, you want to encourage her to choose to eat because she is hungry rather than to fill time. This is a difficult lesson and should be done lovingly and carefully. It will take years to learn or may need to be revisited many times throughout your child's life. It is a concept we all neglect at times, and for our children with Down syndrome, it is one that may make a big difference when they are on their own.

One method for helping your child understand whether or not she is hungry is a ten-minute wait exercise. If you are relatively certain she is not hungry (perhaps because she finished her lunch just a few minutes ago and ate well), ask her if she is really hungry or if she really enjoyed the taste of the food. If she's not sure, set the timer for ten minutes. Tell her if she is still hungry when the timer goes off, you will get her something more to eat. During this time distract her by talking about something, reading a book, or playing a game. She may forget all about it. Visual

timers are good for this because they do not make a sound when the time is up. This is an especially good technique if your child eats very quickly, as it takes up to twenty minutes for your stomach to send messages of fullness to your brain. Older children and teens can learn about hunger by learning to rate it on a scale of 1 to 5 with 1 being not hungry at all and 5 being ravenous.

While you are teaching your child about hungry vs. not hungry, make sure she has a means to communicate when she has had enough to eat. Try a variety of communication techniques (symbols, photographs, sign language) to teach this communication skill. As your child's communication abilities increase, these options still need to be practiced by both of you. For instance, you can teach polite ways of asking for more ("May I have more cobbler, please?") or asking to leave the table ("May I be excused?") rather than grabbing food or leaving the table in the midst of a conversation.

> There was a time when Sheila would just keep eating if I let her. So I introduced the "twenty-minute wait." She was around four or five years old at the time and would keep asking for food. If food in the kitchen wasn't nailed down, it was hers. I started by serving the portions and when she was done, she was done. If she asked for more, which I knew she would, I would tell her that if she was hungry in twenty minutes, she could have more. I would set the timer. If the rest of us finished eating while the timer was still going, I would go about cleaning up the kitchen. When the timer beeped, I asked her if she wanted more. If she said yes, I asked her if it was her tummy that was hungry or if it was her tongue that was hungry. Invariably she would tell me it was her tongue. After a while I began to ask her if her tummy was hungry or if her tongue just liked the taste and feel of the food.
>
> Now when I look back I think this may have been how Sheila began to understand the sense of feeling full. Occasionally she would tell me that her tummy was still hungry. When she did, I gave her another small serving and if she asked for even more, I would set the timer and go through the process again. Sheila rarely asks for seconds anymore. When she does, I give them to her without a lot of thought. When she wants more than seconds—usually of her favorite foods—we begin the twenty-minute wait again.

Early Childhood or Preschool

In early childhood, your child's life begins to expand far beyond her home and family. She begins preschool, meets friends, and the support people involved in her education grow in number and influence. Although you are still at the center of her world, you will begin to occupy less and less of it as she continues to grow up. During this time you will begin to see an increase in risk-taking behaviors and strategies. Some children will dive into life headfirst, while others will take more time and join in after watching a while. Your child will begin to develop friendships, and hopefully have more play dates with children from school. Life in general is *busy*.

THE FEEDING RELATIONSHIP

At this point, the balance of the feeding relationship between you and your child may change dramatically. In many areas, early intervention services (birth to three) are provided primarily in the child's home. However, early childhood services are typically provided in a classroom setting, four or five days a week. This means an increase in the number and frequency of people working with your child on a regular basis. If there were very few support people involved regularly with your family for the first three years, that's about to change. This change in dynamics means it is important to share your values about food, eating, and activity with your child's team (see Chapter 1). Unfortunately, it is probably something you will need to do on more than one occasion each year, depending on the situation.

Your child, of course, isn't interested in all of this. She's busy discovering, trying new experiences, and looking to see what everyone else eats at school, if not attempting to sample it. She may be watching commercials on television, which may influence which foods she wants for her meals and snacks. For instance, it's not likely that a child will decide she wants peanut butter cup cereal for breakfast unless she's seen it somewhere. She's continuing to test her independence with you and is more vocal about what foods she wants to try. You can help with this by talking about healthful choices and allowing for a few of those foods you swore you would never buy in the house such as chocolate or strawberry milk.

MOTOR SKILLS

Children with Down syndrome will progress through textures and chewing stages at very different rates. Some will be close to developing a mature rotary chew at this point, while others may still be "munching." It's important not to rush through the textures or your child may choke. You also need to take it slowly so you can promote the muscle development in her jaw and tongue that are needed for a mature rotary chew. (See Chapter 1.) If your child needs a texture modification, ask your IEP team to help you encourage your child's chewing development. If your child still requires soft or basically non-chew foods as she reaches the end of her preschool experience, talk to your IEP team or physician about having a feeding team evaluate her.

Some activities to encourage other motor skills include:

- **Let your child push the shopping cart.** While not directly related to a healthy lifestyle in function, it's a great upper body exercise for children with Down syndrome. Try to let her steer the cart as much as is safe for those around you.
- **Have her wipe the table, counters, and cutting boards** before and after meals.
- **Ask her to "sweep" the floor.** You may need to accept a less-than-perfect job. Don't let her catch you doing it over after she has finished. Consider using "Swiffers" for your child to push around more easily.

NUTRITION EDUCATION ACTIVITIES

This is a great time to start including fun nutrition education activities. Nutrition education rarely focuses on food and activity only. If planned well, nutrition education activities include other skills such as reading, fine motor skills, and math. Some ideas for nutrition education activities for this age group include:

- **Learn to group foods** (bread group, fruit, vegetable, meat, etc.) You can do this by using real food, photographs, or symbols based on what your child understands. Though it is difficult to do when using real food, always provide the written word along with the object, photo, or symbol. In this way you are enhancing your child's exposure to familiar words. (See "Keeping Track of What You Eat" in Section 4 for an activity related to food groups.)
- **Identify foods at the store.** When you go shopping, talk about the foods and their food groups.

- **Continue to encourage eating for fuel** rather than to occupy time or for the toy surprise.
- **Involve your child in menu planning.** At this point, it's probably most appropriate to have her select an entrée for the meal from a group of your choice.
- **Involve your child in meal preparation:** setting the table, gathering serving dishes, and so on.
- **Involve your child in passing food around the table.** Use serving dishes that she can pass easily.

GROCERY SHOPPING:

- **Send your child on a controlled "treasure hunt" for items on the shopping list.** Give her a photo, box top, or symbol of the food she is looking for. Point out the appropriate aisle as needed.
- **Talk about how to choose produce.** Without going into great detail, you can begin to teach your child about food selection at the store. Examine pieces of fruits and vegetables for bruises, cuts, or signs of age (mold). Be prepared to make some loud exclamations when you find a particularly bad piece. Look for broken eggs together in the egg carton.
- **Let her choose the flavor of an item** you are purchasing such as pudding, cereal, or crackers.
- **Weigh produce together.**

COOKING-RELATED IDEAS:

- **Pour** beans, sand, water, or anything else that can be poured. (Also a good motor activity.)
- **Let her help you measure and pour ingredients** into the mixing bowl or bread maker.
- **Color eggs.**
- With supervision, **use Easy Bake-type Ovens**. A great "cooking" experience. Be sure to declare extreme pleasure over the outcome. She will remember it all her life.
- **Involve your child in preparing a favorite snack.**

Early Elementary (Grades 1–3)

In the early elementary grades, your child's world will explode with choices. There will be choices about friends, after-school activities, and, in some schools, choices about what to eat. Some children will be in inclusive classrooms and schools, while others will be in special education programs. Regardless of placement, your child wants to discover what she can do successfully on her own. You will again need to reassess the roles of responsibility related to feeding, such as whether school staff are letting her make choices or using food rewards. The complicated part is learning what the other adults in your child's life are doing in this area. Chapter 3 discusses the uses and abuses of food rewards; Chapter 12 considers issues related to food and fitness at school.

Having friendships becomes increasingly important to your child's overall wellness at this age. As her interest in spending time with her friends emerges, use the opportunity to teach her how to organize time out with friends so she can do this for herself in adulthood.

Some children with Down syndrome will be involved in community activities after school such as Brownies, Cub Scouts, 4-H, soccer, basketball, baseball, or Special Olympics. Whatever the activity, it is a good idea for children to experience being active while developing friendships. If these opportunities are difficult for you to access, talk to your IEP team about developing a circle of friends or buddy system, or using peer mentors with your child. You can also arrange play dates for your child. Play dates are another meaningful way of developing friendships.

Many children do well when there is an expected routine they can count on. This is also true for children with Down syndrome. It is also important to learn how

After School Schedule: Kids Who Come Straight Home from School

- **Arrive home:** Time to go through backpacks, hang up coats, and share the events of the day.
- **Transition time:** A few minutes to rest, listen to music, or talk about the day (10-30 minutes).
- **After school snack.** More time to chat (20 minutes).
- **Activity:** Time for some exercise! Kids who have been in class all day need to burn off some energy. Some suggestions are playing ball, tag, soccer, swinging, dancing, and so on. (See activity ideas in the Appendix.) Some children need a quieter activity such as reading or doing a puzzle. The important thing here is for children to have some time to regroup. Physical activity is best from a health standpoint, but choose the activity your child needs most emotionally.
- **Homework:** Start homework while dinner is being prepared. This is a good idea if your child has a lot of homework or if it is hard for her to do homework in the evening. If your child has no homework, find a constructive activity to do together such as helping with dinner preparation.
- **Chores:** There are a lot of chores that can be shared and calories that are used doing them. Teach your child about household duties by doing them together. Suggestions include: setting the table, cleaning up after dinner, sweeping the floor, folding laundry, vacuuming, and putting things away.
- **Write the schedule down.** This is especially important if your child is coming home alone for a short period of time. If the schedule is written down, she knows what is expected of her. A written or picture schedule is a good idea for handling after school events for all children with Down syndrome.
- **Overall suggestion:** Limit television as appropriate.

to use free time in an appropriate manner. One way to do this is to provide after school schedules for your child to follow. After school routines provide a framework that encourages your child to use free time wisely, discourages long periods of sedentary activity (watching television or playing computer games), and encourages friends and family to spend time together.

For parents of children with Down syndrome, after school routines require planning and an investment of time for teaching and encouraging the process. It may take a few tries before you establish an effective routine for your child. Every child will need different routines after school—some will need more time outside using unspent energy, while others will need quiet time to regroup after a long day at school. Some children will go to day care centers and others will go directly home. A suggestion for after school routines is provided at the bottom of this and the previous page. In addition, some ideas of activities children with Down syndrome enjoy at this age are included in the Appendix.

After School Schedule: Kids in After-School Care

- **Transition time:** hang up coats, find classroom, and so on. Many programs have a circle or reading time to begin the afternoon.
- **Snack:** Investigate the facility's menu. If the snack choices are not acceptable, do not single your child out by demanding special snacks. Offer to work with them or make donations to improve the menu for all the children.
- **Activity:** Be direct with the staff regarding your expectations. Sending everyone out to the playground for free play is easy, but aerobic activity there may be limited. Encourage the staff to include games for everyone that are aerobic: dancing, tag, duck, duck, goose, and so on. If your child needs some quiet time after school rather than the hustle and bustle of free play, let the staff know how long your child needs to regroup.
- **Homework:** If you want your child to work on homework during this time, consider enlisting a study buddy for your child. If your child is younger, ask if a child from an older age group could read, color, or play educational games with her. You may want to limit which learning activities she is doing away from home so you can keep tabs on particular subjects. Let the staff know what you expect.
- **Going home.** Encourage your child to share stories from the events of the day. Enjoy your child's escapades by showing interest in her stories and using active listening techniques.
- **Transition time:** Allow your child a few minutes of free time to talk with you, listen to music, put things away, and so on.
- **Chores:** For kids in after school care, the most helpful chores are related to meal preparation and clean up. Everyone's invested in getting dinner on the table soon, so it will probably be motivating to help.
- Limit television watching as appropriate.

NUTRITION EDUCATION ACTIVITIES

PYRAMID CONCEPTS

Continue to talk about food groups and categorize various foods. Now is a good time for your child to plan meals with balance in mind. (See Chapter 16.) If you have already introduced the idea of balanced meals and snacks using the food pyramid, have your child begin to plan meals for the family with all their favorites in mind.

Talk with her about your own eating choices. When you are together having a snack that is not balanced, decide how you can change it so it is balanced by the food pyramid. (See the "Snack Balance Activity" in Section 4.) Make lists of balanced snack combinations you and your child enjoy.

What IS the Food Guide Pyramid?

Throughout the book, I mention opportunities to use the Food Guide Pyramid as a way to teach your child about healthy eating. Once your child has started to group foods, she is ready to be introduced to more complex, yet practical ways to use food groups to shape her eating habits. The Food Guide Pyramid is an easy tool for introducing those new skills.

The Food Guide Pyramid was introduced as a replacement for the four food group method many parents grew up with. It is designed to represent the framework of the U.S. Dietary Guidelines for healthy eating in America. The base of the pyramid is built with the food group with the most recommended servings per day, leading up to the tip of the pyramid, with the food group that is the least nutritious. A color-coded version of the Food Guide Pyramid is provided inside the front cover for you to use as a tool with your child. The activities in Section 4 use this pyramid in a variety of activities as well.

Other countries have chosen different representations for their dietary guidelines to fit their culture and food traditions. For example, Canada uses a rainbow and China uses a pagoda. Families from countries that do not use the pyramid may find it is still a useful teaching tool, or may wish to adapt activities to their country's representation of the dietary guidelines.

COOKING

Cooking is a great activity for your child. Make it fun! As parents, we often get waylaid by the nuts and bolts of making meals. Set aside a special time to experience cooking with your child. When you do, make things that are out of the ordinary routine. Making new and different foods rather than the usual ones lets your child know that this is a special time and encourages exploration and learning about new foods. Some ideas include:

- Making edible play dough (see recipe below)
- Making "dough art" such as specially shaped breads or baked dough ornaments. Some great ideas for bread dough activities are included in the book, *Electric Bread for Kids: A Bread Machine Activity Cookbook.*
- Making special cookies
- Making a special cake or cupcakes
- Making "food art" (make a caterpillar out of celery, peanut butter, raisins, and toothpicks or pretzels for legs.)

There is a list of cookbooks in the References and Suggested Reading section for you to consider.

Edible Play Dough

Peanut Butter Play Dough

Ingredients:

- 1 cup peanut butter (creamy is best)
- 3 tablespoons honey
- 1 cup dry milk.

Directions:

- Mix peanut butter and honey together.
- Add dry milk gradually until the mixture is the consistency you want.

Edible Play Dough (Cooked)

Ingredients:

- 2 teaspoons cream of tartar
- 1 cup flour
- ½ cup salt
- 1 cup water
- 1 tablespoon vegetable oil
- food coloring

Directions:

- Combine ingredients except food coloring in a pan.
- Cook 3-6 minutes over medium heat until mixture forms a ball when stirred and does not stick to the side of the pan.
- Remove from heat.
- Put dough on wax paper and wait for it to cool (about 10 minutes).
- Knead dough until smooth.
- Divide into balls for the number of colors you plan to make.
- Add food coloring (food coloring paste is the easiest) and knead into the dough.

Keep in airtight container (plastic bag or bowl) for up to 3 months.

Cooking is also a great time to talk about numbers and use math skills without pressure. As you work together you can structure the cooking activity to include skills related to counting, grouping, and other skills. Some ideas include:

- Count the number of cups, teaspoons, and so forth as you measure them.
- Have your child count as she puts paper baking cups in the pan for muffins or cupcakes.
- Have your child count out the number of baking cups you need for the pan in advance.
- Instead of sifting flour, scoop flour into a tablespoon and count how many tablespoons it takes to fill the necessary number of cups. When pouring the flour from the tablespoon to the cup, have your child shake it gently so the flour falls lightly into the cup. This technique has a similar effect to sifting the flour.
- Have your child find the right number (or the first one and then first two) on the oven to preheat.
- Have you child help you set a timer to how many minutes the food needs to bake.
- Count the number of chocolate chips, nuts, or other smaller foods in the recipe, group them by tens, or group them by smaller cup measurements.
- Group dry ingredients and liquid ingredients separately.

Cooking is also a good time to encourage organizational skills. For instance, make a list of the ingredients or tools you will need to create the entrée you are making. Have her find and mark off the items from the list before you begin to cook.

MEAL PREPARATION

Begin by evaluating whether or not your child is motivated to participate. If she's not motivated to participate, you will not be successful. It is usually easy to be motivated to participate in food-related activities, but it is best to put some thought into planning. If your child enjoys helping you, there are myriad opportunities for participation. If your child is more independent in her learning style ("I want to do it MYSELF"), you will need to plan carefully so she is successful in her endeavors.

In all cases, it is important to build in time to teach and coach your child so she is successful. Choose a meal when you have adequate time to assist your child in the beginning. Here are some areas to consider including your child in the meal preparation process:

- Setting the table (hand-eye coordination, bilateral skills, and learning to gather necessary tools).
- Gathering serving dishes (large motor skills, hand grasp, and upper body strength).
- Adding ingredients to cooking (bread maker, mixer, adding sprinkles, etc.). Pouring encourages medium motor skills, hand-eye coordination, bilateral skills, and counting).
- Peel fruits and vegetables (fine motor skills, bilateral coordination). Begin with foods that are easy to peel such as a banana with the top started, a scored orange, corn on the cob.

- Tearing or breaking foods into smaller pieces (fine motor skills, hand-eye coordination). Have your child tear apart lettuce leaves, break spaghetti noodles in half, or snap peas or beans into smaller pieces.
- Gathering foods when shopping (identifying foods, counting, large motor skills, discriminating between items, and following multiple-step directions).
- Washing food (medium motor skills, hygiene, and food handling skills)
- Washing dishes (medium motor skills, sensory play, hygiene, and food handling).
- Learning about utensils. What do you need to flip a pancake? What do you need to stir pasta?

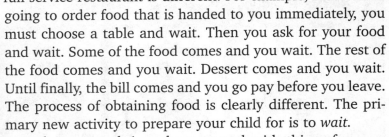

Our son Hans is five years old. His favorite snack time is in the evening. We eat an early dinner and never have dessert because we save it for later. Sometimes we bake bread, sometimes we bake brownies, and sometimes we bake French fries. We didn't think much about including Hans in the process of making the snack until one day he brought us the potholders to get the bread out of the oven. Hans learned the procedure for putting things in the oven and waiting for the timer to go off during this evening snack, but he learned it all backwards! Now he is an expert at gathering the things we need to make our evening snack.

—Nancy Seaborne, Beaverton, OR

RESTAURANT EXPERIENCES

This is a good age to expose your children to more formal restaurant experiences than the local fast food restaurant (if you haven't already). While most Americans visit a fast food restaurant with their child as soon as she is able to eat a French fry, many avoid full service restaurants or struggle with behavior when they do visit one.

Before you introduce your child to a "real" restaurant, it helps to view the experience through her eyes. Does she have a frame of reference for the experience? If most of your restaurant eating has been at fast food restaurants, you will need to explain how a full service restaurant is different. For example, rather than going to order food that is handed to you immediately, you must choose a table and wait. Then you ask for your food and wait. Some of the food comes and you wait. The rest of the food comes and you wait. Dessert comes and you wait. Until finally, the bill comes and you go pay before you leave. The process of obtaining food is clearly different. The primary new activity to prepare your child for is to *wait*.

The next task is to be prepared with things for your child to do while she is waiting. This is a good time to practice conversation or occupy your child with coloring books, games, books, or other things you have brought from home. Even with these pre-planned activities, your child may become restless. If the service is slow, she may decide to visit someone else's table. This is another rule to discuss when visiting a full service restaurant. Do not stop by other tables for a snack on your way back from the bathroom. If your child is still impulsive around food, particularly when hungry, this may be asking for a miracle. It may be best to ask the server if your child's entrée can be served before yours, order an appetizer or salad, or ask for some crackers you can all munch on while you wait.

FOOD SAFETY

It is important to model good food safety as much as possible. While it is unrealistic to believe that no one will ever lick their fingers while cooking or even taste batter with raw egg, there are food safety concepts that young children with Down syndrome can and should learn.

For example, good hand washing is an essential part of food safety and must be modeled and encouraged at all times. Good hand washing skills not only promote food safety, but improved health and hygiene too. Whenever your child helps in the kitchen, the first order of business must be washing her hands. When there is a break in the cooking (going outside while the item bakes), she should wash her hands upon returning and before dealing with any food items.

Hand washing is the most important food safety skill to teach, but it is by no means the only one. You may also want to teach your child that food not on her

A Word about Hand Washing

Good hand washing is more than running your hands under the water. Even if you use antibacterial soap to wash hands, it is important to pay attention to the method used. Studies have shown that the most effective way to kill germs—even better than using antibacterial soaps—is to rub your hands together while washing them. The heat produced from the friction between your hands is what kills the germs and bacteria that can cause food-borne illness or the common cold. For younger children, a good way to encourage the appropriate amount of time (45-60 seconds) for rubbing hands together is to choose a song such as the "Alphabet Song" to sing during this process. Older children will want to use a more "catchy" tune or rap during the process.

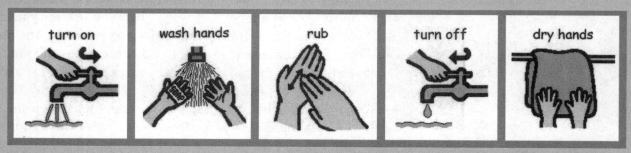

Sometimes a visual reminder of how to wash hands appropriately is all that is needed to remind people to take care when washing hands.

plate (e.g., on the floor, on a chair, or on the ground) is not to be eaten. It is dirty and needs to be thrown away. Food for eating is on a plate, in a bowl, or in a glass. This can be a tough lesson, so be prepared to spend some time on it. Try stopping her in the midst of impulsively reaching for that gummy bear on the floor and then either offer the same food (one gummy bear, not a package) or another enticing food before she gobbles up the one on the floor. Tell her or show her why the dust-covered gummy bear is not good to eat. Later, you can move to incentive charts or verbal praise.

Another food safety concept to teach your child is the importance of keeping hot foods hot and cold foods cold. You may ask her to put the milk away after pouring rather than leaving it out on the table or help you put leftovers away immediately after the meal. You may also want to encourage your child to use her silverware rather than sharing with others. Her friend may have some great pudding in her lunch, but your child should use her own spoon if she's going to taste it. This can be a tough concept and is not always appropriate in some family cultures where sharing food and utensils is widely accepted. Remember to honor family culture. See the Appendix for more food safety concepts to teach.

Upper Elementary (Grades 4-5)

The upper elementary grades are full of emotional growth for children with Down syndrome. Your child may be more interested in the thoughts and actions of others outside your family than before. Her friends at school, as well as the images she sees on television and in movies, will influence her attitudes, preferences, and choices more and more. She may also have difficulty separating reality from fiction or imagination at times. For some children, routines are very important at this age. The structure of the routine, as long as it is not too restrictive, allows her to feel more independence and freedom.

Most children with Down syndrome are able to read at this age. Actual reading levels vary, however, so it is important to provide information in a manner that is easy to understand. Additionally, math is usually a difficult subject at this time. There will be a wide range of skills at this point, due to both ability and opportunity. However, most will be able to count, group, and perform simple math skills. This is important when considering recipes and other nutrition education activities.

Last, and probably the most difficult for many parents, your child may begin to be aware of the fact that she has Down syndrome, if she hasn't already done so. For the most part, your child will focus on her differences as they relate to having a disability. However, be mindful of the differences in body shapes and sizes between people with Down syndrome and those without. For some, body image will become an obsession. She may talk about wanting to "look normal," which we often associate with the facial features common to people with Down syndrome.

This desire to "look normal" also relates to the typical body shape that comes with Down syndrome: a short, stocky build and low muscle tone that makes a person look "soft" or "pudgy." Listen to how your child talks about her appearance. If she is openly making negative comments about her appearance, it is a good time to talk about the differences between all people when it comes to body shapes and sizes. While you may want your child to be healthy and slim, be careful not to make it an obsession for either of you.

It would be nice to believe that since your child has Down syndrome, you will be spared the issues related to body image seen in teens and adults today. Unfortunately, that won't necessarily be the case. I've had a number of conversations at workshops with beautiful young women with Down syndrome who are as obsessed with their body and not gaining weight as other young women. Your child's self-esteem need not be linked to her weight or how she looks if you encourage her to believe in herself for reasons other than appearance.

Our family has always felt that it is important to talk about Down syndrome with our daughter, Eleanor. We believe she deserves an explanation regarding why things are more difficult for her at times. These talks made no sense to her until she was around ten years old.

Suddenly every question dealt with Down syndrome and disability. She was very sad and angry to be labeled. She wanted to know why she has a disability when other children do not. She even went so far as to take several baths a day in the hope she could wash it away. She wrote endlessly in her journals.

Years later, she is still angry about her disability. She wants to fit in with her peers and be a "normal" teenager. She now has a best friend her age who also has Down syndrome, which has helped enormously. In addition, she has focused on something she does well, which is swimming. She trains constantly, has changed her eating habits ("I am an athlete!") and gets satisfaction from the praise she is given by her coach and friends. She has reached a time in her life where her frustration with her disability is mitigated by excelling at a sport. It is important to her that she prove to herself, her family, friends, and classmates that there is something she does very well.

THE FEEDING RELATIONSHIP

The greatest challenge to the feeding relationship between you and your child at this age is the influence of her peers and the media on her eating preferences, style, and attitude about their body. She will begin to want some independence regarding food choices and amounts during this time. You may notice your child taking larger portions than before, as well. It takes careful thought to provide the appropriate balance between your roles within the feeding relationship during this time. This is a good time to:

- Discuss serving sizes: See below for suggestions about teaching this, as well as Activity 7 in Section 4.
- Ask everyone in the family about feeling hungry and full.
- Provide enough food for choices to be made, but not so much that family members will consistently overindulge.
- Limit the amount and types of snacks available in your house while you are encouraging a change in snack habits. Be careful not to become too restrictive or the foods you are trying to limit will become a delicacy to your child (and family) that is gobbled up or hoarded when away from home.
- Check in with your child's IEP team regarding the use of food for rewards. If used in the past, they can still be replaced with other rewards relatively easily. Most children with Down syndrome find "human rewards" (praise, acknowledgement,

and access to special activities) equally, if not more, rewarding than food.

REPLACING FOOD REWARDS

If food rewards have become an entrenched method of providing positive reinforcement to your child at home or at school, it's a good idea to re-evaluate their use. Consistent use of food rewards for good behavior or hard work teaches your child that when she does something well, she should get something to eat. It also teaches her to value the types of foods used for rewards—usually high sugar or high fat delicacies—more than other foods. If you would like to begin to change this practice, here are some ideas you can try:

- Make a list of all the times food rewards are used. You may be surprised at how often your child is eating in the course of a day.
- Make a list of nonfood "motivators" for your child that are currently meaningful, such as: stickers, Pokemon cards, Barbie accessories, sports paraphernalia, verbal praise, "high fives," or doing something special with you or a friend.
- If your child is quite attached to the food reward system, begin by having her earn one sticker or checkmark on an incentive chart before receiving the food reward. As she gets used to this system, increase the number of stickers to two, then three, then five, and so on. When you increase the number of stickers she needs to earn, especially for tasks she has mastered well, tell her you are doing that because she is growing up so fast or doing so well. Make it a goal to need to earn *more* stickers.
- Once you increase the number of stickers or checkmarks to earn for a reward, discuss changing the reward from a food reward to something more tangible. For instance, when she earns ten stickers, she gets fifty cents for a trip to the toy store. She can save her money or spend it right away.
- When you begin this process, it is important to have a visual way for her to follow her progress so she doesn't become discouraged. Use incentive charts to help her track her progress.

Sometimes parents use a special food treat as a reward for good behavior. For example, they may say, "If you don't whine while we are at Grandma's house today, we'll go for ice cream on our way home." While this too is a food reward, it may not be problematic unless you go to Grandma's house every week, offer a reward every time you visit Grandma, or use the same reward for good behavior once a week or more. If you want to decrease your use of food rewards for this type of situation, again brainstorm a list of things your child will be motivated to work for. Perhaps a trip to a special park, playing a favorite game, or having a friend over will be a sufficient nonfood reward.

Changing how you entice your child to do her work or behave the way you want is difficult. Also, sometimes children need to do their work or behave a certain way without a reward. Your child needs to learn to do something because it is what is expected in a certain situation, not because she is going to get something from it.

Snacks and Your Child's Teeth

Keep an eye on what your child is choosing for snacks and what you have available around the house. At this age, popular snacks include candy such as "gummi" treats, Skittles, fruit leather, Phytobears, and other high sugar, *sticky* foods. The good news is these foods help build muscles and overall chewing skills. The bad news is they stick to teeth for hours, which promotes cavities. Use sticky, gooey treats wisely. If you know your child is eating a fruit-chew type snack, have her at least rinse her mouth when she's done, if not brush her teeth. If you send sticky foods such as raisins to school in your child's lunch or for a snack, teach her to get a drink of water when she's done or send a crunchy food such as a carrot, apple, or snap peas to eat afterwards to help remove some of the residue. As with most foods, a little is fine, but a lot can be a problem.

LEARNING ABOUT WEIGHT MANAGEMENT

It is well known that most children and adults with Down syndrome struggle with weight management, for reasons discussed in Chapter 13. Many, if not most children, with Down syndrome will begin to struggle with their weight as they approach and enter puberty. For children without Down syndrome, it is common to be a little "pudgy" in the pre-adolescent phase of life. Before you know it, they hit a growth spurt and that extra weight seems to disappear. Your child with Down syndrome will also gain some weight in the preadolescent phase, but the growth spurt that follows is likely to be less dramatic.

It is important to begin to discuss ways to choose food for fuel and health without commenting on your child's weight. If you emphasize health, energy, and looking good as goals of healthy eating, your child will include not being overweight on her own. If you haven't begun to focus on healthy eating yet, now is a good time to start. Your child's attitudes and values about food and activity are still forming. The fruits of your efforts will be evident later in her teen and adult years. You will be most effective if you begin to establish some habits to encourage your child such as:

- **Complimenting your child when she makes a tough decision regarding taking seconds or thirds.** For instance, if you see her struggling with the decision, validate her choice to not have more. "Dinner was really good tonight, wasn't it? I had a hard time remembering not to eat more, too. You did a great job. We'll make lasagna again soon."

- **Talking about how foods taste.** Learning to enjoy food for its quality rather than quantity is an important lesson for everyone. One way to do this is to wait until you are near the end of the meal and make a comment such as, "This shortcake is really great and filling. How did you make it? What makes it so moist?" or "It's been so long since we had enchiladas, I forgot how good they are. It's hard to only have one, but one is just right. Do you think we should try making them with chicken instead of hamburger next time?"

- **Avoid commenting on how much food her siblings are eating.** As your other children eat with seeming abandon, try to avoid acknowledging the difference in amounts of foods.
- **If your child is very focused on how much his brother or sister is eating, talk about it.** Explain to your child that everyone needs different amounts to be healthy without eating too much. Focus your conversation on your child, not her sibling, and discuss whether or not she is still hungry and use some of the techniques to teach about hungry and full discussed earlier. Talk about how active or inactive she is during the day and whether or not her body needs more food for fuel.
- When you discuss amounts of food to eat, **don't try to scare your child into eating less** by saying, "If you eat like that you're going to be fat." Focusing on a negative outcome such as being fat or overweight is intangible and promotes an obsession with avoiding being fat. For children at this age, it also may promote some embarrassing moments: "Mommy, Aunt Edna took seconds! She's going to be FAT!"
- If one of your children is an athlete, explain how much energy it takes to go to practices once or twice a day. **Encourage your child with Down syndrome to become more active.**
- **If your child complains about being hungry frequently, have her start to rate her level of hunger on a scale of 1 to 5.** One is not hungry at all (but food sounds good) and five is so hungry you feel weak. Once she has rated her level of hunger, talk about what it means. If she is only a little hungry, does she want to wait until later and eat a regular amount of food for her meal or snack or does she want to eat a small snack now so she won't feel hungry?
- **Begin to teach your child about different serving sizes.** For instance, how many pretzels are equal to a serving of potato chips or watermelon?
- **If your child shows an interest, look at food labels** and talk about the seving sizes, fiber, and fat content of different packaged foods.

As your child grows older, this balancing act between metabolism and the "Energy In vs. Energy Out" equation will become more and more evident. Look for ways to keep your dialogue as positive as possible. You can help by teaching your child to eat when she is hungry and focus on the interactions at the meal. Some ways to do this follow.

AFTER SCHOOL & WEEKEND ACTIVITIES

As your child grows, she will want less of your assistance in her daily activities. Even so, she may or may not be ready or willing to call up friends to arrange activities. Learning to make plans to do things with others is an important skill to have later in life and will enable her to be more active as an adult. For instance, calling a friend to go for a walk or arrange to meet her at the gym is an important skill for independence and overall health. One way to make the transition from parent-arranged "play dates" to getting together with friends is to break it down into steps:

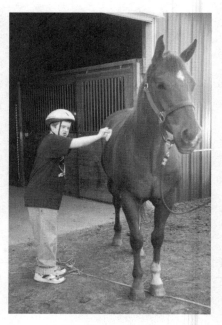

- **Step 1:** With your child, make a list of the types of activities she would like to do with her friends. Remember, you're brainstorming, which means anything is possible.
- **Step 2:** What do you need for these activities? For example, to go to a movie, your child will need money, someone who can drive, and a night that is not a school night. To go bike riding, your child needs safety equipment, a bike, and a friend with a bike. To walk a dog, your child needs a dog (will you buy her one?).
- **Step 3:** With your child, make a list of friends and their phone numbers.
- **Step 4:** Make a list of the kinds of activities that are appropriate for different days of the week.
- **Step 5:** Write a script for what to say on the telephone. Have your child call you and practice by asking you to do something with her.
- **Step 6:** Sometimes it is helpful for the first experience to be a success. Consider making arrangements with someone you know who will be willing and able to accept your child's invitation.
- **Step 7:** Always confirm plans with the other family. It is easy for information to be confused or for misunderstandings to occur when your child makes arrangements with friends. It is a good idea to either call the other parents or ask to speak to them when your child is through with her conversation to clarify and confirm information.

ADAPTATIONS:

- If your child has trouble speaking clearly on the phone, prearrange the time of the phone call with the other family, if possible. Be available to assist with questions.
- If your child has trouble dialing the phone number correctly, put some of her friends' phone numbers on auto-dial.
- If your child has limited speech, you can pre-record the message. Make the call by speakerphone so you both can clarify any miscommunications.
- Send a written invitation with an RSVP enclosed.
- Send an email if her friend regularly uses email, too. You can also follow up with parents regarding activities using email.

Always know where your child intends to go, who she will be with, how they will get there, and when they will be home before she leaves. Don't be afraid to check on them if they are on their own. If your child knows you will check on her, she is less likely to do things that will endanger her. It is also important to be attentive to your child's energy level. If she is tired after a full day at school, don't force her to be active or do challenging things. Save the challenges, both physical and emotional, for the weekend. When she has a lot of energy after school, encourage her to set up activities with friends or join after school activities. It is important not to over-stress your child.

<table>
<tr><td>

NUTRITION EDUCATION ACTIVITIES

</td></tr>
</table>

PYRAMID CONCEPTS: SERVING SIZES

This is a great age to begin discovering serving sizes together. Get out the pyramid definitions for serving sizes, check food labels, or use a diabetic exchange booklet to determine the size of one serving. Unfortunately, each of these resources has slightly different serving sizes for foods. Any one of them is appropriate; only when you are counting calories for weight management do you need to worry about consistency.

Measure the amount of food for one serving and put it on a plate to see what it looks like. You might want to purchase a small food scale with large numbers for

The Rule-of-Thumb for Portion Sizes

While many individual foods, particularly snack foods, have different serving size amounts, it is probably easiest to teach a more generalized rule-of-thumb approach to determining what is "one serving" of a food. Here are some rule-of-thumb techniques to help define an appropriate serving size.

- **Meat:** 3 ounces cooked weight of any meat. Three ounces of cooked meat is approximately the size of a deck of cards.
- **Cheese:** 1 ounce of hard cheese, which is the same as a one-inch cube. Borrow some of those cube counters they use at school to learn about units and counting.
- **Soft cheese:** 1 tablespoon (cream cheese or cheese spread). This is about the size and thickness of a book of matches.
- **Rice, pasta, applesauce, and similar textures:** 1 cup, which is about the same size as a tennis ball.
- **Fresh fruit:** 1 cup, which is about the size of your fist or a baseball.
- **Cereal:** 1 cup, which is about the size of a baseball.
- **Bread:** 1 slice (or bun half), the size of a CD case.
- **Peanut butter, margarine, and other oils:** 1 tablespoon, which is about the size of a book of matches.

While using measuring cups and a scale to weigh and measure foods for serving sizes is the best method, this gives your child something she can visualize to compare the amount of food she is contemplating with the amount of a normal serving size.

easy reading to learn about serving sizes for meat. This is a great exercise for most Americans, actually. One of the main cultural differences between the eating habits of Americans and much of the rest of the world is the size of servings we eat. When you begin measuring and weighing servings of foods, do it for the experience rather than telling your child this is how much she should eat.

What you want is for your child to:

- Recognize portion sizes that are very large.
- Understand when she is eating more than one serving (for instance, a hamburger bun is 2 bread servings rather than one even though it seems like one serving—when was the last time you ate a hamburger without a top bun?), and
- Realize that everyone needs to take time out to weigh and measure foods sometimes to remember what one serving looks like.

Consider taking a picture of the recommended servings for different foods. This is especially helpful for foods called "combination foods." Some examples include tacos, pizza, casseroles, and chef salad. Once you break foods apart into their individual pieces, you will need to use some common sense in determining whether it is a whole serving, half a serving, or an uncountable amount in each food. Use the "rule-of-thumb" serving sizes to guide you.

COOKING

Now is a good time to begin collecting recipes your child likes. Take this on as a hobby with her and begin a cookbook for her that she will always have. You can start by using this cookbook more like a scrapbook:

- Take pictures of entrées your child helps make.
- Take pictures of your child setting the table or in meal preparation activities.
- Copy recipes she likes into the cookbook. Include information about why she liked it or if it is just "OK."
- Write down recipes she is learning to make or can already make on her own in an easy-to-follow format.
- Write down the food groups included in combination foods such as lasagna or tacos.
- Find the price of ingredients on the shopping receipt and write it on the recipe. Have your child add up the cost of the ingredients (use a calculator).
- Decorate the dividers to the cookbook together.
- Make notes regarding what was hard to do.
- Write down descriptions of how to do things in a way your child understands. Some cooking procedures seem obvious, but are difficult to understand. For instance, what is the difference between dicing, chopping, and slicing, or between stirring, beating, and folding?

With this cookbook, you can create a tool that is individualized for your child and helpful to her if she is cooking on her own. No recipe is too easy to be included. One template for copying recipes into your cookbook is provided in the Appendix.

As you share cooking experiences together, remember to teach basic cooking skills and kitchen safety. Some of the "Look and Cook" series of cookbooks have beautiful photographs to illustrate cooking skills such as peeling, chopping, and measuring. Check one out from your local library and read it together. Remember to include steps in the cooking process that you take for granted, such as positioning handles on pots and pans on the stove, not putting metal in the microwave, and using a potholder when removing hot items from the oven, stove, and microwave. These steps should be included in the recipe you create together.

It is also a good idea to include a cooking skill or safety section in the cookbook notebook. In this section, include reminders such as not using a knife or fork to fish burned toast out of the toaster, how to hold a knife when chopping, and how to use a potato peeler or other kitchen utensils.

FOOD SAFETY Hand in hand with cooking are food safety concepts. Include in your cooking escapades discussions about how to store certain foods and how to handle foods that are left over. Some of the earliest concepts are easy:

- What should be put away in the refrigerator?
- What should be put away in the cupboard or pantry?
- What foods need to be cooked before you eat them?
- What foods do not need to be cooked before you eat them?
- What does food look like when it is "spoiled" (moldy, discolored, slimy, smelly, and so on)?

These beginning concepts are important for independence when your child is older. The easiest way to teach your child these basic food safety concepts is to clean up after a meal together. Have her help put foods in containers and back in the refrigerator or pantry. When you are cooking, have her retrieve ingredients from the refrigerator such as cheese, fruits, vegetables, and milk. Discuss whether they are good to use and show her how you decide. If you decide a food is no longer good to keep, show her how to dispose of it.

Middle School or Junior High

Children in middle school or junior high are at a stage where they begin to question the rules by testing, ignoring, or refusing to follow them. Children with Down syndrome also go through this stage, and like many stages of development, they sometimes last a little longer than parents like. You will also see great variances in the interests, communication, motivation, and educational placements of children with Down syndrome. Some are very good communicators, interested in things that are typical for this age group. Others may struggle with communication and appear to have different interests. Some are in special education classrooms, while others attend a full day of general education classes. The variety, complexity, and range of combinations in educational placements grow along with our children.

Regardless of the surroundings or politics of educational placement, children with Down syndrome mature. Once they enter the pre-teen and teenage years, they test the boundaries of their lives, each in their own way.

Our son, who has Down syndrome and autism, does not use speech to communicate. He is now thirteen years old. People who have not known him long sometimes make assumptions about his interests and abilities based on his communication skills and mannerisms. When they do, they are usually treated to a dynamic introduction of "I'm a teenager and you can't tell me what to do." If he doesn't see a reason to do something you ask, he just doesn't. He does not get angry, he does not shout, he does not have a melt down, he simply doesn't. However, if you share with him what is about to happen and why it is important to him, he thinks about it and then joins in. It is clear as he enters his middle school years that he is not going to accept that something must be done "because I said so."

Never underestimate the importance of commitment from your child. If your child does not feel like an important part of what is happening around her, she will not participate. As you look for ways to encourage healthy lifestyle choices for your child, include her in the decision-making. Choose things she will enjoy. Offer more than one option. Schedule challenging activities at a time of day when your child will be more likely to want to participate. Make it fun—for her.

Children in middle school also want to have as much independence and control as possible over things that involve them. Give your child controlled responsibility for meals and snacks as often as you can. This means covertly engineering situations so she is successful the first time. For example, if your child takes a sack lunch to school, let her choose what to pack. However, first stock up on healthy foods that she likes rather than sending her to the store to buy her lunch foods without guidance. Or, give her five dollars to cover her snack purchases at school for the week. She will be able to make her own choices from what is available at school, but be limited by the amount of money she has to use. Or, let her choose what to make for dinner from an array of options. She will learn that you trust her to make the right choices and that she can do things without you hovering over her. That's an important lesson! Of course, it's likely that children with Down syndrome are not quite ready for the level of independence they desire. That's no surprise—no child is at this age.

There are also some behavioral trends that may begin to emerge in the pre-teen and early teenage years that are more specific to Down syndrome. One is the use of "self-talk" to problem-solve situations. Dennis McGuire, Ph.D., clinical social worker, and Brian Chicoine, M.D., medical director, at the Adult Down Syndrome Center in Park Ridge, Illinois, share that the use of "self-talk" is a common process used to work through situations that are stressful or worrisome. You may hear your child passionately talking to herself in the bathroom behind closed doors. If you listen to the conversation, it may be one-sided or even have multiple participants. The content, however, may shed some light on what your child is feeling. Be sensitive in how you approach this situation. You are listening in on a private conversation. In the process, you may learn more about the most stressful things in your child's life than you will from asking her directly.

Things to listen for related to health and eating are comments about appearance, an intense session of self-talk and private role-play followed by excessive eating, or self-talk related to eating or activity. All of these can shed light on emotional eating, excessive worry about body image, or stress about exercise and eating behavior. If your child's self-talk has an emphasis on these topics, you need to evaluate what the source of the stress might be.

Another behavior that may begin to emerge in the middle school years is a type of rigidity in the way things must be done. For some children with Down syndrome, having a routine or order to certain tasks makes it easier to tackle the more difficult things. For example, your teen might insist that dinner be at exactly 5:00 p.m. If dinner is later, she becomes insistent that it must be NOW and begins to set the table. If she does not have dinner at this time, she becomes irritable and unable to cope with the situation, making it difficult for everyone. Dennis McGuire calls the tendency to create sameness in action or behavior "The Groove" because these routines are like well-worn paths, or grooves. Some are related to activities or routines and others are related to preferences. McGuire explains "the most common [groove] centers on personal preferences for things such as music, sports teams, or celebrities. Also common are grooves with issues related to independence as a theme. These are often expressed as 'I want to do _____ by myself and in my own way.'"

Although grooves are not always easy for families to deal with, they do have advantages. Most importantly, the predictability of an established routine promotes independence. As your child creates her personal grooves, she knows what to expect and exactly how to go about doing something. You can use grooves to your advantage by establishing a rewarding routine related to exercise or food choices. For example, introduce an activity such as walking the neighbor's dog on Tuesdays. Encourage your child to do this by paying her or praising her for her helpfulness. Over time, walking the neighbor's dog on Tuesdays will become a habit or a groove—a normal and necessary part of her routine on Tuesday. This same concept can be used for other activities such as:

- joining an exercise class,
- cooking dinner for the family one day a week,
- having a healthy evening snack such as carrots or fruit,
- drinking a bottle of water every day,
- reading the label to determine a serving size for packaged foods, or
- packing a lunch instead of eating pizza for lunch at school.

All in all, these pre-teen and early teenage years are among the most challenging for both parents and children with Down syndrome. Investing your time to include your child in any lifestyle plans—food, activity, or social—is worthwhile. It takes thought, planning, and accommodation to do this. When successful, the outcome is clearly worthwhile. You might have to wait a few years to see it, though.

INCREASING YOUR CHILD'S INDEPENDENCE

As your child becomes increasingly interested in independence, it is easy to see how the responsibilities of the feeding relationship are challenged. It is important for parents and professionals who work with children with Down syndrome to constantly question the balance between choice and control regarding food.

In most cases, pre-teen and teenage children with Down syndrome are not ready for a cart blanche attitude from parents about food. Still, it is probably time to start devising ways to transfer some of the responsibility from parent to child.

This transfer of responsibility depends on your child's desires for independence. One way to do this is to give your child an appropriate responsibility for one meal each week. Since you need to have the ingredients on hand, she must either plan the meal before you do your grocery shopping or choose a menu from foods that are on hand.

If your child is challenging her freedom to make choices about food away from home, you need to be careful not to begin a food battle. Listen carefully to your child's concerns. Try to understand what they mean. Is she feeling over-restricted? Do all the other kids eat from the a la carte menu, but she's expected to eat the school lunch? Does she want to drink soda with sugar rather than diet soda? And underlying most of these questions is: Is she having a hard time "fitting in"? Once you have an idea of what is bothering her, you will have a better idea of how to frame the choices she has. You might decide that she is ready to have a certain amount of money each week to purchase the food she wants at school without any comments from you.

Another technique for avoiding food battles at this stage is to continue a natural, regular conversation about health and healthy lifestyle choices. Talk about your own choices. Will you exercise a little more this week because you know you will eat a lot at Aunt Millie's house this weekend? Share your plans for exercise routines and the different options you are considering. Put your exercise time on the family calendar for the week so your family, and your child with Down syndrome, can see when you are planning to get your exercise. Talk about moments when you thought you might buy a bag of candy because you were upset and then share how you worked through the situation without compromising your health goals. All of this is important teaching when you are beginning to shift the responsibility of the feeding relationship to your child. She needs to hear that you must think about these choices, too. The more typical it seems, the more likely your child is to buy into the process.

Some situations—such as sleepovers, birthday parties, holiday dinners, weddings, and other special occasions—are simply "nutrition nightmares." These are situations where the best choice is to not worry about healthy eating and let your child enjoy the moment. The best thing to do is try to minimize the feeding frenzy kids sometimes feel when they are with their friends. In fact, if your child tells you that she knows she's not making healthy choices, you can pat yourself on the back. She knows it's her choice, and she knows it's not the best choice. She knows a lot.

If the balancing act between you and your child regarding food choices begins in middle school, rest assured it will continue for a long time. Maintain the same level of responsibility you have established at home for snacks, meals, and activities for a while and allow school and time with friends to be unfettered. The goal in doing this is to allow for some independence and to show your child that you trust her. While she may not feel that trust right away, she will feel the control she has over her lifestyle.

PHYSICAL DEVELOPMENT

The middle school years mark the beginning of puberty, and that means many physical changes for children. Girls will likely begin to menstruate, while boys may sprout facial hair and develop new, lower voices. Both boys and girls will experience unfamiliar changes in their hormones that cause mood swings. These hormonal changes influence the onset of acne, which many people associate with poor eating habits. The most direct link to acne and eating is when your child puts her hand on her face while eating or doesn't wash her hands after eating a greasy pile of french fries and rests her head in her hands. Other links to acne from food choices are questionable. However, if your child cares about her appearance, she may choose healthier foods if you link acne to high amounts of junk food.

If you have not had to worry about your child's weight yet, you may need to soon. Somewhere in the middle school and high school years, the effects of a lower basal metabolic rate begin to catch up with most people with Down syndrome. That's not to say that every child with Down syndrome is destined to be very large, by any means. It is merely something to keep in mind as you begin to work through your child's developmental stages. For instance, during this time your child begins to seek independence in her choices. She is offered a greater variety of choices at lunch time—few of which are more healthy than the school lunch. At the same time, her growth rate may slow, which in turn will lower the amount of food she can eat without seeing a change in her weight.

Here are some concepts/activities your child may be ready to learn about at this time:

- **How to use the scale to weigh herself.** Encourage her to weigh herself at the same time of day, one time a week. Weighing yourself more than once a week is too often, as true body weight changes take time to occur. Focus on looking at changes over time rather than from day-to-day.
- **If you think your child is finished growing taller, make a note of the size she is wearing.** She will learn her size best if she is helping you shop for her clothes or shopping on her own. It is probably unrealistic to expect her to stay the same size forever, but if she is changing sizes because she is growing thicker more than once in a year, that is something to talk about. If she has outgrown a favorite dress due to eating habits, think twice before buying another special outfit. Perhaps she will be motivated to exercise in order to fit into that outfit for a special event.
- **Chart the number of minutes of activity along with weight change on a graph.** See Chapter 13 for more ideas to teach about the "Energy In vs. Energy Out" equation, as well as Activity 12 in Section 4.

Regardless of your child's past, present, or future weight, remember that weight alone is not a measure of health or a healthy lifestyle. It is but one component of a complex topic that is best described as "weight management." Proactive nutrition education is one part of successful weight management. Weight management is discussed in further detail in Chapter 13.

PHYSICAL ACTIVITY

Recent surveys indicate that children become less active as they get older. It's not hard to see why there may be a change in activity around middle school. Recreational sports become competitive, weeding out those who do not excel. Children struggle with self-esteem and are less likely to risk trying out for a competitive team or be seen trying to learn a new sport. On top of this, children with Down syndrome may not feel accepted by their peers and may or may not feel shy about participating in team sports.

One way to encourage a sense of accomplishment along with activity is to encourage your child to set some "leisure goals." In the past, you have probably made the phone calls or signed your child up for activities to keep her active and

around other kids. You may have begun teaching her to set up her own dates with friends as well. Now it's time for her to begin to make some goals focused on her leisure time. This means choosing an activity, choosing how often she wants to do that activity, who she will do it with, and how she will get there. If you have your own fitness program, it is helpful to be open about how you make those plans. Try to share this process in a natural way rather than in a lecture or lesson. Your job at this stage is to become a bridge to the activity rather than the activity coordinator.

If you and your child choose to make and keep health-related goals, you can go through this process together. This goal-setting process is discussed in more detail in Chapter 13.

Help your child by providing her with some ideas for activities. Create a resource file with names and numbers of organized sports activities and friends who like to do things with your child. Some ideas for this notebook include:

- Special Olympics. Some states have challenging and well-coordinated Special Olympics programs that last throughout the year. In other states the Special Olympics program is primarily tied to special education classrooms at this age. Call your local Special Olympics Office for more information.
- A local community center with a variety of activities available.
- Your county or city department of parks and recreation.
- Information on classes and programs at YMCAs or other local gyms.
- Information on summer or school break programs offered through the local school system.
- Information regarding summer camps and day programs offered by groups such as Kiwanis or other organizations.

There are two important goals regarding activity for all children with Down syndrome at this age:

- to experience success related to goal setting, and
- to nurture social connections with other kids and adults with activity (rather than food) as a focus.

Both of these will foster a positive self-image as well as important skills for a healthy lifestyle in adulthood. To achieve these goals, your child will need time, teaching, and encouragement from you.

NUTRITION EDUCATION ACTIVITIES

The focus of nutrition education activities in middle school is to begin to set reasonable, attainable goals related to food. For some, this may mean setting goals to learn to cook favorite dishes. For others, it may mean setting goals related to eating habits, such as choosing balanced meals and snacks or learning to define appropriate serving sizes. It is very important to work *with* your child on goal setting rather than dictating what areas she should work on. Involving her in the process not only increases what she learns, but may gain her commitment to participate in setting and working toward the goals.

PYRAMID CONCEPTS

Combination Foods. This is a good time to begin talking about *Combination Foods*. Combination foods are foods that include more than one food group in a serving. Foods such as pizza, lasagna, tacos, French toast, and hamburgers are combination foods. One serving of each of these foods will not only be higher in calories than a food from one food group (such as an apple), but they are typically nutrient dense foods. An activity about combination foods is available in Section 4.

Nutrient Density

Nutrient Density is a term used to describe foods that have a high number of nutrients such as vitamins, minerals, and fiber per calorie. They are the best bang for your nutritional buck because of the density and variety of nutrients they contain. Combination foods tend to be nutrient dense because they include more than one food group. Foods that are not combination foods can have a high nutrient density also. Some of them include:

- broccoli,
- most berries,
- liver, and
- nonfat milk.

Servings: Size and Number. Serving size is something you will work on with your child and for yourself all the time. If your child develops a new favorite food or menu, wait for a teachable moment and look at the label for the serving size together. When you do, also take note of the number of calories in a serving. Perhaps one serving is very high in calories. Whether it is or not, it may have very few nutrients. If it's a food from the *Sometimes* group, you will want to talk about how many servings of bread or fruit this new favorite is the equivalent of (That is, how many servings of bread or fruit could you eat and consume the same number of calories). Also discuss the fact that by eating something with very few nutrients and a lot of calories, you are fueling your body with watered-down energy. While you may get calories from it, you won't get the same vitamins, minerals, and fiber that fresh fruit provides. So even if you eat the right amount of calories to keep from gaining weight, your body will be short on the necessary nutrients for it to work its best.

Foods from the "sometimes" group that have few vitamins and minerals to offer can substitute for other foods in calories, but not in the quality of those calories. These foods are often described as providing "empty calories" because of their poor nutritional quality. Eating a lot of foods with empty calories means you have to eat more nutrient dense foods and calories to get the vitamins, minerals, and fiber your body needs to function.

SCIENCE OF NUTRITION

A wonderful way for your child to become aware of her eating and activity habits is to write down all food and activity for at least one twenty-four hour period. Chapter 13 includes a food record and goal-setting activity that can be used for this purpose in class or at home.

If you do this activity at home, try to get the entire family to participate. The more people who are participating, the more fun it is for everyone, and the less your child with Down syndrome will feel singled out. It is also a much better learning experience to see food and activity records for other people and what they mean for them. The learning outcomes from this type of activity for your child include:

- seeing a list of how much food she ate,
- seeing a record of how often she is physically active,
- finding out whether her meals and snacks are balanced,
- learning whether her activity and the amount of food she ate during this time would promote weight gain, loss, or mainte-nance if she did it every day,
- discovering how many food groups or servings of food she can eat each day,
- being introduced to the details of how "Calories IN vs. Calories OUT" works for each individual.

Remember, each child with Down syndrome will learn different things from the same activity. For some, participation in this activity means identifying foods and their groups. For others, it will mean an understanding of how calories and activity affect a person's weight. Regardless, there are ways to include everyone.

SHOPPING & MENU PLANNING

If your child is interested in helping with shopping or menu planning, let her. The key to effective education in any area of life is taking advantage of teachable mo-ments when they arise.

From the cookbook of favorite foods you have been compiling together, begin a new section for favorite menus. Have your child plan menus for different meals and snacks using the methods described in Chapter 16. Once the menu is written, list the foods you need to make the menu. Cross off the foods you already have in the house. Re-copy the list of foods that have not been crossed off. As you copy them, group them by categories found in the grocery store: fruits and vegetables, pasta, canned fruits and vegetables, frozen foods, dairy foods, meats, and dry in-gredients (such as spices and flour). Grouping things on the list in this way makes it easier for your child to find everything she needs. Examples of ways to modify or organize your shopping list for your child's success are provided in Chapter 16.

Once you are home with these items, copy down the price for each from the store receipt onto the back of the menu. By keeping track of the cost of foods, your child will eventually have a record of approximate cost for making some of her favorite combinations of foods.

Chapter 16 discusses menu planning and balance and shopping systems in greater detail.

COOKING

Once again, what you emphasize when practicing cooking with your child depends on her interests. It is important for your child to practice using all the appliances in the kitchen. She should learn to safely:

- use a microwave,
- use the oven,
- use the stove,
- operate the dishwasher,

- operate the can opener (manual or electric),
- use the toaster or toaster oven,
- use the crockpot,
- use a knife,
- operate a mixer, and
- use the garbage disposal, if you have one.

Work on these skills together in a natural way rather than in a scheduled, task-oriented manner. Learning these skills is an educational activity, but it is also a time for you to communicate with each other. Doing cooking-related activities together gives you the opportunity to see first-hand which tasks are frustrating or difficult and which ones come more easily to your child. Chapter 15 discusses teaching people with Down syndrome how to cook in more detail.

Sometimes parents ask why it is important to teach children with Down syndrome how to use all the kitchen equipment when they can learn to make just about anything they want using a microwave. It is true that most foods can be made in the microwave or purchased already baked in a store deli. Just as it isn't reasonable to expect your child to cook everything from scratch, it is also unreasonable to expect her to never use a stove, oven, or crockpot. Knowing how to safely use all the equipment in a kitchen helps reduce the opportunity for accidents if your child decides to experiment.

FOOD SAFETY

As your child becomes more independent, it is important to teach additional basic food safety skills. Some things will always happen in a kitchen, even if they aren't sanitary. Those are the sorts of things we have to live with. No one is perfect. But there are some basic food handling concepts that will help everyone stay healthier and also avoid spreading any food-borne illnesses, such as salmonella, in the kitchen. These are the basic rules to teach your child (see the Appendix for more detail):

- Wash your hands before you prepare any foods.
- Wash your hands again after you sneeze or cough.
- Wash cutting boards, counter tops, and utensils with hot soapy water after preparing each food and before starting the next one.
- Keep fresh fruits and vegetables separate from uncooked meat and poultry.
- Keep hot foods hot and cold foods cold. (Hot foods should be heated to at least 160 degrees F (71 degrees C). Cold foods should be stored at 40 degrees F (4 degrees C) in the refrigerator.) Bacteria grows quickly in foods that are lukewarm or room temperature.
- When in doubt, throw it out! If you don't know if a food is still good or not after storing it in the refrigerator a while, throw it away. Don't risk eating spoiled food.

These simple rules will go far in promoting food safety for your child and family.

SUMMARY

The middle school years are a time to take advantage of teachable moments that lead to independent activities. For children with Down syndrome of all abilities, stretch your imagination to find ways your child can increase her independence in developing leisure skills, cooking-related skills, and understanding how to make healthy food choices. Goal setting is one way to foster independence while creating a situation that is likely to be successful. These successes, no matter how small, will foster a feeling of capability. Focus on what she *can* do right now without worrying about what you hope she will be able to do in the future.

High School

When your child reaches high school, the greatest changes may involve you, her parents, rather than her development. Your child is nearing the end of her educational career. First and foremost in your mind are all the things yet to learn and the transition to life after high school. Given the complexity of the next stages of life, it is understandable that working on health-related goals or promoting wise food and activity choices may not be on your short list of things to do. However, if you have been working together on these areas of life prior to high school, you will continue to promote a healthy lifestyle as a routine part of your family's lifestyle. If you have not, there are some tips in the next chapter for starting to work on these things later in life.

For your child, the high school years can be anything from the most exciting social time to a bridge to a job and greater independence. Some young adults with Down syndrome will be in general education classrooms or special education classrooms in the school building. Some will be in vocational programs, either at a vocational training center or in job training placements with a job coach.

Regardless of your child's school placement, she will still need a group of friends to connect with on a regular basis. If you are feeling unsure about your child's opportunities to find friends to spend time with, check with local agencies such as the ARC, your park and recreation office, United Cerebral Palsy Association, Special Olympics, the local Down syndrome support group, or even the local hospital that sponsors disability-related programs or a Down syndrome clinic in your area. Some groups have weekly or biweekly social gatherings for people with

disabilities. While it may not be what you think is best for your child, you may find she enjoys it. Let your child decide.

You will also be dealing with issues related to making the transition out of school. Transition to *what* is the great unknown. Your child may have some ideas about what she would like to do, where she would like to live, and how she would like to live her life after high school. Some young adults will want to go on to a postsecondary program. Others will not have the interest or funds to do so. Some will have realistic expectations about jobs and lifestyle, while others may not. It's not uncommon to hear a teenager with Down syndrome express her desire to become a movie star, for instance. While that may not be unattainable, it is not easy to accomplish.

How do you, as a parent, handle all of these important concerns as well as promote a healthy lifestyle? It's not easy. There are so many things to consider at one time. It may help to first realize that it is unlikely that your child will leave the public school system ready to: a) obtain a good job, b) live away from home, and c) develop a strong circle of friends to spend time with. This is a reasonable belief since children who do not have Down syndrome rarely are ready for all the responsibilities included in that list immediately out of high school.

You may want to use these last years in the public school system to obtain training for independent living skills such as cooking, shopping, and getting around in the community. Unfortunately, given the present state of nutrition education in the schools, it may be difficult for your child to learn the basics needed for a healthy lifestyle. For a student in general education, the current nutrition education is brief and provides little understanding of the effects of eating habits on weight or lifestyle over time. For students in special education, there is more instruction on the mechanics of cooking, shopping, budgeting, and menu planning, but even less attention to choosing foods for health. The programs I have seen designed to teach these skills in special education classes tend to offer high fat, high sodium, high calorie recipes and options. There is usually some instruction in menu planning for a variety of foods, but without an explanation of why different foods are important for your body. Last, I see few ideas in any education setting for promoting positive, healthy, social gatherings.

Unfortunately, this puts most of the burden of teaching your child how to live a healthy lifestyle on you. Making choices about serving sizes, appropriate amounts, and food quality is going to be learned from how you and the rest of the family lives. This is why it is easier to promote healthy habits through example than it is to expect others to teach and encourage them. Of course, it is difficult to promote this value in your children when healthy habits are not practiced at school or by friends at school.

What's the solution to this? I'm not sure. The Cooking Buddy program described below and sports-oriented activities offer avenues to hopefully expose your child to some healthy habits. If your child is interested and able, consider going to a heart-healthy cooking class together or joining Weight Watchers for the lifestyle education portion.

Promoting health and healthy lifestyles is an important area of need for teens and adults with disabilities. The good news is that policymakers have recently begun to focus on making health-oriented programs accessible to people with disabilities. Look for programs and lifestyle education opportunities to emerge in your community through DD Councils and other traditional support organizations in the next few years.

As your child begins to set her sights on independence or the end of school, start easing her into the everyday process of being independent and healthy. Many of the suggestions and activities listed previously in this section are designed to do just that. Most important, take time to learn what is most important to your child. Now is the time to begin to envision her choices when you are not there. By understanding what her priorities are, you can encourage her and augment her plans in ways that will encourage a fulfilling life after school.

THE FEEDING RELATIONSHIP

Even though your child is on the edge of adulthood, you are still her parent. Your responsibility for what and how much food is available, as well as where and when it is provided is still valid. Likewise, your child is responsible for whether she eats the food, and if so, how much. This remains the case until your child leaves home. If you are planning for your child to live away from home, it is time to encourage her to begin to take responsibility for her own food choices.

PHYSICAL DEVELOPMENT

Most children, with and without Down syndrome, meet with a frustrating reality in high school: some people can eat everything in sight without gaining weight and others cannot. For your child with Down syndrome, this may be even more frustrating. It might help if your child understands that her disability plays a role in this difference between her and another student. In this discussion point out that she has stopped growing taller, while her friends without Down syndrome are still growing. This means that her body does not need as much energy to get through each day, not only because of her metabolism, but also because she is done growing. Explain to your child that people with Down syndrome do not burn calories as quickly as people who do not have Down syndrome. This means it takes less food to meet the calorie needs of her body. If your child isn't ready to hear this, remember it for another time. It's important for your child to understand why things are different if she is struggling with comparisons between her eating and others.

Explaining the difference in metabolism to your child may seem like a very complicated topic. It's not really. Mia Peterson, a young woman with Down syndrome, explains it this way to her friends who do not have Down syndrome:

> *"Let's pretend you and I are exactly the same height, weight, and age. If you have a cookie and I have a cookie that is exactly like yours, it will do different things in our body when we eat it. When you eat the cookie, you will burn the calories from the cookie faster than I will. The reason is my metabolism is slower than yours. My body takes longer to use the calories than yours does because I have Down syndrome."*

Mia likes to use this story to lead into a longer conversation about why being healthy is important to her. She knows that because she has Down syndrome, it is very important for her to be mindful of how much and what types of food she eats if she wants to be healthy.

PEER PRESSURE AND EATING HABITS

Probably the greatest influences on the lifestyle of teenagers with and without Down syndrome is the media, their friends and teachers, and support people. Most teenagers with Down syndrome I meet have favorite musicals, plays, bands, television shows, and movies. Some can recite movies for me from memory. It would be silly to think these same teenagers are not influenced by the messages sent by advertisements. When you watch television advertising, you can see how your child might get the idea that Britney Spears can drink can after can after can of soda without it affecting her physique; or believe it's perfectly normal to eat four or five pieces of pizza for dinner *every* night; or think that it's OK to go to the local fast food place for lunch every day and have a "super-sized" meal.

Friends, respected teachers, and support people play an equally influential role. If your child only sees her friends eating without restraint at the pizza parlor or eating super-sized meals at fast food restaurants, she will likely decide that this is acceptable behavior all the time. In addition, if gatherings with friends are focused around food, then she may decide that there must be food and free-for-all eating at all social gatherings. These examples may seem extreme, but they are not uncommon assumptions for any teenager who is beginning to feel her independence.

As you talk about being independent and making choices about eating with your child, try to bring some realism to these images. Yes, it is easy to eat foods from a fast food restaurant every day, but it is expensive. Yes, it does look like people drink a lot of soda, but how many calories *is* that? Focusing on calories is something that is best used for teaching purposes. If your child seems to be unduly persuaded by media images, caloric comparisons are quite dramatic. Here's something to use as a demonstration:

- Using the equations in the Appendix, calculate the calories your child needs to maintain her weight. Do the same for yourself.
- Each of you choose a meal from your favorite fast food restaurant.
- Using the nutrition information from the restaurant (available by asking at the counter or from the restaurant website), determine the number of calories in the meals you chose.
- On a piece of graph paper, choose a column to represent your child. Color in the number of boxes that represents the estimated calorie needs for your child. (Each box represents 100 calories.) Do the same for yourself, but leave a large space between your columns.
- With a different color, shade the number of boxes equal to the calories of the meal your child chose from the restaurant menu. Do the same for your meal next to your calorie needs.
- How many calories are left for you to consume the rest of the day (if any) without exceeding your estimated calorie needs?

If there are calories left for you to eat, determine how much food it represents. Talk about how you would feel eating so little for the rest of the day. Talk about what happens if you eat more than your estimated needs every day. Try to bring the discussion to the topic of whether or not the people they see in the media or their friends could actually eat this way every day without gaining weight.

COOKING

At this stage of life, the focus of any nutrition education related activities needs to be on creating independence. One way for your child to experience cooking for others, as well as having guests for dinner, is to participate in a *Cooking Buddy* program.

To establish a Cooking Buddy program, you need two or three other teenagers with or without disabilities and the support of a parent. The purpose is to practice creating affordable menus, experience making and eating new dishes, and practice cooking skills. At each meeting, the cooking buddies draw pre-selected recipes from a hat to make for the next meeting's meal. Recipes should be chosen by a coordinator or parent who has gathered a list of potential recipes. (You need a "hat" for the salad, main entrée, and dessert or whatever menu structure you want to follow.)

In the time between meetings, each participant makes a shopping list, buys the ingredients, records the price of the ingredients, and makes the dish for the meeting. The group then meets at a host home (which changes each week). The person who is hosting the group provides drinks and sets the table as if for special guests. The visiting participants bring their entrée to the host's home for the meal. Once everyone arrives, they sit down and enjoy their meal and each other! It is a great time to share the trials and tribulations of cooking attempts or the awful smell of a recipe that seemed like it would be scrumptious.

When someone makes an entrée your child likes, she can add it to the collection of recipes in her cookbook. Each cook provides information, including the recipe, any additional instructions or tips to make it easier to make, the cost of ingredients, the nutrition information for the recipe, and a rating of the difficulty of the recipe. A detailed outline of this program can be found in Section 4.

SUMMARY

The high school years typically represent the end of your child's education in the public school system. Evaluate what skills you would like her to learn while there are still resources available for teaching them. (See Chapter 12 for information on working on nutrition education at school.) If your child is focused on her upcoming independence, she will welcome the assistance. Some teens and young adults may not be interested in what happens after high school. In this situation, it is even more important to seek coaching and system building from community- or school-related resources for independence in job, home, and lifestyle to help build a bridge to the next stage.

Adulthood

Once your child is an adult, you will probably have a good idea of what her life will look like. You know what her strengths and weaknesses are; what she has learned; what is difficult for her; what makes for a great experience; what frightens her.

Most likely, you will be making decisions and plans about where your child will live. There are as many solutions to this question as there are families. Some adults with Down syndrome will spend time at a postsecondary program, learning skills that will enable them to live more independently. Some families will purchase a home through the "home of your own" program (Section 8 housing); some will move into a duplex or town house arrangement with the adult with Down syndrome living in one area while her parents live in the other; some adult children will move into apartments on their own or with a roommate; some will move to group home settings, both large and small; and some will continue to live at home.

POSTSECONDARY PROGRAMS

Most postsecondary programs include instruction for independent living. These programs are constantly reviewing what they are teaching students regarding healthy lifestyles. There is a growing realization that this aspect of independent living cannot be overlooked. Before you register your child for a postsecondary program, ask questions regarding food selection and nutrition education. Learning the program's method of promoting healthful lifestyles is just as important to your child's overall success as learning to manage laundry, money, and work.

GROUP HOMES

If your child is living in a group home or if you are considering one, talk with the administrator and staff development person about attitudes regarding food and activity. Consider asking the following questions:

- Are the people who live in the group home involved in menu planning? Cooking? Shopping? It is important for your child to be involved in this process.

- Does the menu structure allow for more than one entrée and a variety of side dishes for each meal? A variety of entrées and side dishes provides more choice and control over food selections for your child.
- Does the staff of the group home support, model, and encourage healthy choices? You don't want your child to receive confusing messages. If your child believes smoking is bad, for instance, and the majority of the workers are smoking, she may change her opinion because the people she spends a lot of time with, and who are important in her life, think smoking is OK. "Do as I say, not as I do" doesn't work very well.
- Are a variety of healthy foods available for snack options?
- Is there a way to encourage the people who live there to eat appropriate amounts?
- Are opportunities for physical activity such as low-impact aerobics, walking, or biking available? If so, how often?

You need to find out whether the lifestyle you value and have worked toward with your child is supported in the group home environment. In group living settings, there is a real struggle for families, workers, and people with disabilities between the need to give residents the freedom to choose and the need to structure the environment to avoid regular excesses. You will want to learn the values of the group home setting and decide if they are compatible with yours and your child's.

LIVING IN THE FAMILY HOME

Evaluating the environment in your own home is much less stressful than interviewing others. If your adult child is living with you, is your home conducive to healthy living for her? Is better health a priority for everyone living there? It is important to send a consistent message about health and exercise to your child. If you expect her to engage in a regular exercise routine, you must have one too.

Although you may think that it will be easiest for your child to attain a healthy lifestyle at home, this may not necessarily be the case. A 1998 study of 283 adults with Down syndrome found that more adults who lived at home were overweight than those who lived in a group home setting. The study does not mention any other living situation. There are some fundamental differences between living in a group home and at home with parents that probably contribute to the weight differences found in the study. For instance, food is more available at home, parents are more likely to give in to persistent food requests due to exhaustion, and parents may simply be focusing on other aspects of life. In the group home, there are restrictions on when food is available (so they can meet their budget) and staff rotates every eight hours. They are able to come in fresh and focus on appropriate choices and behavior for residents because they are paid to do that.

Consider creating family menus for everyone to use as a reference. (See Chapter 16.) You can give this responsibility to your child as appropriate. Create menus for meals and snacks with everyone in mind. In the end, you will find your grocery bill is less than it was before. Also ensure that your child stays physically active, as discussed on pages 177-78.

SUPPORTED AND INDEPENDENT LIVING

If your child is living in an apartment alone or with roommates and with or without a supported living coach, the atmosphere of the living situation depends on those who live there. If at all possible, however, persuade your child to make menus to plan what she will eat for the week. Ask her counselor or job coach to work on this with her using the ideas in this book. Menus are a highly useful tool for adults with Down syndrome living on their own. If your child uses

a menu, the menu determines the food items on the shopping list, helps her eat healthy foods, and provides the security of knowing what will be eaten that day.

When cooking for one or two, and when cooking is a lot of work, it is easy to make only a few things that you are comfortable with, such as macaroni and cheese, sandwiches, or a microwave dinner each night. One way to encourage your child to experiment with her cooking skills is to plan a dinner together once a month. The idea is to try at least one new food or entrée at the meal. Your child can make it, you can make it, or you can make it together. It is always easier to do something new and different with a friend. It is also a good idea to set up a Cooking Buddy program for your child and her friends who are living on their own or getting ready to move out. It's a great way to combine a social event with learning.

When I was in high school, I never really cared much about what my parents had to say about healthy eating. I especially felt this way when I was a senior and after I graduated from high school. I think I was sad a lot. Everyday when I went to work in the deli, I would bring home a candy bar, a donut, and a soda pop. Sometimes I brought home an entire meal. I watched a lot of television while I was home by myself. My younger sisters were at school and my parents were at work. I was lonely. But I didn't listen to what anyone said about my eating or exercising. All I cared about was me. Later I realized my family was right about the way I was behaving about my health. Things started to turn around when I started running cross-country, which is a two-mile event.

When I moved out of state to live in my own apartment, the clothes I had worn in high school began not to fit me anymore. Every time I came home and tried on clothes I would cry and have a fit about it. My mom would talk to me about my weight all the time. Every time I came home we had to have a sit-down conversation about my weight. I didn't like it. I also didn't want my parents to know or think I knew that they were right. So I began to work on learning about nutrition and healthy lifestyles on my own.

Later I started running, walking with friends and family, and training for a bike ride across the state of Iowa on a bike for two. Once I started doing all that activity, my clothes started fitting better.

What encourages me to stay as healthy as I am now is the nice comments people give me about how I look now that I have lost the weight I gained. I look good and I want to keep it up. This helps me feel more confident about myself when I speak in front of people. It also has kept me interested in being active in things like running and biking. My life now is so much different than it was when I finished high school.

FOOD AND THE WORK ENVIRONMENT

When your child is an adult and out in the workplace—regardless of the type of work she does—there will be new people and situations that influence her food choices. Some jobs are very rigid and routine based. In this situation, your child most likely has a job coach who influences what she does during her breaks at work. Ask your child's job coach what her job schedule is like. If she has something to eat during her breaks, find out what her food choices are. Is she selecting from a vending machine? Going to a grocery store? Is she bringing her snack from home? Are there other options for break time than eating (such as going for a walk, listening to music, or making a phone call)? Look for ways to offer choices about activity (eating or walking) to your child during work breaks whenever possible.

Many adults with Down syndrome secure jobs in foodservice, such as at a fast food restaurant, grocery store deli, or full service restaurant. Sometimes jobs in foodservice come with the added benefit of either reduced-price or free food when you work a full shift. Given that most adults with Down syndrome have limited income due to the restrictions on Social Security Income and Medicare benefits, this is a good benefit. However, if your child is choosing high calorie foods to eat on her break, you may find yourself with a dilemma. Again, if your child has a job coach, solicit her help in encouraging your child to make a variety of choices. You may also seek the assistance of the manager or assistant manager. Perhaps they can set up a method to structure the foods available at break time to promote less calorie-dense foods. Talk with your child about the options available to her and how to make selections that promote a nutritionally balanced and healthful meal or snack using activities in Section 4.

PHYSICAL ACTIVITY

We've all heard stories about children with Down syndrome who were good students but then couldn't find anything to do once they graduated from high school. The prospect of having your adult child sit at home, watching television and eating to pass the time while waiting for an opening in a job training program or some other work situation is not a welcome one.

This is when your child's network of friends or the skills she learned in the process of calling friends to make arrangements to get together come in handy. Encourage your child to make a calendar and fill it with activities that she enjoys. There are many benefits to regular activity for anyone. One known benefit is an

improved sense of well-being. People who include a regular aerobic activity in their routine generally handle the ups and downs of daily life better than those who do not. If your adult child is not currently active, sit down with her and talk about different activities she might enjoy. Make sure you include a social component to these activities—such as finding an exercise buddy or taking an exercise class with a group of friends. Here are a few ideas to consider:

- Join a walking club. Walking clubs often have group walks with a pin you can purchase as a memento. Your child might enjoy collecting the pins and displaying them on a walking vest or baseball hat to show her accomplishments.
- Sign up for community aerobic classes or start your own.
- Make exercise dates with friends and do aerobics tapes in the living room.

- Join a local health club or YMCA. Visit the club beforehand to evaluate whether or not it is a welcoming and inclusive environment for your child.
- Hire a personal trainer at the health club or YMCA. Your child may find the partnership of a personal trainer or coach very motivating and rewarding. Again, be selective about who works with your child.
- Find a walking partner and schedule a regular time to walk around the neighborhood, park, track, or mall together.
- Encourage your child to ask neighbors if she can walk their dogs. There's a growing business in walking dogs for people who are too busy. If your child is good with animals, this may be a good opportunity for many reasons.

These are just a few ideas of ways to create an exercise routine your child will enjoy. (See Chapter 14 for more.) These activities will, of course, only work if she is a part of the process of choosing the activity and setting up the schedule. Some things will elicit a twinkle in her eye that means she thinks it's a great idea. *Those* are the types of activities to seek.

Conclusion

If nutrition education and encouraging healthy lifestyle choices have been a part of your family routine for some time, your child has probably been exposed to and developed routines consistent with those values. If not, it's not too late to make changes. It's never too late for anyone—whether they have Down syndrome or not—to learn new skills, develop new interests, or change habits in a positive, or negative, way. If you are contemplating making changes or introducing concepts regarding healthy lifestyles to your adult child, it may be easier to develop a plan by reading through the next chapter first.

The definition of a healthy lifestyle changes as we age. What is important to us when we are younger—such as being able to compete in sporting events— is not as important in our adult years. The definition also changes as our body shows signs of aging and we are forced to modify our activities. Regardless of your child's age, there's absolutely no reason to believe she cannot choose to be healthier and experience great success.

CHAPTER 11

Beginning in the Middle

When it comes to health, everyone makes changes throughout their lives. For instance, if you learned that your cholesterol is 300, you would probably visit a registered dietitian and an exercise specialist for a program to reduce cholesterol. And when your children move away from home, you will need to learn to cook for one or two instead of for a larger family. Many of us must learn ways to be more active to prevent weight gain. Choices and decisions about health and healthy lifestyles are ongoing. We make adjustments at every turn. So do our children with Down syndrome.

If nutrition education, weight management, or promoting a healthy lifestyle for your child with Down syndrome has not been a priority before, don't worry. Now is a great time to start. Learning, as you know, is a life-long process. It's not a linear activity. Learning and developing healthy habits is most successful when people are motivated or interested in the topic. If you are motivated and interested now, you will be a better role model and teacher than you would be if you were acting out of obligation or guilt.

The previous chapter offered a progressive plan beginning in infancy for introducing your child to nutrition education and skills promoting healthy choices for food and activity. Let's look at how you can use that information regardless of where you begin your quest to promote healthy living.

Deciding Whether to Make Changes

No matter how old your child with Down syndrome is, it is possible for him to make changes that will lead to a healthier life. It is important to remember that no one leads a "perfect" life when it comes to health and wellness. That is partly because no one really knows what "perfect" is. It is also because we are all human and invariably we have a habit or two that isn't the healthiest. It's normal.

Whether your child is in elementary school or an adult, making changes that promote better health requires some planning. By asking him to consider making new choices, you are challenging his concept of a typical day or the choices within the day. Therefore, the first thing to do is to decide what is important. Ask yourself some questions such as:

- Why is it important to make changes?
- What brought this need to my attention?
- What do *I* need to learn to be able to be successful?
- Does my child have significant health problems related to our lifestyle? Which ones are the most immediate? Diabetes or celiac disease require immediate action, while promoting activity to prevent weight gain or even obesity can be done over time.
- Does my child express a need to make these changes? For instance, if he complains about his weight and is overweight or wants to be more active, he is expressing a need to make some changes.
- Do I need to make some changes? How are my habits getting in the way of my child living a healthier lifestyle? For instance, if your favorite snack is potato chips and you always have a plentiful supply around the house, how might that affect your child's choices for snack? Are there changes you can make in your daily routine that will send a healthier message to your child?
- Are my expectations for my child with Down syndrome the same as they are for my other children? For me? Do your best not to send double messages. If you want your child with Down syndrome to make changes to promote a healthier lifestyle, then encourage your other children to be healthy too.
- Does my child seem depressed?
- Does my child have activities with friends or people he enjoys besides his family?
- Specifically, what outcome do I want from teaching my child about nutrition and healthy lifestyles?

Your answers to these questions drive what you do next. Obviously, if your child is in a medical crisis that requires dietary intervention, you need to implement some sort of survival plan while you learn more. If your child is expressing a desire to make some changes or wants to work toward moving away from home, you need to make some plans now—even if *you* are not ready. If the desire to make changes is primarily yours, ask yourself what changes you need to make in your own life first. This allows you to lead by example, which is a wonderful teaching method for children and adults with Down syndrome. Making your efforts to improve your health obvious will entice your child to take note.

Talk It Over and Prioritize the List

Once you have decided what is important for you and your child, prioritize the list. This is most effective if you involve your child in the discussion. Of course you don't start the discussion by saying, "John, you've been looking a little tubby to me. I am going to make some changes around here to help you lose that flabbiness." That will put him on the defensive. The discussion you want to have with your child is about health and lifestyle. Here are some better examples of conversations starters:

- *"John, I want to do some things that will help our family be healthy. Would you like to help me make some new menus that will be healthy for our family?"*
- *"John, I was thinking we all could use some more activity. I've been feeling out of shape for a while. What do you think we could do to be more active? I found this list of things we could do at the community center. What do you think?"*
- *"John, I know you have been thinking a lot about when you get to live on your own. I was thinking that you and I could start cooking together. Would you like to do that?"*
- *"John, you seem sort of bored on the weekends. I am too, sometimes. Would you like to find a team you could play on to make some new friends? I have a list of places where Special Olympics Teams meet or we could go on a Buddy Walk next week together. What do you think?"*

Of course, all these conversation starters seem a little contrived. You may not need them to start the conversation. Your child may say something that gives you a natural opportunity. The important part is that when you suggest changes that will affect your child, you are not focusing on his needs or problems in a negative light. Including the entire family or yourself in the project starts a dialogue that gives your child an opportunity to be involved without feeling like a failure.

Don't Single Out Your Child

Remember, if you choose to set mandates such as "you have to sign up for a team sport for each season," the rule must be set for everyone in the house. Rules must be the same for everyone—there are no special rules for your child who has Down syndrome. This is especially important for middle school students and older. Your child will know if the rules are different and may feel slighted. He may act out with rebellious behavior. He may resent the seemingly relaxed attitude you have toward his siblings. A healthy lifestyle for children and adults with Down syndrome has the same components (good eating, regular activity, social activities, and so on) as a healthy lifestyle for people without Down syndrome.

Once you and your child have chosen an area to begin, read through Chapter 10 for ideas of how to encourage, teach, and support your child. If you choose to begin by increasing activity, read through Chapter 14, which will help you consider and plan for changes in activity. If you begin by planning menus, read Chapter 16, as well as the nutrition education activities offered before. Your child will need to learn some basic nutrition concepts to plan nutritionally balanced menus. The point is: choose your starting point, find an activity to begin with, and then introduce additional topics from the foundational skills (learning the pyramid, planning activities, and so on) over time. Take advantage of teachable moments that present themselves whenever you can rather than creating a battlefield between you and your child.

Evaluate the Feeding Relationship

Once you have jumped in with both feet, take time to read about the feeding relationship in Chapter 3. The feeding relationship describes the dynamics between you and your child when it comes to food and mealtimes. It is not a relationship between you or your child and food. This feeding relationship between you and your child defines how you handle certain situations and provides a way to set up natural, yet unnoticeable structure to promote healthy choices.

The Feeding Relationship

Adults (Parents and extended family members)
Adults are responsible for **what, where, when,** and **how** food is presented.

Children (Persons with Down syndrome, regardless of age)
Children are responsible for **how much** and even **whether** the food is eaten.

Care Givers (Babysitters, Speech-Language Pathologists, Physical Therapists, Occupational Therapists, Teachers, Educational Assistants)
Support people are responsible for **what, where, when,** and **how** food is presented within the known parameters of your family as long as it does no harm to the child.

If eating or exercising has become a battle between you and your child, you will need to focus on rebuilding mutual trust. This is most easily done by focusing on an area that has not become filled with tension. Choose something you can be positive about and focus on the success your child has with what he is learning. For instance, if you have been battling with your child over increasing his activity each day, consider changing your first steps to something related to food choices. Maybe he ate less at snack today or is taking an interest in helping with the cooking. If so, you will do best if you introduce activities he is interested in and engage in fewer battles as a result. If it's hard to find an area that feels positive to you, take heart. There is always a positive. If your child is interested in being healthier—even for a fleeting moment—that is what you focus on. Praise him for becoming aware that he can make a difference in his own health.

When I teach weight management classes to adults who do not have Down syndrome, everyone shares one good thing about the week before. Sometimes people have trouble thinking of even *one* thing that went well. At that moment, I can look at them with a big smile and say, "You are *here*. You cared enough about yourself to come tonight. That's a big step."

The same is true for your child with Down syndrome. Even the smallest outward commitment to making a change is important. If you or your child feels as if you have not done anything good lately, look for it. It is there, but it may be a very subtle, small thing. Working on an area where you are not currently at odds has a greater chance of success than choosing to promote change in an area where you are already fighting. After you learn how to work together as positively as you can, it is easier to revisit earlier areas of conflict.

Goal Setting

Goal setting is an important part of making changes. If your child is in elementary school, the goals are primarily focused on your own choices. When your child is young, the best way you can encourage a change in his attitude and priorities is to change your own. He will watch you begin to exercise, see that you're having fun playing badminton instead of avoiding it, and he will begin to think that running around batting a birdie in the air is fun. And if it's fun, you can bet that your child will want to be squarely in the middle of it.

If your child is in elementary school, you can make early goals for yourself, such as learning to plan meals, involving your child in the kitchen, learning new activities everyone can join you in, and so on. If your child is in middle school or older, you must set your goals together. Some changes will be primarily for you alone, while others will be for your child. Whatever you do, make sure you have your child's agreement if you are planning to encourage him to make changes too. Information about goal setting with your child is provided in more detail in Chapter 13.

When you begin focusing on healthy lifestyles in the middle of the life cycle, goal setting is very important for both of you. Setting short-term goals that are easy to reach builds your confidence that you can work toward a long-term goal. These smaller goals provide the structure you both need to move forward without getting lost or discouraged in your attempts. Changing habits is no small task. Be kind to yourself and your child, yet be determined.

GOALS FOR THE ENTIRE FAMILY

Sometimes the best way to promote healthier habits for your child with Down syndrome is to promote changes for the entire family. This is especially true if family habits are likely to promote unconscious eating (eating without thinking about what or how much you are eating).

Beginning in the Middle: an Example

Amy was fourteen when I met her. She was in the sixth grade. She loved to shop and dressed impeccably. She had a few friends at school, but none that she did things with on the weekends. Amy was very interested in making her own choices about food, but had little nutrition knowledge. Her mother wanted to encourage her, but did not know where to begin. She had started by trying to teach Amy to eat low fat foods. Amy didn't like those foods and did not understand why it was important. She began to dislike "eating healthy" so she would eat mostly candy and other forbidden foods.

Since Amy wasn't interested in exercising, we decided to focus on learning to make a meal a week. The first task was to write a menu. I asked Amy if she wanted to learn to cook in ways that were good for her body, or if she just wanted to learn to cook. She thought it would be good to make menus that people liked. As we talked, she began to realize that eating healthy foods does not mean giving up all foods. It means eating a mixture of foods from all the food groups. I told her it would be a few weeks before she would get to start making her menus, so we mapped out a plan of action:

Step 1. Food Guide Pyramid [Activities 1 and 2 in Section 4]
Step 2. Understanding combination foods [Activity 3]
Step 3. Meal and snack balance [Activities 5 and 6]
Step 4. Writing a balanced menu [Chapter 16]

If Amy had not wanted to wait to learn basic nutrition skills before writing menus and making her meals, we would have started by having her make a menu that included one favorite food for each member of the family rather than learning how to balance meals. Later we would go back and pick up information about the Food Guide Pyramid to enhance Amy's menu writing abilities.

Anytime is a good time to consider making changes for better health. The most difficult part is deciding to make a change. Once you have decided, your child will too. You might have to wait until he sees the benefit through your own changes before he's ready to join you. Be positive. Remember, you are his coach and his best teacher and lead the way with patience.

CHANGING THE ENVIRONMENT

Sometimes it makes the most sense to change something about your family's environment in order to accomplish a nutrition-related goal. For example, once or twice a month your husband and children go to the movie store on a Friday afternoon to rent enough movies to fill a weekend and more. When they return, they are eager to begin the movie marathon they have planned. The ritual begins with ice cream sundaes during the first movie. During the second movie, they bring out the popcorn. And on it goes throughout the weekend. A few healthy activities such as soccer games sneak into the movie festival, but the focus of the weekend is on the five or six movies the gang is devoted to watching before they must be returned Sunday evening.

How could you change this scenario? Some ideas include:

- Reduce the movie festival to once a month, then once every six weeks.
- Create a new rule that food cannot be eaten in the family room where the television is. The sundaes and popcorn are still options, but they must be eaten away from the movie. Probably the number of snacks will decrease, as well as the amount eaten.
- Start a rule that everyone must go for a walk between movies. If it is too late at night, you could have everyone do an aerobics video or play a game of indoor tag between movies.
- Make a relish tray of fruits and vegetables for the evening. Family members can go into the kitchen and grab a baby carrot or slice of apple easily and not miss much of the movie if they need to eat.
- Create a menu of selected snacks or desserts for your family to choose from. There's no need to do without, but keeping food in the room where food belongs (the kitchen) will help decrease the total amount of food eaten.
- Schedule fun activities such as a game of badminton or koosh ball darts or a bike ride during the day time when there are no other activities.

Slowly, over time, you will see a change in the movie festival. Even if the number of movies your family manages to watch in a weekend remains the same, the focus will change from the food *and* movie to just the movie. Eating and watching television or movies are two different activities.

A common, similar situation is the problem of young children eating in front of the television. Often when kids are young, they watch a number of videos or television shows. Some are educational and some are pure entertainment. Especially when it is raining or snowing outside, television can become a big part of a child's day. If they are eating snacks while watching television, they may begin to feel as if the two activities are inseparable.

What kind of family-oriented goals can you make to change this scenario over time?

- Take note of when your children are eating in front of the television. Do they always eat something when watching a show or video? Sometimes? Rarely? If they don't eat in front of the television all the time, take note of when they do and what videos or television shows they are watching to see if there is a pattern.
- Make a new family rule: no eating in the family room (or wherever the television is). You may want to split the rule into two parts: no drinks and no food.

■ Make a poster or visual method of saying "no eating" or "no food" or "no drinking" on the doorway leading into the room.

Usually when you add new rules to the household it takes time for everyone—including you—to learn them. Mistakes happen. Rather than scold offenders, remind them what they have to do. "No eating in the family room. Come into the kitchen to eat your snack."

When we moved to a new home, we had to make some new rules. In our old home, we allowed eating and drinking anywhere except the bedrooms. In this new home, we wanted to keep food in the kitchen and family room. Our television is in the living room. Our son who has Down syndrome and autism had just learned to use a straw in a pop can. He felt very independent with his drink. He would pick it up, take a sip out of the straw, walk into the dining room (which is adjacent to the living room), and become very interested in the video that was on. At this point, he would "forget" he was carrying a pop can and just let go of it. This was not a good thing.

I announced that the new rule for everyone was that drinks—including pop, coffee, tea, milk, and even water—were to stay in the kitchen area only. This was hard on all of us, as my husband and I were used to taking our coffee and tea mugs with us as we meandered through the mornings. It took a lot of reminding and cajoling to get everyone to follow the rule. For Andy, we put a sign on the doorway from the kitchen to the dining room with a symbol for "no pop." When he would start to take his pop out of the kitchen, we would point to the sign and remind him, "no pop."

But that wasn't enough. We then made a symbol for the kitchen island that said, "Put pop here." Now we could tell him visually and verbally where to place his can of pop. It took a while, but soon we were only pointing to the symbol on the counter. Now he knows that his pop can goes on the corner of the kitchen island. That's his place for snacks and drinks and to watch or help me cook. He doesn't need the symbol anymore. He just knows. Every now and then, when we aren't paying enough attention to him, he begins to meander around the kitchen island with his can of pop, waiting to see if we will notice. When we ask him, "Where do you think you are going?" he smiles that sneaky smile and puts the can down on the counter.

CHANGING ATTITUDES

It is much easier to engineer changes in the environment than it is to encourage changes in attitude. It is both easier to accomplish and easier to devise a plan of action. Changing unhelpful attitudes that are expressed by other family members is extremely hard. For instance, if someone in your family tends to categorize foods as "good foods" or "bad foods," or if they constantly refer to particular foods as "making you fat" (while proceeding to pinch your tummy), these will be very difficult things to change. This is because there is no way for you to change another person. You can only change yourself.

In the examples above, whoever is in charge of household rules (usually a parent) can change the environment in order to affect eating habits. However, attitudes expressed through word choices have to come from within each person. It's not impossible; it's just hard. For instance, if you would like to stop foods from

being categorized as "good foods" and "bad foods," you will need the understanding of the person who uses that language. Talk with him or her about how important it is for your child to learn about healthy eating without worrying about whether he is being "good" or "bad." Explain that you understand the meaning is focused on the health effects of a particular food, but that it's important for your child with Down syndrome to understand that all foods are OK, even if some are more nutritious than others. No one food is going to be the sole reason that someone is overweight, has diabetes, or is not in good shape.

Once everyone understands the concerns about "good food" vs. "bad food" (or other words you may want to avoid using), you can all work together to avoid using those phrases. What will you replace them with? Rather than replace the actual word use, focus on replacing the thought process. When you are getting a snack for the evening, you can talk about the balance of the snack, the food group it is from, whether you've eaten a lot of "sometimes" foods today, and so on. Another method is to focus on hunger rather than the food item when a person is snacking. If you see them grabbing more chips, instead of saying, "That's a bad food that will make you fat," you can say, "Are you still hungry or do you just want to eat? Let's walk around the block and if you're still hungry when we get back, you can feel better about having a snack." Yet another method is to have an appropriate amount of "healthy foods" in the house. In other words, the balance of what foods are available should reflect the balance you want your family to eat. If your goal is to promote more nutrient-dense foods than empty-calorie foods, it is wise to have a higher percentage of nutrient-dense foods such as fresh fruit, pretzels, juice, or beef jerky available than chips, cookies, and soda.

Conclusion

Anytime you attempt to promote change in your child's life, even when it's good, you must put thought into your strategy. Only very young children will not notice a change in the rules or food choices available. Older children, teenagers, and adults have far too many life experiences to draw from to accept that things have changed "just because." This is true for everyone, whether or not they have Down syndrome. However, the teens and adults with Down syndrome I know constantly remind me that they are very interested in being as healthy as they can be. They merely want to be in control of what that looks like.

CHAPTER 12

Food and School

While my son looks forward to what they serve at school for lunch, I do not! My son gains weight every school year. We believe it is directly related to what is served at school. A few times a year, my husband or I visit Charley at school during lunch. It's an easy time to visit, meet his friends, and he seems to enjoy it. This year I noticed he chose 2% milk to drink with his lunch. This was something we had talked about at home—drinking nonfat milk rather than 2% milk. When I asked him about it he said he wanted "blue milk like the guys." Sure enough: 2% milk comes in a white carton with blue writing, but nonfat milk is in a white carton with pink writing, something that is apparently very important to fifth grade boys.

School, and all the things that happen there, is a major part of your child's life once she reaches kindergarten age. Once she has begun attending classes all day, a good portion of her day is out of your direct supervision. This means that she will consume at least one meal while she is away from home, and also encounter a variety of other food-related activities such as birthday parties or classwork involving edible rewards. This chapter will explore food and activity concerns associated with school, such as school lunches, physical activity, and nutrition education.

School Lunch

Lunchtime at school is a very important time of the day. Next to recess, it is the most unstructured time and is filled with myriad social and skill-learning opportunities. Whether they are eating a lunch purchased at school or one packed at home, lunchtime is one of most children's favorite times of the school day. It is also one of the most overlooked times for natural learning for children with and without Down syndrome.

REGULATIONS AND LAWS

Before discussing the learning opportunities available during school lunchtime, it is important to understand what school lunch programs are and how they operate. Understanding the regulations and process of school lunch programs makes it easier

to know how this time can be used to naturally encourage new social, communication, and motor skills for children with Down syndrome.

The relationship between school lunch and breakfast programs to students with disabilities is not direct. If your child needs accommodations and modifications to meals provided at school, which a few children with Down syndrome do, you must first navigate a complicated maze of legislation. The first and most important thing to know about your school's food programs is whether or not they are "reimbursable" programs. Some schools, especially very small ones, do not participate in United States Department of Agriculture (USDA) School Lunch Programs for reimbursement. Therefore, these school lunch programs are not regulated by the USDA. If your school provides lunch, but does not use the USDA School Lunch Program, modifications are still available, but specific guidelines do not currently exist.

The federal law that covers modifications and accommodations to school lunch programs that *are* regulated by the USDA is Section 504 of The Rehabilitation Act of 1973. Section 504 is a part of a civil rights law and one of its provisions requires meals to be modified for children who have a disability restricting their diet. The regulations to implement these modifications are issued by the USDA as the Child Nutrition Reauthorization Act of 1998 (PL 105-336). This law regulates school breakfast and lunch programs, as well as many other child nutrition related programs. These regulations also apply to child nutrition programs providing reimbursement to daycare facilities and snacks provided for after school programs for children. The USDA's nondiscrimination regulations apply to students who have "a physical or mental impairment which substantially limits one or more life activities, has a record of such an impairment, or is regarded as having such an impairment." The most common diet-related disabilities include diabetes, celiac disease, and food allergies that result in severe, life-threatening reactions (such as anaphylactic shock).

Although most children with Down syndrome fit the USDA's definition above, not every child with Down syndrome requires a dietary modification. Specific rules are provided by the USDA to determine which students do require modifications. Students requesting dietary modification must:

1. meet the definition for disability as defined by the Individuals with Disabilities Education Act (IDEA) or USDA, and
2. have a physician's statement of need (see boxed text).

MODIFICATIONS FOR STUDENTS WITH DOWN SYNDROME

Low Fat Diet. An easy and often appropriate school lunch modification for children with Down syndrome is a low fat diet for weight management, providing 20 percent or less of their total daily intake from fat sources. If your child is struggling with her weight, you can obtain a physician's statement for a low fat diet for her. This does not prevent her from food-swapping or choosing to eat a lot of candy during the class party, but it may change her entrée for school lunch. However, the criteria for lunches provided by schools with a School Lunch Program are improv-

Physician's Statement of Need

A physician's statement of need or prescription must include:

- **Your child's disability and an explanation of why the disability restricts your child's diet.** Example: "Bobby Smith has Down syndrome and celiac disease, which is a life-threatening intolerance to gluten in food."
- **A description of the diet** (1500 Calorie Diabetic Diet, Gluten-Free Diet for celiac disease, or 1500 Calorie Low Fat Diet for Weight Management)
- **The major life activity affected by the disability.** Examples: "Untreated celiac disease results in malnutrition, GI distress, and possibly behavioral symptoms" or "Bobby Smith is diagnosed as being 200% his Desired Body Weight (DBW). He has a significant risk of medical complications secondary to his obesity."
- **The food or foods to be omitted from your child's diet and food or choice of foods that can be used as substitutions.**

It is a good idea to keep a copy of the physician's statement in your child's permanent school records and also attach it to your child's Individualized Education Program (IEP) each year. In some situations, your IEP team may ask for an updated physician's statement. Generally, however, these conditions do not change over time. It is also a good idea to create a set of forms describing your child's dietary restrictions for classroom teachers and other school personnel. The forms for writing a 504 Plan for students who have diabetes is available in the Appendix. Modify these forms for your child's dietary need (celiac disease, peanut allergy, or calorie restriction for morbid obesity).

ing all the time. Menus are written to follow the U.S. Dietary Guidelines, which means 30 percent or fewer of total calories for the meal come from fat. The difference between 20 percent fat calories and 30 percent fat calories may not be obvious. The menu changes will be as easy to implement for the foodservice staff as possible, which makes sense. For example, your child may be given nonfat white milk, rather than 2% chocolate milk, depending on the menu.

Texture Modifications. The regulations for texture modifications are not as specific. USDA recommends a physician statement for texture modifications such as mechanical soft foods (chopped meats, soft foods, and chopped vegetables), pureed foods (baby food texture), or thickened liquids. Any texture modifications made to your child's food at school should be determined by a feeding team or speech-language pathologist and listed in the modifications and accommodations section of your child's IFSP or IEP.

One year when I inquired about appropriate foods to celebrate my son's birthday, I learned that a friend in his class needed texture modifications. His lunch, prepared in the cafeteria, was taken to the classroom where it was blenderized by the teacher or an educational assistant. Later I learned that the blender was washed in the classroom sink, where they had no hot water! (Hot water was later installed to classrooms.)

I was so stunned I didn't know what to say. The food had to taste awful. By the time it was served it would be very cold. On top of that, there were so many food safety issues it was frightening. The good news is there were easy solutions for this situation that not only improved the taste of this student's food, but his safety as well. Some of these solutions included having the foodservice staff puree the student's meal in the cafeteria, keeping cold foods cold, and hot foods hot to decrease the risk of food-borne illness. Because this was done in the kitchen, the foodservice staff also cleaned the equipment using acceptable methods for minimizing the risk of food-borne illness from cross-contamination. These changes are indeed small, but important both for food safety and food quality.

If your child has accommodations for food textures on her education plan, it is advisable to ask some questions about the procedures staff will follow to modify the food. Sometimes procedures that seem reasonable to staff are not conducive to food safety. If your child's food is to be chopped or pureed at school, ask the following questions:

- Is there a written procedure for how my child's food will be modified?
- What equipment is available for snacks and parties?
- Where will the equipment be cleaned? Who is responsible for this?
- Is the food being served at temperatures that are safe and appetizing?
- What are the food safety procedures for temperature in the school?
- Is this plan approved by the foodservice manager (the person in charge of the operations for the school's foodservice rather than the person who puts the food on the plate or the cook) or a dietitian? This will ensure food safety measures are being followed.

In general, you want texture modifications that are made to your child's food done as close to the time of service as possible. Foods should be blenderized or chopped in the kitchen by staff trained in food safety, heated or chilled to a safe temperature, and served to your child as close to where they are prepared as possible. School foodservice managers can help create a plan that will promote food safety for your child while providing the necessary accommodations.

Other Modifications. Chapters 6 and 7 cover modifications for children with Down syndrome and diabetes or celiac disease. If your child has any other food allergy or intolerance that is not life-threatening or if you choose to follow a specific type of diet (such as Feingold, vegetarian, or yeast-free), the regulations do not require the school to make modifications. Individual school districts may consider this type of request on a case-by-case basis.

Bringing Lunch from Home

Many families choose to send a lunch from home with their child. Sometimes this is the easiest way to control food allergies or special diets. Sometimes families choose to send lunch from home because their child prefers it, they can send food they are comfortable with, or they can save some money. Regardless of the reason, sending lunch to school with your child offers lots of opportunities for teaching about healthy eating, as well as lessons you'd rather your child not learn, such as the trading value of one of your specialties.

When your child is in early elementary school, there are a variety of non-food related concerns to consider:

- Can she open the containers food is sent in?
- Will she be able to keep foods cold if necessary?
- Is there a place to warm things up?
- Will she need assistance in setting up her meal?
- Does she have a socially acceptable and desirable lunch box or bag?

Many of these issues can be worked around, but only if you think of them ahead of time. Ask if there are lunch monitors who can help with the milk carton or a Tupperware container if your child is having trouble. Consider ways you can make it easier for your child to open foods, such as loosening the lids of items such as yogurt, or opening and rewrapping foods such as granola bars that come in foil or plastic packaging. Send finger foods and foods that are easy for your child to manage, as well as tasty and healthy.

Soon, your child will be very interested in what you are including in her lunch each day. She may or may not approve of the decisions you have been making. This is a good time to fill out a "favorite food list" specifically for lunches (see Activity 4 in Section 4). Find out what she's dreaming she can have as compared to what you are already sending. You may be able to make some compromises that will keep her happy. As you do this, it's also a good idea to uncover *why* these foods are important to her. Perhaps it is because she sees her friends bringing them or because some foods have greater bargaining clout at the lunch table. Schools usually have a policy to discourage food sharing or swapping, but it is part of the school experience. If you discover your child is swapping her lunch items for something better, find out what that "something better" is first. You may find that your child is making some good choices while having fun with her friends. Regardless, talk with your daughter, and perhaps the staff at school, about the importance of eating only her food.

THE ANATOMY OF A SACK LUNCH

There are few rules to packing sack lunches. Here are a few food-related tips to consider:

- Choose foods that will still be enticing four hours after you pack them.
- Use the guidelines for menu balance discussed in Chapter 16 (three of the five bottom food groups must be represented for the meal to be balanced).
- Send a generous, but not over-generous amount of food. You will want to send enough food to accommodate her varying stages of hunger.
- Send a variety of foods: entrée, such as a sandwich, something crunchy, a fruit, and a drink. If your child doesn't like, or can't

chew sandwiches, try string cheese, tortilla wraps, cold pasta salads, or a thermos of soup or chili.

- It is a good idea to include one "sometimes" food or delicacy that is less healthy but preferred. In many ways, this is a good opportunity to teach about the balance of the "sometimes" foods in a meal.
- When your child is young, include a note, draw a picture, or leave something special in her lunch to let her know you are thinking about her.

I always wrote a note in water-based marker on the inside of my son's lunch box each day. The notes would say things such as, "Good luck on your spelling test!" or "Earn lots of stars so we can go swimming tomorrow!" Tom would quickly open his lunch box to see the message and wipe it off with his napkin before anyone noticed. One of his teachers suggested it was embarrassing to him, so I stopped writing the notes. After three days, Tom came storming into the kitchen after school demanding an explanation for the missing notes. For him, the notes were important even if they were quickly removed.

School Lunch As a Learning Opportunity

Lunchtime at school is one of the main social events of the day. Eating is only a small part of what is going on in the room at any one moment. Children are learning social skills, communication skills, sorting skills, fine motor skills, and much more.

The obvious opportunities for children with Down syndrome to learn at lunchtime are related to social and communication skills. Your child may be able to pick up these skills informally, as the other students do. Or it may help to specify what skills she will learn in her IEP or IFSP.

Any goals you write into your child's IEP must be related to either academic concepts she is learning or to functional life skills. For example, learning to use utensils, learning to carry a tray, and learning to serve herself from the school salad bar are all part of the functional life skill of managing lunch independently. If she has money-related goals on her IEP, consider short-term goals related to purchasing food in the cafeteria or student store as naturally occurring opportunities to practice. Or if your child has decided she can help herself to anyone's lunch as well as her own, write some goals and objectives to teach the expected behavior along with a behavior plan. However, weight management or diabetes management are not appropriate areas for instruction in your child's IEP. It is important for staff to be able to assist and support your child if she has a 504 plan related to her diabetes, but not to teach her about weight management unless it is a part of the classroom curriculum already.

LUNCH BUDDIES One way to set the stage for success at lunchtime is to create a circle of friends or lunch buddies. Lunch buddies are fellow students who want to sit with your child, be her friend, and support her. Students who participate as lunch buddies need coaching about what is expected to be successful. If your child's team decides to set up a lunch buddy system, build in a time to get together and talk about what works and doesn't work and to hear what the buddies and your child think needs to be different. Kids have the best ideas about what is fun and what will work. Use the opportunity to learn from them.

The amount of coordination, coaching, and assistance a buddy system needs depends on your child. Some buddy systems need almost no adult intervention to be effective. All they need is a structure and purpose. Other students need to be taught how to be a good communication partner or tricks they can try in tough situations. Regardless, buddy systems are an easy-to-implement method of encouraging learning during lunchtime with minimal adult intervention.

Here is an example of one lunch buddy program:

Rachel, a third-grade student with Down syndrome, has a large group of friends who signed up to be in her lunch buddy group. In fact, her group is so large they have to take turns sitting with her. Each Monday, names are drawn from a jar to decide who will participate in the Lunch Bunch for the week.

Rachel's mother is concerned about Rachel's ability to be polite at meals. She has a hard time not taking food from other people's plates. When she sees a food that looks good to her, she takes it, no matter where it is or whose plate it is on. Rachel's IEP goals and objectives include:

- Rachel will eat foods from her lunch or snack only.
- Rachel and a buddy will set the table for Lunch Bunch activities.
- During Lunch Bunch activities and given visual cues from a buddy, Rachel will use a napkin to wipe her face when appropriate. Visual cues include:
  - A buddy points to her own mouth when she has Rachel's attention.
  - A buddy moves Rachel's napkin closer to her.
  - A buddy says Rachel's name and then wipes her own mouth.
- Using natural cues only, Rachel will participate in passing food around the table. Types of natural cues include:
  - Being given a condiment basket to pass to a buddy.
  - Responding to a request for an item near her from a buddy.
  - Requesting that a buddy pass an item to her (pepper).
- Rachel will participate in one activity for cleaning the area used for the Lunch Bunch including:
  - Wiping the table with cleaning solution,
  - Returning chairs to the table,
  - Recycling or throwing away wrappers and unwanted food, and
  - Putting containers and lunch boxes away.

The Lunch Bunch eats at a special table in the cafeteria that has room for four people. It is important that only four people sit at the table during lunch. If more are at the table, the food is too easy for Rachel to reach. As the year progresses, the IEP team hopes to include six people at the table at a time.

If Rachel resists the impulse to take food from someone else at the table, she receives a sticker on a chart. When the chart is full, she earns a previously chosen reward. Rachel's friends in the Lunch Bunch each have a personal goal (which

may or may not be on an IEP) that they are working toward during lunch time. For instance, one buddy struggles with being on time for lunch. Another is working on not interrupting others in conversation. They are also working toward a pre-selected reward individually and as a group. These children may or may not be receiving special education services. They help choose the goals they work on.

Before the Lunch Bunch began, they met with a teacher who explained what was expected and where to find supplies. The group, including Rachel, practiced with plastic food and the condiment baskets. In addition, Rachel's buddies were coached about being good communication partners to Rachel. They were coached in ways to praise her and how to respond when her behavior or response was inappropriate. ("That's not the relish basket, Rachel, the relish basket is the green one." Rather than "No, not that one, try again.") Once the group was working, they had a meeting during lunch every two weeks. During that meeting, they talked about what was working and what was hard. They also talked about ways to make it more fun for everyone to learn.

Special supplies used for the Lunch Bunch included:

- placemats,
- a full place setting (plate, glass, and utensils),
- condiments in separate baskets such as salt, pepper, sugar, ketchup, and relish packets,
- a specific set of cleaning supplies,
- a centerpiece (usually made in a class art session).

It's easy to see how a lunch buddy program can be used to meet other IEP-related objectives in different areas as well. There are many communication opportunities (commenting, telling jokes, talking about weekend activities, using AAC systems, and so on). While this group's focus was on the mechanics of mealtime and manners, there are no restrictions on how a group of buddies can be used in a situation like this. Setting up a Lunch Bunch takes some creativity and time, but maintaining it is easy. Students involved take pride in the project and even improve on it. They may also build friendships that last long after lunch is over.

BUYING FOOD ITEMS

Learning to buy things is a needed skill for your child. Your child can practice this skill by purchasing her lunch, drink, or snack. Some schools use paper tickets which children buy before school. Others use a debit card system that keeps track of the amount of money students have in their lunch accounts. Both offer opportunities for a range of activities involving managing money:

- Adding the cost of lunches together to determine how many tickets to buy.
- Multiplying to determine how many tickets to buy.
- Subtracting the amount of money needed from the amount given to determine change.
- Counting off the number of meals used on a debit card so your child doesn't run out.

If your child is learning about numbers, you can make a graph or tally to keep track of the number of lunches she has purchased with her debit card. If there are ten lunches on the card and she has used eight, how many days are left until she needs to bring money again?

If your school uses a debit card system, your child can practice:

- locating her card in a pocket chart,
- running the card through the machine (a fine motor skill), and
- putting the card back in the pocket chart.

If your child is learning to read her name, consider asking the teacher to put her photo or a special symbol next to her name. See if the teacher will put her pocket (with her name on it) in a row with only 3 or 4 other pockets in the same row. This reduces the number of names she needs to choose between to find her own.

Some schools use a Personal Identification Number (PIN) instead of a card to charge lunchtime purchases (meal or drink). In this case, your child can practice:

- pushing the buttons on the machine,
- entering the right sequence of numbers with a visual cue and reducing the cues needed to get the numbers correct.

In some instances (or if your cafeteria just accepts money) you might want to give your child the opportunity to pay for purchases with coins and dollar bills. Goals in this area that might be included on a child's IEP include:

- When provided with the exact change at home, Jenny will give it to the cashier when prompted to buy a carton of milk.
- When given two quarters and two dimes, Jenny will select one quarter and one dime to pay for a carton of milk.
- When given a container of quarters and dimes, Jenny will match the number of quarters and dimes needed to pay for a carton of milk to a card with the right number of coins represented on it.

One of the deals we have made with our son, Connor, is that if he has a good week in school Monday through Thursday, he can buy hot lunch at school on Friday. Friday is Pizza Day at school. The school uses a computer to tally the meals purchased. When the students come through, they punch in their personal code, which we cleverly named his "Magic Pizza Number."

While unpacking his school bag one day I found a half-empty bag of Doritos. This seemed rather odd because: 1) he doesn't like them—or he didn't anyway, 2) we rarely eat food like that at home, 3) it was a day he takes a homemade lunch, and 4) he is only authorized to buy his lunch in the cafeteria on Fridays.

Using my "concerned Dad" voice I asked him where they came from. He was very excited to tell me, "I bought them! They are very yummy, Dad, have some!" Then, realizing this may not be a good thing, he added, "I bought them for you, my sweet Dad."

Trying not to smile, I asked him how he paid for them. He assumed a superhero type of pose and proclaimed, "With my Magic Pizza Number!"

OTHER SKILLS IN THE CAFETERIA

Depending on your child's school, there are probably a variety of other useful skills your child can work on during lunchtime. To learn about these skills, you may need to visit the school and observe the typical routines before, during, at the end, and after lunchtime.

- **If your child takes a lunch to school, pack a lunch that takes a little while to eat.** For instance, a friend of mine makes sure any chips she sends are in small pieces rather than unbroken. She knows her son will eat them regardless of their size and it takes him longer to get them out of the bag. You could cut foods such as fruit and sandwiches into smaller pieces and provide foods that require some assembly at the lunch table, such as assembling a fresh pita sandwich.
- **Pack foods that take longer to chew,** such as bagels, pretzel rods, jerky, granola bars, and celery sticks with peanut butter.

Of course, it is important not to frustrate your child in your quest to lengthen the time it takes her to eat. Be reasonable yet creative with your ideas.

If your child consistently and creatively finds ways to increase the amount of food she has for lunch by bartering with friends or charming the cafeteria worker, for example, your best option is to discuss this issue with the team. When you do, make sure the cafeteria worker and any other lunchroom staff are involved in the plan.

> Our daughter's school allows twenty minutes for lunch. We asked for a double lunch period for her because she takes a long time to get through the lunch line and arrange her foods once she has them. It is hard for her to carry her tray and get all the condiments she needs on the first trip. She often needs to go back to get everything. Being independent and doing these things herself takes longer for her. The only way she was able to eat in one lunch period was for an adult to help her, which she hated. Her IEP team suggested this accommodation and it has worked well.

EQUIPMENT ACCOMMODATIONS

Another very common area of frustration at lunch for children with Down syndrome is managing the milk cartons and eating utensil, which is called a "spork." Milk cartons are difficult to open and difficult to drink from. The opening is different from a glass and some students have trouble drinking from a straw. The spork is a combination of a spoon and a fork made from plastic. The prongs of the spork often break easily, which is frustrating and makes it difficult to continue to eat. In addition, plastic ware has a flimsy, thin handle. Many children with Down syndrome do better with a built-up handle or thick-handled utensils. If your child has trouble with these areas, ask for accommodations in her IEP. A glass for drinking her milk and assistance opening the carton are easy solutions. You might want to send your own silverware to school for her to use rather than using the plastic ware provided by the school.

READING ACCOMMODATIONS

For children who are learning to read or struggling with reading, talk to the foodservice staff about the signs that label the foods. Some schools offer a choice of entrée to students. Your child needs to understand the label for the entrée to choose what she really wants. Signs should be uncluttered, include the name of the food or entrée, and perhaps have a symbol (clipart, drawing, photo) of the food for quick comprehension. If your child is using symbols or photos for communication in the classroom, it is best if any symbols used in the cafeteria are consistent with the system she is already using. These adaptations will help your child move more quickly through the line. It helps other children move quickly through the line too.

Making Healthy Choices at School

Children with Down syndrome entering middle school typically encounter the biggest change in eating environment since they first started eating lunch at school. Many, if not most middle schools, offer the typical school lunch program as well as an "a la carte" menu. These additional offerings vary from school to school. Typically the new menu includes items such as pizza, nachos, cookies, ice cream, and a variety of bottled drinks. Unlike with the school lunch program, which is often still available, there are no guidelines regarding the food students choose. These a la carte programs often bring needed revenue into the overall school foodservice system, which is good. But they also represent a dilemma for parents and students: what do I choose?

Be ready to make some agreements with your child regarding the expanded choices. It is important to include your child in the development of the plan so she will be more likely to follow it. You know your child best. Strike a deal that promotes health, but will reduce the likelihood that she will break the agreement or find ways to buy extra food. It is hard for anyone to resist the impulse to eat favored foods at this age. Be reasonable when making your agreement.

Some parents find it easier to deal with the a la carte menus if they send snacks or other healthier options to accompany the nachos. One mother sends fruit and a bottle of 100 percent juice with her child to school with the agreement that she can purchase the entrée from the "cool side" of the cafeteria. Others make agreements with their children to take a lunch from home two or three days a week and purchase a drink at school to accompany it.

Many parents find it necessary to monitor the amount of money available to buy food each day. If it is possible to purchase and the impulse is strong, your child will probably buy it. Talk with your child about the financial aspects of this too. For example, you might explain, "We can't afford for you and your brother to buy lunch at school more than twice a week. You may each have $5 a week to spend on lunches. After it's used up, you need to bring your lunch, regardless."

Regardless of how you handle this situation, it is easiest if you make agreements and plans that include both positive and negative consequences with your child's input *before* she enters this environment. Setting the rules beforehand helps create a set of boundaries and routine from the beginning, making it less likely you will need to impose more restrictions later.

If your child has her own source of money, it will be harder to impose rules or monitor spending without support from school staff. Even if your source of information is the school staff, try to handle it in a way that your child does not feel as though she is under the scrutiny of the food police. You may want to focus your attention on helping her develop spending plans for her money away from school. As those plans progress, you will "discover" that she doesn't have the money she should, which will open up a natural opportunity to talk about where it's going. Remember, using money to obtain things that are otherwise restricted is a normal behavior. Treat your child with Down syndrome in the same way you would treat your other children who are making similar choices.

While it helps to talk about healthy choices and how to eat well at school with these expanding options, it's still hard. Your child will want to do what she perceives everyone else is doing. Whether or not that perception is true is questionable, but it is true to her.

Other Opportunities for Food at School

TREATS FOR SALE

In some schools, the cafeteria or student union is open at different times of the day offering delicacies that are hard to resist such as donuts, candy bars, and soda. It isn't uncommon to hear that children with Down syndrome are frequent visitors, whether or not they have the money to purchase something. Unfortunately, yet understandably, these visits are sometimes profitable for the child whether or not she has money.

If this is a concern for you and your child, or if you want to limit the type or amount of food your child purchases, visit with the foodservice staff to discuss this situation and any others related to foodservice. You may need to create a list of acceptable purchases for your child to help foodservice staff honor your request. If the school has a computerized purchasing system, you may be able to put restrictions on your child's purchases. However, don't rely solely on that mechanism for success. Work with the foodservice staff or school administration to devise a plan that works for your child. Try not to over-control the situation. There is a very delicate balance between over-control and learning to make choices for your child. If the restrictions are too severe, she may act out with frustration while watching her peers purchase foods she is restricted from having.

We've been working for a year on slowing Scott's weight gain. During the summer, things went well. But when he returned to school, he started gaining weight again. Then I learned that the cafeteria worker was giving him seconds when he asked. He would do a chore for her and his payment was food. He loved it and the cafeteria worker was happy, but I was not! In her defense, the cafeteria worker did not know we were working on Scott's eating habits and weight. We talked about it and came up with another way to pay Scott for helping her in the cafeteria.

VENDING MACHINES

Many high schools and some middle schools have vending machines stocked with snack foods that do not promote healthy eating: candy, soda pop, chips, and other high sugar and high fat foods. Some vending machines also offer healthful choices such as breakfast bars, fresh fruit, or bottled water. The content of vending machines in schools is highly variable from year-to-year and between schools. These vending machines may be off limits at certain times of the day, or available for use all day long.

For students with Down syndrome who are included and very independent during the school day, vending machines may be a temptation. Unless your child has an educational assistant with her all day—including between classes and recess—it will be next to impossible to control whether or not she takes advantage of these machines. The best option is to talk about it with your child, find out what she is thinking, and discuss her options. Be very careful to promote her independence and yet attempt to create some structure or control over her options. You can limit the amount of cash she has available, but if she takes her own money, there is little you can do about it. Remember, the more controlling you are, the more likely your child is to do exactly the opposite of what you want.

In some schools, teachers may suggest that your child's IEP include goals related to using a vending machine. While learning to buy something from the vending machine may seem like a great activity for fine motor and money skills, it can lead to expectations of a sumptuously sweet treat each day. If staff is insistent about teaching vending machine skills and/or you think your child needs to learn them, look for some nonfood opportunities that are easy to build into the classroom day. For example, your child could use vending machines for postage stamps, machines to make ID tags, or selected machines that dispense water and juice.

FOOD AS A LEARNING TOOL

In some classrooms, teachers use candy or other food treats to motivate their students to learn. For example, students might use Cheerios or candy such as M&Ms to work out addition and subtraction problems and then be allowed to eat their work. Or they might be given a handful of different-colored candy or cereal, count how many of each color they have, and then graph the results. If the entire class is doing these activities, it's probably not a great idea to intervene unless they will be using food in this manner frequently enough that your child expects to eat whenever she does math problems. If you feel food is used too often for all the children in the class, offer ideas of other fun objects students can count, add or subtract, categorize, and graph. If, however, this is the individualized instruction your child is receiving during time away from her classroom, it is the same as offering a food reward and should be discussed with the IEP team. Regardless, make your thoughts about using food for educational activities or rewards known early in the year and before it is a problem whenever possible. Unfortunately, it is likely a topic you will need to address year after year.

PARTIES AT SCHOOL

School is a great place to learn and develop friendships. And parties are a natural part of school. Classrooms have parties for birthdays, holidays, and sometimes because they have earned a special party by working together on a goal. If your child has a food-related medical problem such as celiac disease or diabetes, provide your child's teacher with information regarding how to manage these parties. However, for most children with Down syndrome—even those working on weight management—a party is a time to relax food restrictions and allow them to enjoy the event.

While this may seem contrary to your long-term goal, it is actually an important part of learning how to handle everyday life and common situations. Talk to your child's teacher about ways to ensure that the focus of the party is on the goal met, the birthday person, or other nonfood activities. It is important for your child to experience the camaraderie of accomplishing a goal as a group or celebrating a special event without feeling isolated by imposed food restrictions.

As your child learns to focus on the reason for the party rather than the food served at the party, she will learn that parties are about people, not food. This lesson will be very helpful as she generalizes it to activities outside of school. You can help reinforce this lesson by asking your child what happened at the party and showing interest in the games, the goal met, or the people who were there rather than asking her about what she ate. If she is learning to listen to her body and how hungry she is to determine what she eats at mealtime, she will also learn to correct for days like this by skipping her after school snack or eating less at dinnertime.

Activity at School

The amount of energy-using activity children are involved in during school hours varies widely. It depends on your school's physical education program, as well as your child's interest and ability in participating. Some students are in general education physical education programs, while others participate in adaptive physical education programs. Both can be effective depending on the teacher. (See Chapter 14.)

Another opportunity to expend energy is at recess and lunchtime. Again, the amount of activity your child is involved in will vary with her interest and the opportunities that are available during recess and lunchtime. Some schools feel these times are for "free play" or downtime from formal activities, but other schools provide opportunities to be involved in more organized activities such as walking programs or intramural sports. An example of a school-wide walking program is provided in Chapter 14.

Although recess and lunchtime may appear to be the perfect time for some aerobic activities for your child, take into consideration her current threshold for fatigue. If she is working hard to make it through six hours of school, then perhaps it is appropriate for her to be involved in activities that are soothing and quiet during these times. For example, she may enjoy going to the library and looking at books or learning to make friendship bracelets on the playground with her friends. Or she may be perfectly happy just walking around with a couple of friends checking out the boys. If she comes home with energy to spare, you might want to look into ways she can be more active during recess and lunchtime. Some examples might include playing four square, tetherball, or participating in lunchtime sports or walking programs.

If your child needs support to be involved with other students or has an educational assistant with her at recess time, you may want to discuss your child's activity during this free time with the IEP team. Many children—particularly those with the dual diagnosis of Down syndrome and autism or those who need AAC systems to communicate—may want to be involved in specific activities but need some support to be successful. If your child is yearning to be with others, there is no reason her IEP goals and objectives cannot extend to recess and other nonacademic times of the day.

Nutrition Education in the Classroom: Adapting Lessons for Life

It would be great if we could rely on our children's schools to teach them the basic nutrition and healthy lifestyle concepts they need to know as adults, but this is unfortunately not very likely for kids in general education or special education. Remember, if your child is included in the general education classroom, her IEP will be written with an eye toward helping her make progress in the general education curriculum. It is not designed to teach her everything that is useful for her to know. So, if the general education curriculum doesn't provide a practical or in-depth focus on nutrition and healthy living, then it is difficult, if not impossible, to include those kinds of goals on her IEP.

EARLY ELEMENTARY SCHOOL

Each school district has a health curriculum that suggests what concepts should be taught in the nutrition module, but content and design varies widely from school to school and even between classrooms. Typical nutrition-related activities provided in the general education curriculum during the early elementary years include:

- Learning about food groups,
- Introduction to the Food Guide Pyramid,
- Servings for food groups in the pyramid,
- Serving sizes,
- Nutrients: vitamins and minerals (grade three),
- Energy-providing nutrients,
- Foods from different cultures & nations,
- Signs of spoilage in foods (primarily fresh foods at the store).

If your child is in a general education classroom for nutrition education activities, you may need to make suggestions for curricular adaptations. Regardless, there are ways for every child, regardless of ability, to participate in nutrition education activities. Below are a few suggestions that may be appropriate for your child.

VISUAL CUES

Many children with Down syndrome need visual cues to support them as they work through activities that are new for them. Photos, plastic foods, and color-coded systems can provide those cues without a lot of personal attention. For example, when I teach young children about food groups, I use a pyramid that is colored:

- Bread: Brown
- Vegetables: Green
- Fruits: Yellow
- Milk: Blue
- Meat: Red
- Sometimes: Purple

For every lesson I teach, I use the same colors for each food group. In the beginning, when children are grouping foods, the writing with the name of the food and the border around the photo or symbol cards are the same color as the corresponding area of the pyramid. For instance, a photo of strawberries is either glued to yellow construction paper or printed with a yellow border with the word "Strawberry" in yellow (the yellow usually needs to be printed in bold face font or have a dark background to be seen). In this way, the child has a food with a visual cue (the color yellow) to help her place it in the right food group (fruit). When using plastic or rubber foods, glue or draw a color spot on the food to assist your child.

I use this same color-coded pyramid for categorizing combination foods, building menus, and even keeping track of what is eaten in a day. (See the Food Guide Pyramid on the inside of the front cover of this book.) In this way, people who may not be able to read the words can most likely get the foods in the right group. While it is important to always have the name of foods and food groups along with a photo or symbol printed on cards and labels, it is equally important to give your child a way to accomplish the learning activity if the reading is difficult. In this instance, literacy is the secondary lesson and nutrition concepts are the primary lesson.

FOCUSING ON IMPORTANT CONCEPTS

In most schools, the curriculum begins to expand to human body systems and nutrients around grade three or four. Consider some modifications to keep your child active and interested; there is a lot to learn! Keep in mind what is most important for your child to know. If the class is learning the names of various vitamins and minerals and what they do in the body, the important concepts for your child with Down syndrome to learn may be different. For instance the modified primary concepts for your child might be:

- Food is energy and fuel for your body.
- Protein is used for growth and repair of your skin and organs.
- Carbohydrate is for energy.
- Fat is for flavor, vitamins, and energy.
- Vitamins and minerals are necessary for your body to work right.

LATER ELEMENTARY SCHOOL

In grades four and five, common concepts covered in general education include:
- Calories and metabolism,
- Nutrients: Protein, Carbohydrate, Fat, Vitamins, Minerals, and Water,
- Food labels,

- Healthy eating,
- Using calories through activity and sports.

This sounds like a lot of information, but it is often covered in a week or two in most general education classes. Talk with your child's teacher to find out what they will cover and how it will be presented. You may want to suggest adaptations to the material that reinforce the most important points for all children. Some ideas include:

- **Calories and Metabolism:** Everyone's body uses calories at a different rate. You can guess how many calories your body uses to do different activities using charts that tell you how many calories are used for different activities. This guess gives you an idea of how many calories to eat each day without eating too much.

    Because this activity requires some sophisticated math skills, your child may benefit from working with a buddy, using a calculator, or merely gathering the information with someone else doing the math. Modify the activity so your child can successfully learn the concept of calories. Again, the math involved is a secondary learning activity that is not necessary for learning about calories and how they affect energy.

- **Nutrients:**
    - *Protein:* is needed for growth, repair, and the health of your body's muscles, organs, and skin.
    - *Carbohydrate:* is the fuel for the body. It gives you energy and helps you make your body move. If you don't get enough fuel for your body, you are tired all the time.
    - *Fat:* carries important vitamins and provides flavor and energy (calories) to food. Since fat has more calories than protein and carbohydrate, it is important not to eat a lot of foods with a lot of fat. One teaspoon of fat has two times as many calories as one teaspoon of carbohydrate or protein.
    - If your child is learning to do complex math, include activities to calculate calories of foods from their protein, carbohydrate, and fat values on labels. What is important is that your child understands fat has double the calories of protein and carbohydrate. Modify the activity so your child is learning in a manner that is appropriate for her understanding and ability.

- **Vitamins & Minerals:** are very important. By eating a variety of foods from all the food groups, your body gets all the vitamins and minerals it needs to work right. Vitamins and minerals help you to see, use calories, and make your bones strong, among many other things. Vitamin and mineral pills (supplements) are OK to use if you follow the instructions, but they never replace our need for eating a balanced diet.

■ **Water:** Water is very important for our body. Without water our body can't do most of the things our organs, muscles, and brain are meant to do for our bodies to work right. It is important to drink plenty of water (6 eight-ounce glasses) each day. If you are an athlete, you should drink a glass of water before a workout, practice, or game and at least two glasses of water afterwards so your body stays hydrated.

An illustrated and easy-to-understand version of these concepts is provided in the Section 4.

MIDDLE SCHOOL AND BEYOND

Nutrition education activities in general education during middle school and high school usually involve learning more about the relationship between calories and daily activity, but with little tangible application to daily life. For example, students may keep food and activity diaries for three to five days, then use a computer program to analyze the calories, vitamins, and minerals they have eaten and used for those days. In some schools, follow-up discussions and activities are provided for students to investigate their own nutritional status.

In schools that offer Home Economics classes and sometimes in Child Development classes, there may be some discussion about meal planning or label reading. However, because few students are making their own meals or planning to in the near future, these lessons are easily forgotten and rarely applied to daily living.

In general, students in general education receive very little useful instruction regarding building a healthy lifestyle and personal wellness. Much of this instruction is done incidentally for students who participate in sports by the coaches. If your child is included in a class that covers nutrition education topics, try to encourage teachers to take the time to provide adequate modifications and accommodations for your child, because it is a very important topic for her to learn and master.

Homework Time

Many schools begin assigning homework in the early elementary years. The amount of time children with Down syndrome spend on homework will vary, but this is when study skills begin that last throughout your child's education. Use good judgment when deciding whether to provide a snack during homework time for your child. If you do decide to provide a snack, offer snacks that are healthy rather than indulgent. For example, try a small serving of dried fruit, pretzel sticks, baby carrots, or snow peas rather than cookies or ice cream.

Sometimes offering a snack at or near homework time helps motivate your child to focus on her school work. It is not always best to wait until later to provide a reason to do something. She may need the social time associated with eating a snack before she can sit down to do homework.

It is sometimes easy to forget that in order to think well, we must eat well. This means eating healthful foods as well as not being hungry. In general, a person should eat every three to five hours. If homework time falls more than five hours after a meal, then a snack is a good idea. However, if your child associates eating and homework (or doing any schoolwork), then you need to separate the two activities.

Conclusion

There are many natural opportunities for your child to learn about food at school. Your child makes decisions about what to eat and how much to eat all the time while she is at school. In fact, lunchtime is a natural and easy time to incorporate many learning activities in a way that is fun for everyone involved. Work with your child's teachers, the foodservice staff, and others to make good use of a topic that is motivating to everyone and has a great impact on decisions and attitudes later in life.

CHAPTER 13

Weight Management

For families of children and adults with Down syndrome, weight management is one topic we will all address at one point or another. In fact, this may be the first chapter some parents turn to looking for ideas and suggestions. The good news is that being overweight or obese is not inevitable. However, promoting and maintaining a healthy weight requires thought and tenacity for people with Down syndrome and those who support them. The concepts preceding and following this chapter are integral parts of effective weight management for your child with Down syndrome. This chapter concentrates on strategies, research, and techniques specifically related to managing weight, planning to lose weight, and promoting health.

Weight Trends in Children with Down Syndrome

Generally, children with Down syndrome have a slower rate of growth in the first few years than children who do not have Down syndrome. This is due to many health and medical influences, such as congenital heart defect, premature birth, lower birth weights, genetics, and the influence of low oral motor tone on feeding. This means many infants and toddlers with Down syndrome are smaller and lighter than average. Sometimes parents spend a great deal of time encouraging their babies to eat so they will gain weight. Once the heart is repaired and

appropriate therapy and modifications are made to feeding, however, young children with Down syndrome settle into a natural rate of growth for height and weight. Although each child grows at a different rate, in general, children with Down syndrome are shorter and huskier than those without.

In addition to the differences in growth rate, there are also differences in basal metabolic rate. Studies on metabolism show that

children and adults with Down syndrome have a lower basal metabolic rate (BMR) than people without Down syndrome. This decrease in BMR is approximately 10-15 percent. This means that when a person with Down syndrome is at rest (lying down and asleep), he uses 10-15 percent fewer calories than a person of the same age, weight, and height who does not have Down syndrome.

Because of the way estimated energy needs are calculated, the best illustration of what this difference in BMR means in practical terms comes from estimating calorie needs for adolescents and adults. The same concept, however, applies to young children who are in good health. For example, a typical 16- year-old girl who is 5 feet 4 inches tall and weighs 125 pounds has a BMR of approximately 1,392 calories per day. A young woman with Down syndrome who is the same age, height, and weight has a BMR between 1,183 and 1,253 calories per day. Remember, BMR indicates how many calories the body burns *at rest*. Any calories used for sitting, walking, and even digesting food are added to this amount. The difference between what the typical teenager and the teenager with Down syndrome burn at rest is 139-209 calories. This may not seem like much; it is equivalent to the calories provided by a small and medium-sized apple. Yet, if the 16-year-old with Down syndrome consumes merely that 10-15 percent more calories for one month, it means 4,170-6,270 extra calories in a month, which translates to 1-1¾ pounds of potential weight gain in a month and 12-21 pounds over the course of a year. (You gain one pound when you consume 3,500 more calories than your body needs.)

From my observations of children and adults with Down syndrome of all ages, particularly at conferences where I can view a number of kids at one time, I have concluded that the reduced BMR usually begins to catch up in adolescence. This is a time when children naturally "pudge up" before they experience a growth spurt. For children with Down syndrome, the actual rate of growth during that spurt may be slower than it is for other children. (This seems possible since children with

Definitions of Overweight vs. Obese

There is a very important practical difference between being overweight and obese.
- **Overweight** is defined as being over 110 percent of a person's desired body weight range.
- **Obesity** is defined as being over 120 percent of a person's desired body weight range.

People who are overweight can still live a relatively healthy lifestyle without losing weight. The extra weight typically does not create a direct health risk. When a person is obese, the chances increase that the extra weight puts them at greater health risk for weight-related health problems such as diabetes, mobility issues, and so on.

Down syndrome do not grow to be as tall as their nondisabled peers.) In addition, at least one study has shown that children with Down syndrome finish growing sooner than the typical child. Consequently, the extra weight that an adolescent with Down syndrome actually needs for his growth spurt is less than parents expect. The growth spurt may end before you are aware it was in full swing. This is a very important time for focusing on eating for health and fitness and developing an interest in an active lifestyle.

Whatever the reasons, I do know that fewer parents struggle with their children's weight prior to their teenage years, but almost all parents and children with Down syndrome struggle with weight during their teenage and adult years.

When to Be Concerned about Your Child's Weight

One study considered the food choices of children with Down syndrome as compared to their nondisabled peers. The researchers discovered that children with Down syndrome in the study compensated for the lower calorie need naturally when they were allowed to choose what, how much, and whether or not they ate as defined in the feeding relationship (Chapter 3) rather than having food timing, amount, and selection strictly mandated for them. In other words, the children in this study were offered meals and snacks appropriately, and the children with Down syndrome ate fewer calories without being coached by their parents or caregiver. They ate what their body needed.

This information tells us that children with Down syndrome can make accommodations for their lower calorie need naturally, but only if we allow them the freedom of listening to their bodies when it comes to eating. This natural accommodation may account for the impression that younger children with Down syndrome often seem to remain appropriate for their weight and height.

The best advice is to keep an eye out for a change in your child's weight for height as plotted on a growth chart. The type of chart is not as important as watching the trend for the percentage. In other words, you are watching your child's rate of weight gain over time—either up or down—on the growth charts.

For instance, at age 5, your child might be on the 50th percentile for height and 60th percentile for weight on the growth chart for children with Down syndrome. Ordinarily, you could presume that he will follow those same percentiles in the coming years, with a little swaying back and forth in either direction. A sustained change in weight to the 80th percentile (sustained over the course of 6 months or more) or a continued gradual increase in this percentile with height remaining relatively the same over 6 months on the chart would indicate a change in rate of weight gain that could lead to being overweight. Likewise, if your child's rate of weight gain *decreases*, when his weight has been appropriate, it is important to investigate why.

Remember, no matter which growth chart is used, some children will naturally fall in the extreme top and bottom percentiles. Usually a good look at a child's parents will confirm the genetic influence on the child's growth. Remember, you are looking for unexpected changes in growth status (percentile) after your child's weight percentile has stabilized (around age four or five).

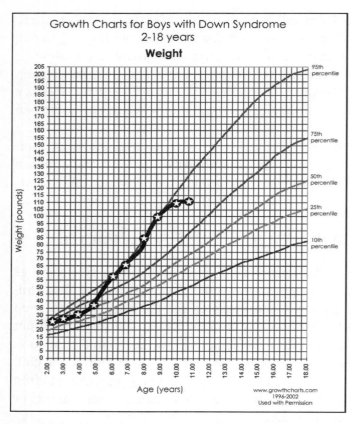

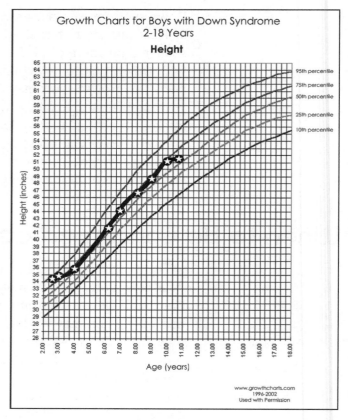

This is an example of the rate of growth for a boy with Down syndrome. Up until he was five years old, his weight hovered around the 50th percentile and his height on the 75th percentile on charts for boys with Down syndrome. His growth was following an expected, reasonable pattern. Once his heart was repaired (between age 5 and 6), his weight jumped to the 95th percentile. The change in growth rate is clear and very dramatic. In the last 3-4 years, his mother has been working with him—and the rest of the family—on food and activity choices. In the last year, these efforts to make healthy choices have blossomed. Her son is making thoughtful choices when making lunch and having snacks. As you can see, his weight has stabilized. He is eating enough calories for growth, but not to gain weight. He and his family have worked hard to maintain the same weight for the last two years.

Our battle with Stephen's weight began shortly after his VSD was repaired when he was five years old. In the year following his surgery, he gained eleven pounds, which was one-fourth of his body weight. After five years of very little activity and literally stuffing him with calories to prepare for surgery, being sedentary had become a habit. We knew we had to take action.

We started by trying to increase his activity. He loves water, so we began therapeutic swimming. He also played Challenger baseball and took therapeutic horseback riding lessons. By the end of second grade, it was clear that simply keeping him active wasn't enough. We had to look at food, too.

Stephen loved to take his lunch to school. I thought it was because he enjoyed my carefully planned, healthy lunches. I soon learned that he traded his grapes and Cheerios for Doritos and potato chips daily. The final straw was when we received a notice from the school cafeteria telling us we owed money for several school lunches he bought. It seems the little rascal had eaten what he wanted from his lunch or traded it away and proceeded through the lunch line claiming he forgot his money. While I was secretly applauding his ingenuity, this had to stop.

I talked with a lot of people about the situation. One friend asked me what Stephen's "choices" were for lunch. It was such a light bulb moment for me. Stephen had no real choice or control over the situation at all except in ways that were unacceptable. Once I let him choose between grapes and carrot sticks or yogurt and a turkey wrap, his eating habits at lunch changed. Stephen's weight gain slowed over the course of the year. The following year he gained only half a pound and grew an inch! He is still overweight, but he is slowly but surely getting taller while maintaining his weight.

Weight Management for Weight Gain

Weight management is more than preventing or slowing weight gain, although that is the most common concern for children and adults with Down syndrome. It can also mean promoting weight gain for children who are underweight and having trouble reaching a healthy weight as they grow taller. This happens most often in children with Down syndrome who have medical concerns, particularly as children are waiting to have heart surgery.

What Is Failure to Thrive?

Failure to thrive is a medical term used to describe infants and young children (usually up to three years old) who do not grow as much as expected for their age and gender, based on established growth rates (such as the growth charts for children with Down syndrome). Most children with Down syndrome who qualify for this condition are experiencing extreme medical conditions such as waiting for heart surgery, Hirschsprung's disease, or other anomalies. In most cases, babies with Down syndrome who are struggling to maintain or gain weight take off dramatically once the underlying medical condition is corrected.

Often families have spent a great deal of time and energy encouraging their child to eat. Once the underlying medical condition is corrected, they are relieved to see their child eating. It is comforting to see your child eating and gaining weight after a long struggle. It is important, however, to modify your family's feeding style so your child's weight will stabilize once he is healthy.

Determining Adjusted Desirable Body Weight (ADBW) Range

If your child is still growing and you are unsure whether or not he is overweight, you might find it helpful to calculate his *Adjusted Desired Body Weight Range (ADBW)*. If you know by looking at your child that he is overweight or obese, you might want to think twice before doing this. If you are working on your child's eating habits, knowing he is 180 percent of his ADBW may not be very motivating. In my opinion, the best use of ADBW for growing children is for very young children or pudgy babies who are good eaters before it is clear where they will fall. Ideally, your child's weight will be between 90-110 percent of the ADBW range. Information on determining your child's ADBW range is available in the Appendix.

When to Be Concerned about an Adult's Weight

Adults with Down syndrome have, of course, finished their growth. Exactly when this occurs is unclear, but it appears that people with Down syndrome finish growing in height earlier than those without Down syndrome, perhaps as early as sixteen years of age. As parents, however, we do not think of our children as adults until closer to age eighteen or twenty. There is no real difference between the late teens and early twenties when considering a healthy weight or eating for a healthy lifestyle. In fact, it is basically a part of the transition process that follows the same sort of timeline for transition to adult life in school. You should be thinking about what you want your child's lifestyle to look like when he is an adult beginning at age thirteen at the latest.

In theory, your adult child's weight should remain approximately the same for the rest of his life. That's not very realistic for anyone with or without Down syndrome. There are a number of studies documenting the prevalence of obesity and overweight in adults with Down syndrome. These studies suggest the incidence of obesity and overweight is slightly higher for adults with Down syndrome (45 percent of men and 56 percent of women) than in the general public (20 percent of men, 25 percent of women). Over time, the incidence of obesity and overweight in adults with and without Down syndrome is becoming more similar. This is not because we are reducing the number of people with Down syndrome who are overweight, however. Rather, it is because those of us without Down syndrome are catching up.

Health care professionals often use a very general rule-of-thumb to determine desired body weight for adults:

- *Men:* Start with 106 pounds. For every inch over 5 feet in height, add 6 pounds. This is your desirable weight, plus or minus 10 percent. For example, the desired weight range for a man who is 6 feet tall is 178 pounds, plus or minus 18 pounds, or 160 to 196 pounds. (6 feet is 12 inches over 5 feet. So, 6 times 12 equals 72. Adding 72 to 106, you get 178. Ten percent of 178 is 17.8, or about 18 pounds, so the desirable weight is between 178 minus 18 pounds [160] and 178 plus 18 pounds or 196.)

- *Women:* Start with 100 pounds. For every inch over 5 feet in height, add 5 pounds. This is your desirable weight, plus or minus 10 percent. For example, the desired weight range for a woman who is 5' 5" is 125 pounds, plus or minus 13 pounds, or 112 to 137 pounds.

- Using this method, people are considered overweight if they are between 110-120 percent of their DBW and obese if over 120 percent DBW. (Multiply the desirable body weight for your height by 1.10 to find out if your are overweight, and 1.20 to find out if you are considered obese. For example, the six-foot-tall man above would be obese if he weighed 214 pounds because 178 (his DBW) times 1.20 equals 213.6.)

Unfortunately, there is no rule-of-thumb for folks who are under 5 feet tall.

Body Mass Index (BMI). Another way to evaluate whether someone is overweight or at an increased health risk due to their weight is to use the Body Mass Index (BMI). BMI is a mathematical equation that estimates the amount of muscle and fat in a person's body based on studies of large numbers of people. Your BMI number tells you whether your weight falls into a range considered optimal for good health and longevity. For children, the optimal ranges for BMI change throughout the growing years (see BMI charts for boys and girls age 2-20 in the Appendix). The American Academy of Pediatrics (AAP) and the Center for Disease Control (CDC) have developed guidelines for health care professionals to refer to when a child's BMI falls into a high-risk category. For children with Down syndrome, these recommendations need to be considered along with information specific to known health risks for people with Down syndrome.

For adults, a BMI of 20-25 is considered a *very low risk* for health problems related to weight such as heart attack, stroke, and high blood pressure. A BMI in the *low risk* category means weight management may be appropriate, and a BMI in the *moderate risk* category means weight management is highly recommended. Again, the health risks associated with a high-risk BMI for people without Down syndrome may not be the same as for people with Down syndrome.

The trouble with using any of these measures for evaluating your child's weight is that they do not take into account the differences in body composition and stature for people with Down syndrome. For example, the rule-of-thumb method does not accommodate for the short stature seen in Down syndrome. The weights obtained using this method for people with Down syndrome would be very difficult to obtain and maintain and are not appropriate to use as a point from which to compute percentage overweight.

Using BMI as a measure is not any more specific. BMI for people with Down syndrome is based on body measurements that are affected by muscle tone. Thus, the measurement obtained is not corrected for the lower muscle tone found in people with Down syndrome.

The best answer to evaluating your adult child's weight is to use a measure of common sense:

- **Rely on your *eyes*.** Does your child look overweight or obese to you? Remember, a person with Down syndrome, even if working out regularly, may appear more "soft" than someone without Down syndrome. Be kind in your assessment.
- **Adjust the rule-of-thumb approach by adding 10 percent.** For example, if a woman is 5' 3", the maximum DBW for her would be 127 (115 + 12 = 127) if she does not have Down syndrome. Allowing for an additional 10 percent, or about 13 pounds, the adjusted range is 114 to 140 pounds.
- **Watch for sudden changes in clothing size.** Weight gain can happen slow or fast. Your child's habits will determine the rate of weight gain. However, even a gradual weight gain will feel like a sudden change in clothing size. If your child seems to be increasing in girth rather than height and consistently requires larger sizes, you need to evaluate the situation.

■ **Plot your child's growth using all the methods described above** (DS Growth Charts, CDC Growth Charts, BMI, ADBW) and keep track of them over the years. The best information about your child's health risks related to his weight will be discovered when analyzing this long-term information.

Keep in mind that some adults with Down syndrome will not have to worry about their weight or use corrected desirable weights. For the most part, however, modifying methods of determining desired weights is appropriate. All these methods of determining desired weight for people with Down syndrome should be considered guides rather than absolute measures. There is no one perfect weight for anyone, including people with Down syndrome.

Use these methods as markers to evaluate changes in your child's weight or lifestyle. Be cautious if you find yourself trying to compare your child's body composition to another adult with Down syndrome. Some spend dozens of hours each week working out to be in shape to reach a goal such as Karen Gaffney, who swam the English Channel as part of a relay team. Others participate in little activity outside of their daily routine.

Underlying Medical Reasons for Weight Change

If your child is unexpectedly gaining or losing weight, it is important to rule out medical reasons for the change in weight.

Medical Conditions that Contribute to Weight Gain
- Hypothyroidism
- GERD
- Medications that promote weight gain as a side effect

Medical Conditions that Contribute to Weight Loss
- Undiagnosed diabetes
- Undiagnosed celiac disease
- Hyperthyroidism
- Cancer
- Infection
- Unrepaired heart defect
- GERD

Healthy Weight and Children with Down Syndrome

The best approach to weight management for children with Down syndrome, in my opinion, is to seek a healthy weight. What is a healthy weight for a person with Down syndrome? It is the weight achieved and maintained when a person, with or without Down syndrome, is living a healthy lifestyle. It is not always within the "desirable body weight" range. Sometimes it's above this range and sometimes below. It is, however, a comfortable weight that is easily maintained, is comfortable when active, and does not present an immediate health risk to an individual.

For children who are not done growing, a healthy weight is one that promotes optimal growth when leading a healthy lifestyle. This means that if your child is overweight, your goal is *not* for your child to lose weight. While he is growing, your goal is to promote healthy eating and activity, and to slow the rate of gain or maintain his current weight until he has grown into it. It is extremely unwise to restrict caloric intake to promote weight *loss* in children who are still growing. However, if your child's weight is a concern and he is still gaining weight, it is fine to work on ways to reduce calories in and increase calories out to slow and stop weight gain. When you do this, it is a good idea to talk it over with your physician or a dietitian for coaching and encouragement. Food choices become very important to make sure your child gets the nutrients he needs when you are limiting foods. It is *not* a good idea to reduce calories in and increase calories out to promote weight *loss* except in extreme situations. It is extremely unwise to promote weight *loss* by calorie restriction alone in a growing child.

Generally, the goal is to fuel your child with enough calories from a wide variety of foods to *maintain his current weight* while he grows. Restricting calories to promote weight *loss* compromises his nutrition status, the type of fuel his body and brain uses, and ultimately his educational performance, as well as his behavior. To determine how many calories per day your child should be taking in, use either of the equations for estimating calorie needs in the Appendix. Use the number calculated for your child as a guideline for how much your child can eat to maintain his growth and weight without losing weight. You may find it helpful to visit with a registered dietitian who works with children who are overweight on a regular basis. You may need to work together to modify the strategies for your child and family.

Children whose weight puts them at medical risk for injury or disease may need to consider *losing* weight. This should only be done with strict supervision of your child's pediatrician and in consultation with a registered dietitian. Look for a dietitian who specializes in childhood obesity to work with you. Unsupervised, long-term weight loss in children affects growth, development, and cognitive abilities and development.

Healthy Weight in Adults with Down Syndrome

A healthy weight for an adult with Down syndrome is one he can maintain while leading a healthy lifestyle. This sounds ambiguous, but it's not. For instance, if your child is leading a sedentary lifestyle and consistently overeating, those two habits are not conducive to a "healthy lifestyle." In this instance, you should work with your child to improve his activity and eating habits—not to create a perfect body or perfect habits, just improve them—which will likely result in either stopping weight gain or losing weight. You will first notice that his clothes fit better or are no longer tight. As the process continues, so will the changes in your child's weight and muscle tone. (Remember, in this chapter, we are using the word "adult" to refer to someone who has finished his growth, whether he is still in his teens or older.)

No More Diets

As a society, we are just learning the effects of "dieting." In the 1950s and 1960s, dieting wasn't common. Children raised during that time did not have their caloric intake scrutinized, though they were chastised if they didn't finish the food on their plate. Parents were not dieting, nor were they concerned about regular aerobic exercise. In addition, Americans in general were not significantly overweight or obese.

Today, 70 percent of all Americans are considered overweight and about a quarter of Americans are obese. Fewer than 40 percent of Americans exercise regularly. It's common for parents to be dieting, trying one fad or another. Some parents are focused on leading a healthy lifestyle, practicing healthy eating, and regular exercise—sometimes to an extreme.

We have learned a lot about weight gain and weight loss in the last forty years. One of the key facts we know is that *dieting*, or seeking a quick fix for losing weight, rarely results in lasting change. While it is possible to follow a restricted calorie and arduous exercise program for a period of time and obtain results, daily habits are not changed. In addition, following diets for a short-term solution leads to what is called the "diet cycle." The diet cycle describes how it feels to follow a very restrictive eating and exercise plan. You begin the diet—a specific eating plan which may or may not be appealing to you—with high hopes. Then you begin to feel deprived because the eating plan is so restricted. After a while, you give in and eat things that are not on the eating plan (otherwise known as bingeing). Immediately after the binge, and sometimes during, you feel guilty because you broke your diet, which leads to beginning the diet once again.

The Diet Cycle

Historically, people with Down syndrome have been victims of diets imposed by others. In years past, group homes and institutions placed people with Down syndrome who were considered overweight on restricted calorie diets, often without their knowledge. Sometimes the calorie restrictions were as low as 800 calories each day. There was no attempt to involve the individual in the process. The person with Down syndrome had no choice regarding his diet. This often resulted in behavior problems such as taking food from others, hiding food, stress from feeling hungry all the time, and basically feeling punished for being overweight. In short, weight management was done *to* them rather than *with* them.

In recent years, policy changes—even in restricted living situations—have loosened to avoid this approach. People with Down syndrome have more choices about how to live their lives and are involved in the decision-making process. It is no longer appropriate for a healthcare professional to choose to limit caloric intake without involving the person with Down syndrome in the decision. In addition, living situations are less institutional: group homes are owned by parents, private organizations, or churches rather than the state and county. Adults with Down syndrome are living in a greater variety of living situations: apartments, fraternities, supported living situations, and even in their own house.

These changes are all positive. But even with good changes, there are problems. With the increase in choice and control, some adults with Down syndrome disregard any concern for health. This is most likely because they do not know what the alternatives are and they are enjoying their right to choose. People working with adults with Down syndrome often believe that imposing *any* diet is not respectful of the individual's right to choose. There are two extremes in handling food choices: 1) lack of structure and complete freedom of food choices, or 2) complete control of choices by caregivers or support people. We must learn to seek the middle ground: promoting healthy lifestyles through education and structured choice-making.

As you consider weight management for your child, at any age, remember this: You must have his commitment to the idea for it to work. Focus your efforts on teaching your child how to make choices in ways that use his strengths and interests to promote health rather than on a short-term specific goal for weight loss. This focus on a healthy lifestyle will help everyone see weight management for what it is: as one of many important components of a fulfilling life.

The Process of Change

Weight management is the process of managing the areas of life that affect weight in order to maintain a healthy weight. In other words, the term weight management can be used for people who need to gain weight, lose weight, or maintain their weight. If you and your child have not dealt with weight management before, try to keep in mind that it is a life-long process. There is no one moment where you can proclaim the project "done" and live life with abandon. In short, it is a lifestyle, a healthy lifestyle.

You can't change habits over night. Studies on behavior suggest that for sustained change to take place, a new habit must be in place for about three weeks. Even then, the new behavior is fragile; old behaviors are easy to start up again.

It helps to understand the stages of change to understand how to promote successful change for you and your child. There are five stages to making changes in behavior:

1. **Precontemplative Stage.** In this stage, people are usually unaware of the need for behavior changes. You are aware of the potential for concerns related to health and lifestyle, but nothing has triggered you to the need for action.

2. **Contemplative Stage.** In the contemplative stage, you are aware there is a concern. You begin to consider what type of change may need to be implemented.

3. **Preparation Stage.** People in the preparation stage are ready to take specific action. Plans and goals are first created in this stage.

4. **Action Stage.** It is time to commit to, and act on, specific goals and objectives that lead to a long-term goal.

5. **Maintenance Stage.** The maintenance stage is an ongoing one. In this phase, people make plans to maintain the success they have achieved in the previous stage.

If you have decided to promote a healthy lifestyle for your child with Down syndrome, you are probably in the third stage. There are some changes you can make without having any commitment from your child: creating healthy menus, changing the mix of foods available for snacks, and planning family activities that focus on people and activity rather than food. Any changes that require commitment from your child, however, will require patience. While you are ready to set goals and get moving, your *child* is in the first stage: the PREcontemplative stage or not contemplating change at all. This doesn't mean you can't make some changes in your own life during this time. Modeling the expected behavior is a big part of teaching children with Down syndrome of any age. It's unrealistic to ask your child to live a healthier lifestyle than the rest of the family, or you.

The negotiations that take place between you and your child as you promote the idea of making healthy choices are delicate. Proceed cautiously. It is important to look at the motivation for making changes from your child's point of view. What you find motivating is not necessarily what will motivate your child.

Designing plans for a healthier lifestyle for teens and adults with Down syndrome must include all of the key elements of a successful wellness plan. People with Down syndrome will not be interested in all the detail that goes into planning, though. Although your child will benefit and most likely enjoy a program designed with the above key elements in mind, he may not be motivated by them. The key elements your child will most likely find motivating are similar, with a few additions:

- FUN (Fun)
- Making friends (A social component)
- Having choice and control (Variety)
- Independence (Challenging but not competitive activities)
- "Cool stuff" in the form of rewards (Appropriate rewards)
- More energy
- Clothes fit better (if style conscious)

Successful Wellness Plans

There are key elements to any successful wellness plan. When these elements are built into the plan, people are more likely to make long-term changes leading to healthier lives. A well-designed wellness plan includes:

- FUN
- A social component
- Variety
- Challenging but not competitive activities
- Precautions to decrease risk of injury
- Appropriate goals
- Rewards
- Opportunities to compete against one's own personal best, but not others
- Family and friends
- Support of family and the medical community

Of course, there are also many health-related, long-term reasons for participating in a wellness program. While important, they are not likely to be interesting to your child with Down syndrome. Examples include:

- Longer life
- Better health
- Weight loss
- Increased muscle tone
- Body image
- Disease prevention

Although all of these are good reasons to live a healthy lifestyle, they're not likely to be motivating to your child. They are not very effective motivators for people without Down syndrome, either. This does not mean your child does not want these things. Rather, they are the effects of long-term changes and most are not visible. In the workshops I've conducted, I find that the adults with the most obvious need to make some changes are the most knowledgeable, and the most resistant to change. Through these discussions, I have learned that adults with Down syndrome who are overweight are tired of well-meaning people telling them what to eat and what not to eat.

When you and your child finally meet at that third stage, the preparation stage, it is very important to let your child lead the way with your almost subliminal guidance. Try to think of yourself as his coach and cheerleader rather than the "enforcer." Not only will you understand your child better, but he will be more successful. You will, however, need to provide a structure to his options and set him up for success, especially in the beginning and perhaps for a long time. Always offer more than one choice, including a choice that is not the healthiest. Making healthy choices doesn't mean making perfect choices.

If your child's first response to anything you say is to do the opposite, it is important to plan ahead. You may need to sweep your home of problem foods such as foods your child consistently eats too much of before he realizes he even ate something. It will be very helpful to make a plan together ahead of time so your child knows what will happen. Create a list with your child of three to five small changes in eating or exercise habits. Have him choose one as his goal. For instance, if you both agree to eat only one normal-sized serving at dinner, consider hanging a sign that says "no seconds" or represents this goal visually.

Your child may belligerently fight the new rule. Your job, which is harder than it seems, is not to react. Hopefully, you have already worked out effective consequences for angry outbursts. In addition, work out a tiered reward system: one reward for not taking an extra serving, despite expressing anger, and one for good-humoredly not taking an extra serving. In time—which may feel like years—the meltdowns and negotiations will decrease if you are consistent and use methods that are motivating to your child. Remember: the key to success is for *your* child to decide to make the change in his eating habits, even though he's going to fight it.

The process of change takes time for everyone. For children and adults with Down syndrome, it may take more time. People with Down syndrome who have established "grooves" or routines will have the most difficult time changing any aspect of their routine. Be kind. Go slowly. Be respectful of your child's life as you encourage him to make changes that ultimately change his lifestyle.

The Importance of Friends

A study of Body Mass Index measurements in adults with Down syndrome found that people who had friendships had a lower BMI than those who did not have a good network of friends. In addition, a survey of 183 adults with Down syndrome asked participants what they felt was the most difficult part about exercising. The clear answer was "finding someone to do something with." All of this means that socialization is a very important aspect of physical activity for teens and adults with Down syndrome. It also points out that people with Down syndrome may participate in exercise and other activities for different reasons than we do ourselves. This means that you should look at activities through your child's point of view if you want to help him create an effective, active lifestyle that is fun for him.

GETTING STARTED

There's a lot of preparation to getting started with a weight management program. The first step for you, the parent or professional, is to take a look at your child's current schedule. You began this process when you were in the contemplative stage. Now you will take this information one step further. Consider things such as:

- When are his meals?
- Does he have a snack each day? More than one? What times are they?
- If he has a snack each day, what is the purpose for the snack? Sometimes snacks are necessary because meal times are far

apart. Sometimes snacks have been built into an individual's daily routine because it is the classroom, work, or day care routine. If the latter is true, what are some other options for your child that he might enjoy as much?

- What activities is he involved in now?
- What activities are available? List everything imaginable. You can narrow your list later.

Once you have considered these and other questions you have, read through Chapter 4 (Nutrition 101), Chapter 10 (Nutrition Education), and Chapter 14 (Fitness and Activity). These chapters will guide your thoughts about timing of meals and snacks, appropriate serving sizes, activity ideas, and activities that

work into the daily routine and promote learning about healthy lifestyles. In addition, there are some nutrition education activities to teach concepts related to menu planning, goal setting, serving sizes, and more in Section 4.

As you read these chapters, list the ideas that sound hopeful. Start bringing home different foods to try. This piques everyone's interest. To look for activities, call resources in your community such as the Arc, the community parks and recreation program, Special Olympics, Easter Seals, UCP, and other possibilities. Gather cookbooks that might be interesting for you or your child to use. Try a new recipe on a whim. Collect easy-to-make lower fat foods and dishes from the store: different frozen meals, soup mixes, and so on. What you want to do is have information at your fingertips when your child is ready to try something new. When you bring home new foods or try new recipes, you begin to create an atmosphere of experimentation and curiosity. Everyone's trying this new thing. What do we think about it? As your child begins to show interest in making changes, include him in your investigations and experimentations.

Goal Setting 101

As you begin to work toward change, it is important to set goals. You need to set both long-term and short-term goals for you and your child. In many ways this is much like an IEP or IFSP. The difference is that you are responsible for much more. You, with your child, determine the *Present Level of Performance,* the *Long-Term Goal,* and the *Short-Term Objectives.* In addition, you will evaluate your progress much more often.

If your child is young, you will do this on your own, though your child will drive what goals are set. If your child is older and making a determined effort in this area, he will set his own goals. In either case, you must consider yourself the *coach* rather than the *instructor.* Regardless of age, your child must lead the way in these changes—either by making choices or by planning and implementing his own healthy lifestyle approach to weight management.

It is important to choose your goals carefully if your child is to be successful. Successful goals are:

- 100 percent achievable,
- Easy to visualize as successful,
- Discrete—each goal defines one step.

Goals are not multi-layered. They do not have subcategories or multiple steps, nor are they interrelated. Activity-related goals are confined to activity. Food-related goals are confined to food-related activities such as cooking, snack choices, and so on. To accomplish a short-term goal, your child will do *one* thing and only one thing.

Especially for teenagers and adults with Down syndrome, the process of setting and attaining goals is a great experience. When goals are written well, your child will consistently meet or exceed them, providing a great sense of accomplishment.

In general, goal-setting to promote behavior change works best with the following structure:

1. Set weekly goals.
2. Set one goal for food-related behavior and one for activity.
3. Set daily goals that lead to the weekly goal.
4. Create a way to keep track of success. Visual methods of record keeping are very motivating.

SAMPLE WEIGHT-RELATED GOALS

There are three types of weight-related goals. Goals aimed at:

1. stopping weight gain,
2. maintaining current weight, and
3. weight loss.

It is very important to choose weight-related goals that are realistic and achievable. If your child is slowly gaining weight over time, begin by slowing the rate of weight gain and then stopping weight gain. Being able to do that is a crucial step to success. Sometimes stopping or slowing weight gain takes a while.

Anytime your child chooses a goal aimed at losing weight, keep the rate of weight loss reasonable. A rate of one-half pound to one pound a week is a safe, reasonable, and effective rate of weight loss for anyone who has finished growing.

The overall goal of any wellness plan must be to make changes that support a healthy lifestyle rather than a focus on a specific weight. It is perfectly fine for the weekly goal to be to maintain current weight.

GETTING YOUR CHILD INVOLVED IN GOAL SETTING

Learning to set achievable goals and working toward them is a key element to self-esteem. However, for some children and adults with Down syndrome, participating in goal setting may be difficult. Perhaps your child has not been taught how to set goals. Perhaps he has trouble with communication. Or perhaps your child has a dual diagnosis such as Down syndrome and autism, which makes this process seem out of reach.

These are all things you need to consider as your child's parent. If your child uses augmentative communication or complex curricular adaptations, seek help from people who work well with your child. Feel free to reach beyond the people who work with your child on a daily basis to enlist the help of someone who has been a pivotal person in your child's life in the past: a speech-language pathologist, a special education teacher, a general education teacher, or a friend who has a special connection with your child. It is likely they will enjoy an opportunity to be that pivotal person again. The hardest part is asking them.

Safe Rate of Weight Loss

It is very important to set goals that are consistent with a healthy rate of change in weight. A reasonable goal is one-half to one pound of weight (one-quarter to one-half a kilogram) each week as an average over time. Anything more than two pounds of weight change in a week is probably too dramatic of a program to foster long-term changes.

For example, one pound of weight is equal to 3500 calories. To lose one pound a week requires a calorie deficit of 3500 calories over the course of the week. That is, you need to take in 3500 fewer calories per week than your body is accustomed to getting. This is a change of 500 calories per day. This change in calories is obtained by either increasing calories out (activity), decreasing calories in (food), or a combination of both. To lose more than one pound in a week, it is easiest to increase exercise. For instance, 40 minutes of extra walking in a day will use approximately 350 more calories in a day. These 40 extra minutes of walking do *not* need to occur at one time. They can be eight five-minute walks, or four ten-minute walks. Each additional walk or other activity in a day adds to the number of calories *used*.

It is helpful to determine approximately how many calories are needed for your adult child to maintain his weight. Use the equations in the Appendix to estimate your adult child's calorie needs.

To summarize: A safe rate of weight loss for adults is considered one-half to two pounds a week using a combination of *decreasing* the number of calories IN and *increasing* the number of calories OUT. A faster rate of loss may serve to reach an ultimate weight goal faster, but research shows changes will not be sustained.

If you are concerned that the concepts underlying goal-setting are tough for your child, simplify them. For instance, it is not necessary for your child to think of goals by himself. Choose an area to work on together. Then offer three or four choices you know he can do successfully. Ask for his ideas for a few more similar goals. If he doesn't have any, let him know it is OK. For some people with Down syndrome, the choice may need to be more immediate: "What activity will we do today?" (offer three or four options). Maybe the choices need to be visual. Offer activity choices using symbols or photographs.

If your child's choices are immediate or symbolic, you may be determining the goals and parameters. This can be done at any age. For example,

1. Jon will increase his physical activity by choosing an afternoon activity to do with his friend Bob. Choices include: walking the dog, going to aerobics, going on a hike, or riding his bike.
2. Jon will choose snack foods from his snack menu. I will offer snack foods that are low in fat that he likes.
3. Jon will explore different low fat entrées for lunch. I will offer these new dishes as "side dishes" to see how he likes them before working them into the menu on a regular basis.

Weight Loss Success
By Yvonne Gustafsson

Jenny Gustafsson, 28 years old, has lost 58 pounds with Weight Watchers since February 2001. She had already lost 7 pounds before she started Weight Watchers. She has gone from 222 pounds to 157 pounds. Her goal is 150 pounds.

Jenny started gaining weight in her late teens. She was tested for hypothyroidism and the test came back positive. Even though she got medication for the condition, she kept gaining weight. The jobs that she had after graduating from high school were jobs where she did not move very much. At home she also liked activities where she could sit still. She liked to eat and when her siblings lived at home there was always junk food available. I tried to control what she ate and bugged her a lot, which didn't do any good. About a year before Jenny started Weight Watchers, I finally realized that my bugging wasn't going to make any difference. I stopped worrying about what she ate and let her make her own choices. Also about the same time Jenny got a new job at a retail store. She now works there three or four days a week. It is a job where she is on her feet and moves a lot. In January of 2001 Jenny expressed her wish to lose weight. She wanted to have a smaller stomach. We talked to Dr. Brian Chicoine at the Adult Down Syndrome Center and he mentioned that some of his patients with Down syndrome were having success with Weight Watchers. In February, Jenny started going to their meetings and doing the program. It was an immediate success and she was very excited. I asked Jenny some questions about her weight loss:

1. What do you like about Weight Watchers?
   The meetings, Becky my leader, and seeing other people who want to lose weight.

2. What is hard about losing weight?
   To keep eating healthy food.

3. What has helped you to lose weight?
   To keep my food journal and count my points every day. (By following the point system, Jenny has learned that healthy foods have low points and junk food has lots of them.)

4. How do you feel now that you have lost so much weight?
   A lot better. I have more energy. I have better balance and I can dance. I know it is healthy. I can fit into my old prom dresses and swimsuits.

5. How do you like getting compliments?
   I like it. I feel happy.

6. What advice do you have for people who want to lose weight?
   Avoid sweets and fat. Eat healthy snacks like pretzels and popcorn. Eat bread, bagels, and muffins that are made from whole wheat and bran. Eat food that has fiber.

WEIGHT MANAGEMENT AND MEDICATIONS

Some medications prescribed for long-term use for children and adults with Down syndrome have side effects that can affect your child's weight. Your physician should be aware of these side effects, though he may not mention them. Some medications, such as Ritalin, can decrease appetite. For some children, this decrease in appetite causes weight loss or stops even normal weight gain. Some medications, such as risperdal and SSRIs, increase appetite—and subsequently promote weight gain—for all people. In a few cases, this is more dramatic for people with Down syndrome.

If your child begins taking a new medication, talk to your physician or pharmacist to find out whether weight gain is one of the common side effects. If so, it is important to think about how to change family eating habits to reduce this effect for your child. An increase in appetite caused by a medication feels no different than typical hunger. It can seem unnoticeable to the person taking the medication. The solution may involve learning to eat lower fat, high fiber foods to provide bulk (see information on "High Fiber Diet" in the Appendix), drinking more water, or tightly structuring meals and snacks to minimize the feeling of hunger. This is not easy for people without Down syndrome, so it will be difficult for your child too.

When my son began a medication well-known for inducing weight gain in children with Down syndrome, my husband and I discussed how we would try to minimize the probable weight gain. Andy has always been a "good eater," so we were concerned that he would become a *very* good eater. We chose to focus on the snacks that are available to him. We modified the foods we offer Andy for grazing from pre-packaged high fat foods to his favorite fruits and vegetables. In the process, we learned that he is more interested in the "crunch" of the food than he is in the specific food. In the morning we prepare a large plate of broccoli, celery, sliced apples (sprayed with lemon juice), baby carrots, and snap peas. In this situation, we set the goals, but Andy still makes choices. He chooses how much of the crunchy buffet to eat. Each time the amount of medication changes, his voracious appetite changes too.

Our goal for weight management was to minimize weight gain from medication without frustrating Andy. We knew that if Andy was frustrated, he would seek food in inappropriate ways. While he has gained some weight, he does not look unhealthy. In fact, we think the added weight looks good on him. We did not realize how thin he was before.

One reason this method has worked well for Andy is because we chose foods we already knew he liked. Use the "Family Food Favorites" worksheet in Section 4 to help you create a solution for your child. Look for what is motivating to your child about the snack. Is it really about the food and how hungry he feels or is he more interested in your attention? If your attention is as important as the snack, find ways to change the focus of that time from food to an activity or game. While you may still have a snack, if he really wants your attention, he will eat less because he is more interested in having fun with you than he is in the food.

What if Andy was not interested in raw vegetables? Again, the key to snack choice is in knowing what your child likes to eat. Your child may not like raw vegetables, but he may like fresh or canned fruit, air-popped popcorn, pretzels, or another snack item that is not loaded with calories. Most important is to respect that your child feels hunger, but also find ways to minimize his focus on that hunger, especially if it is induced by medication.

Food-related goals are not as simple as weight-related goals. There are many areas of focus for your child to choose from. Some reasonable first goals include:

SAMPLE FOOD-RELATED GOALS

1. I will keep a food record 5 days this week.
2. I will not take second portions at lunch.
3. I will learn about serving sizes by weighing and measuring the foods I eat.
4. I will take half the serving of dessert that I want.
5. I will try different diet sodas, tea, and sugar-free flavored water and make a list of the ones I like.
6. I will drink a sugar-free drink instead of regular soda once each day.
7. I will make a menu for my snacks this week. (See Chapter 16 for more on menus.)
8. I will make a menu for my meals this week.

Before your child can make appropriate food-related goals, he will need enough nutrition education to understand healthy choices. This means you may need to do some homework regarding healthy cooking, reading labels, and designing tasty, low fat, high fiber meals. Some recommended books for learning about nutrition and cooking are listed in the References and Suggested Readings list. Once you have done your homework, practice making goals for yourself and working on improving your lifestyle. We all know people with Down syndrome do best with appropriate role models. More importantly, you shouldn't ask your child to live up to a higher standard than you do yourself. Learning about nutrition and working to improve your personal health will remind you how difficult it is to make changes.

Once you have done your homework, you can focus on your child. Start at the beginning. Teach him about nutrition, balanced meals and snacks, and how to fuel his body so he feels good before talking about calories and limiting high-fat foods. It is far easier for your child to make changes to reduce the unhealthy choices if he understands what he *can* choose. As time goes on, the food-related goals your child makes will become more specific and complicated.

SAMPLE ACTIVITY-RELATED GOALS

The next chapter discusses the relation between physical activity and a healthy lifestyle in more detail. Since activity is an integral part of weight management, though, we need to at least touch on it here. Just as food and weight-related goals must begin small and be realistic, so must goals for activity. Some ideas for beginning activity goals include:

1. I will go to my doctor this week to get his permission to start an exercise program.
2. I will get the schedule for aerobic classes at the YMCA.
3. I will call my friend, _____, and ask if he would like to take an aerobics class with me.
4. I will go for a walk around the block after work on Tuesday and Friday.

Over time, your child will need to make different activity-related goals. They must be reasonable, specific, and clear. For example:

    5. I will go to aerobics at the YMCA at 2:00 p.m. on Monday, Wednesday, and Friday.

    6. I will go for a 30-minute walk on Sunday afternoon with Mrs. Smith's dog.

Including the specific day, time, and duration of an activity in the goal allows your child to plan his week. When he makes his list for that day, he knows he is supposed to be at the YMCA at 2:00 for his aerobics class. Without those details, your child will delay when he exercises or what day he goes.

Activity 10 in Section 4 can help your child learn about setting goals and food records. Please note that your child does not have to be able to read or write well—or at all—to participate in this process. He can check the food groups he eats at meals and snacks. He can paste symbols or photos of the foods he eats on a food record. Whatever works best is what you want. The goal-setting activity is primarily based on writing the goal on a piece of paper. Let him dictate that to you. Be his secretary. After he has chosen his goals for the week, you can rewrite them in a visual manner if you need to. There's no reason this process has to be perfect, nor is it an academic exercise. Use your child's abilities to encourage and promote his participation in the process.

MEASURING SUCCESS

Keeping track of your child's success is just as important as setting goals. It is highly motivating to be able to see progress. There are many ways to keep track of success. Some are more visual than others. Graphs, charts, and other easy-to-understand methods are quite effective.

Some visual methods of record keeping and goal tracking are outlined in Section 4.

Another way to measure success, especially if your child chooses to increase his physical activity more than change his eating habits, is to keep track of measurements. Some key areas to measure include:

- chest,
- waist,
- hips,
- thighs,
- calves, and
- upper arms.

Keep track of these measurements. They will not change quickly, but changes should be evident in about four weeks. One method of comparing changes is to add measurements together and look for a change in total number. The other, of course, is to compare measurements for different areas of the body. Some people find it much more motivating to keep track of the number of inches lost rather than monitoring weight. Regardless of what you and your child choose to measure, follow these guidelines:

- Weigh or measure no more than once a week.

- Weigh or measure at the same time of day.
- Have your child wear similar clothing each time you weigh and measure.

Some other considerations include having your child face away from the scale so he can't see the number, making sure others aren't watching, and protecting your child's privacy during the process and when considering whether or not to share the information. It's not your decision who knows about your child's success or struggle in the weight management game; it's his.

The method of monitoring success is not as important as making it motivating and easy-to-see and understand. When your child is feeling low and unmotivated to go for his walk, he may find renewed interest by looking at the graph of his increased activity and decreased weight or measurements. Use the method he is most interested in—or use them all. There are no rules.

If your child is working toward a reward, you can track the successful steps toward that reward. In fact, some young people with DS will probably be much more motivated by seeing how close they are to their reward than by looking at an abstract graph of their weight change. Consider putting a picture of what your child is working for on his chart and plot his steps towards it. The closer he gets, the more motivated he will be. Building in short-term and long-term rewards is an important part of maintaining interest and motivation.

Don't Be a Parent, Be a Lifestyle Coach!

We were invited to a special event months in advance that our son was extremely excited to attend. Our son is attending a post-secondary program and lives away from home. A few months before the event, we bought him a new suit and had it tailored to fit him perfectly while he was visiting. He looked stunning. When he returned from school a month before the event, the suit barely fit! It was hard for him to wear the pants comfortably.

I explained to him that we had gone to a lot of trouble to get the suit fitted for him. There wasn't time to fit it again—and what if it didn't fit the next time he came home before the event? If he didn't fit the suit, he wasn't going to be able to go. He said, "I know it is what I've been eating at school, Mom. I need to change the way I eat and get some exercise."

When he came home the next month, the suit fit him beautifully. He has never changed his eating and exercise habits like that before. It took something that was important to him for him to apply what he already knew how to do. I am very proud of him.

When it comes to weight management, it is essential for parents to act more like a coach than a parent. You don't want to become the food police or the family drill sergeant. It's not fun. Your job is to provide the support, tools, opportunities, and guidance for your child to make changes that lead to a healthier life. Here are some guidelines to consider:

- Work as a collaborator or partner rather than a dictator.
- Model the expected behavior. Coaches show their protégé the way by their example as well as their words.
- Talk about choices you are making out loud. For instance, if you choose to eat a smaller portion of sloppy joe for dinner so you can have birthday cake without feeling guilty, talk aloud about that decision.
- Involve your child in helping *you* make decisions about activity and food to meet your personal goals. Involve him in the process in someone else's life.
- Use strategies that match your child's interests and readiness for change.
- Use strategies that make sense to your child.
- Affirm your child as much as possible.
- Give advice sparingly. Wait until he asks as often as you can.
- Provide a menu of choices that promote change.
- Be optimistic. Focus on what your child can do and plan for success.
- Avoid arguments. Don't create a battlefield.
- **LISTEN.** Your child will have a lot to say as he works through his new choices and lifestyle changes.
- Never ask more from your child than you can do yourself.

The best advice comes from Mia Peterson, a young woman with Down syndrome:

> *"It is up to us to stay healthy, exercise, and eat well. Parents can encourage us, give advice, and remind us now and then, but they can't make us do anything. Only we can."*

A Note to Parents

The topic of weight management is a very difficult and personal one for all parents—and perhaps especially so for parents of children with Down syndrome. We feel responsible if our children are overweight. Often when I watch teenage and adult children with Down syndrome perform, deliver a public address, or participate in a community service project with the local parent group, I listen more to the audience than I do the presentation. If a person with Down syndrome is overweight, all of his accomplishments seem to be washed away as strangers express disdain about his appearance and health. These are valid concerns, but they do not negate the accomplishments or personality of the individual. I believe we must include and proudly accept *all* children—even those who are obese. We must not exclude or judge children and adults with Down syndrome because of their weight. If we do, we destroy any successes we have painfully gained for self-determination and the inclusion of our children with disabilities in society.

Of course, I am not suggesting that healthy weight and healthy lifestyles be ignored in favor of academic or social accomplishment, or inclusion. I am suggesting that life is a balance of all of these things. If we, as parents, promote healthy lifestyles—by living them ourselves—for everyone in our family, it is much easier. To do this, it is important to include everyone in the process.

At times, as you attempt to guide your child toward a healthy lifestyle, you will find yourself asking difficult questions: is this a teachable moment, a parent moment, or is it a lost cause nutritionally speaking? Of course, you must use your discretion. Our burden as parents is to capitalize on the teachable moments in a way that is positive, supportive, and destined for success as often as possible. Do your best.

TEACHABLE MOMENTS

What is a teachable moment? Teachable moments are times when your child:

- shows an interest in learning,
- asks questions,
- attempts to help you.

Teachable moments are times when you and your child are not:

- rushed,
- tired,
- upset,
- hungry,
- sick,
- distracted.

A teachable moment can be planned or unplanned. It can be as simple as talking through your decisions. For example, "I had a really big lunch today at the restaurant so I think I will take smaller portions for dinner tonight." Or, "Since Thanksgiving is next week, I'm going to walk for an extra ten minutes every night. That will help me burn some extra calories before our dinner." Verbalizing what the options are ahead of time usually works better than waiting until the heat of the moment when the temptation is already there—for example, when the chocolate is right in front of your child.

Usually, you will not be able to use your child's mistakes as teachable moments. For instance, it would generally *not* be a good idea to point out to your child that he should have kept to his exercise schedule if he didn't want to gain weight at the moment that he is standing on the scale and finding out that he weighs more than he did last week. Telling your child (or anyone else) "I told you so!" rarely leads to behavior change or a feeling of competence.

PARENT MOMENTS

What is a parent moment? Parent moments are times when you must either structure the choices by eliminating some or you must make decisions for your child. These moments can be tough. Sometimes there are hurt feelings on both sides.

When your child is young, there are many parent moments. This is when the feeding relationship discussed in Chapter 3 is most helpful. You are responsible for *what* your child eats. To confine how *much,* you must limit the amount available.

When your child is older, these moments may turn into a power struggle. These are hard on everybody.

Sometimes it is far more destructive to try to create a healthy option than to allow your child to enjoy a situation where overeating is likely. There are lessons to learn from experiencing life during events such as:

- birthday parties,
- holiday celebrations,
- sleepovers,
- special occasions.

These are infrequent situations that have few constraints for all participants. A sleepover or birthday party is a time to enjoy friends and the time together rather than worry about food choices. It is just as important to learn how to enjoy these situations naturally—without hoarding or being over-focused on food because no one is watching over you—as it is to learn to make healthy choices at other times.

Conclusion

Weight management is a tricky subject for everyone, including children and adults with Down syndrome. It is an area that demands compassion, empathy, positive behavioral support, appropriate teaching methods, and, most importantly, creativity, to be successful. While the basic mechanism of managing weight is easy to understand, the process of implementing effective strategies is complex and time consuming. There is no one way to success. The secrets to success will be found in your child's interests. The best strategy is to work collaboratively with your child. Remember, successful teamwork is a very dynamic process.

CHAPTER 14

Fitness and Activity

Being active is an important part of a healthy lifestyle. Not only does regular physical activity burn calories, but it also has benefits such as:

- decreased appetite,
- better sleep,
- increased sense of well-being or self-esteem,
- reduced stress,
- increase in metabolism,
- decreased blood pressure,
- decreased resting heart rate.

All of these things help your child live a happier, healthier life. They can also indirectly improve the quality of your family time together. The key is for activity to be a natural and fun part of your family's routine so everyone gets adequate amounts everyday.

Activity Levels in Children with Down Syndrome

When your child is very young, her most important activity is learning: learning to roll over, crawl, walk, run, and jump. Encouraging your child's gross motor development is the natural way to include activity in her life. This, of course, hap-

pens throughout the day as a part of everyday play. Teachers and therapists involved in your child's early intervention and preschool programs may offer guidance for encouraging your child's gross motor development.

Even if your child is slow to begin walking, if she's exploring her environment, crawling around, and using her body throughout the day, she is doing her job and is likely active enough. Your job is to provide an

engaging and stimulating environment at home and at school that she wants to be involved in. If there are things for her to do that are appropriate and engaging, she'll exhaust herself in the process. The physical therapist involved with your early intervention team should be able to give you some effective guidance in this situation.

As your baby grows into an unstoppable toddler and preschooler, you will need to be mindful of the type of activity she is engaged in throughout the day. While *you* may be exhausted from being with her all day, you may find that most of *her* activity was not aerobic in nature. (See the sidebar below.) It was a sad day when I realized that pushing my son on the swing and going on the merry-go-round or teeter totter was not aerobic for him, though it was for me. At this point, you must begin to consider how you will promote an active lifestyle that your child will enjoy for years to come.

Types of Exercise

Aerobic Exercise is oxygen-requiring exercise. It uses whole body movements that last over time and require you to breathe harder. The extra oxygen is used by your body to convert the food you eat to energy for your body to continue the activity. Examples of aerobic exercise include: walking, dancing, swimming, and biking.

Anaerobic Exercise is exercise that uses an intense and short spurt of energy. The primary action is the use of muscles. Examples of anaerobic exercise are: weight training, lifting boxes, sprinting in track races (less than 10 minutes), or stop-and-go sports like soccer or softball.

Low Impact Exercise is exercise that is weight bearing, usually aerobic, and gentle on the joints and skeletal structure of your body. Examples of low impact exercise include: walking, riding a bike on a paved surface, swimming, and water aerobics.

High Impact Exercise is weight-bearing exercise that is hard on the joints and skeletal structure. Examples of high impact exercise include most aerobic dance classes, running, and jumping rope.

Strength Training is a specific type of exercise, with or without weights, designed to improve the strength and tone of muscles. Sometimes this is done with free weights; sometimes it is done with resistance equipment such as Nautilus weights or exercise bands.

Like most children in developed countries, children with Down syndrome tend to become less active as they grow older. There are many reasons this happens. For instance, when a child starts full-day school, she has five or six hours of mostly sitting during her day. In addition, after a long day at school, many children with Down syndrome then sit down to long periods of homework.

Another factor for many children is interest in television and video games. While many shows are educational, research has connected this increase in television watching and playing video games to childhood obesity. Of course, television watching is not unique to children with Down syndrome, but they may watch even more TV than usual due to social barriers. For instance, when children with Down syndrome are young, including them in after school activities is often easy to do. In early elementary school years the goal of team sports is to learn the game. Soccer starts out as "kick and chase," and baseball begins as t-ball. But as children get older, the games become more competitive and it may be difficult for your child to keep up. Even if the group is open to your child's participation, she may not want to participate because it is becoming too hard.

It is not only the pace of the games and activities that get in the way. For some children with Down syndrome, there are physical barriers that may make it difficult to be active with a group of nondisabled peers. For instance, children with Down syndrome often have low muscle tone, so you may need to be more purposeful in the activities you choose for your child. For instance, playing "wheelbarrow" with friends or pushing a wheelbarrow while doing yard work are good ways to build upper body and shoulder strength. This then makes it easier for your child to participate in many different activities.

Another common concern is flat feet or ankles that bend inward (pronated ankles). Both of these affect your child's comfort and ability to run when participating in activities, especially if your child's ankles are pronated with her shoes on. You can ease the effects of flat feet or pronated ankles by making careful shoe selections. According to Patricia Winders, PT, the most important features to look for in a shoe for your child are:

- flexible soles (they should be bendable in your hands),
- a long, wide, arch support (not just a bump),
- a firm heel counter,
- a firm medial counter,
- not too wide,
- not high tops (they don't promote the strength needed by the ankles to keep them straight), and
- lightweight.

I've found that flexible soles are very difficult to find as my son gets older. Most tennis shoes for teenagers are hard as a rock and completely unbendable by hand. There are a few brands that are flexible, but they change frequently. If your child has a good pair of shoes and her ankles still seem to be pronated, visit a physical therapist or an orthopedist with some experience with people with Down syndrome to see if you need to consider an insert for her shoe.

The list of reasons for a decrease in activity as children become older is long and varied. Some are societal and some are specific to children with Down syndrome. Regardless, the more you can encourage and support your child to be active and decrease her interest in more sedentary activities such as watching television and videos, the healthier she'll be.

Promoting Active Lifestyles

HOW MUCH ACTIVITY IS ENOUGH?

Despite the often accepted decrease in activity for children with and without Down syndrome, there really aren't any reasons your child has to follow that trend. Your goal is to find ways to encourage her to be active throughout the day, throughout life.

There is no magic formula to know how much activity is enough. However, many experts recommend that children get at least an hour a day of physical activity. For adults, the recommendations are the same as for all Americans: thirty minutes of aerobic exercise three times a week and at least thirty minutes a week of strength training.

Are these goals realistic? Only you and your child know the answer. If your child is leading a fairly sedentary routine, then what is important is changing that routine to include more activity. It does not mean the new activities need to be group or organized activities. Everyday opportunities to start building activity into your child's life at any age include parking farther away from the door, using the stairs, and going for a short walk together in the evening.

If your child has a physical disability that limits her ability to be active in the usual ways, look for other sensible ways to increase her activity. For instance, there are aerobic videos for people who are unable to walk and many park and recreation programs have water aerobic programs and equipment for people with limited movement. It is always difficult to have to look for one more modification, though. So be reasonable with yourself and your child. Brainstorm a list of ideas and work at investigating options as you are able. What is important is to look for ways that your child can be active regardless of her limitations.

Of course if your ultimate goal is stopping weight gain or encouraging weight maintenance, your child will likely need more activity to accomplish those goals than merely walking a little further or using the stairs. There are many ideas to help you carve out a plan for encouraging your child to be more active throughout this chapter.

HOW MUCH ACTIVITY IS TOO MUCH?

Of course, it is always possible that your child is getting too much exercise. For children, evidence of being overworked is usually behavioral. They may be difficult to wake in the morning, irritable, or stubborn. If your child is involved in an active sport every day after school and is having difficulty in school, grumpy, or sleepy all the time, the demands of school and activity may be too much.

For adults, the same rule of thumb applies. If your child is having difficulty at school or work, sleeping more, or showing signs of stress, you will want to look at her daily routine. The recommendation for teens and adults *without* Down syndrome is a maximum of an hour a day of organized exercise. In other words, unless someone is an athlete in training for a competition, an hour a day of exercise is a lot.

Another form of overexertion can occur if an activity is too hard or you are exercising too hard for your fitness level. The fitness level of kids with Down syndrome is often misjudged by folks organizing activities or conducting gym class. One way to decide if your child is exercising too hard is to monitor her heart rate once during physical activity. You then compare her actual heart rate with her *target heart rate*, which is determined by first computing her *maximum heart rate*, as described below.

Maximum Heart Rate. Maximum Heart Rate (MHR) is the maximum work your heart can do. It is used as a guide to determine how hard your heart is working during exercise. For people without Down syndrome, MHR is generally predicted by the equation: 220 − age = Predicted MHR in beats per minute. A person who is 18 years old has a MHR of 202 beats per minute (220-18=202).

People with Down syndrome have a lower MHR than those without. Recently a group of researchers determined a formula to predict MHR for people with Down

Activity Pyramid

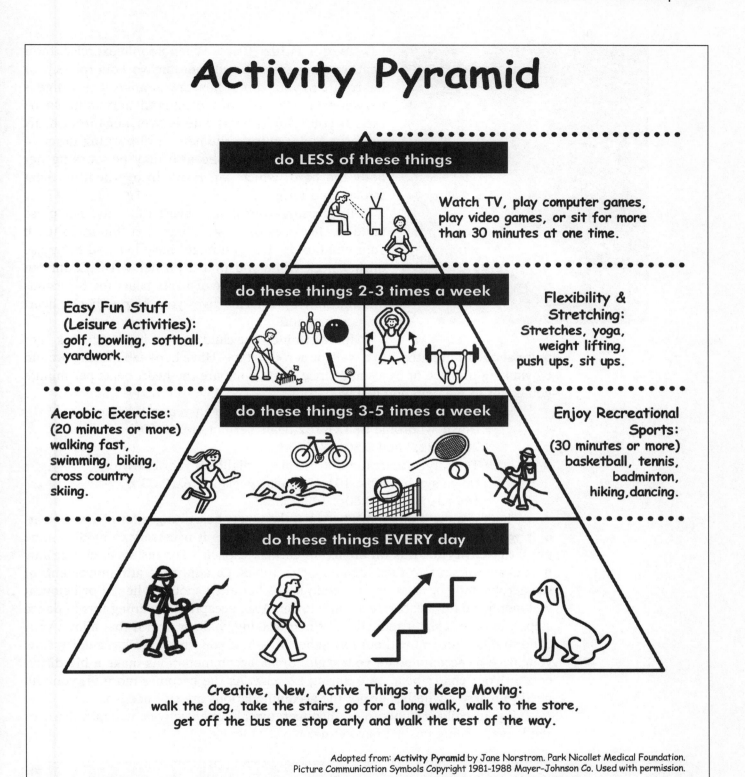

do LESS of these things

Watch TV, play computer games, play video games, or sit for more than 30 minutes at one time.

do these things 2-3 times a week

Easy Fun Stuff (Leisure Activities): golf, bowling, softball, yardwork.

Flexibility & Stretching: Stretches, yoga, weight lifting, push ups, sit ups.

do these things 3-5 times a week

Aerobic Exercise: (20 minutes or more) walking fast, swimming, biking, cross country skiing.

Enjoy Recreational Sports: (30 minutes or more) basketball, tennis, badminton, hiking, dancing.

do these things EVERY day

Creative, New, Active Things to Keep Moving: walk the dog, take the stairs, go for a long walk, walk to the store, get off the bus one stop early and walk the rest of the way.

Adopted from: **Activity Pyramid** by Jane Norstrom. Park Nicollet Medical Foundation. Picture Communication Symbols Copyright 1981-1988 Mayer-Johnson Co. Used with permission.

syndrome: Predicted MHR = 210 - (0.56 x age) - (15.5 x 2). For example, the Predicted MHR for a person with Down syndrome who is 18 years old would be: 210 - (.56 x 18) – (15.5 x 2) = 169 beats per minute.

Once you know your child's MHR, you can figure out her Target Heart Rate—which enables you to determine if she's exercising too hard.

Target Heart Rate. When people exercise, their heart rate increases. A good aerobic workout raises your heart rate to your target heart rate range. This range is between 60-80% of your predicted maximum heart rate. If your child's heart rate is over her target heart rate, she is not getting the benefit of burning fat calories from her exercise. She also may be working her body too hard, which can result in overheating, heat stroke, and fatigue.

To measure your child's heart rate, find her pulse either on her neck or wrist, or have her find it. To teach your child to do this, you might have her find her pulse on her neck while you find it on her wrist. Count out loud together the number of heart beats for 6 seconds and multiply by 10. This gives you the number of heart beats per minute.

To determine your child's target heart rate, take her pulse about 10 minutes into a walk or aerobics tape. Have her keep moving around by walking in place or in a small circle. Then compare the heart beats per minute you count to the equation below.

- The target heart rate for the above eighteen-year-old without Down syndrome is: 121-162 beats per minute. (0.60 x 202=121.2 and 0.80 x 202=161.6.)
- The target heart rate for the above eighteen-year-old with Down syndrome is: 101-135 beats per minute. (0.60 x 169=101.4 and 0.80 x 169=135.2.)

There is quite a difference between the target heart ranges for eighteen-year-olds with and without Down syndrome. This makes it necessary to modify some physical activity for this difference in cardiac capacity. For instance, choose low impact aerobics rather than high impact aerobics. Or adjust the arm movements of the aerobic tape or class. If your child keeps her arms shoulder height or below, it will help keep her heart rate slightly lower. Also, accepting lower leg lifts in dance steps will offer a slight reduction. When walking, walk at a pace that allows your child to talk with you without losing her breath. If you fitness walk regularly, slow your pace to accommodate your child. Small accommodations make a big difference in your child's heart rate during exercise. As she becomes more fit, you will need to reassess whether or not the accommodations are still needed.

If your child is stubborn or uncooperative about an activity, you may discover she is really being pushed beyond her physical limits.

My nine-year-old son with Down syndrome is fully included in regular education. This includes physical education class. Up until this year, he was in special education and had Adapted P.E. Now his P.E. teacher reports to me that he will not participate with the other kids. I observed his class, and they do around fifteen minutes of continuous, intense cardiovascular exercise without a break. He came over to me, exhausted. When I measured his heart rate after a few minutes of resting, it was 156 beats per minute. I believe it is not a behavior problem, but simply that he is at his maximum and needs a break.

Exercise and Medical Concerns

Always check with your child's physician before starting a new exercise or physical activity. This is especially important if your child has heart concerns, obesity, or has been very inactive for a period of time. If your physician has any concerns or guidelines for your child, it's best to find out before you begin.

If your child had a heart defect that's been repaired, exercise is probably not a concern. Regardless, check with your child's cardiologist to see if there are any exercise restrictions for your child. If your child has a heart defect that has not yet been repaired or cannot be repaired, do not start any new exercise program without consulting with your child's cardiologist. It is important to be aware of and make accommodations for any restrictions your child may need to prevent injury.

Opportunities for Activity at Home

Throughout your child's life, and especially when she is young, it is important for you to join in activities with her. Your child with Down syndrome will learn to value activity if you value it and the best way to teach her that is to do things together. Having a friend to do activities with is especially important for adults with Down syndrome because the social component of activity is a stronger motivation than lower body fat or better fitness.

Sometimes parents struggle when brainstorming a list of activities their child may enjoy. A list of leisure and physical activities enjoyed at different ages by people with Down syndrome is included in the Appendix. Use these lists as a springboard for considering what types of activities your child and family can enjoy together. If you are still short of ideas, talk with your child's P.E. or Adapted P.E. teacher, contact a leisure specialist at your local park and recreation department, or contact the leisure and recreation division of TASH.

There are some key factors that may increase your chance of successfully promoting activities for your child regardless of age:

- Have lots of friends there.
- Make it fun.
- Make it challenging, but not competitive.
- Minimize the risk for injury.
- Vary the activity.
- Choose activities that are appropriate for your child's ability.
- Schedule activities thoughtfully. Don't over schedule your child.
- Show interest by watching or asking questions.
- Build in rewards (new clothing, pins, equipment, and so on, but not food). See below for a national incentive program that may be motivating for older children.

As always, be kind to yourself. Keeping activity fun for you and for your child is very important. However, if adding activity to your child's life becomes one more thing to worry about, it will be a burden to everyone, sending the opposite message than the one you want to promote. Try not to over schedule yourself or your family.

PRESIDENTIAL
SPORTS
AWARD

This award incentive program is open to children and adults aged 6 to 106 years old. It is based on keeping logs of activity, with a goal of 50 hours of a specific activity (or specific combinations of activities). A wide number of sports are included, from walking, bicycling, dance, and swimming, to golf, basketball, lawn bowling, and soccer. There is also a family award program for families who like to do things together. Participants log a specified number of hours (usually at least 50) of a selected activity and mail in the log book along with $5.00 (in the United States) or $7.00 (in Canada) to receive a patch, certificate of achievement from the president, and other goodies. Residents of countries other than the United States may also participate in the program, for a slightly higher fee. See the Resources at the back of the book for information about log books and award programs.

Making Time for Activity at Home

During the school year, there may be very little time left for formal physical activities after school, especially if both parents work and nobody gets home much before 6 p.m. Then you probably have supper, homework, and bath time to fit into your schedule. In this situation, when you may feel as if you don't have one spare minute to spend making the beds that you didn't make in the morning, the best way to get your child to exercise is to figure out ways to incorporate physical activity into your daily routine. Here are some ideas:

- **Give your child some daily chores with a physical component:** setting the table, fetching needed condiments, filling cups with ice and carrying them one by one to the table before supper; sweeping up, carrying dishes to the counter, or helping load the dishwasher after supper; throwing toys back into the toy box, carrying the recycling to the curb, walking from door to door "checking" all the locks in the house before bedtime.

- **Involve your child in the "work" of shopping.** Let her push the grocery cart, help you put your purchases on the conveyer belt, carry bags into the house. If your child is old enough, and you discover you have forgotten an item in Aisle 2 when you are in Aisle 11, send your child back to get it (or go with her).

- **Use physical activity to break up homework time.** Put on a CD and have a short dancing or marching break in between the reading and math homework, or after so many minutes of work. Play a short game of "Simon Says" with lots of jumping around when your child's attention is flagging. Let your child bounce on the bed, if such antics are allowed in your house. Or let her spin around, if that is something your child enjoys. (One mother with a nine-year-old with Down syndrome reports that her daughter decided on her own to spin around before homework time because it "wakes up" her brain.)

Just Keep Moving, Please

Infants and small children do not need exercise programs. They exercise naturally because they are in constant motion as they develop gross motor skills and explore their world. Climbing up on the sofa requires considerable exertion when you are only two feet tall.

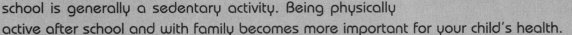

Once your child has mastered the fundamental gross motor skills, her attention will turn to activities. For young children, whole body activities that use arms, legs, and trunk muscles are best. Some examples are climbing on playground equipment, running in a wide open space, riding a trike and later a bike, soccer, golf, T-ball, basketball, and swimming.

As your child begins to spend more time at school, she'll spend less time being physically active. This is because school is generally a sedentary activity. Being physically active after school and with family becomes more important for your child's health.

Regardless of the activity you and your child choose, the biggest challenge is keeping it motivating and fun. For example, walking is a great exercise, but few children with or without Down syndrome find it fun. Here are some ways to add spice to a family goal of going for a walk:

- play tag (catch a friend or sibling),
- play chase,
- run to...(a place in the park or person who is a distance away),
- alternate walking and running to reach a destination,
- walk to the playground from home,
- walk to a friend's house to see if she can play.

Regular exercise increases strength, improves posture, increases endurance, and improves aerobic fitness. Exercise decreases depression, and there is nothing like brisk exercise to break up a bad mood.

People do not do things simply because they know they are good for them. If they did, it would be difficult to find a parking space at the gym, and the parking lot of the local fast food place would be empty. People who exercise regularly do so because they made it fun and then they made it a habit.

The first step is to make it fun. Go for a family walk. Play a game of soccer. Go bike riding. Swim at the neighborhood pool. Then turn the fun activity into a regular habit. Change activities to keep it fun and interesting. Whatever form your physical activity may take, remember the key is to just keep moving.

By Patricia C. Winders, PT
Author of *Gross Motor Skills in Children with Down Syndrome*

- **Change the rules related to watching TV or videos or playing computer games on a school night.** The rule could be as simple as: everybody gets up and does something during commercial breaks: wandering around the room, hopping like a frog, going upstairs to put pajamas on, bouncing on a trampoline. Or you could suggest games for everyone to play when the commercial begins: a game of leapfrog, holding each other's legs to do wheelbarrow walking, playing volleyball with a balloon, walking from chair to chair in a variation of "musical chairs" until the commercials stop. (For videos or computer games, you could set a timer to indicate activity breaks.) Of course, whatever nutty thing your children have to do during commercial breaks, you have to do too.

Opportunities for Activity at School

By the time your child enters elementary school, she has mastered many skills related to being active. At school, the number and type of opportunities to promote activity broaden. There are opportunities during school and after school that may capture your child's interest. This section discusses a few opportunities that are available in most communities or for you to consider asking your child's school or PTA to provide.

PHYSICAL EDUCATION AND ADAPTED PHYSICAL EDUCATION

Structured opportunities for physical activity during school hours typically occur during physical education and adapted physical education classes. Realistically, these opportunities may not amount to much aerobic activity each day depending on how often classes are offered and how they are conducted.

Adapted Physical Education (APE) varies in how it is delivered from school to school, city to city, and state to state. Generally, the purpose of APE is to either provide modified or separate physical education services designed to promote the development of fundamental motor skills and patterns, physical and motor fitness, and skills in aquatics, dance, individual and group games and sports (including intramural and lifetime sports).

If your child receives APE, it may be in conjunction with the general P.E. class or separately. It is not always necessary for children with Down syndrome to have Adapted Physical Education. Many physical educators are able to modify the instruction and design of P.E. classes to include children with disabilities. If your child's doctor has recommended restrictions on your child's physical activity, you will want to list those restrictions in the accommodations and modifications section of the IEP. For instance, a child with an unrepaired heart defect may need to limit the amount of running, jumping, or other strenuous activity she does, or a child who has been diagnosed with atlantoaxial instability may need to avoid jumping on a trampoline, doing summersaults, and other activities that may strain her neck.

As with all educational placements, advocate for a situation that will be challenging and fun for your child. Hopefully, your child will be active during her physical education class, while having an opportunity to try different sports and games. A positive experience will encourage your child's interest in lifelong activity.

A number of professional organizations focus on appropriate and inclusive physical education and activity for children with disabilities (see Resources). If you would like assistance designing or advocating for an appropriate school-based program for your child, contact the National Association of Sport and Physical Education or a certified recreation therapist. (See resources for contact information.)

RECESS

When I listen to parents share stories about their children, I am stunned to hear how many teachers restrict recess for students who have not finished an assignment or have misbehaved during class. While there are many education-related questions for a child with Down syndrome in this situation, it is unlikely that the punishment (not going to recess) fits the crime. This is particularly true when your child is distracted or acting inappropriately—both of these are signs that your child needs a break. Recess is an unstructured play time that gives your child a break she deserves from the constant demands of structured activities. If your child's teacher suggests restricting recess as a punishment, work to find other positive reinforcers or punishments to replace it. Use the information in the box below for ammunition.

Why Recess Is Important

The National Association for Sport and Physical Education's Council on Physical Education for Children has published a position paper on the purpose of "Recess in Elementary Schools." Listed among the recommendations is:

- Recess should not be viewed as a reward, but a necessary educational support component for all children. Students should not be denied recess as a means of punishment or to make up work.
- Recess should not replace physical education. Recess is an unstructured playtime where children have choices; develop rules for play; and release energy and stress.
- Adults should direct or intervene when a child's physical or emotional safety is an issue. Bullying or aggressive behavior must not be allowed.

The one remaining mystery for me about recess is the timing. It seems that every school has recess following lunchtime rather than lunch following recess. Physiologically, children will get more from recess if they are active prior to eating. For children who need to develop weight management skills, being active prior to eating reduces the impact of hunger, thus promoting smaller portion sizes. In addition, a study of plate waste from school lunches found that students wasted significantly less food when they had recess before eating lunch. This was due in part to the physiological component of activity. More importantly, students were not in a hurry to leave the lunch room to get to recess. They took more time to eat their food and chose more appropriately.

Why is lunch before recess? I don't know. However, if your child is struggling with weight concerns, you might be able to negotiate a change in lunch time for her and her classmates.

SCHOOL-WIDE WALKING PROGRAMS

One mother of a young boy with Down syndrome asked me whether there are any school-wide walking programs to encourage activity during recess, or before and after school. She was looking for a way to build in a reward-based walking program for her son who was struggling with his weight. As a result, I found a number of walking programs designed for schools. One of the most complete packages designed for school-wide or individual classroom participation is produced by Fitness Finders, Inc. They have three programs:

- **The Feelin' Good Mileage Club.** This program is designed for kindergarten through sixth grade.
- **The Mega Mileage Club.** Designed for older students and adults. Participants exercise on their own and accumulate team miles to reach U.S. destinations or countries around the world.
- **Families in Training.** Families work together to reach mileage goals they set.

Each of these programs comes with forms to organize groups, incentive ideas, and ways to include information in the classroom. Examples include teaching fractions by walking-quarter mile segments, tracking the group's progress around the world, walking the miles to a selected country a classroom is studying, and competitions between other classrooms as well as other schools. Miles are tracked in a very visual way and few accommodations need to be made for children with Down syndrome. See the Resource section for more information.

While these programs are designed for organized groups, some parents have worked with school staff to establish an informal walking club before school and at lunch. Regardless of what type of walking program is used, it is a great way to encourage kids to move during their free time.

PRESIDENT'S CHALLENGE: PHYSICAL ACTIVITY AND FITNESS AWARDS PROGRAMS

The President's Challenge is designed for children from ages 6-17 and is primarily organized through physical education classes. The program includes five different awards:

1. **The Presidential Lifestyle Award (PALA)** rewards an active lifestyle for students who are active for 60 minutes per day, five days per week, for six weeks. Students can repeat this award throughout the year.
2. **The Presidential Physical Fitness Award (PPFA)** recognizes an outstanding level of physical fitness. Students who score above the 85th percentile on all five items of the President's Challenge receive this award.
3. **The National Physical Fitness Award (NPFA)** is awarded for achieving a basic, yet challenging level of fitness

by scoring at or above the 50th percentile on all five items on the President's Challenge.

4. **The Participant Physical Fitness Award (PA)** is for students whose scores fall below the 50th percentile on one or more items on the President's Challenge. The Participant Award honors those who attempt the test.

5. **The Health Fitness Award (HFA)** is awarded for students who reach a healthy level of fitness.

New to this program are accommodations for people with disabilities, as well as additional programs focused on promoting active and healthy lifestyles. After reading the current requirements and accommodations, I don't see any reason why a student with Down syndrome cannot work to qualify for one of these awards. The President's Council on Physical Fitness and Sports provides detailed information about the challenge tests, accommodations for students with disabilities, and instructions on how to score the tests and apply for the awards. In addition, instructions for testing accommodations and submitting applications for students with disabilities are covered in detail. Students who earn a Presidential Challenge Award receive a patch to acknowledge their achievement. For more information, contact:

> The President's Council on Physical Fitness and Sports
> 200 Independence Avenue, SW
> Room 738H
> Washington, DC 20201
> www.fitness.gov
> *or*
> The President's Challenge
> 400 East 7th Street
> Bloomington, IN 47405-3085
> 800-258-8146
> www.indiana.edu/~preschal
> preschal@indiana.edu

After-School Activities and Community Programs

Especially in the elementary school years, there are myriad after school and community-based programs your child may enjoy. Unfortunately, it may be a challenge for your child to be included on your local soccer, T-ball, or hockey team. Technically, community programs without performance criteria are required to include children with disabilities under the Americans with Disabilities Act (ADA), but they may never have done so before. This means you must decide how important it is to you and your child to be a part of that team. In addition, community teams are not required to include people with disabilities at a higher percentage than naturally occurs in the community.

If you decide to challenge a local team to include your child, try to keep the debate away from your child so she can enjoy the activity and her friends. Heated debates and discussions about methods to accommodate your child should be done with other team parents outside of the team members' hearing. This helps the kids remain positive and accepting, rather than getting caught up in the politics of the adult-oriented debate. Remember, if it is not a positive experience for your child, you may defeat the purpose of including her.

Contact your local Parks and Recreation Department for a listing of classes and clubs in your neighborhood. Some community-based programs have regularly scheduled activities for teens and adults as well. Many Park and Rec programs have inclusion specialists available to you if you need assistance. In some cases, the program may be able to provide an assistant to the class coordinator for your child.

FINDING INCLUSIVE RECREATION OPPORTUNITIES

It is not always easy to find a community fitness club that is both inclusive and welcoming. Often, however, you will find that the local YMCA values including people with disabilities. Call ahead for a tour and inquire about inclusion specialists and other opportunities. The YMCA is also a place where you may be able to hire a personal trainer for your adult child if she is interested in working out in a club environment.

If you are looking for a center-based opportunity for your child to be active, it's a good idea to visit with the director of the club first. The box on pages 252-53 lists some questions to guide you in evaluating the inclusiveness of a program. The checklist is designed to help you determine what barriers to inclusion are in a community recreation program. Knowing what barriers exist will help you decide whether or not a program will be welcoming for your child. If there are many barriers, you will need to decide whether or not you want to advocate for change in that program.

SPECIAL OLYMPICS

Special Olympics International, Inc., is a well-known, community-based, volunteer organization to promote physical activity through sports for people with mental retardation. To be eligible to participate in Special Olympics (SO) programs a person must be at least eight years old and identified as having one of the following conditions: mental retardation, cognitive delay (as measured by formal assessment), or significant learning or vocational problems due to cognitive delay that requires specially designed instruction. Actual practices and games vary, but athletes in SO typically meet once a week for practice in sports skills and then periodically have competitions with local, regional, and state teams.

The Unified Sports Program of Special Olympics is designed to bring people with and without disabilities of similar age together as a team to compete in Special Olympic competitions. The Unified Sports program began in 1987 with the purpose of fostering integration of people with mental retardation into school and community sports programs.

The type of sports and team (unified or traditional) vary from community-to-community based on the local organization, volunteers, and participation.

LITTLE LEAGUE CHALLENGER DIVISION	The Challenger Division of Little League Baseball is the fastest growing Division in the league. In this division, players with disabilities are paired up with a "buddy" who does not have a disability. To sign your child up for participation in Challenger Baseball, or to volunteer as a "buddy," call the Little League regional office nearest you. To start a Challenger Division in your community, call your local Little League president or a member of your league's board of directors.
WALKING CLUBS	Many areas of the country have walking clubs that offer both organized walks completed at your own pace, or year-round walks that can be done at any time. Organized walks may offer t-shirts or award pins for finishing the walk. Some clubs offer awards for completing a certain number of walks that are recorded in a log book. Walks sponsored by chapters of the American Volkssport Association are rated as to difficulty, with some suitable for wheelchairs and strollers. For more information on walking clubs, contact the American Volkssport Association (see Resources).

Common Trouble Spots in Physical Activity

STOP, DROP, AND FLOP	The "stop, drop, and flop" behavior is one most parents of children with Down syndrome can count on when things aren't going well. The behavior is not limited to young children, although adults with Down syndrome often take a more subtle approach. Instead of flopping down on the ground when they don't want to continue with an activity, they may find every possible place to sit down and resist getting up again. If you run into this situation, ask yourself these questions:

- Does your child think this activity is fun?
- Does she have a friend who is involved in the activity?
- Does she understand the game?
- Is she tired?
- Is she too hot?
- Do her clothes (particularly her shoes) fit well?
- Is she hungry or thirsty?
- How was her day at school?
- Is she over-exerting herself? (check her heart rate)

Persistent encounters with "stop, drop, and flop" or refusal to participate in a once-preferred activity may mean your child is not interested in the activity, it is too competitive, or she's exhausted. Your child may be extremely interested and motivated to participate—to the point of overexertion. Her behavior may be because she has worked so hard she is exhausted and needs a break. Make sure you check her heart rate to see if it exceeds her target heart rate, as described above. If so, it is important to modify her participation (length of participation or intensity of activity) so she is participating at a reasonable level without losing her motivation.

GETTING STUCK IN A GROOVE	If your child has not previously been very active, you will likely encounter some resistance when you first attempt to persuade her to increase her activity. Especially if she is a teenager, by now she probably has set routines and ideas—or grooves—about how her day should be spent. Any changes in activity—social or exercise-related—will require her agreement and commitment.

Evaluating Inclusion in Community Recreation

Administrative Policy and Practice

- Does the agency mission statement reflect a philosophy that promotes inclusion?
- Is an inclusion philosophy, or attitude, promoted in all literature provided to the public (such as brochures, public relations advertisements, etc.)?
- Does the agency seek the opinions of parents, advocacy groups, consumer review boards, and other inclusion-oriented persons?
- Do staff members have education and/or experience with inclusion?
- Are staff given supervision, opportunities for continuing education, and feedback regarding inclusive techniques and practices?
- Is this feedback and support a part of regular evaluation and support efforts?

Logistical and Environmental Considerations

- Do the programs group same-age peers with and without disabilities in activities together?
- Do modifications for physical accessibility allow for flexibility?
- Are adaptations for individuals with hearing, vision, mobility, and other impairments readily available?
- Are sponsorships available?
- Does scheduling occur at times and places that are convenient for participants and families?
- Is scheduling readily accessible for people with disabilities, including access to public transportation?
- Are children enrolled in programs that are chronologically age-appropriate?
- Are budgets sufficient to support successful inclusionary efforts?
- Is there an effective communication system between staff members?
- Do key players in the inclusion process communicate regularly?

Techniques and Methods

- Is there an assessment of skill, experience, and interest levels of participants with disabilities as part of the program planning and assessment procedures?
- Do inclusive programs use effective inclusion strategies and techniques? These may include partial participation strategies, companionship training, task adaptation, cooperative learning, and teaching new social and recreation skills with appropriate behavioral teaching techniques.
- Are there ongoing modifications of activities and materials? When appropriate are reductions in adaptive devices and techniques encouraged when participants no longer need them?

- Is there an ongoing monitoring and evaluation of the program?
- Are there staff who are well trained in how to conduct the program?
- Is the staff given adequate preparation, administrative support, and sufficient staff assistance?
- Is there a welcoming orientation for participants and families as they are introduced to inclusive programs and adaptive strategies?
- Are families invited to participate in activity assessment, evaluation, and the activities themselves?

Individualized Programming

- Are activities selected based on the needs, preferences, and interests of participants?
- Are adaptations geared to the individual, and as typical as possible?
- Are adaptations designed to promote and increase independence within the activity?
- Are adaptations oriented toward enhancing mastery of recreation and social skills?
- Is there a plan to fade adaptations out when possible?
- Do activities help develop skills, leisure knowledge, positive attitudes, and an awareness of what resources are available to the participant?
- Are these skills easily transferable to community opportunities, settings, and time availability of the individual?
- Are allowances made for personal challenge and dignity of risk?
- Is there a wide variety of choice in activities available?
- Is there a variety of choice in level of participation (ranging from spectator participation to interactive) in activities?

Checklist by Stuart J. Schlein, Ph.D., C.T.R.S. and Linda Heyne, Ph.D., C.T.R.S. Reprinted from DISABILITY SOLUTIONS, *Volume 1, Issue 1, May/June, 1996, pp. 4-5.*

Look for social gatherings that are more active or that focus on something besides eating. Gatherings that focus on dancing, bowling, billiards, or playing board games, tend to focus more on the people than the food as compared to a group barbecue or ice cream social. The more active your child is in school activities, the easier this is to accomplish. Consider options such as participating in team sports as the manager for one of the school varsity teams or participating in a community intramural group through the Department of Parks and Recreation. Whatever the activity, attempt to choose activities where your child will feel welcome so she can develop a social network as well.

When attempting to change your child's activity level, it might be helpful for her to set goals or make leisure plans either on her own or with you. General guidelines for goal setting are discussed in Chapter 13.

OBESITY-RELATED PROBLEMS

If your child has a weight problem, it may interfere with her ability to participate in some activities. Some common concerns are trouble with gait, ankles that turn in, trouble finding shoes that fit comfortably, muscle and joint pain, hip pain, and back pain, along with the same obesity-related problems people without Down syndrome face.

In these situations, consider low-impact activities. There are videos for "arm-chair aerobics," low impact dance classes and videos, and water aerobics classes. Walking, swimming, and riding a bike or tricycle are also low impact activities, but for some, they will take more physical work than is possible.

Although obesity can be an obstacle, it is not an unmanageable one. Again, remember that doing things with friends can be a powerful motivator, so if your child is not interested in doing anything as a family, look into activities with other young people her age.

The Bottom Line

The bottom line is simple: Get everybody moving and have *fun* doing it. Be active yourself and you will encourage your child to be active. Maintaining an active lifestyle will be a challenge for children and adults with Down syndrome throughout their lives. Keep the focus on making friends and having fun while being active as much as possible. Not only is keeping active important for health, but when your child is engaged in a physical activity with friends, that's one less time the activity will be centered around food.

CHAPTER 15

Cooking Corner

There isn't a lot of talk among parents of children with Down syndrome about cooking skills. Parents of children who are young tell occasional stories about adventures in the kitchen—coming upon their child with a dozen eggs cracked into a bowl to make breakfast, for example, or finding their child perched on the counter with all his favorite foods surrounding him. The tales from parents of teens center around experiences with the microwave oven such as blown-up hot dogs or frozen dinners cooked until they are a melted plastic mess. Once out of the school system, I hear very few stories about meal preparation. Meal preparation, or cooking, is an important part of life, however. It is too often ignored, treated as one more chore, or skimmed over in planning for our children's futures.

Everyone can cook. Not everyone enjoys cooking, but everyone *can* cook. In addition, every person with Down syndrome can cook. Perhaps this belief is borne out of my own love of food and all you can do with it. I became a registered dietitian because I enjoy creating food as well as understanding how food affects our bodies and our emotions. As a child, it seemed as though the world revolved around food and I wanted to be a part of it. Some people will find my interest in food strange, which is why they didn't go into a food-related profession. We all have interests we developed as children that, when cultivated, enhance our lives as adults. My lifelong interest in food drives my belief that every person with Down syndrome *can* cook—that there is a way to modify the process of making something to eat in a way that will be successful for your child.

Cooking can be defined many ways. Making delicacies with a toy oven run by a light bulb is cooking. Making frozen meals in a microwave is cooking. Making an entrée such as Hamburger Helper™ from a box is cooking. Making pasta sauce from scratch is cooking. Even making cookies from a refrigerated bucket of pre-portioned cookie dough is cooking. There are so many ways to cook that there is at least one method of cooking that your child can successfully use—with or without supervision—at each stage of his life.

Introducing Your Child to Cooking

Ideally, your child should be introduced to experiences preparing food at an early age. Sometimes children make cookies or popcorn in preschool, but with increasingly strict food safety laws, these natural food explorations are not as easy to do in a school situation as they once were. The best experiences for young children occur when you are preparing food for them in your own kitchen. Of course, to include your child in meal preparation requires a teachable moment. If you are not in a hurry, look for ways your child can assist you. Some ideas are listed in Chapter 10.

Simple Rules for Working Safely in the Kitchen

1. Tie long hair back out of your face.
2. Take off dangling jewelry, such as long necklaces or bracelets.
3. Whenever possible, use flame-resistant oven mitts when taking things out of the oven.
4. Try not to wear baggy or loose clothing that can catch handles or drag through what you are cooking.
5. Keep things that easily catch on fire away from the stove and oven (paper, sheets of plastic wrap, mail, and so on).
6. Clean spilled grease and oil from stovetop burners when they are cool.
7. Make sure pot handles are pointing inward, so people walking by can't knock pots off the stove.
8. Wipe up spills on the floor right away so no one slips.
9. Use a stepladder or stepstool to reach things in high cupboards or on high shelves.
10. Know where the fire extinguisher is in the kitchen. If you can't find one, ask your parents to buy one.
11. Check the battery in the smoke alarm twice a year (when you move the clock ahead or back an hour for Daylight Saving Time is a good time).
12. Wear shoes when you cook. If you drop a knife, heavy can, or spill hot liquid while cooking, your feet won't get hurt.

SETTING UP THE KITCHEN

There are some things you can do to enhance your child's independence in the kitchen. Many of the modifications made to the kitchen are appropriate at all ages. Consider:

- **Get a stepstool that brings him up to the counter so he can work alongside you and see what is happening.** Even if he is merely observing, he will learn more by watching you with his head above the countertop than if he is trying to pull himself up to peek.

- Place **non-skid liner** such as Dycem or Contact brand nonadhesive ultra gripliner under bowls and cutting boards to reduce slippage.

- **Purchase measuring cups and spoons that are color-coded with large printing.** (For example, the tablespoon might have a blue handle, the teaspoon a red handle, and the half-teaspoon a yellow handle.)

- **Use color dots to mark temperatures** on the oven and stove dials.

- **Use color dots to mark the "start" buttons** of the microwave, food processor, bread machine, and other appliances. If you use color coding, it is wise to use the same color for "start" and "stop." One suggestion is to use green to signify "start," and red for "stop."

- **Purchase appliances and tools that are easy to manipulate.** For example, electric can openers take a lot of coordination. The Grippers™ brand of kitchen appliances are designed for people who have trouble with fine motor activities. They are easy to hang onto and easy to manipulate.

- **Purchase a volumetric beaker with a measuring bar for measuring liquids, a tabletop liquid measure cup**

(see photo), or color code the lines on a glass measuring cup. The measuring bar and table-top measuring cups are designed so you can see where the liquid is without having to get down to eye level with the measuring cup. If you use a traditional glass cup measure for liquids, color code the lines to add cues regarding where the liquid should be. The purpose in color coding is to allow your child to focus his attention on the task of cooking rather than reading. He will still have the printed word on the appliance or measuring cup, but the color coding removes any doubt he may feel.

- **If you use color-coded measuring equipment, try to purchase measuring spoons and cups that use the same color for ½ , ¼, and so on.** Regardless, mark recipes and directions with the color so your child knows what he's looking for.
- **Purchase removable, color-coded labels to mark foods in the freezer or refrigerator.** This will come in handy for labeling foods that are stored. Color code the labels by week for the refrigerator and month for the freezer. It is easier to toss out all the containers with the blue label when they are old than to look over all the labels for a specific date and decide if it's time to throw something out.
- **Use visual and audio timers for cooking.** Visual timers do not ring when time is up, but they may be easier to operate and keep track of for some. Audio timers may need to be digital or easy to operate. Use what makes sense for your child's abilities by accommodating your child's fine motor skills.
- **Purchase potholders that go over your hand like a mitt.** Choose styles without a lot of extra material that are soft and easy to move your hand in. Stiff oven mitts make it difficult to feel when you have a good grip on the pan.
- **Label shelves in your refrigerator and pantry with pictures and words to make it easy to find things.**
- **Keep spices and other baking supplies in organizers and bottles that are labeled and easy-to-read.** Find pictures or other visual methods to label things for children who are early readers.
- **Keep knives sharp.** A dull knife is much more dangerous than a sharp one.
- **Purchase colored cutting boards.** Use one color for meats and another for vegetables and fruits. This will be helpful in decreasing cross-contamination of foods.
- **Purchase spoons, spatulas, and other utensils that are easy for your child to hold. Some will need thicker handles than others.** Wooden spoons may be a good choice to avoid melting. The Good Grips® series of utensils is very good and easy to use.
- **Pre-measure spices and other dry ingredients for favorite meals.** Label and store in containers for use later.

COOKING METHODS

It is important to remember that any method of cooking is fine. Whether you choose to teach your child to use microwave meals, make meals from cans or a box, cook from scratch, or take out food doesn't matter. What matters is that your child realizes that he can prepare a meal (yes, calling for take out is preparing a meal).

You and your child will determine what the best combination of cooking methods is for him throughout his life. What we must avoid is denying our children opportunities to experience the type of cooking *they* are interested in. For instance, micro-

Using Visual Strategies in the Kitchen

A visual strategy is a method that uses symbols, photos, or color cues to make it easier or possible for someone to do something. For instance, your child's speech-language pathologist or teacher may have suggested labeling your house with photos and symbols paired with words during preschool and elementary school. Use this same strategy to help things go smoothly in the kitchen. Even if your child reads well, using visual strategies on recipe cards, around the kitchen, and to label things in the kitchen is one more way to present instructions. This is helpful when your child is working hard to learn something new. Visual systems, such as color-coded measuring tools, reduce frustration with reading. It's easiest to learn when you are able to focus on one skill at a time. Reading need not be a limitation in learning to prepare some foods independently.

wave meals are great. They are easy, they have directions, and they provide appropriate serving sizes. But what if your child wants to cook French fries, a frozen pizza, or cookies? All of these require different skills than using the microwave. If he does not learn how to make a favorite food properly and is determined to do it himself, it could be a disaster. This doesn't mean you are required to act on his every whim. It does mean telling him that you will work on a skill together, and eventually make a recipe together. It also helps if you tell him a particular day you will do this.

Some people with Down syndrome will never be interested in cooking, while others will not want to stop. If your child is simply not interested in the cooking process, he may still need to learn some skills, depending on the type of support he will need when he lives away from home. For instance, if he moves to a group living situation, he may not need to be involved in the cooking, but will need to help with the chores involved in cooking. Include him in shopping trips, cleaning the kitchen, and setting the table. If you want your child to live more independently, he will need to learn how to prepare his own meals. It's helpful to come up with a combination of meals he can purchase pre-cooked (from the deli, at the local store, or from a restaurant nearby) and easy-to-prepare meals such as frozen dinners. When you do, be clear about the amount of food to purchase and eat at a meal. It will be important to remain involved in what your child is eating when he moves out of your home—the easiest foods to obtain are rarely the least expensive or healthiest.

COOKBOOKS

Finding cookbooks appropriate for children and adults with Down syndrome is no easy task. Not only is it difficult to find cookbooks that are written at an appropriate reading level, but most recipes are written to yield four to six servings. Understanding and choosing to eat appropriate serving sizes is an important concern for people with Down syndrome. Those who live in apartments are preparing foods for one or two. Those who live in group situations may be cooking for six or more people.

Additionally, some cookbooks written for people with disabilities are appropriate for literacy and cooking skills, but the recipes included are hardly innovative or interesting. I am not convinced that every person with a disability needs or wants to learn how to make "Ants on a Log" (celery with peanut butter and raisins) or tomato soup from a can. For one thing, not everyone likes raisins. To top it off, soup now comes in ready-to-eat containers.

I've collected dozens of cookbooks—both designed for people with disabilities and not—and have not yet found one I can wholeheartedly endorse. See the References and Suggested Reading list for some cookbooks that might be useful. Choose cookbooks that fit your child and family.

MAKE YOUR OWN COOKBOOK

The best solution is to make your own cookbook. In fact, when I asked a group of parents of teenagers and adults with Down syndrome what they do with their child regarding cooking, all were making some sort of individualized recipe collection, including writing down the steps to microwaving a frozen dinner because the writing on the box was too small.

It makes sense to begin creating a cookbook when your child is young and shows an interest in helping with meal preparation. You can both refer to the recipe as you make the meal. Some people work best using note cards (5x7 cards are easy to handle), while others do best with regular notebook-sized pages. Whatever the size, shape, or method of recording your recipes, it's a good idea to laminate the pages or keep them in protective sleeves. Cooking is a messy business, after all.

There is some key information that should be included for every recipe in your recipe book, including:

- the name of the recipe,
- how long it takes to make this from start to finish,
- how many people the recipe should serve,
- the size of one serving,
- a general idea of cost,
- a specific list of ingredients,
- a specific list of tools and utensils needed,
- specific steps to make the recipe (you may need to break cookbook recipes into smaller steps),
- directions for storing leftovers,
- a rating for how good it is, and
- possible foods to accompany the dish to round out the meal.

Of course, as you begin to create your recipes, you won't have all this information. Gather it over time. If your child is young, some of this information or the way it is presented will change. However, the more information you gather, the more useful the cookbook will be for your child.

In addition to recipes, also consider including steps related to other mealtime tasks in the cookbook. For instance, list the steps to setting the table, running the garbage disposal, taking out the trash, and so on.

MODIFYING RECIPES

A template for a recipe page is provided in Section 4 for you to use to begin collecting recipes for your child. Even young children who are in the early stages of reading can have recipes to follow. Use symbols, pictures, and labels from boxes to create some of the first recipes.

A Note about Directions

Among all the cookbooks I have reviewed, only one includes a step in the directions that is vital for every cook to know. In her book, *Cooking Made Easy,* Eileen Laird lists "Wash your hands" as the first step to every recipe. It seems like a simple thing, but including this step in a recipe does two things: it keeps the chore of washing hands from being a battle and it reinforces that it must *always* be done. If your child is making three recipes in a row, it's better for him to wash his hands three separate times than it is to not wash them at all.

In addition, it is important to include reminders to turn off appliances and directions for food storage in the recipe. If your child doesn't need the reminder or has already performed the step, he will pass over it. Consider including a page in the recipe book with steps for cleaning the kitchen after cooking. This is especially helpful for items such as cutting boards or difficult-to-clean pots and pans. (See the Appendix for a list of food safety concepts to teach.)

Be sure to include any individualized directions your child might need. For instance, in her book, *Visual Recipes: A Cookbook for Non-Readers,* Tabitha Orr mentions heating water in a coffee machine rather than on the stove. I thought this was an innovative way to boil water for things such as oatmeal. However, the book does not list the steps for performing this task. Another example is frozen meals. If your child eats a particular brand of frozen meal often, list the directions on a separate recipe page. The writing on boxes is very small and this will help

Write and illustrate recipes in a method that makes sense to your child. Preparing foods is a skill of its own. It can be taught separately from literacy skills. As your child's reading skills change, so will your recipes. It makes sense not to use challenging words or multi-step directions in your recipes. Use words, symbols, and directions that are not challenging for your child as he learns to prepare foods. For now, let him focus on learning to prepare foods rather than on reading.

For adults who do not read, having a personal cookbook is still a good idea. Whether living at home or in a group situation, there will be things your child will want to do in the kitchen. He may want to learn something new or need help remembering how to do something he's done before. In these moments, having an individualized, personal cookbook will be very important. Include lots of photographs, pictures of your child, and labels or box tops from specific foods in the recipe. Your child will probably be very proud of his personal cookbook. Being able to do things on your own and obtain support without interrupting others is a great boost to self-esteem. For more information on creating a picture cookbook, see *Constructing a Picture Book,* listed in the References and Selected Readings.

There is no one right way to organize your child's recipe collection. It is important to organize them in a way that makes sense to your child. Ideas include:

- by recipe collections to create a menu (that is, first list the favorite menu, then the recipes for each dish in the menu),
- by food group,
- by entrée,
- by meal,
- by cooking method,
- alphabetically.

Include your child in making the cookbook as much as possible. He will be more excited about using the recipe collection if he has a part in creating it. Consider taking photographs of recipes and meals your child creates to include in the cookbook. You may even want to consider taking photographs of your child as he cooks to illustrate the recipe cards.

Grocery Shopping

Grocery shopping is an important component to cooking. Just as with cooking, there are a number of levels of participation. There are many skills and lessons that fit naturally into the process of grocery shopping for children with Down syndrome which can be found in Section 4. Older children and adults

with Down syndrome who have had limited experiences grocery shopping may benefit from some of the early grocery shopping activities as well. Playing "I spy" or having a scavenger hunt for items on the grocery list make the job fun and encourage problem-solving skills in the store.

As you begin to teach your child, it is helpful to choose one store to use for your grocery shopping escapades. Your child will be more successful in a familiar store where he can reliably predict where new items on his list can be found. Additionally, as your child becomes more independent, or if he wanders away from you, the familiarity of the store personnel will be helpful. Our first grocery shopping experiences were very positive, thanks to the help of our neighborhood Safeway store manager. She had experience with people with disabilities and played a key role in shaping the attitudes of the people who work in the store toward my son.

Grocery shopping must be planned in advance to be successful. First, the shopping list is created from a weekly menu. The menu you create takes into account your budget, time, and choice of meals. (See the next chapter.)

Second, make sure the shopping list is organized into categories that make sense to you and your child. One way to organize shopping lists is to group needed items in the following categories on the list:

- Bread
- Dairy

- Fresh fruits and vegetables
- Canned vegetables
- Canned fruits
- Canned juices
- Soups
- Pasta and rice
- Cereal
- Snack foods
- Frozen entrées
- Frozen juice
- Frozen desserts
- Frozen vegetables and side dishes
- Fresh meat
- Soda
- Medicine

Design "the list" in a way that makes sense to your child.

- Early readers may do better with one item per card with photos, words, or both. If you have Internet access, images of many items can be found online. As the list becomes more complicated, color code the index cards by food group (grains = brown; vegetable = green; fruit = yellow; meat = red; dairy = blue; sometimes = purple) or category.
- Pre-readers can participate by using a symbol system attached to the basket. When an item is found, it is removed from the list or strip.
- Use pre-printed shopping lists that already separate items by category or create a template for one of your own that has enough room for your child to add to the list himself.
- Organize the list items in the order they are found in your store. That is, if customers enter the store through the produce section and then proceed to the dairy section, list fresh fruits and vegetables first, followed by dairy products.
- Paste labels to the list to provide specific information about the item and brand.
- If numbers are difficult, use three labels, symbols, or photos to list three of one item.

Once the shopping list is written, you are ready for the actual shopping trip. As with anything, you want to set your child up for success. If your child is new to having duties during your shopping trip, keep his list very short and choose items that are important to him. If your child shows absolutely no interest in shopping and will not participate, you need to decide if this is a battle worth fighting. However, if your child's goal is to live on his own, he will need to be able to do this. To live independently, you need to be able to shop successfully from a planned menu and list and stay within a budget.

Tips for Making Visual Shopping Lists

Including visual cues in your shopping list takes a little time. Once you have collected the photos, symbols, or labels you need, it becomes much easier. Here are some methods for collecting visual tools for shopping lists and recipes.

- Many food manufacturers have web pages on the Internet where you can download photos to get a label or image of a product. To save an image from a web page, position the mouse arrow over the image and right click. A menu will appear on the screen. One option will be "save picture as." Choose this and save the file to a folder in your computer. You now have the image in your computer to use for your shopping list.
- Scan images or create pages of color copies at the copy store to make the list less cumbersome.
- Save labels from food items you purchase at the store as you use them. You can tape or glue them to the shopping list, copy them, or scan them to print from your computer.
- It may also be helpful for early readers if the categories of the shopping list are color-coded. For example, fresh vegetables and frozen vegetables can be written in green; fruits in yellow; dairy in blue; bread in orange; cereal in brown; pasta in black; and so on.
- Make reusable stickers of the images with a sticker-making machine or by printing the images on reusable sticker paper.
- Use a Polaroid or digital camera to take photos of items you need. An I-zone camera by Polaroid makes reasonably good one-inch photos that develop quickly. I-zone cameras have a variety of different types of film available including sticker film. Trim off the extra paper, peel off the backing, and you can stick the image on the shopping list.
- Cut pictures of grocery items from advertisements in magazines and newspapers.
- Use your imagination and collect symbols, photos, or labels that will make sense to your child and also make the shopping process a success. The most important part about shopping is to plan for success with each trip.

CHOOSING FOODS AT THE GROCERY STORE

You have your list, you have your money, you have your calculator to add up the prices. As your child gets older and shows an interest in grocery shopping or cooking, it is time to begin teaching him how to choose foods at the grocery store.

Food Containers. When purchasing any packaged food at the store, inspect it for damage or signs of tampering. Do not purchase packages with holes or cans with dents (especially dents on the seam of the can) or cans that are bulging (top or bottom popping up instead of laying flat) no matter how much they are marked down.

Bread. If purchasing "day old" bread or bakery products, look for signs of mold. Never buy a product with a damaged wrapper or package.

Fruit. Show your child how to look for signs of spoilage in different fruits. This includes bruising, shriveling due to dehydration, or broken skin.

Vegetables. Show your child how to look for signs of spoilage. This includes mold, discoloration, and damaged leaves or broken skin.

Milk and Dairy Products. Show your child how to look for the "use by" date. Additionally, teach your child not to eat foods just because the expiration date is coming. While it is important to throw out old foods, you do not want to encourage him to eat something up to avoid throwing out spoiled food. Rather, focus on purchasing reasonable amounts of food.

Eggs. Show your child how to open the egg carton to see if any are spoiled or broken. If your child has good fine motor skills, teach him to turn each egg in the carton to check for eggs that are broken, but dried, on the bottom side.

Meat. Show your child how to look for the "sell by" date. It is important to point out the difference between the "use by" date on the label of dairy products and the "sell by" date for meats.

There are many other grocery tricks people practice at the store. As you shop with your child, take advantage of teachable moments, when he is showing an interest, to teach him the things you feel are important for his success at the grocery store.

Shopping Skills at School

There are multitudes of skills for shopping that can be embedded in your child's work at school. In some situations, you may need to suggest the community application of a skill such as adding the prices of foods using a calculator, but learning calculator skills can be done at school. Here are examples of math-related skills that can be added to your child's IEP:

MATH SKILLS

- Using a calculator, Ian will add a list of 3 different whole numbers together and copy the total onto a piece of paper in the following progression:
  - one-digit whole numbers,
  - two-digit whole numbers,
  - three-digit whole numbers,
  - four-digit whole numbers.
- Using a calculator, Ian will add a list of number values with two decimal places, similar to money:
  - 2 number sets
  - 5 number sets
  - 7 number sets
  - 10 number sets
- Ian will demonstrate knowledge of matching prices to money by selecting bills and coins to equal the amount added on his calculator.
- Ian will demonstrate knowledge of higher and lower prices by
  - Matching the words "higher" and "lower" or "more" and "less" to three- and four-digit numbers.
  - Selecting the higher or lower price from a group of 2, 3, and 4 prices.

> ❑ Naming the higher or lower price verbally or by using AAC method.
- Given visual and verbal cues, Ian will record the weight of 4 different items using a produce scale.
- Given visual and verbal cues, Ian will demonstrate the difference between increasing and decreasing weight by adding or removing items from a produce scale.
- Ian will demonstrate correspondence of more and less weight to higher and lower price by matching the higher price to the higher weight and the lower price to the lower weight.

READING SKILLS

You may also want to consider teaching your child about the jargon found on food labels. In some situations, these words could be considered survival words for your child to learn to sight read. Remember, learning to read or manipulate numbers can continue throughout life. If your child finishes school without some of these skills, he may be interested in learning them later. By using visual strategies and multi-layered teaching strategies (such as "Match, Select, and Name" found in *Teaching Reading to Children with Down Syndrome* by Pat Oelwein), an adult can continue to add to his personal vocabulary just as we all do. Consider which of these terms are important for your child to identify on labels and include them in his survival words reading program.

LABEL LINGO

WORD ON LABEL	MEANING
- Free - No - Zero	The product contains none, or insignificant amounts of, something. For example, "Sugar free" means there is no sugar or sweetener (though there will likely be a sugar substitute). "Cholesterol Free" means there is no cholesterol in the product, and so on.
- Low fat	There are 3 grams or less of fat *per serving*.
- Low saturated fat	Less than 1 gram of saturated fat *per serving*. (There may be many grams of mono or polyunsaturated fats)
- Low sodium	There are less than 140 milligrams of sodium *per serving*. This is important for people who are on a "No Added Salt" or 4 gram sodium diet.
- Low cholesterol	There are less than 20 milligrams of cholesterol *per serving*.
- Low calorie	There are less than 40 calories *per serving*.
- Lean	Less than 10 grams of fat, less than 4 grams of saturated fat, and less than 95 milligrams of cholesterol *per serving* of this meat product.
- Extra lean	Less than 5 grams of fat, less than 2 grams of saturated fat, and less than 95 milligrams of cholesterol *per serving* of this meat product.
- Light	The product contains one of the following: ❑ ⅓ fewer calories than the regular product, ❑ ½ the total fat of the regular product, or ❑ ½ the total sodium of the regular product.

Leaving the Nest

Some young adults with Down syndrome will attend postsecondary school programs or other training programs for independent living. These programs are designed to help young adults with disabilities learn to manage living and working in the community with supports that are gradually reduced. However, the most common complaint I hear from parents who have children enrolled in these programs has to do with problems in teaching about meal management and grocery shopping. When you develop support systems for your adult child, ask questions such as:

- How much time is allowed for planning menus each week?
- How much time is spent preparing and planning for grocery shopping?
- Who is responsible for monitoring the menu planning and grocery shopping process?
- Who is responsible for ensuring that adequate time, preparation, teaching, and support is provided for menu planning and grocery shopping?
- We have been working on easy-to-prepare, healthy menus. Will the support personnel follow the dietary parameters we want for our child? (Be prepared to list them.)

Grocery shopping from a menu is an important skill for people who live on a budget. Adults with Down syndrome will likely always be on a budget. Therefore, this is an essential skill to teach, adapt, and modify for your child, regardless of where he lives.

If your child lives in a group home setting or another structured setting, talk with the support staff about including your child if he is interested in the menu planning and meal preparation process. Make sure there he has an effective method of communicating his preferences, his pleasure or displeasure, and hunger. Some suggestions of ways to do this are discussed in Chapter 9.

Although many people without Down syndrome do not follow a formal menu planning process, the structure and planning involved is a necessary component to helping your child manage his life, as well as to promoting healthy eating habits. If you do not address this in a thoughtful, consistent manner, it will be a huge stumbling block to your child's success away from home. While it may not be worth the battle at home, it is an essential issue for support people at postsecondary programs and other living situations away from home to tackle.

CHAPTER 16

The Art of Menu Planning

Everyone in charge of cooking plans meals. Some spend ten seconds planning; others, ten hours. For some it comes quickly; others labor over the details of the meal. Regardless, planning what to eat is part of the adult responsibility in the feeding relationship. It is one of the areas of the feeding relationship that you will begin to shift to your child through example and strategic activities over time.

Menu planning saves time, money, and stress, but the most important benefit is typically overlooked: satisfied customers. When family members know that food they like will be prepared, they are more likely to happily join mealtimes and even consider trying new foods. Additionally, if you have a method of menu planning, you will find it easy and natural to begin involving your child with Down syndrome in the task. Menu planning is not taught in most school settings, especially if your child with Down syndrome is included in a general education setting. The benefits of meal planning outweigh the cost in time for most parents.

Successful menu planning for your family is more than randomly choosing foods that sound as if they will go together. There are many philosophies to menu planning, but it doesn't need to be complicated. It involves considering:

- food preferences of family members,
- age appropriateness of food,
- appropriate foods for special dietary needs (gluten-free, weight management, and so on),
- appropriate foods for chewing ability,
- family members' skills with utensils,
- appearance of food,
- amount of time to prepare food,
- temperature of food when served.

Step One: Food Preferences of Family Members

The first step involves creating a master list of everyone's favorite foods. Include columns for: Main Dishes, Breads & Cereals, Vegetables, Fruits, Dairy, and "Sometimes" Foods.

Using the Family Food Favorites table in Section 4, fill in everyone's favorite foods for each category. To reduce confusion later, it is helpful to color code the foods by family member. It might be easier to fill out a separate sheet for each family member in the beginning and combine foods in the table later. Foods and entrées that more than one family member like should be in a separate color from the others. Here's one color system, for an example:

- Foods more than one person likes: black.
- Mom's favorites: blue
- Dad's favorites: brown
- Elizabeth's favorites: green
- Jack's favorites: red

This will be your master list for creating menus and strategically introducing new foods to your family. As your family's preferences change, you will need to update the list. Once every six months or so will do unless there are dramatic changes. This activity is also provided for you to do with your child in Chapter 10.

ACTIVITIES TO INVOLVE YOUR CHILD

- **Have your child help you create the list of favorite foods.** Start by discussing what foods she likes best. When you have done this a few times, add other family members to the discussion. Have her choose the color coding for each person. As handwriting skills increase, she can write the list, or parts of it, with you. If your child is a prereader use symbols, photos, or labels of favorite foods to glue into the chart. If you do this visual version, you might need to make it poster-sized so there is enough room.
- **When categorizing the favorite foods, talk about foods that are considered "combination foods" (pizza, casseroles, and so on), if appropriate.** If she is interested in this, put symbols next to the combination foods to signify the food groups, as in the Activity 3 in Section 4. That is, pizza is a bread, vegetable, dairy, and meat. As you do this, your child may learn to identify different food groups within foods. This is a helpful skill for evaluating snack and meal menus for balance.

Step 2: Check the Calendar

We all lead busy lives. Sometimes the addition of IEP meetings, private therapy, and special after school activities makes a day feel out of control. Maybe every day feels out of control. For some people, too much structure feels oppressive or causes problems when plans change without notice.

If you have not used a menu planning process before, the evening meal is the easiest place to start. It's usually the most hectic, so the structure of menu planning will be more helpful to you. As you grow comfortable with the process, consider expanding it to include lunchtime if family members pack lunches from home. Creating a snack menu is also a helpful tool to most families. It is comforting to know what is available and appropriate for snacks on any given day.

When you begin to plan menus, take a look at your calendar and make a note of which days you need to eat quickly, which days are more leisurely, and who will be at the meal. Now list the days of the week on a sheet of paper. Circle any day you are willing and able to spend thirty minutes or more making dinner.

ACTIVITIES TO INVOLVE YOUR CHILD	<ul><li>**Look over the family calendar together.** Ask your child about activities that are or are not on the calendar that she is involved in.</li><li>**If your child will be out doing an activity during a meal-time, talk about where and what she will eat instead.**</li></ul>

Step 3: Let's Play Poker

In today's world, menu planning only works if it's done with an element of flexibility. In fact, an easy way to structure menu planning is by thinking of it as a game of poker. This is because:

1. it's easiest to plan for just five days a week rather than all seven,
2. when you do, it's best to create a full house: three meals that take preparation, two that require next to no preparation, or vice versa.

When you do have more time for preparing meals, prepare twice as much and freeze the extra for another day. You can plan to use the frozen extras on a day when there is little time for preparation, but everyone is home. However, don't fill up all your days you are home with labor-intensive meals because things will undoubtedly change. You want to create a list with enough flexibility that you can move meals around if things change.

Some families, often those with three or more children, have planned cooking days each month. On these days they make weeks' worth of casseroles, bread, waffles, and other entrées that can be frozen for future use.

> Cooking ahead of time can be a real timesaver for large families and also with special diets! For me, the most important things are to get organized and set about three hours aside for me to get cooking. At the end of three hours, I want everything cooked, put away or at least cooking, and the cleanup done.
>
> We have just purchased an upright freezer. Our chest-type freezer made it difficult to keep track of what was in there. We have rows set up on the top shelf for lunches. I have one shelf that is marked clearly "Non-GF," as we do not all have celiac disease. As my supply of prepared meals starts to look depleted, I start thinking about what day I have the time to cook and start making sure I have all the cooking ingredients I need.

Once you have a good idea of what's coming up the next week, you can write your tentative menu for the week and the list of foods you'll need to prepare them. This list will become your shopping list. When you write your menu use the "family favorite" list for menu ideas. Beyond planning balanced menus, your primary goal is to have at least one favorite food for each family member in every menu. This helps ensure there is at least one thing each person will eat at a meal.

Shopping list	Monday	Tuesday	Wednesday	Thursday	Friday

I've been doing this for so long now that I only need to plan for the main meals. The side dishes and desserts or snacks that satisfy everyone's various tastes quickly fall into place. There are times, however, when some menus are not as successful as I'd like. When this happens, we get out the "family favorite" worksheet and start over. Usually what I learn is that someone's tastes have changed!

ACTIVITIES TO INVOLVE YOUR CHILD

- **If you decide to swap days for a menu, share why** you changed Tuesday's menu to Thursday.
- **If you are running late getting a meal started, let your child decide whether she is willing to wait another hour for her expected meal, or whether she'd rather eat something else sooner.** This will only be successful if either answer is all right with you.

Step 4 : Evaluate the Menu

The next step is to evaluate the menu you have created for:
- food preferences of family members,
- age appropriateness of food,
- appropriate foods for special dietary needs (gluten-free, weight management, and so on),
- family members' skills with utensils,
- nutritional balance of the menu (see below),
- appropriate foods for chewing ability,
- appearance of food,
- amount of time to prepare food,
- temperature of food when served.

There are many ways to evaluate menus for nutritional balance, ranging from basic to complex. Because menu planning is an easy and natural time for nutrition education, it is best to model a method that your child will find easy to use as she learns to help with the menu planning. (See the Menu Planning activity in Section 4.) A method of evaluating menus that is often overlooked in nutrition education programs is to consider balance. This method focuses on obtaining the most nutrition from a menu in a way that is relatively quick and simple.

With this in mind, "balance" is defined as:

- Including three of the five bottom food groups (grains, fruit, vegetable, dairy, or meat) for each meal (breakfast, lunch, and dinner).
- Including two of the five bottom food groups for a planned snack. Planning for snacks is one way to begin to change how you view them. Rather than being impulsive moments of "cupboard cruising," they become nutritionally important, planned events. See "Are Your Snacks Balanced?" in Section 4 for more information.

Once you have looked at the menu together and are satisfied that it meets the criteria for nutritional balance, talk about other concerns that are important for your family. They might include:

- Other special concerns that are important for someone in your family, such as gluten sensitivities, diabetes, or trouble with textures.
- Whether or not there are enough lower fat options for family members who are trying to lose weight.

It's usually best to write menus and shopping lists in pencil so you can easily make changes without having to recopy the menu.

ACTIVITIES TO INVOLVE YOUR CHILD

- **After you have finished the menu, have your child check that each day's menu has at least one food that each family member likes.**
- **If your child is learning food groups, use the pyramid activity in Section 4 to categorize foods for nutrition balance.**
  You don't have to do this every day. Make use of teachable moments when your child is interested in helping with the meal or talking about menus. Sometimes this is a good way to talk through your child's frustration about wanting to eat a favorite entrée every day. If reading, writing, and communicating is difficult for your child, use symbols to represent the menus. Work with just one meal and one menu at a time. In doing this, there is a natural way to introduce the concept to your child and build on it.

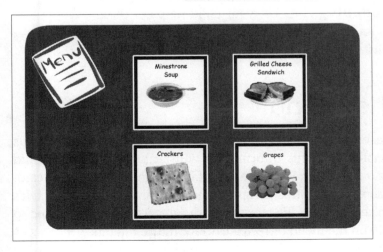

- Use words, symbols, labels, or photographs to post the menu for the meal. This helps your child prepare herself for what is coming.
- Use the symbols on your menu list. Have your child take those symbols and place them within the color-coded pyramid to show food groups and menu balance. If your child is learning food groups, talk about that. If your child is ready to learn about nutritional balance, talk about it as you put the symbols in place.

Step 5: Make a Shopping List

Once you have created your menu, it's time to make the shopping list. If you generally follow your menu plans and shop from your list (rather than purchasing things that look good at the time), you will notice it takes less time to shop, it is easier to stay within your grocery budget, and it takes less time to prepare meals. I have to admit to being reluctant to believe this as a student. It wasn't until I began practicing a loose system of menu planning that I realized it was true. This is a difficult admission for a person who resists structure. Refer back to the previous chapter, for suggestions about making a shopping list your child can use.

ACTIVITIES TO INVOLVE YOUR CHILD

- **Go through the pantry and refrigerator for ingredients you need for your menu and create the shopping list.**
- **When you go shopping, give your child a portion of the list to gather in the store.** When your child is young, this may mean choosing one food from a category of foods, such as bagels, to cross off the list. Even if you go together to get the foods, it is important to learn to shop from a list. Shopping lists can be visual or written. There are more ideas for shopping in Chapter 15.
- **Read the weekly food advertisements for the store where you do your grocery shopping.** You might want to do this before you create your menu to give you ideas for the week. Cut out photos of the foods you will purchase to use for a visual shopping list. Talk about unfamiliar or uncommon foods when you see them.
- **Go through coupon books and ads together, looking for coupons for your shopping list.** Let your child help cut them out for your shopping trip. As a reminder, put a star or some sort of mark next to items on your list that have coupons.

Step 6: Price and Rate the Menu

Once you have purchased the foods for a menu, keep track of how much foods cost for each entrée. Keeping this information will be helpful as your child begins to practice shopping on a budget. Write the cost of ingredients on the recipe card. In some cases, it is cumbersome to keep track of spices and other smaller ingredients. It's probably most important to keep track of the more expensive items (meat, cheese, and so on). Write the cost estimate on the menu or recipe card for future reference.

After you have served the meal, rate how everyone liked it. Your child can poll family members to see what they thought of the meal. Have your child keep your family's favorite menus—especially the ones *she* likes most—in a notebook for future reference. There's no need to recreate the wheel each week.

Give Your Child Increasing Responsibilities

It is easy to see how you can begin very early to include your child in this process. One of the greatest benefits of sharing this responsibility with your child as early as possible is that you can share your values regarding healthy eating. While you are writing menus, shopping, or clipping coupons, you can have light-hearted discussions about nutrition balance, serving sizes, healthy eating, and making realistic choices about food and activity. When you do this, remember your child will be looking to see that your actions fit your words. For instance, if you tell your child that it's important to use margarine instead of shortening in cooking, make sure you do that yourself. Or, if you tell her to watch how much caffeine she drinks in soda, be careful about how many cups of coffee you drink each day. Your messages about food, nutrition, and activity must be consistent, and obvious by your own personal choices.

As your child becomes independent, she may rebel in her food and menu choices for a time. That's typical of all children. Most likely she will come full-circle and return to the habits and values she learned when menu planning with you.

As your child begins to understand what menu planning is all about, here are some activities that can help her take on more responsibility:

- Have your child create the menu, evaluate it for balance, and make the shopping list for one day of the week.
- If your child takes her lunch, have her create a lunch menu and shopping list for school following the steps above.
- Have your child use the same type of system for developing snack menus and a shopping list for appropriate snacks.
- If you are embarking on a new weight management program, choose new entrées to try from a low fat cookbook together.
- Have your child participate in choosing menus from a cookbook with photographs if reading is difficult.
- If a special event is coming, have your child plan the menu and shopping list. For example, a birthday party, the Fourth of July, Memorial Day Picnic, and so on.

The Bottom Line

Beyond saving time and money, a primary reason to make menu planning a habit is to teach your child with Down syndrome some necessary skills. When students with Down syndrome are included in general education classes, their exposure to topics such as menu planning are usually limited or nonexistent. While the benefits to inclusion far outweigh the benefits of learning about menu planning at school, it is a skill your child will need to have to live as independently as possible. In addition, if you consider that children with and without Down syndrome learn more about day-to-day household management from the examples of their parents, how can you avoid developing a menu planning routine?

Section Four:
Learning Activities

This last section includes a variety of activities for teaching nutrition concepts. These activities are written as group activities with everyday life in mind. Some will be easy for families to use and others will be too contrived or perhaps involve too much detail. Use the activities that fit your family's values and lifestyle or modify them so they do. In addition, not every person with Down syndrome or his family needs to do each activity. Your child may not be interested in learning about balanced snacks, while others will find the topic fascinating.

The activities are written in a lesson plan format to encourage educators, parent group leaders, dietitians, nurses, physicians, coaches, and health educators to include nutrition education materials designed for people with Down syndrome and related disabilities.

Key elements to each lesson include:

- ***Uncluttered design:*** Many nutrition education materials are beautifully designed and fun to look at, but most have too much information or too many distracting images on a page. Children and adults with Down syndrome may be distracted by this extra information or find it difficult to locate the information they need.

- ***A literacy-friendly font:*** In other words, the font uses letter shapes more consistent with handwriting than typical manuscript fonts such as "Times New Roman."

  This is a literacy-friendly font.

  This is not literacy friendly.

- ***A visual component along with the text:*** People with Down syndrome learn to read at different rates and attain different levels of ability. It is important to provide information in a way that encourages reading and literacy, but also is understandable to early readers. Whenever possible, include package labels, photographs, or symbols such as Mayer-Johnson's *Picture Communication Symbols* in nutrition education activities. Sources of visual tools or software for making them are listed in the Resources.

- ***The use of color to provide visual cues:*** The activities in this book are designed to teach new food-related skills. However, completing an activity also means being able to read the words, pictures, or symbols involved and do something with them, such as grouping similar foods or placing a food in the correct spot on the Food Guide Pyramid to determine the balance of a menu. Providing color-coded materials will help your child or student be successful regardless of literacy skills or previous exposure to the topic. The color-coding system I recommend is the one used on the pyramid inside the cover of this book:

  - Bread, Cereal, Grain Group: Brown
  - Fruit Group: Yellow
  - Vegetable Group: Green
  - Meat and Meat Substitute Group: Red

❑ Milk Group: Blue
❑ Sometimes Group: Purple

You can color the entire area in the food guide pyramid for activities using the food group, or use the color cuing in a more subtle way by adding a colored outline of the food group box.

These methods are helpful for people who are emerging readers, nonreaders, or people who have not worked with food groups before. They make it easier to focus on teaching nutrition education concepts rather than literacy skills.

Learning should always be fun. Learning about nutrition to promote a healthy lifestyle really means discovering how food fits into life. Viewing it as an adventure and discovering new things together makes it more interesting not only for your child, but for you as well.

Making Food Cards or Picture Food Models

Many of the learning activities in this section require food cards or photo food models. A *food card* is a visual representation of the food: a label from the product, a box top, a photograph from a magazine, or a line drawing. Each picture or symbol also has the name of the food written in a literacy friendly font or handwritten. You may want to type or write the name of the food in the color of the corresponding food group (see above for recommended colors). A *photo food model* is a little different. These are photographs or drawings that are done to scale, which means they are the same size as the serving size they depict. Photo food models are difficult to make. Sources for them are listed in the Resources. Food cards are appropriate for most activities. If you are focusing on serving sizes with your child, however, using food models may be a good idea.

HOW TO MAKE FOOD CARDS

There are many ways to make food cards. Make food cards that will be durable enough for your child. Some children are very careful with materials, while others are not.

DIRECTIONS FOR COMPUTER USERS

Choose durable paper stock. If you are making food cards on a computer, use card stock paper. You can cut and paste images into a drawing program. This may allow you to draw a color-coded box around the image or fill the background with color. Otherwise, print the images at a reasonable size with the words typed below. Cut the cards square and color the edges with felt pen to color-code them for the pyramid activities. Programs and web pages with drawings and photographs of food are listed under "Visual Supports" in the Resources.

MAKING FOOD CARDS BY HAND

To make food cards by hand, choose colored tag board or thick construction paper the color of the food group codes for the background. Cut squares of an appropriate size for your child to handle. Glue photos from magazines, boxes, or labels to squares of the matching background color (for instance, glue a photo of a milk carton to a blue square and photos of fruits to yellow squares), or draw pictures of food on the squares. Print the names of the foods beneath the pictures.

LAMINATING FOOD CARDS

Laminating your food cards will keep you from having to make them over and over. You can use a hot or cold laminating machine or sheets of laminate available at most office supply stores. When using cold laminate and sheets of laminate, you may not be able to apply Velcro if you are using a PECS type system. (It won't stick.) If you plan to glue something to the laminated cards, contact paper is the best cold laminating method to use.

Laminators and sticker makers are popular with scrapbooking enthusiasts and can be found in many craft stores. They make stickers (with laminated or unlaminated tops) and magnets, and can laminate symbols. The most popular model is the Xyron Sticker Maker & Laminator, which comes in a variety of sizes (www.stickermaker.com). Another similar product is the Brother Bakster and LX series of cool laminators (www.brother.com/usa/laminator/laminator_cntr.html).

Making food cards takes some time. In most situations, however, you only need to do it once and you will have the set of learning tools you and your child need to learn about healthy eating.

Activity 1: Learning to Group Foods

DESCRIPTION:

This color-coded activity can be used for any lesson using the Food Guide Pyramid. For instance, grouping foods is taught with the additional color cue. If your child cannot yet read, but can identify colors, he can learn to group foods, plan menus, and categorize foods of all kinds using the color-codes to guide him.

NUTRITION OBJECTIVES:

- To group foods according to the Food Guide Pyramid.

INCIDENTAL LEARNING OBJECTIVES:

- Categorize foods by groups using pictures or symbols.
- Match food pictures or symbols to food names or words to put in the pyramid.
- Match by foods to group by color ("put green on green," matching the border or background of the vegetable name and picture).
- Add sight words of favorite foods to reading vocabulary.
- Count the number of foods in each food group in the pyramid.

MATERIALS NEEDED:

- Color-coded Food Guide Pyramid (see inside front cover of the book)
- Color-coded photos, package labels, or symbols of foods (see instructions for making food cards in the introduction to Section 4). Each food card should also include the name of the food printed on the front

DIRECTIONS:

1. Choose the primary objective of the activity (grouping, menu planning, color, and so on). Only teach one thing at a time.
2. Have your child place foods in their food group.
3. Check placement by matching color borders (brown to brown, and so on).

SUPPLEMENTARY ACTIVITIES:

Use this pyramid and the color code system any time you use the Food Guide Pyramid. Continuing to use the same teaching tools throughout will help your child focus on new concepts rather than worry about the change in format.

My Food Guide Pyramid

Sometimes

(soda, ice cream, french fries, chips, candy, and so on)

ICE CREAM

Milk

Adults: 2 servings a day
Kids: 2-4 servings a day

Yogurt

Meat (beef, fish, chicken, & dried beans)

5-7 ounces (after cooking) a day

Vegetable

3-5 servings a day

Fruit

2-4 servings a day

Grain (bread, noodles, crackers, cereal, rice)
6-11 servings a day

The Picture Communication Symbols © 1981-2002 Mayer-Johnson, Inc., Solana Beach, CA, USA. All rights reserved world wide. Used with permission.

fruit roll	fruit	grapefruit	grapes	pineapple	apple
banana	strawberry	orange	broccoli	celery	lettuce
vegetables	tomato	cucumber	carrot	chicken leg	steak
lunch meat	meatball soup	hamburger	fishburger	ham	milk
milk	cheese	yogurt	bread	bread	rolls
spaghetti	asparagus	pastry	pancakes	cupcake	cake
candy bar	chocolate	crackers	soft ice cream	scrambled egg	egg on toast
waffle	toast	pizza	taco	salad	ketchup

The Picture Communication Symbols © 1981-2002 Mayer-Johnson, Inc., Solana Beach, CA, USA. All rights reserved world wide. Used with permission.

Activity 2: Learning the Food Guide Pyramid

DESCRIPTION:

The following pages are designed to introduce food groups, the Food Guide Pyramid, number of suggested servings, and serving sizes. There is a lot of information on these pages. It's best to introduce one topic at a time. For instance, focus the lesson on the pyramid, number of servings, *or* serving sizes rather than introducing all of these concepts at once.

OBJECTIVES:

- Name food groups in the Food Guide Pyramid by writing (or placing a food photo or symbol on) the name of the food group on the pyramid.
- Select or name three foods from each food group.
- Write or gather symbol cards to represent the number of servings for each food group.
- Explain what it means to eat foods "sometimes."

INSTRUCTIONS:

1. Copy a set of handouts for each person.
2. Color the foods their usual colors or your own unique design. Color the pyramid as shown on the inside front cover of the book.
3. Cut out individual foods to make food cards for other activities.
4. To make food cards, follow the instructions in the introduction to Section 4. You can use package labels of favorite foods or draw pictures of favorite foods together to use as food cards. The more individualized the food cards available, the more interested your child will be.
5. Talk about the foods in each group. Share which ones you like and which ones you don't eat very often. Make natural conversation about foods. Match the color of the border or background of each section of the pyramid with the border or background of the corresponding food group.
6. Talk about the meaning of "sometimes." (Sometimes means you don't have something from that group every time you eat. If we only eat them "sometimes," they stay special, too. But if we eat a big serving all the time, they are not special anymore, and they make it harder to eat healthfully.)

SUPPLEMENTARY ACTIVITIES:

- With tape, make a large pyramid with the corresponding sections on the floor.
- Place photos or empty packages of foods in the appropriate group.
- Make a separate box to the side of the pyramid for combination foods.
- Talk about the food equation that makes up that combination food—for instance, taco = tortilla (bread) + hamburger (meat) + beans (grain) + lettuce (vegetable) + cheese (dairy) + tomato (vegetable) + salsa (sometimes). This is explained in more details in the combination foods activity. (See Activity 3 on page 292.)
- Gather photos or symbols so you have enough to represent the number of recommended servings for each group and place them in the pyramid on the floor.
- Measure the suggested serving size of different foods. Put them on a regular-sized dinner plate, bowl, or glass to see what a serving size looks like.

My Food Guide Pyramid

Sometimes
(soda, ice cream, french fries, chips, candy, and so on)

Milk
Adults: 2 servings a day
Kids: 2-4 servings a day

Meat (beef, fish, chicken, & dried beans)
5-7 ounces (after cooking) a day

Vegetable
3-5 servings a day

Fruit
2-4 servings a day

Grain (bread, noodles, crackers, cereal, rice)
6-11 servings a day

Water
6-8 glasses a day

The Picture Communication Symbols © 1981-2002 Mayer-Johnson, Inc., Solana Beach, CA, USA. All rights reserved world wide. Used with permission.

What goes in the **Milk** Group?

skim milk

2% milk

chocolate milk

cheese

yogurt

cream

sour cream

How much is 1 serving?

 1 cup of Milk

The Picture Communication Symbols © 1981-2002 Mayer-Johnson, Inc., Solana Beach, CA, USA. All rights reserved world wide. Used with permission.

What goes in the **Meat** and **Meat Alternative** Group?

chicken

cheese
(cheese can be a meat or dairy if you
eat at least 1 ounce)

lunch
meats

eggs

nuts

beef

turkey

tuna

How much is 1 serving?

 2-3 ounces of meat
(after it is cooked)

OR

1 egg

OR

2 ounces of nuts

The Picture Communication Symbols © 1981-2002 Mayer-Johnson, Inc., Solana Beach, CA, USA. All rights reserved world wide. Used with permission.

What goes in the **Vegetable** Group?

broccoli

tomato

tomato juice

celery

peppers

asparagus

green beans

spinach

carrots

How much is 1 serving?

1 cup of raw vegetables
OR
½ cup of cooked vegetables

The Picture Communication Symbols © 1981-2002 Mayer-Johnson, Inc., Solana Beach, CA, USA. All rights reserved world wide. Used with permission.

What goes in the **Fruit** Group?

watermelon

cherries

apple

banana

pineapple juice

pear

orange

grapes

strawberry

How much is 1 serving?

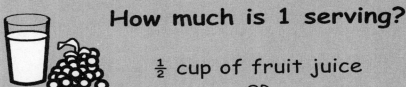

½ cup of fruit juice
OR
½ of a large piece of fruit
OR
15 grapes or raisins

The Picture Communication Symbols © 1981-2002 Mayer-Johnson, Inc., Solana Beach, CA, USA. All rights reserved world wide. Used with permission.

What goes in the **Bread** and **Cereal** Group?

noodles

bread

challah

english muffin

hot or cold cereal

muffin

crackers

hamburger bun

rice

How much is 1 serving?

  ½ hamburger bun OR
1 slice of bread
OR
 ½ cup of noodles OR
⅓ cup of rice

The Picture Communication Symbols © 1981-2002 Mayer-Johnson, Inc., Solana Beach, CA, USA. All rights reserved world wide. Used with permission.

What goes in the **Sometimes** Group?

candy

soda

french fries **or** onion rings

ice cream treats

cake

cookies

oil

chips

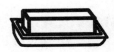

butter or margarine

How much is 1 serving?

One medium-sized serving of a dessert OR candy
OR
1 cup of chips
OR
a small French fries

The Picture Communication Symbols © 1981-2002 Mayer-Johnson, Inc., Solana Beach, CA, USA. All rights reserved world wide. Used with permission.

Activity 3: What's a Combination Food?

DESCRIPTION:

Combination foods contain ingredients from more than one food group and are usually main dishes. Pizza, tacos, hamburgers, casseroles, and similar entrées are considered combination foods. To use the Food Guide Pyramid for determining macronutrient meal balance or food groups eaten in a day, it is important to know what is in a "combination food."

OBJECTIVES:

- Your child will name three foods from his favorite food list that are considered combination foods.
- Your child will select or name the food groups that are included in these three favorite foods.
- Your child will place food symbols, photos, labels or word cards in the appropriate food groups for a combination food on a pyramid. Your child will count the number of food groups represented in each combination food.
- Your child will build a "food equation" with food symbols, photos, or words to represent the food groups included in other combination foods.

MATERIALS NEEDED

- Photos, boxes, or symbols of many different types of combination foods (pizza, hamburger, lasagna, tacos, and so on)
- A blank food pyramid or one made with tape on the floor
- A bulletin board, tape to post symbols on the board, or "Post It Poster Board" to create food equations is helpful
- The handout with examples below

INSTRUCTIONS:

1. This is like playing a game of "food math." In order to understand what food groups are in combination foods, you must be able to identify the foods in an entrée. Make a list of some of your child's favorite combination foods.
2. Cut out pictures of the foods from magazines or print photos from the Internet or a program such as *Picture This*. (See Resources.) Page 298 may also be photocopied and the food items cut apart to complete the sample exercises on the following pages.
3. Find photos or make word cards for the main ingredients in a combination food (Pizza = bread + vegetable + meat + cheese).
4. Put the "food equation" together like a math problem.
5. Once you have the correct food equation, count the number of different food groups in each food. You may want to place the photo/symbol/word cards in an empty, color-coded pyramid to help your child visualize what this looks like.
6. This activity leads into planning balanced menus, which is done using a pyramid as an evaluation tool.

What Food Group is Pizza?

Lots of foods have more than one food group in them. Things like Pizza, tacos, hamburgers, and spaghetti all have more than one food group. How do you know what food groups you ate? You pick it apart!

Pizza		crust		tomato		pepperoni		cheese		sausage		mushroom
	=		+		+		+		+		+	

Pizza is made of the crust, tomato sauce, cheese, pepperoni, mushroom, and sausage.

How does this fit in the Food pyramid?

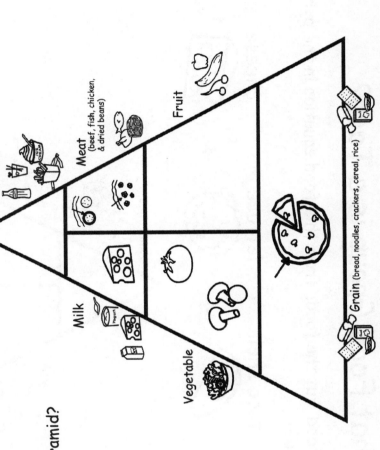

Sometimes

Meat (beef, fish, chicken, & dried beans)

Fruit

Milk

Vegetable

Grain (bread, noodles, crackers, cereal, rice)

The Picture Communication Symbols © 1981-2002 Mayer-Johnson, Inc., Solana Beach, CA, USA. All rights reserved world wide. Used with permission.

What Food Group is a Taco?

Taco is another combination food. Put the foods from this food equation in the pyramid. How many food groups are in a taco?

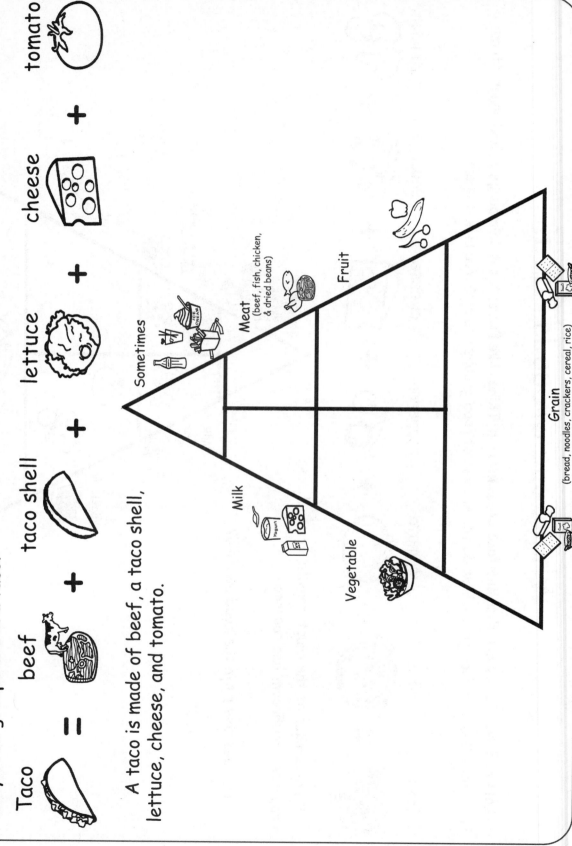

Taco = beef + taco shell + lettuce + cheese + tomato

A taco is made of beef, a taco shell, lettuce, cheese, and tomato.

The Picture Communication Symbols © 1981-2002 Mayer-Johnson, Inc., Solana Beach, CA, USA. All rights reserved world wide. Used with permission.

Complete the Food Equation

Now you try to complete the food equation for some combination foods. Each box needs a food.

Can you finish the food equation for a hamburger?

hamburger  = [ ] + [ ]

Can you finish the food equation for a cheeseburger?

cheeseburger 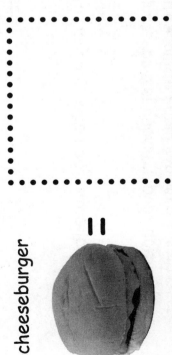 = [ ] + [ ] + [ ]

The Picture Communication Symbols © 1981-2002 Mayer-Johnson, Inc., Solana Beach, CA, USA. All rights reserved world wide. Used with permission.

Casseroles are always made of more than one food group, which means they are a combination food. Lasagna is a casserole.

Can you make the food equation for Lasagna?

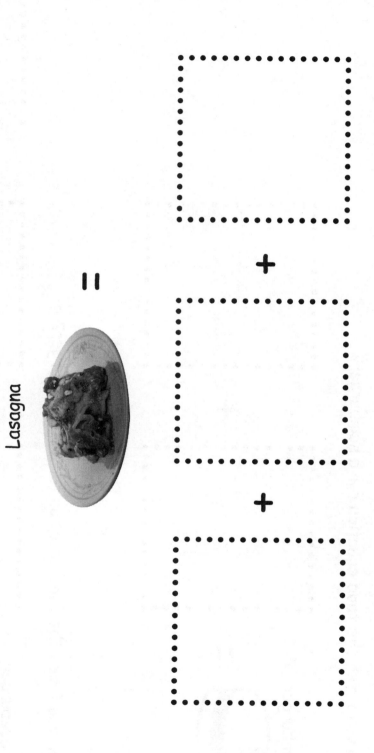

Lasagna

The Picture Communication Symbols © 1981-2002 Mayer-Johnson, Inc., Solana Beach, CA, USA. All rights reserved world wide. Used with permission.

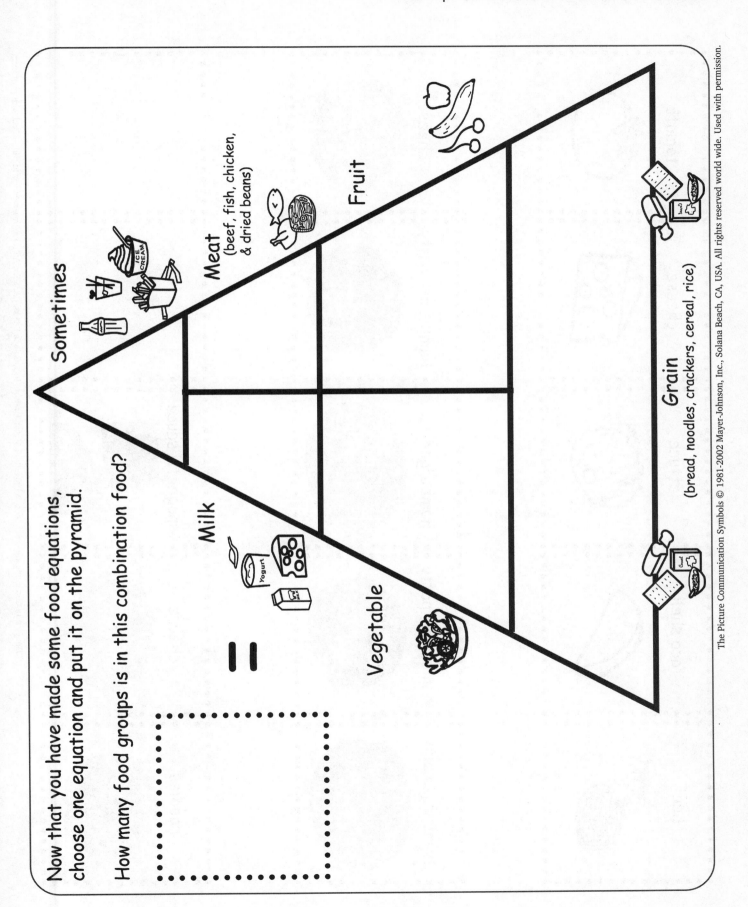

Now that you have made some food equations, choose one equation and put it on the pyramid.

How many food groups is in this combination food?

The Picture Communication Symbols © 1981-2002 Mayer-Johnson, Inc., Solana Beach, CA, USA. All rights reserved world wide. Used with permission.

tomato

cheese

lettuce

taco shell

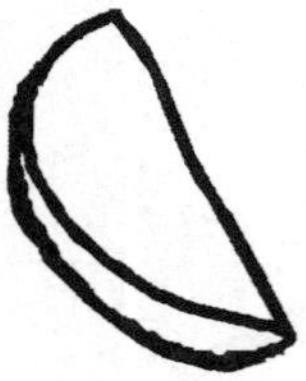

beef

cheese

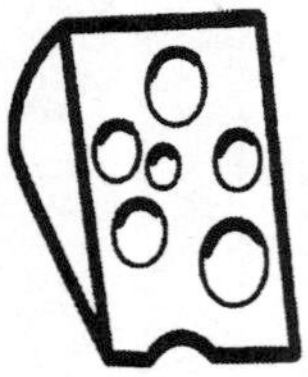

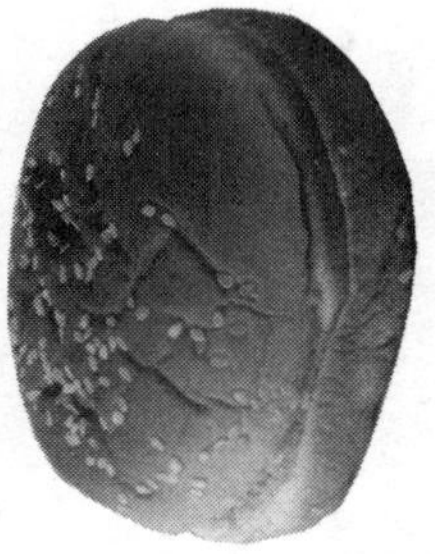

hamburger patty

hamburger bun

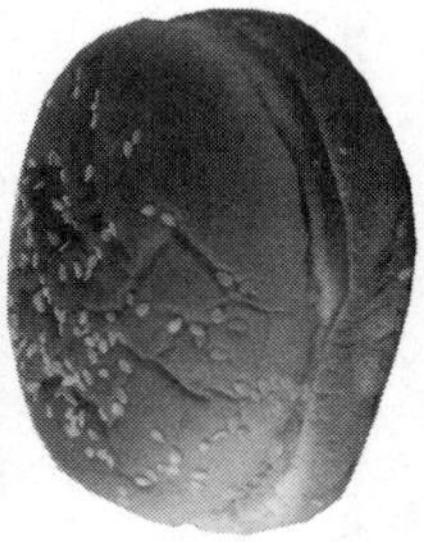

hamburger patty

hamburger bun

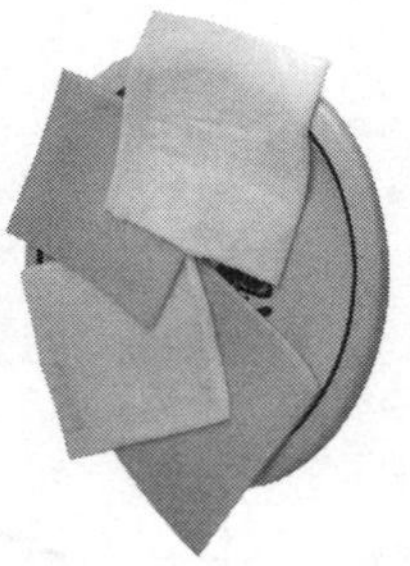

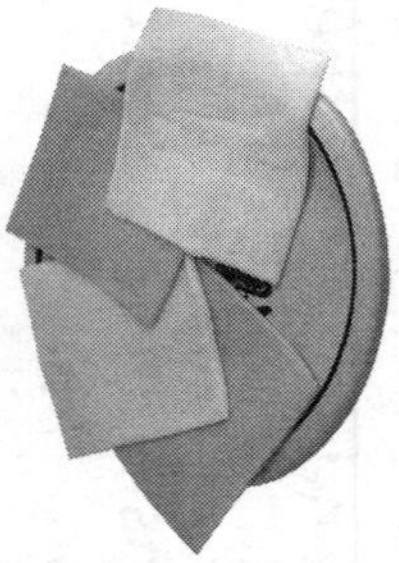

spaghetti sauce

cheese

noodles

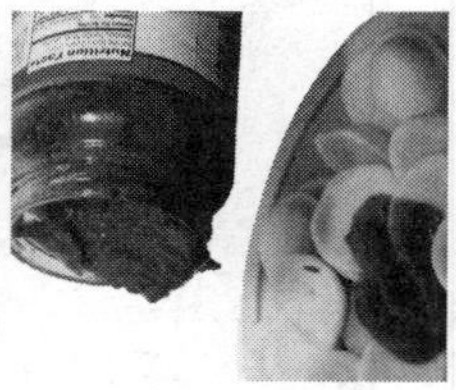

The Picture Communication Symbols © 1981-2002 Mayer-Johnson, Inc., Solana Beach, CA, USA. All rights reserved world wide. Used with permission.

Activity 4: Family Food Favorites

DESCRIPTION:

Knowing what people like to eat is one of the first steps in successful menu planning. It is also a great way to start conversations about different foods. Not everyone likes the same things! These directions are written for a child who is not yet writing or who can focus better on the activity if someone takes notes for her. Feel free to change the activity in ways that will make it more motivating for your child. The process of information gathering is the main objective.

MATERIALS NEEDED:

- Colored pens, felt pens, crayons, or pencils
- Family Favorite Form (below) or a piece of paper

INSTRUCTIONS:

1. Discuss with your child your desire to make meals that have food that everyone will want to eat. Your goal is to provide at least one favorite food for each person at mealtimes.
2. Show your child the pens and have her choose a color.
3. Talk with your child about her favorite foods. As she tells you a food, write it in the appropriate column of the list. Ask her to help you categorize the foods.
4. Ask your child to help you find out the favorites of other family members. She can ask them what their favorite food is while you write it down.
5. Before you begin your interviews, have your child select colors to represent each person.
6. Dutifully record the responses of each person interviewed. Try to remain in the background, only providing cues when needed.
7. When you are done, talk about the list.
8. Copy the list to a new form to reduce confusion. Underline foods chosen by more than one member with their color code. For instance, Apples may be written in red (Mom) and underlined in blue, purple, and green (Sam, Amy, and Dad).

For this list to be effective, it is important to update it on a regular basis. Usually once every six months is appropriate, but if you find fewer and fewer people eating the meals you make, you might want to begin the process again.

Breakfast Foods	Lunch/Dinner Main Dishes	Fruits	Vegetables	Bread, Grain, and Pasta	"Sometimes" Foods

The Picture Communication Symbols © 1981-2002 Mayer-Johnson, Inc., Solana Beach, CA, USA. All rights reserved world wide. Used with permission.

Activity 5: Are Your Meals Balanced?

DESCRIPTION:

Eating balanced meals is the easiest way to get the most nutrition value from meals. Getting the right balance of vitamins and minerals is important, but so is eating meals that have the right balance of carbohydrate, protein, and fat. The following activity will help you and your child create menus that are balanced for the macronutrients: carbohydrate, protein, and fat. Having a balance of these nutrients helps us avoid running out of energy at unexpected times. Drops in blood sugar can lead to inappropriate, stubborn, or aggressive behavior. This can be avoided by learning to plan meals with a blend of macronutrients. In addition, if menus are planned using a variety of foods over the course of the week, it is more likely that vitamin and mineral needs will be met as well. Note: Serving sizes and unique entrée combinations are not the focus of this activity. Allow your child to be creative in his menu planning. He will test your dedication to the definition of a "balanced" menu by making unique selections.

MATERIALS NEEDED:

- Food cards, drawings, or pictures of foods from magazines
- Copy of an empty food pyramid
- Blue painter's tape to make a pyramid on the floor, if desired

INSTRUCTIONS:

1. Explain to your child and family the importance of eating foods that provide the right balance of food groups at the right times in the day. Eating balanced meals helps the energy from your food last longer so you don't get tired, hungry, and grumpy before you eat again. To make your meals balanced, you need to have some carbohydrate, protein, and fat in every meal. The easiest way to know whether you have a little bit of each of these in your meal is to look at the food groups.
2. Divide your family into groups. If this isn't possible, do the activity together, allowing your children to lead the menu creation process.
3. Gather food cards, drawings, or pictures of food.
4. As a group, create a balanced meal from the foods in the photos.
5. Place the foods in their corresponding food group in the pyramid.
6. Evaluate for balance by asking: "Are three of the bottom five food groups represented?" If not, what food can be added to create that balance?
7. Decide if this is a menu you would like to try as a family.
8. Once your child demonstrates an understanding of the "balance" concept, create and evaluate some menus using his favorite foods. Remember, any combination is acceptable.
9. Write down meal combinations in the pyramid titled "You're the Cook!"

DISCUSSION TO ACCOMPANY HANDOUTS:

In order to fuel your body so it works well, it is important to plan balanced menus. One way to decide whether a menu is balanced is to look at how many food groups it has. A meal (breakfast, lunch, or dinner) is considered balanced if it has three of the bottom five food groups in it. That is, it must have three food groups not including the "sometimes" group.

EXAMPLES:

Jenny is making dinner. She decided to make macaroni and cheese, chips, ice cream, and a soda for dinner.

- Question: What are the food groups represented in this menu?
  - Answer: 3 sometimes foods, 1 bread, 1 milk.
- Question: Does it have three of the five bottom food groups?
  - Answer: No.
- Question: What can we add to make Jenny's menu balanced?
  - Answer: Add anything from a food group other than bread, milk, and the sometimes group to balance this meal. Peaches, for example, would balance this menu.
- Question: What can we take away to keep the meal from being too big?
  - Answer: Jenny's menu with peaches added to it is a lot of calories for one meal. The foods in the sometimes group are high in calories. She can take away the chips or ice cream, or she can drink water, milk, or juice instead of soda.

Mark is making a lunch. He has decided to have a waffle with peanut butter and syrup for dinner with a soda to drink.

- Question: What are the food groups represented in this menu?
  - Answer: 1 bread, 1 meat (the peanut butter), and 2 sometimes.
- Question: Does it have three of the five bottom food groups?
  - Answer: No.
- Question: What can we add to make Mark's menu balanced?
  - Answer 1: Add anything from a food group other than bread, meat, or sometimes to balance this menu.
  - Answer 2: If Mark drinks juice or milk instead of soda, he will have a balanced meal, too.
- Question: Is there anything you would take away from this menu?
  - Answer: Mark might want to drink milk, juice, or water instead of soda for a healthier looking menu.

Sylvia is making breakfast. She has decided to have a chicken sandwich (with lettuce and tomato), orange juice, and hot chocolate (made with milk).

- Question: What are the food groups represented in this menu?
  - Answer: 2 breads (the top and bottom of the bun), 1 meat, 1 fruit, and 1 milk.
- Question: Does it have three of the five bottom food groups?
  - Answer: Yes.
- Question: What can we add to make Sylvia's menu balanced?
  - Answer: Nothing. It is balanced already.
- Question: Is there anything you would take away from this menu?
  - Answer: No.

Kyle is making a frozen dinner with lasagna, broccoli, and garlic bread. He is going to have water to drink with his meal.

- Question: What are the food groups represented in this menu?
  - Answer: 2 bread (the noodles and the bread), 1 meat, 1 milk (the cheese in the lasagna), and 1 vegetable.
- Question: Does it have three of the five bottom food groups?
  - Answer: Yes.
- Question: What can we add to make Kyle's menu balanced?
  - Answer: It doesn't need anything to be balanced.
- Question: Is there anything you would take away from this menu?
  - Answer: Kyle has done a good job of planning a healthy meal.

Note: Activity 3 can help your child learn to break apart the food groups in combination foods such as casseroles, tacos, or sandwiches.

How many food groups does it take to make a nutritionally - balanced meal?

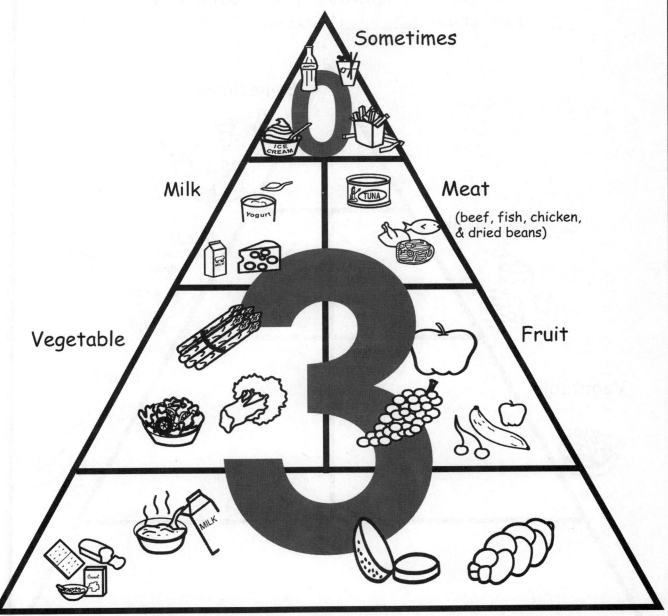

The Picture Communication Symbols © 1981-2002 Mayer-Johnson, Inc., Solana Beach, CA, USA. All rights reserved world wide. Used with permission.

You're the Cook!

What will you make for Breakfast, Lunch, or Dinner today?

This menu is for   Breakfast   Lunch   Dinner (circle one)

I will eat it at: _____ (fill in time)

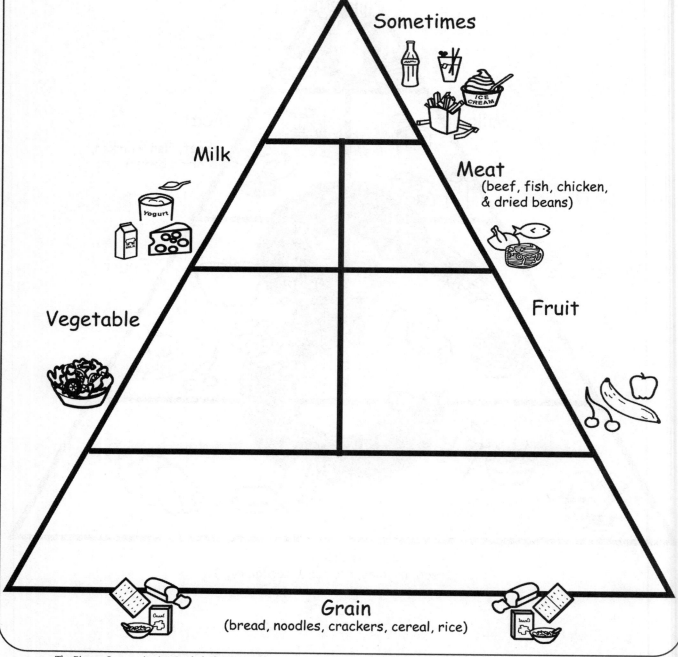

Sometimes

Milk

Meat
(beef, fish, chicken,
& dried beans)

Fruit

Vegetable

Grain
(bread, noodles, crackers, cereal, rice)

The Picture Communication Symbols © 1981-2002 Mayer-Johnson, Inc., Solana Beach, CA, USA. All rights reserved world wide. Used with permission.

Activity 6: Are Your Snacks Balanced?

DESCRIPTION:

Most people equate eating a snack with unplanned, unregulated eating. People who eat to promote healthy lifestyles, however, know that planning for snacks is just as important as planning for meals.

Generally, snacks should be small, and are only necessary if meals are spaced more than five hours apart. In addition, snacks should not be chosen from foods primarily in the sometimes category. Using a method similar to the one for balancing meals described in Activity 5, snacks can be balanced by ensuring that at least two of the bottom five food groups are represented. In doing so, your child will be eating a better balance of carbohydrate, protein, and fat than she would if she chose foods from the sometimes category, which are often full of calories, but low on nutrition value.

Note: Serving sizes and unique combinations are not the focus of this activity. Allow your child to be creative in her menu planning. She will test your dedication to the definition of a "balanced" menu by making unique selections. As your child gains confidence in choosing a variety of snack combinations that are balanced, talk about using appropriate serving sizes for snacks when planning.

MATERIALS NEEDED:

- Food cards, drawings, or pictures of foods from magazines
- Copy of an empty food pyramid
- Blue painter's tape to make a pyramid on the floor, if desired

INSTRUCTIONS:

1. Divide your family into groups. If this isn't possible, do it together, allowing your children to lead the creation of snack combinations. Be sure to write down the ideas you come up with on the family favorite sheet. It will be helpful to you later.
2. Gather food cards, drawings, or pictures of food.
3. As a group, create a balanced snack from the foods in the photos.
4. Place the foods in their corresponding food group in the pyramid.
5. Evaluate for macronutrient balance by asking: "Are two of the bottom five food groups represented?" If not, what food can be added to create that balance?
6. Decide if this is a snack that any of you would like to try.
7. Once your child demonstrates an understanding of the "balance" concept, create and evaluate some snack combinations from her favorite foods. Remember, any combination is acceptable.
8. Write down snack combination ideas in the pyramid titled, "You're the Cook!"

DISCUSSION TO ACCOMPANY HANDOUTS:

In order to fuel your body so it works well, it is important to plan balanced menus. One way to decide whether a snack is balanced is to look at how many food groups it has. A snack is considered balanced if it has two of the bottom five food groups in it. That is, it must have two food groups not including the "sometimes" group.

EXAMPLE:

Sarah is going on a trip to the zoo. There will be a long time between lunch and dinner so she wants to take a snack along. She has decided to take a bag of Doritos, soda, and some peanut M&Ms with her.
- Question: What are the food groups represented in this menu?
  - Answer: 3 sometimes foods.
- Question: Does it have two of the five bottom food groups?
  - Answer: No.
- Question: What can we add to make Sarah's menu balanced?
  - Answer 1: Sarah can take some beef jerky instead of chips. She can also take some peanut butter crackers instead of peanut M&Ms.
  - Answer 2: Adding a bottle of water along with the soda or instead of the soda would be healthier for an outside activity.
- Question: Is there anything you would take away from Sarah's snack?
  - Answer: All three of the foods can be taken away from her snack to make a healthier one.

Howard needs to take a snack with him to work. He wants to try to eat healthier than he has been. He has decided to take an orange and a soda for his snack
- Question: What are the food groups represented in this menu?
  - Answer: 1 fruit, 1 sometimes.
- Question: Does it have two of the five bottom food groups?
  - Answer: No. It only has one.
- Question: What can we add to make Howard's snack balanced?
  - Answer: Add a bag of pre-portioned snow peas or another snack item from any food group except sometimes or fruit.
- Question: Is there anything you would take away from Howard's snack?
  - Answer: It would be healthier for him to drink water or juice, but if he only has one soda each day, this is a reasonable snack choice.

Georgina buys her snack at the vending machines at work for her break. Today she decided to try a can of Slim-Fast® instead of a soda and a package of animal crackers.
- Question: What are the food groups represented in this menu?
  - Answer: Slim-Fast® and other drinks are hard to put into food groups because they have all sorts of vitamins added. However, we are going to think of drinks like this as being similar to an Instant Breakfast® drink and call it 1 milk.
- Question: Does it have two of the five bottom food groups?
  - Answer: No, but it qualifies as a balanced snack because it has added vitamins. It is like having a glass of milk with vitamins.
- Question: What can we add to make Georgina's menu balanced?
  - Answer: We can add some beef jerky or fruit.
- Question: Is there anything you would take away from Georgina's snack?
  - Answer: No.

Note: Slim-Fast®, breakfast drinks, and meal replacement drinks such as Ensure® can generally be counted as balanced. Meal replacement bars are trickier. Nutri-Grain®, for instance, will qualify for a balanced snack combination (grain and fruit), but not for a meal. Most of these bars will need to be evaluated on an individual basis. In this case, it is most important to base the decision on your values about food and whether or not your child is likely to eat these types of snacks to avoid cooking in the future.

Julie went to the vending area at the hotel for a snack. She decided to buy a bag of microwave popcorn and a candy bar.

- ■ Question: What are the food groups represented in this menu?
  - ❑ Answer: 1 sometimes and 2 grains (the popcorn bag says it serves 2).
- ■ Question: Does it have two of the five bottom food groups?
  - ❑ Answer: No.
- ■ Question: What can we add to make Julie's snack balanced?
  - ❑ Answer: Add another food from anything except the grain group.
- ■ Question: Is there anything you would take away from Julie's snack?
  - ❑ Answer: It would be good for Julie to share her popcorn or take half of the bag home.

How many food groups does it take to make a
nutritionally - balanced snack?

Sometimes

Milk

Meat

(beef, fish, chicken,
& dried beans)

Vegetable

Fruit

Grain
(bread, noodles, crackers, cereal, rice)

The Picture Communication Symbols © 1981-2002 Mayer-Johnson, Inc., Solana Beach, CA, USA. All rights reserved world wide. Used with permission.

You're the Cook!

What will you make for snacks today?

Times I need to have a snack: AM, NOON, PM, Bedtime.
(circle one)

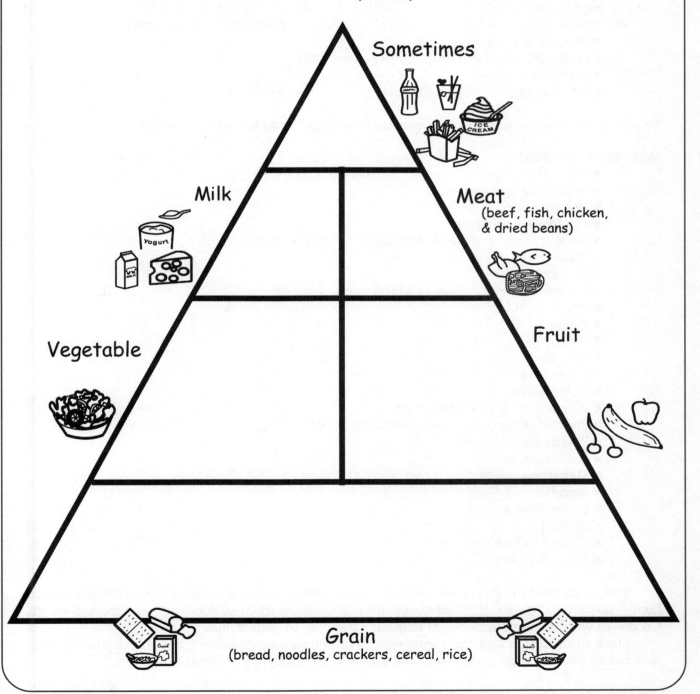

Sometimes

Milk

Meat
(beef, fish, chicken,
& dried beans)

Vegetable

Fruit

Grain
(bread, noodles, crackers, cereal, rice)

The Picture Communication Symbols © 1981-2002 Mayer-Johnson, Inc., Solana Beach, CA, USA. All rights reserved world wide. Used with permission.

Activity 7: How Much Is in Your Serving?

DESCRIPTION:

One of the easiest ways to eat less is to make sure the amount of food you are eating is really "one serving." Most people decide how much they are going to eat by using their eyes to measure. But this is not a very accurate way to gauge a serving size. Why? When you are hungry, your eyes might estimate "one cup" as being larger than it actually is. And when you are not hungry, or working hard to lose weight, your eyes might underestimate the size of "one cup."

What your eyes see as being "a serving" of a food is influenced by many things:

- how hungry you are,
- what type of plate, bowl, or cup you are using,
- your mood, and
- whether or not you like the food.

This activity helps you teach your eyes what "a serving" looks like on your dishes.

MATERIALS NEEDED:

- Measuring cups
- Measuring spoons
- Dietary scale
- Liquid measuring cup
- Deck of cards in a box or tied together with rubber band
- Tennis ball
- Baseball
- CD jewel case
- One-inch cube
- Plates
- Bowls
- Glasses
- Coffee cup
- Boxed cereal
- Play dough or raw hamburger
- Pieces of fruit (apple and orange are good)
- Pitcher full of water
- Peanut butter
- Margarine
- Bread
- Cooked pasta
- Cooked rice
- Cooked vegetables
- Salad dressing

This is the most fun if it is done as a discovery activity with a lot of people. Use foods that your family eats often. The foods listed above are merely suggestions of foods to measure and weigh. Choose to weigh and measure foods that have meaning to your family.

Place all the dishes and measuring devices on the counter or table. Some things you will measure before you use them, others you will measure after they are portioned.

Divide the foods among participants so that everyone is serving at least one food. It is often a good idea to have more than one person serving cereal, pasta, rice, and ice cream. These are foods that different people often take different amounts of. For practicing serving sizes of meats and cheese, use leftovers or make mock meats and cheeses out of play dough.

Once each participant has dished up the amount they typically eat as one "serving," the real fun begins. Measure the portion on the plate, in the bowl, or glass using the appropriate measure. Write down how much each person served and compare it to serving sizes on the box or in the Food Guide Pyramid. (See handout.) It is very rare for a person to always be accurate when estimating serving sizes.

OTHER ACTIVITIES:

1. Compete to see who gets the closest to a proposed serving size.
2. Compare servings to visual equivalents:
   a. Deck of cards = 3 ounces of cooked meat
   b. One-inch cube = one ounce of cheese
   c. CD jewel case = one slice of bread
   d. A paper matchbook = one tablespoon of margarine or one tablespoon of salad dressing, mayonnaise, or oil.
   e. Tennis ball = size of an apple or pear serving or 1 cup of rice.
   f. Baseball = size of a peeled orange, a cooked potato serving, or 1 cup of cold cereal.
3. Compare equal servings in different containers.
   - In other words, measure one cup of a cereal such as corn flakes. Pour the measured cereal into a common cereal bowl and see how much room it uses.
   - Next, pour the cereal into a smaller bowl to see how it looks.
   - Last, pour the cereal into a larger than usual bowl.
   - Talk about how different the serving sizes look. How do you feel about the amount of cereal in the small bowl as compared to the large bowl? Does it seem as if you are getting more?
   - Repeat this with other types of dishes using servings of different foods. What does 3 ounces of cooked steak look like on a dessert plate? On a dinner plate? Which one looks like you are eating more?
4. Is it more or less?
   a. Have someone measure 3 or 4 servings of pasta or rice and place them in 3 or 4 different types of plates and bowls.
   b. Bring them out labeled "Exhibit A," "Exhibit B," and so on.
   c. Have people write down which one has the most and which one has the least rice.
   d. Compare answers before revealing they are all the same.
   e. Repeat with juice or water.

Practice evaluating how much you are eating during light-hearted moments at dinner or another meal by comparing what is on your plate to the visual comparisons or by actually weighing and measuring your servings. It can take quite a while to learn how different containers or dishes can change the appearance of a serving. Remember, even if you are fairly accurate at estimating now, it is important to check your serving sizes periodically by measuring and weighing what you are eating. Your "serving" may get bigger or smaller over time with your mood, hunger, or the flavor of the food.

Refer to the guide below for suggested serving sizes.

What Makes a Serving?

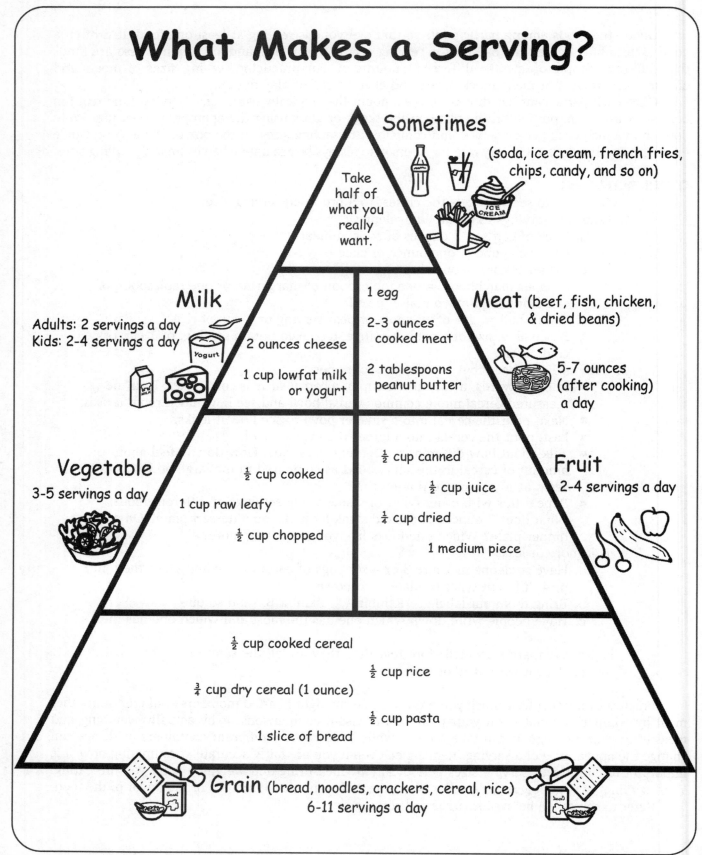

Sometimes

(soda, ice cream, french fries, chips, candy, and so on)

Take half of what you really want.

Milk

Adults: 2 servings a day
Kids: 2-4 servings a day

2 ounces cheese

1 cup lowfat milk or yogurt

1 egg

2-3 ounces cooked meat

2 tablespoons peanut butter

Meat (beef, fish, chicken, & dried beans)

5-7 ounces (after cooking) a day

Vegetable

3-5 servings a day

½ cup cooked

1 cup raw leafy

½ cup chopped

½ cup canned

½ cup juice

¼ cup dried

1 medium piece

Fruit

2-4 servings a day

½ cup cooked cereal

½ cup rice

¾ cup dry cereal (1 ounce)

½ cup pasta

1 slice of bread

Grain (bread, noodles, crackers, cereal, rice)
6-11 servings a day

The Picture Communication Symbols © 1981-2002 Mayer-Johnson, Inc., Solana Beach, CA, USA. All rights reserved world wide. Used with permission.

Activity 8: Be a Water Expert

DESCRIPTION:

Water is a very important part of a healthy lifestyle. However, it is often something we take for granted. Without enough water, your child may experience headache, change in appetite, and become very grumpy. In addition, children, teens, and adults with Down syndrome need water to avoid medical concerns such as constipation.

Your child needs to understand why water is important, how it affects her health, how it affects how she feels if she doesn't get enough, and how to tell if she needs more water.

INSTRUCTIONS:

The following activity is written with a group in mind. However, you can do this at home with only your child by adapting the discussion that accompanies it. Read through the activity to learn the basic information needed. Include that information with your child as you do the activity.

MATERIALS NEEDED:

- 3 clear plastic bottles (1 or 2 liter bottles work best) with labels removed
- 2 cups corn syrup
- Red sprinkles (very fine sprinkles, not the crystallized ones)
- 2 cups of hot water
- Funnel (optional)
- 2 quarts of water in a separate jug with lid
- 8-12 empty drinking glasses
- Small container of food coloring
- Towels (optional, but a good idea)

INSTRUCTIONS:

1. Ask the group or your child:
    - Do you drink water?
    - Do you like to exercise?
    - Do you like to play games like soccer or go hiking?
    - Are you thirsty *right now!?*
      If your mouth is dry *right now,* then you are about 2 percent dehydrated and you need a drink of water. This means you are short 2 percent of the water your body needs.
2. Explain: Water is an essential nutrient for your body. It helps your body work right. It helps your blood move through your veins, and it helps your kidneys wash out things your body doesn't need. It helps keep you cool when you are hot because of the weather or because you are sweating a lot during a game of soccer.
3. There are lots of ways to get water. Do you know some?
   Some examples include:
    - from drinking water or other fluids that have water in them,
    - from the foods you eat, and
    - your body produce some water when it turns food to energy.
4. How much water do you need each day?
    - 2.5 liters (about 2 quarts)

■ 40 ounces of it should come from what you drink unless you are a serious athlete and then you need more. The rest will come from the foods you eat. *Have your child pour the 40 ounces of water from the jug into drinking glasses to count how many glasses of water it takes to drink 40 ounces. Talk about different types of containers or ways to get that much water (a small bottle of water is usually 15 ounces).*

PREPARE BEFOREHAND OR TOGETHER:
■ Fill one clear plastic bottle with enough light corn syrup that it can be seen when you hold it up for the group. Put cap on.
■ Fill one clear plastic bottle with very hot water. Put cap on.

DEMONSTRATION SCRIPT:
Tell the group or your child:
"The amount of water you drink makes a difference in the way your body works. When your body has plenty of water, your blood looks like this:"
Hold up bottle with hot water and shake it to show the water moving around freely.

"When you are dehydrated, or do not drink enough water, your blood is a little bit thicker; it looks something like this":
Hold up bottle with corn syrup and move it so that the syrup oozes around.

"Think of how much more work it is for your heart to pump the thicker blood around in your body."

"Water also makes a difference in how the many nutrients and other important things in our blood work in our body."

"Let's pretend these sprinkles are vitamins and minerals that your body needs to work well. When you don't drink enough water, it takes a lot longer for these vitamins and minerals to get into your blood stream."
Pour red sprinkles into the corn syrup bottle. They should sit on top and be difficult to mix up; they will not dissolve readily. Move the syrup around to illustrate the point.

"But when your body has enough water, the nutrients from food can get into your bloodstream really fast. Look at the difference."
Pour red sprinkles into the bottle with hot water (hot water helps accentuate the point you're trying to make). Shake it so the sprinkles dissolve.
"You can see what a difference drinking enough water makes to how your body works and how you *feel* every day."

1. How do you know you need more water?
■ You are thirsty or have a dry mouth.
■ You are tired.
■ You have a headache.
■ You feel like you just can't wake up in the morning or all day.
■ You are moving slower than you usually do.
■ You just don't care about anything.
■ You are not hungry, but you should be.

■ It is hard to think about things you usually enjoy thinking about, like calling a friend or what you will do the next day.

If you are doing a sport or on vacation where it is hotter than you are used to, you may feel fine at the beginning of the day. If you do not drink enough water, you may begin to feel some of the things listed above after a while. You may not even start to feel a head-ache or sluggish until after the activity is over or you have come inside from the heat.

2. What will you do if you are feeling thirsty or have any of the other signs of being thirsty during or after exercise or being out in the heat?
   A. Drink.
      ❑ If you know you are going to be playing hard in a sport or exercise, drink at least 2 cups of water a few hours before. Drink 1 cup of water for every hour you are playing the game or exercising. Then drink at least 2 cups of water in the hour after the game or exercise.
      ❑ If you are from somewhere cool like Oregon or Maine and you visit a hot place like Arizona, San Diego, or Texas, drink at least 2 cups of water before going out for a long walk or to play in the pool. You should also drink some water when you come inside from the heat, and while you are outside.
   B. Get the most fluid you can from food. Most foods have water. Which ones are the best? (Brainstorm a list of ideas together.)
      ❑ Watermelon
      ❑ Oranges
      ❑ Cucumber
      ❑ Celery
      ❑ Most fruits and vegetables
3. Sometimes foods take away more water than they give to your body. What foods do you think might do that? (Brainstorm a list together.)
   ■ Alcohol
   ■ High fat foods such as chocolate, butter, oil, cakes, cookies
   ■ Foods with a lot of salt such as jerky and chips
   ■ Most baked goods, such as bread

SUPPLEMENTARY ACTIVITIES:
■ Get some old magazines and cut out photos of foods that are good sources of water. Make a poster with all the photos. With this as a guide, spend a day or two keeping a list of the foods you and your child eat from this list. You can also make check marks when you eat a food that is a good source of water.
■ If you are taking a vacation to a much warmer climate, make a list of ways to keep from getting dehydrated. How will you pack water when you are out sightseeing? What foods can you order from restaurants that will help? What will you do if you start to get a headache? Don't forget to talk about the possibility of needing to locate the bathrooms at new locations when drinking more water.

Activity 9: Keeping Track of What You Eat

DESCRIPTION:

For children, learning about foods and amounts can be a lot of fun. Rather than looking at it as a way to monitor the amount your child is eating, look at it as an adventure of discovery and learning. What your child learns will shape how he feels about food and eating later in life. Learning to keep track of foods is an activity that can be worked into math, reading, and life-science (health education) concepts.

For adults, becoming aware of the food you eat during the day is one of the first steps to successful weight management for a healthy lifestyle. One of the first steps to making healthful changes is understanding how you are eating. Beginning the process by keeping a detailed food record is overwhelming for everyone. The first step is to learn to keep track of what you are eating.

INSTRUCTIONS:

1. Copy the handout on the following page.
2. Color code the food groups as needed for reading level.
3. Before you and your child eat, make a check mark in the triangular box of the food groups represented at the meal. You may want to review lessons about food groups, the Food Guide Pyramid, and combination foods beforehand.
4. Compare what you check at the end of the day to what is recommended. Is it more or less than you thought? Is there a food group you didn't eat? If so, is it one you dislike?

SUPPLEMENTARY ACTIVITIES:

- Count the number of servings and graph them by food groups. Draw a line across the bar graph where the number of recommended servings is to see if you ate more or less (see handout).
- This can also be the first activity that leads to learning to keep a food record. The next step would be to work on goal-setting together (see next activity).

Keeping Track of Food Groups

Put a "✓" or "✗" in a box for each serving you eat from a food group.

Sometimes

Milk
(2-4 servings)

Meat (2 servings)
(beef, fish, chicken,
& dried beans)

Vegetable
(3-5 servings)

Fruit
(2-4 servings)

Grain (6-11 servings)
(bread, noodles, crackers, cereal, rice)

The Picture Communication Symbols © 1981-2002 Mayer-Johnson, Inc., Solana Beach, CA, USA. All rights reserved world wide. Used with permission.

How Does Your Food Measure Up? Graph Your Servings!

Bread, Cereal, Pasta, Crackers, Rice	Fruit and 100% Fruit Juice	Vegetables and Vegetable Juices	Milk and Dairy Products	Meat, Kidney Beans, Soy Beans, Tofu, and other Legumes	"Sometimes" foods: Soda, Diet Soda, Candy, Chips, Ice Cream	Combination Foods (taco, pizza, etc.)
★★★★★★	★★★★★★★	★★★★★★	★★★★★★★★	★★★★★★★★	★★★★	★★★★★★

The Picture Communication Symbols © 1981-2002 Mayer-Johnson, Inc., Solana Beach, CA, USA. All rights reserved world wide. Used with permission.

Activity 10: Setting Goals

DESCRIPTION

Setting goals and keeping track of them is a very important part of making successful changes, as well as building self-esteem. Learning to set a reasonable, easy-to-reach goal takes time. However, once learned, it is the foundation for planning for changes, learning new skills, and organizing your schedule.

If your child has decided to set goals for making changes in her eating style, one of the earliest challenges you will face together is choosing a method for writing and keeping track of the goals she sets. This must be done in a manner that shows respect both for her desire for change and her literacy skills. Remember, this is not the time to focus on improving literacy, writing, or math skills. Your focus and your child's interest must be on setting goals to promote a healthy lifestyle.

If your child is not yet able to read, but very interested in changing her eating habits, it is still appropriate for her to set goals. Use picture or sticker-oriented record-keeping methods to write goals or be her secretary and write them for her.

This set of handouts and instructions is designed to help you and your child through the process of setting goals and evaluating their effectiveness. Most goals will require a way of keeping track of choices your child makes related to the goals set. For goals made about food and activity choices, use the record-keeping handouts provided in Activity 11. In addition, your child may want to use the tools provided in Activity 12.

More information about goal setting is available in the section titled "Goal Setting 101" in Chapter 13.

MATERIALS NEEDED:

- Goal setting and goal evaluation handouts
- Felt pens, highlighters, pens, pencils, photos or symbols of food
- Calendar of the month with holidays noted
- Weekly calendar with special events noted
- Weekly calendar with hourly grid
- Stickers

DISCUSSION:

Discuss the reasons for goal-setting with your child, covering these points in words that make sense to her:

"When you decide to make changes to improve your health, you have to do four things":
- Decide to make changes for yourself (not others) that will last a lifetime,
- Discover, through learning more about good health habits, what kind of changes to make,
- Write down a plan for success,
- Break the plan down into small, weekly steps that are easy to reach.

"Together, you and I can":
- Discover what areas you and I can improve in our own lives,
- Make a plan to do it,
- Create and evaluate goals each week that are easy to reach.

"I would like to be your partner [unless she is doing this with another group] and for you to be my partner. As partners, we play a big role in each other's success. Not because we will be able to make each other do anything, but because we will work together as a team to reach our individual goals. Your goals will be different from mine, but we can talk about what makes it hard, or the choices we made in different situations."

SETTING PERSONAL GOALS:

Successful goals:

- are 100 percent achievable,
- are easy to visualize as successful,
- define only one step.

Make Them Easy to Reach. A good goal is one that has a 99.9% chance of happening because it is so easy to do! For example:

- I will eat an apple instead of a bag of chips after school on Monday. OR
- I will walk the dog around the block three times on Tuesday and Thursday.

Why make goals that are super easy to reach? Because it is important to set goals that you know you will be successful doing. It's no fun to make goals you can never do. If a goal is too big of a change, you might do half of the goal, which is much better than before, but not feel like you are successful because you didn't reach the goal you set. If you do *better* than your goal because it was easy, then you have the satisfaction of doing *better* than anyone expected! In fact, you may reach your rewards faster that way, too.

Make Them Specific. Another important part of writing goals is to make them very specific. For example:

- I will eat a fresh fruit for lunch 3 times this week: Tuesday, Friday, and Saturday. OR
- I will ride my bike 2 times this week for 20 minutes: Monday and Friday.

Schedule Your Goals. To write goals with specific days in them, you must have a calendar to work with. You want to be able to do what you set out to do. Try not to schedule yourself to walk the dog on a night when you will not be home.

INSTRUCTIONS:

- Get the goal-writing worksheets.
- Tell your child, "We can both make goals to make changes to be healthier every week. We can help each other make sure they are easy-to-reach, but heading in a healthy direction."
- Fill out the worksheets together.
- Tell your child, "When the week is over, we will talk about how we did on our goals by answering the questions on this handout. Together, we will discover why something was really hard or why something was easy. Then we can make goals that will be 'just right' the next week and build on the things you accomplished this week."
- Last, make sure you and your child build in rewards for yourselves as you make your goals. For example, "When I walk 20 minutes twice a week for 3 weeks in a row, I can buy myself a new music CD for my Walkman."

SUPPLEMENTARY ACTIVITIES:

Set up a way to keep track of successfully met goals. Some ideas are provided in Activity 12.

My Goal-Setting Sheet
Activity Choices

What I will do: _____

_____

How I will do it: _____

_____

Who I will do this with: _____

_____

When I will do this: _____

Su   M   T   W   Th   F   Sa

How did it go?

Did you meet your goal?   Yes   No   Almost!

What I liked about this goal: _____

_____

What I did not like about this goal: _____

_____

The Picture Communication Symbols © 1981-2002 Mayer-Johnson, Inc., Solana Beach, CA, USA. All rights reserved world wide. Used with permission.

My Goal-Setting Sheet
Food Choices

What I will do: _____

_____

How I will do it: _____

_____

Who I will do this with: _____

_____

When I will do this: _____

Su   M   T   W   Th   F   Sa

How did it go?

Did you meet your goal?   Yes   No   Almost!

What I liked about this goal: _____

_____

What I did not like about this goal: _____

_____

The Picture Communication Symbols © 1981-2002 Mayer-Johnson, Inc., Solana Beach, CA, USA. All rights reserved world wide. Used with permission.

My Goal-Setting Sheet
Activity Choices

What I will do: 1. I will walk to the store on Monday and Wednesday.

2. I will go to exercise class two times.

 How I will do it: 1. I won't take the bus.

2. I will take the bus to the gym.

Who I will do this with: 1. I will do this alone.

2. I will go with Kathy.

 When I will do this: 1. Mon and Wed. 2. Tues and Sat.

Su   M   T   W   Th   F   Sa

How did it go?

Did you meet your goal?   (Yes)   No   Almost!

 What I liked about this goal: I liked being outside when I walked to the store. It was fun to see Kathy at class.

What I did not like about this goal: I was tired on Wednesday and Thursday. It was hard to get up Thursday morning.

The Picture Communication Symbols © 1981-2002 Mayer-Johnson, Inc., Solana Beach, CA, USA. All rights reserved world wide. Used with permission.

My Goal-Setting Sheet
Food Choices

What I will do: <u>I will fill out a food record 3 days.</u>

How I will do it: <u>Use this sheet. I will keep it in the kitchen.</u>

Who I will do this with: <u>Kathy</u>

When I will do this: _____

Su   M   (T)   W   (Th)   F   (Sa)

How did it go?

Did you meet your goal?   Yes   No   (Almost!)

What I liked about this goal: <u>It is interesting to see what I eat.</u>
<u>I was surprised.</u>

What I did not like about this goal: <u>Remembering. Keeping</u>
<u>this where I can find it.</u>

The Picture Communication Symbols © 1981-2002 Mayer-Johnson, Inc., Solana Beach, CA, USA. All rights reserved world wide. Used with permission.

Activity 11: Using Food and Activity Records

DESCRIPTION:

Food and activity records provide a lot of information. Because these records contain a lot of information, they must be introduced slowly. The first step is covered in Activity 9. In that activity, your child learned to pay attention to what foods he ate and what food groups they represented.

In this activity, that same information is used to create a food record. In addition, your child can write down the number of minutes he exercises purposefully each day. It is not necessary to exercise every day. It is, however, important for your child to write down when he does exercise to count it toward meeting his goals for the week.

It is important to choose a food record format that fits your child. There are four different food record templates provided. You can also use the checkbox system provided in the "Keeping Track" activity (Activity 9) alone if you will only be recording food intake at first.

Each food record has space to record four different topics:

- foods eaten,
- water intake,
- mood rating for the day, and
- information about exercise.

One format uses boxes for your child to check for each serving from a food group he eats.

One format includes a blank pyramid for your child to write down the foods eaten inside the food group box.

One format does not count water intake or strength training.

One format includes a grid to write down foods eaten and amounts.

The differences in formats are primarily to accommodate reading and writing skills. Choose the method that best fits your child's skills without creating frustration. You want him to focus on the information, not on the task of writing it down. If it is difficult to write down and record, then he won't want to do it. Use stickers, photos, checkmarks, or whatever else works to get the information on paper. If these formats are not appropriate for your child, make one that works for him.

MATERIALS NEEDED

1. Food and activity records appropriate for your child
2. Felt pens, highlighters, pens, pencils, photos or symbols of food
3. Calendar of the month with holidays noted
4. Weekly calendar with special events noted
5. Weekly calendar with hourly grid
6. Stickers

INSTRUCTIONS

1. Try to write down which food groups you have eaten foods from each day. Make sure to include the number of times you eat foods from the "sometimes" food group too. You can keep track by making check marks, putting stickers in the food group area, or writing down the foods you eat.
2. There are different types of food records you can use. Choose the one that makes the most sense to you; some take a lot of reading and writing. Others do not. They all do the same thing: help you keep track of what you are eating.

3. Remember, as you keep track of the food you eat, there is no right or wrong answer. Everyone likes different foods. When you write down what you eat, then you know what you might want to change if it doesn't fit your idea of a healthy lifestyle.

4. At the end of the week, take a look at all your food records and compare them to the goal you set for yourself with the goal-setting sheet. How did you do? Did you do what you set out to do last week? If so, that is a successful goal and you can be very proud. If not, you were still successful because you wrote it all down. Writing things down is one of the hardest parts about learning to understand what you eat. Pat yourself on the back for being willing to write it down!

5. Don't forget to write down when you exercise! Writing it down on your food and activity record is the only way you will remember if you met your goal.

6. Don't forget to reward yourself for goals that you have met. Making changes is hard!

EXAMPLE:

Courtney has decided to make some changes in the way she lives her life. She wants to be healthy and fit.

First, Courtney wrote some goals for the week. She logs them in the top portions of the goal-setting worksheets. (See completed sample worksheets on the next two pages.)

Courtney has decided to keep a food record to remember what she eats. Take a look at the "Sample Food Record" (on page 329) that lists what Courtney ate. Following this list of foods eaten are two ways that Courtney might record her daily intake on a food pyramid. (See these completed examples on pages 330 and 331.)

At the end of the week, Courtney looks at her goal sheets which she filled out at the beginning of the week and writes down how she did by completing the bottom portion of the sheets (completed samples on next two pages). She talks about how she did with her Mom and her friend Kathy, who is also trying to make some changes. When they are done, Courtney writes new goals for the next week on new goal-setting worksheets.

NEXT STEP:

Visualize Your Success! (Activity 12).

Sample: Courtney's Goal Sheet

My Goal-Setting Sheet
Food Choices

What I will do: <u>I will fill out a food record 3 days.</u>

_____

How I will do it: <u>Use this sheet. I will keep it in the kitchen.</u>

_____

Who I will do this with: <u>Kathy</u>

_____

When I will do this: _____

Su   M   (T)   W   (Th)   F   (Sa)

How did it go?

Did you meet your goal?   Yes   No   (Almost!)

What I liked about this goal: <u>It is interesting to see what I eat.</u>
<u>I was surprised.</u>

What I did not like about this goal: <u>Remembering. Keeping</u>
<u>this where I can find it.</u>

The Picture Communication Symbols © 1981-2002 Mayer-Johnson, Inc., Solana Beach, CA, USA. All rights reserved world wide. Used with permission.

Sample: Courtney's Goal Sheet

My Goal-Setting Sheet
Activity Choices

What I will do: 1. I will walk to the store on Monday and Wednesday.

2. I will go to exercise class two times.

 How I will do it: 1. I won't take the bus.

2. I will take the bus to the gym.

Who I will do this with: 1. I will do this alone.

2. I will go with Kathy.

 When I will do this: 1. Mon and Wed. 2. Tues and Sat.

Su   M   T   W   Th   F   Sa

How did it go?

Did you meet your goal?   (Yes)   No   Almost!

 What I liked about this goal: I liked being outside when I walked to the store. It was fun to see Kathy at class.

What I did not like about this goal: I was tired on Wednesday and Thursday. It was hard to get up Thursday morning.

The Picture Communication Symbols © 1981-2002 Mayer-Johnson, Inc., Solana Beach, CA, USA. All rights reserved world wide. Used with permission.

Sample Food Record

On Tuesday, Courtney ate the following things:

BREAKFAST
1 cup Fiber One cereal

$\frac{3}{4}$ cup milk

1 slice toast

1 tbsp. margarine

1 $\frac{1}{2}$ tsp. jam

$\frac{1}{2}$ cup orange juice

SNACK
donut with chocolate icing

Diet Coke

LUNCH
$\frac{1}{2}$ turkey sub sandwich

(which is $\frac{1}{2}$ hoagie bun, 1 tbsp. mayo, lettuce, 2 slices tomato,

sweet pickles, 3 ounces sliced turkey)

1 apple

1 bag chips

1 cup skim milk

DINNER
Meat Lover's pizza

salad

ranch dressing

1 garlic bread stick

SNACK
1 big bowl popcorn with butter

(Following this page are two examples of ways to record food intake.)

Courtney's Food Record (Sample 1)

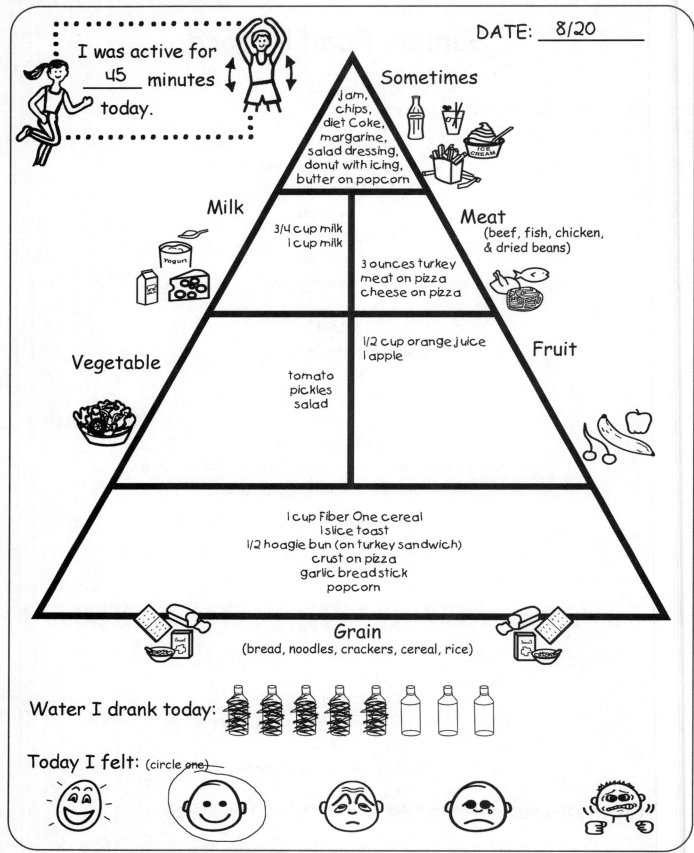

DATE: ___8/20___

I was active for ___45___ minutes today.

Sometimes
jam, chips, diet Coke, margarine, salad dressing, donut with icing, butter on popcorn

Milk
3/4 cup milk
1 cup milk

Meat
(beef, fish, chicken, & dried beans)
3 ounces turkey meat on pizza
cheese on pizza

Vegetable
tomato
pickles
salad

1/2 cup orange juice
1 apple

Fruit

Grain
1 cup Fiber One cereal
1 slice toast
1/2 hoagie bun (on turkey sandwich)
crust on pizza
garlic breadstick
popcorn

(bread, noodles, crackers, cereal, rice)

Water I drank today:

Today I felt: (circle one)

The Picture Communication Symbols © 1981-2002 Mayer-Johnson, Inc., Solana Beach, CA, USA. All rights reserved world wide. Used with permission.

Courtney's Food Record (Sample 2)

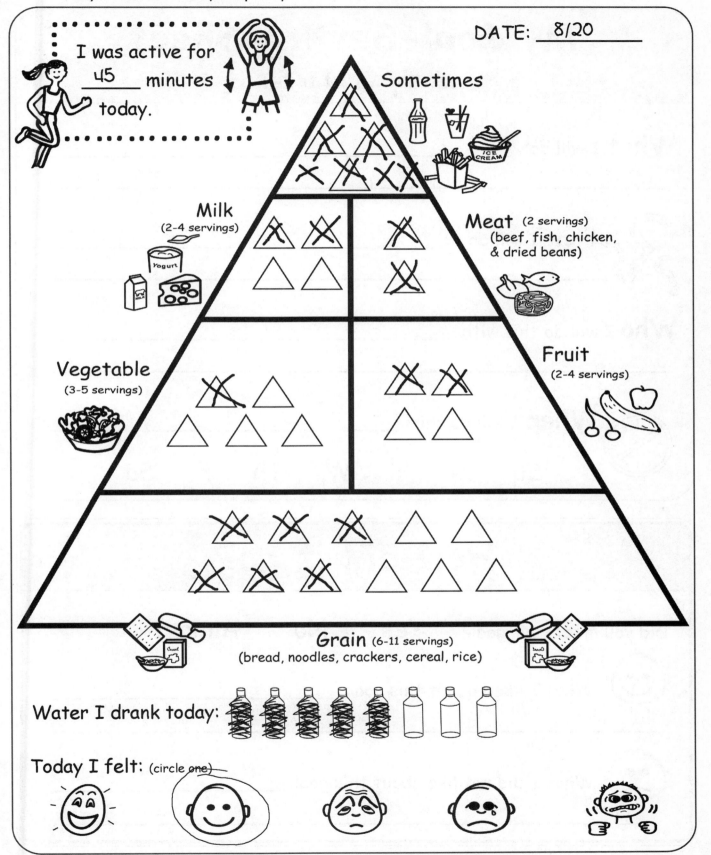

I was active for __45__ minutes today.

DATE: __8/20__

Sometimes

Milk (2-4 servings)

Meat (2 servings)
(beef, fish, chicken, & dried beans)

Vegetable (3-5 servings)

Fruit (2-4 servings)

Grain (6-11 servings)
(bread, noodles, crackers, cereal, rice)

Water I drank today:

Today I felt: (circle one)

The Picture Communication Symbols © 1981-2002 Mayer-Johnson, Inc., Solana Beach, CA, USA. All rights reserved world wide. Used with permission.

My Goal-Setting Sheet
Activity Choices

What I will do: _____
_____

How I will do it: _____
_____

Who I will do this with: _____
_____

When I will do this: _____

Su   M   T   W   Th   F   Sa

How did it go?

Did you meet your goal?   Yes   No   Almost!

What I liked about this goal: _____
_____

What I did not like about this goal:_____
_____

The Picture Communication Symbols © 1981-2002 Mayer-Johnson, Inc., Solana Beach, CA, USA. All rights reserved world wide. Used with permission.

My Goal-Setting Sheet
Food Choices

What I will do: _____

_____

How I will do it: _____

_____

Who I will do this with: _____

_____

When I will do this: _____

Su   M   T   W   Th   F   Sa

How did it go?

Did you meet your goal?   Yes   No   Almost!

What I liked about this goal: _____

_____

What I did not like about this goal:_____

_____

The Picture Communication Symbols © 1981-2002 Mayer-Johnson, Inc., Solana Beach, CA, USA. All rights reserved world wide. Used with permission.

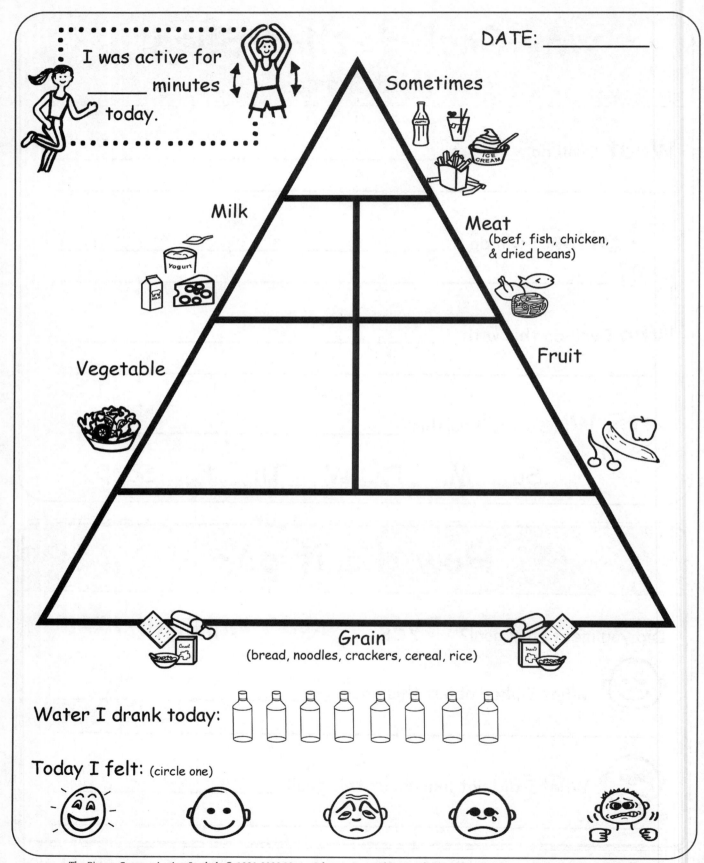

DATE: _____

I was active for _____ minutes today.

Sometimes

Milk

Meat
(beef, fish, chicken,
& dried beans)

Vegetable

Fruit

Grain
(bread, noodles, crackers, cereal, rice)

Water I drank today:

Today I felt: (circle one)

The Picture Communication Symbols © 1981-2002 Mayer-Johnson, Inc., Solana Beach, CA, USA. All rights reserved world wide. Used with permission.

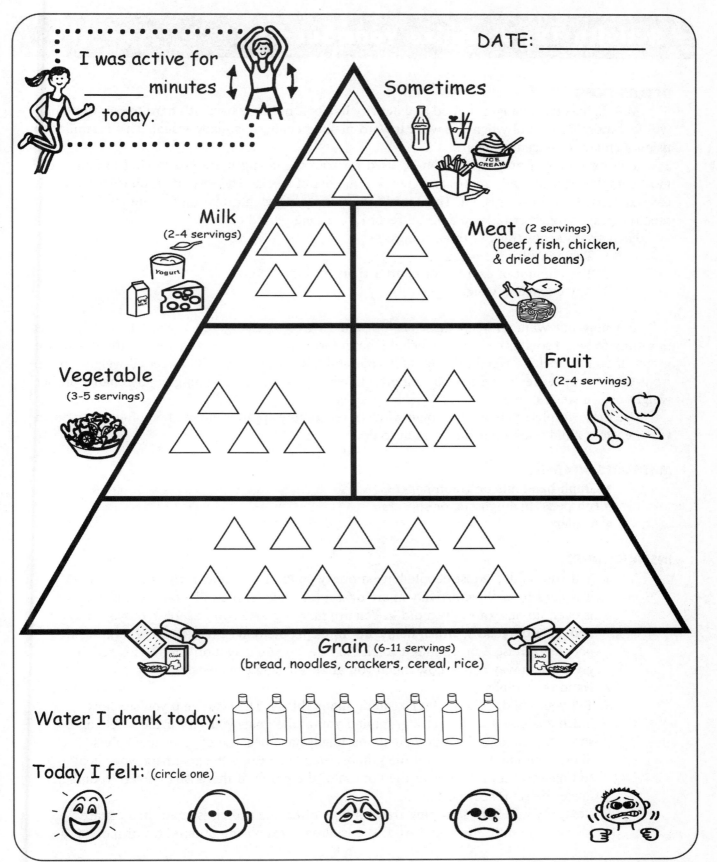

I was active for _____ minutes today.

DATE: _____

Sometimes

Milk (2-4 servings)

Meat (2 servings)
(beef, fish, chicken, & dried beans)

Vegetable (3-5 servings)

Fruit (2-4 servings)

Grain (6-11 servings)
(bread, noodles, crackers, cereal, rice)

Water I drank today:

Today I felt: (circle one)

The Picture Communication Symbols © 1981-2002 Mayer-Johnson, Inc., Solana Beach, CA, USA. All rights reserved world wide. Used with permission.

Activity 12: Visualize Your Success!

DESCRIPTION:

Making lifestyle changes in food and activity habits is not only hard, it's hard to *see*. Your child will feel more successful when the work toward making changes is made visual. This is similar to using a childhood incentive chart.

Two examples of graphs that can be used for tracking changes are provided. The first is the most complex. It has small squares and covers a number of weeks. The second graph is larger and is easy to use with a sticker system. This second graph only keeps information for one week. You can tape the graphs together to keep a visual record for a long period of time.

Each graph keeps track of three things:

1. The goals for the week
2. The amount of exercise or extra activity each day
3. Any change in weight

You may not want to keep track of your child's weight change on a chart like this if it is upsetting to her. If so, it is easy not to include that information by covering the "0" on the side of the graph. If you do include weight changes for your child, don't put your child's actual weight on the front of the graph. Her weight is not important. What you will be graphing is any change in her weight over a week's time.

Use these graphs or create your own with stickers or any appropriate method of marking down whether your child does what she sets out to do.

MATERIALS NEEDED:

- Graph handouts or graph paper
- Felt pens, highlighters, or stickers
- A ruler

INSTRUCTIONS:

1. Tell your child, "Most people have a pretty good idea of how active they are. But it is hard to *see* how active you are over a few days. It feels like once the exercise is over, no one knows you did it. You are marking when you exercise on your food and activity records, which helps. But most people don't exercise every day. Most people exercise 3 or 4 times a week. So how do you stay motivated? This activity gives you a way to see how much you are exercising each week."
2. Hand out graphs.
3. Tell your child, "These graphs can do many things. They can help you see how much exercise you are getting, remind you of the goals you set for the week, and show any changes in your weight you might have because of your new habits."
4. Show your child how to use the graphs. Step One: Copy the goal from your goal-setting sheet into the box at the bottom of the graph. If there isn't enough room, make the sentence shorter.
5. Next, if your child is keeping track of how often she exercises, color in a square for every minute she exercises. If she is already exercising 30 minutes or more at a

time, color in one box for every 2 minutes. Each column is one day. You might want to write the date at the top or bottom of each one to minimize confusion.

6. Next, if your child wants to see how exercising more effects her weight, write down how much she weighs today on the back of the graph. Make a mark by the "0" on the graph to indicate her starting weight. Your child should only weigh herself once a week. Weight changes slowly, so there is no point in getting overly anxious about it. If she gains a pound the next week, put a dot on that day of the week one square up from the "0." If she loses a pound, put a dot for that day of the week on the square that is down one square from the "0." Use a ruler to connect the dots.

EXAMPLE:

Look at the graphs that have been filled in for Courtney on pages 338-39. Courtney decided to keep track of her weight and how much she exercises each week.

She wrote her goals for the week in the box:

1. "I will walk to the store on Monday and Wednesday instead of riding the bus."
2. "I will go to aerobics with Kathy on Tuesday and Saturday."

Courtney did all of those things. It took her 20 minutes total to walk to the store and walk back. Her exercise class with Kathy is 25 minutes long. Can you see how she filled that in on the graph? Courtney did a total of 90 minutes of extra exercise in her first week. She was a little tired on Wednesday and Thursday. How would you make it a little easier not to get tired?

Courtney also wanted to track her weight change. She has a digital scale that tells her how much she weighs. According to her scale, she lost ½ pound this first week. Can you see how she connected the dots to make the line?

If the amount of food you eat does not change, but you are exercising more, soon you will see that your weight will begin to go down. If you are eating less and exercising more, it will also go down. If you are exercising more and eating more it will probably stay the same.

Remember, sometimes your weight goes up and down and you didn't really gain fat. If you eat a really salty meal like pizza or fast food, you may gain two or three pounds in a day! But it is because the extra salt in the food made your body hold on to more water. Those same two or three pounds will disappear in a couple of days. That is why a food record can be helpful! You can look back at what you have eaten to see if there is a reason for losing or gaining weight.

As time goes on, you can tape the graphs together and make a big long graph of all your exercise. Put the graph on your mirror or on the wall to remind you how great you are doing. Visualize your success!

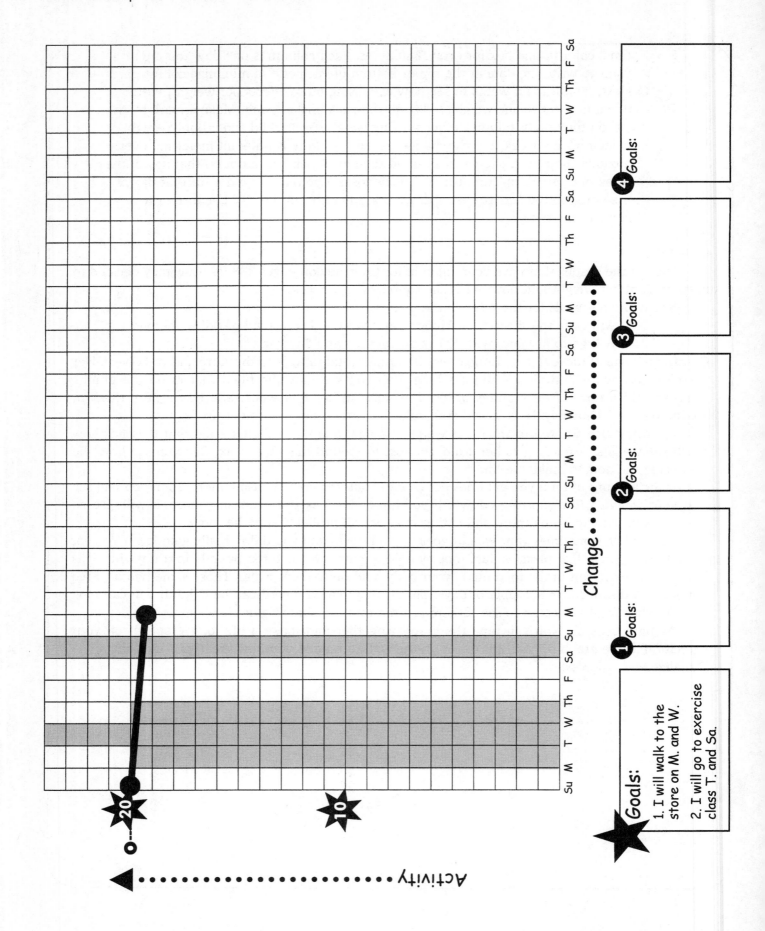

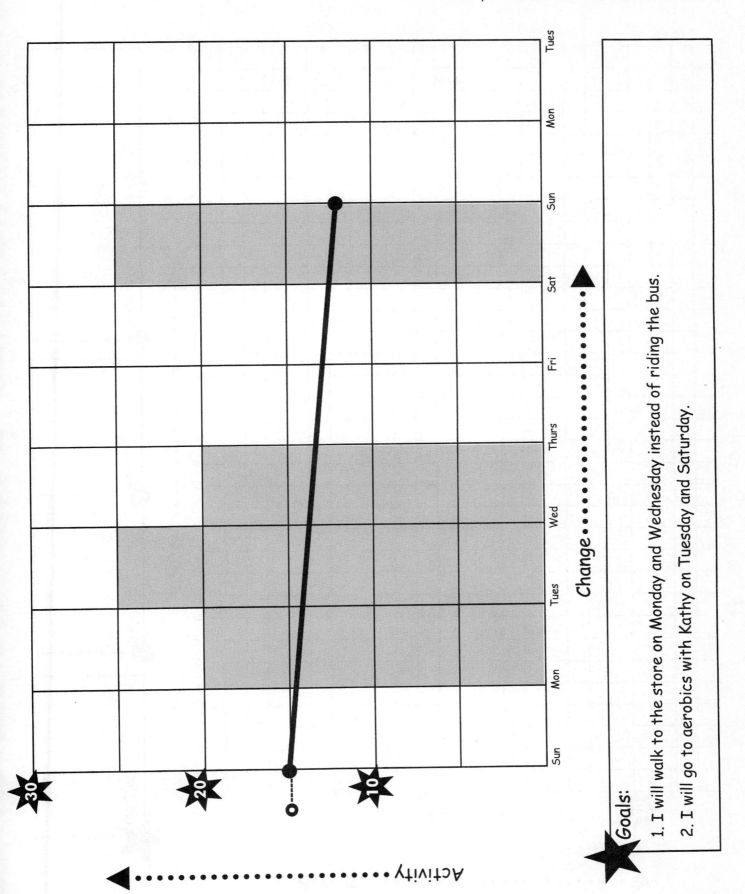

Activity

Change •••••••••••••••••••••••• ▲

Goals:

1. I will walk to the store on Monday and Wednesday instead of riding the bus.

2. I will go to aerobics with Kathy on Tuesday and Saturday.

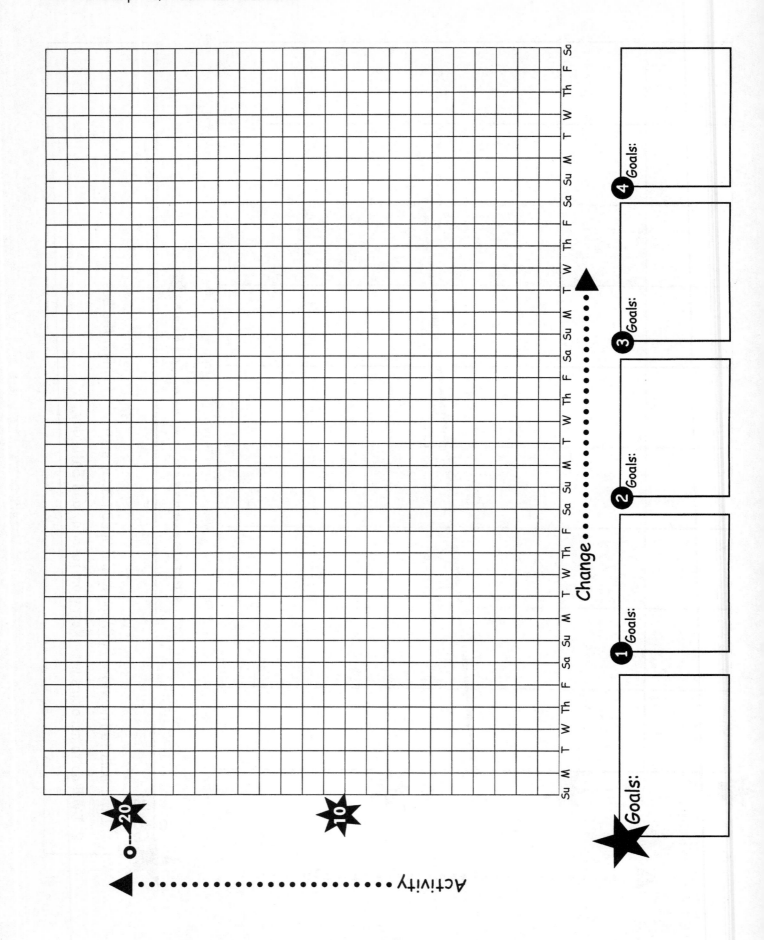

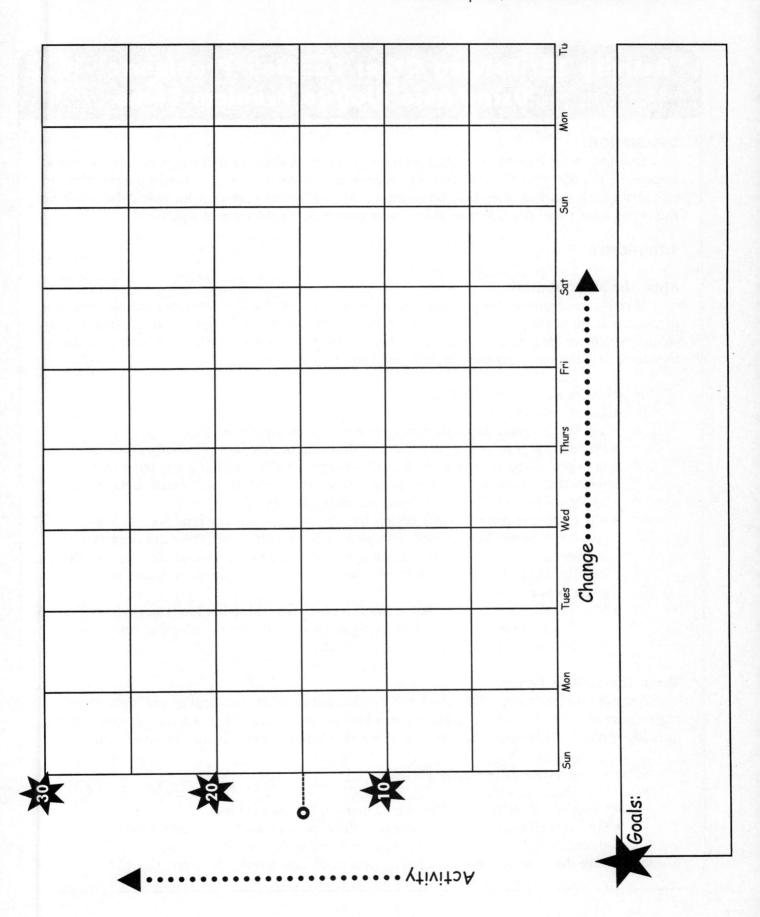

Activity 13: Solving Other People's Problems: Using Role Play to Problem-Solve

DESCRIPTION:

Learning to see how to make simple lifestyle changes is always easier when you are looking at someone else's life. These role plays are exaggerated to make them fun, but offer opportunities to talk about basic nutrition concepts. Brainstorm solutions for each person with your child and have fun at the same time. When you've solved these problems, create some of your own!

SITUATIONS:

Max, the Meat-Maniac

Max, the meat maniac, believes that meat is the only food that will do him any good. He wants lots of muscle to impress the girls. Max eats a steak for breakfast, three hamburgers for lunch, and a whole chicken for dinner. He eats other foods along with his meat, but he doesn't like to. He only eats them if they come with the meat, like the bun for a hamburger.

What advice do you have for Max?
Possible solutions include:
- Tell Max to get a life. Girls aren't attracted by muscle alone.
- Protein that is in meat is important for building muscle. But your body needs more than protein to make muscle. It needs energy to build it with. Energy comes from foods that have carbohydrates, such as pasta and bread. So Max needs to eat a variety of foods to be able to build the muscle he wants.
- The protein in meat is important for building muscle. But any time you eat more calories from any kind of food than your body actually needs, the extra calories become fat. Eating an entire chicken is probably more calories than Max needs in a day. He should try eating half of what he wants to eat for protein and add some vegetables to start.
- Max can eat meat, but he should balance his meals with other foods so his body has all the vitamins it needs to work right. He can practice by using the meal balance sheets in Activity 5 to plan his meals.

Terry, the Truffle Tyrant

Terry, the truffle tyrant, LOVES chocolate. She will not eat a meal without at least three chocolate truffles next to her plate. She eats them between bites of other foods. Terry believes every food should taste like chocolate. Sometimes she puts jam on her chocolate bar and says she has eaten a fruit.

What advice do you have for Terry?
Possible solutions include:
- Chocolate is really good! But there's more to life than chocolate!
- Start including other foods along with the chocolate, such as strawberries or chocolate milk, or even mix a chocolate cereal with a healthier cereal.
- Save the chocolate for a treat after each meal. Just a little chocolate, though!

- Eating a variety of foods is important to stay healthy. Terry might feel tired every afternoon because her diet is full of so much sugar and not much healthy food. She could practice balancing her meals by using the handouts in Activity 5.

Lazy Larry

Lazy Larry doesn't like to exercise. He doesn't like to walk two steps farther than he absolutely has to. He likes to sit in his apartment, watch television, and eat Twinkies. Larry has gained some weight since he moved in with his friends. He doesn't go anywhere except to his job. His meals are restaurant take-out, fast food, or frozen pizza.

What advice do you have for Larry?
Possible solutions include:

- Larry could use some friends. He should find out what some of his work partners like to do. Maybe go to a movie with someone or join a club. He needs to ask someone to help him learn how to make plans like this.
- Larry can make a list of the things he might like to try for fun. Then he will have an idea of what he could do besides sit and watch TV.
- Larry can use the goal making sheets in Activity 10 to write down what he wants to do each day.
- Larry and his friends could host a cooking buddy meeting. Cooking buddies are discussed in Chapter 15.
- If Larry doesn't want to change, then there's probably not much to do. Larry needs to be a part of the solution and decide to want to make changes to be healthier.

Careful Carrie

Careful Carrie never makes a decision if it's not on her list. She has a list for everything: what to do, what to eat, and where to go every day. Some days, Careful Carrie forgets to put lunch on her list of things to do. When that happens, she doesn't eat lunch. Sometimes Carrie puts too many things to do on her list. She puts walking on her list even though she is very tired. She feels she cannot take things off her list, so she goes walking. Then she is very tired the next day.

What advice do you have for Carrie?
Possible solutions include:

- Take a notepad to make lists from and write "Eat lunch," "Pack lunch," or "Lunch" at the top of every page.
- Write a note for the refrigerator, mirror, or door that says, "If it is after 8:00 p.m., do not go for a walk. It is OK."
- Before making a daily list, Carrie should write down the dates that things need to get done on a calendar. Then she should only add to the list the things that *must* be done that day.
- Carrie could ask for help when her list is too long.

Gorging George

Gorging George doesn't know when to stop eating. When he really likes a food, he will eat many servings. The other day, he had four chicken parmesan sandwiches because they were new on the menu and tasted so good! Another time he went to a "make your own ice cream sundae" party and made three banana splits because he thought the sundaes were pretty and it was a lot of fun to make them. Often George says his stomach hurts after a meal or before he goes to bed.

What advice do you have for George?

Possible solutions include:

- George can take one serving of food when he sits down to eat a meal. When he finishes, he can:
    1. set a timer for 20 minutes,
    2. brush his teeth,
    3. go for a walk,

    If he is still hungry when the timer goes off after doing other things during that time, he can have another serving.

- He can "rate" his hunger on a scale of 1-5 before a reasonable-sized meal to help him decide how hungry he really is. He may learn that he wants to eat more just because there is more.

- If he is eating more just because there is more, he can package up extra food before he sits down to eat. Then the food is not easy to get to.

- George should see a doctor if his stomach keeps hurting to make sure nothing is wrong.

Working with Groups

NOTES TO GROUP LEADERS:

Working with groups of children, teens, and adults with Down syndrome is no different than any other group activity. It requires planning, preparation, and luck. All of the nutrition education activities in Section 4 can be done individually, in groups, in general education settings, in self-contained special education settings, in group homes, or at a conference.

Following are some examples of how nutrition education activities can be adapted to a group format. As you develop your idea, refer to the design elements suggested at the beginning of Section 4. Additionally, I've found there are some key elements to creating successful learning opportunities for children, teens, and adults with Down syndrome in a group setting. These include:

- **Fun.** If it's not fun, why participate?
- **Interaction.** Participants are more engaged if they are interacting with each other and with the group facilitator.
- **Creativity.** Use current, age-appropriate themes from popular game shows or events.
- **Modification.** The best group activities are ones that have modifications and accommodations built in. For instance, providing pictures, color-coding, and words as a part of the activity makes it easier for everyone—whether or not they can read—to participate.
- **Support.** Any group with more than four or five people with Down syndrome included must have support. The best situation is when support is provided from others in the group. Even in this situation, however, you may need a floater, or someone who will stay on the outskirts looking for folks who need assistance.
- **Teach, don't test.** This is an important element in choosing your theme. My experiences with a pilot test of a spin-off from the popular game show "Who Wants to Be a Millionaire?" helped me learn this lesson. In designing the activity, we gathered incentives, used music from the television show, and modified the "life-lines" participants could use. But not one person with Down syndrome would agree to be a participant! We quickly modified the game to be more like "Family Feud" between a brother and sister without Down syndrome. All of a sudden, the room of 75 teens and adults with Down syndrome came alive as they collaborated on the answers for the person they were supporting. My lesson? Don't put anyone on the spot—it feels like a test. People do better collaborating on a group project and presenting their results than they do in the spotlight.

With all this in mind, here is an example of teaching concepts about combination foods, menu balance, and hydration in a group setting. The theme is: Healthy Survivor.

DESCRIPTION:

The television show *Survivor* offers a format that is fun and collaborative in nature, yet competitive. After dividing the group into tribes, give them a few minutes to choose a name for their tribe. Each tribe is then given a brief nutrition lesson, after which the tribe problem-solves a scenario relevant to the topic. When done, the tribe presents their solution to the problem. The combined tribes decide whether the group was successful in their quest to "outwit, outlast, and outplay" the situation to create a healthy solution. If so, they are crowned "Healthy Survivors"! There are no winners or losers, which makes it easy to play.

Below are the instructions for the tribe facilitator and the scenarios for groups to work through. These activities are based on the nutrition education activities for understanding combination foods, balancing menus, and getting enough water.

MATERIALS:

- Post-it Self-Stick Bulletin Board (found at office supply stores)
- Paper food models or food cards of a wide variety of foods that are not typical for meals and 12 photos of a glass of water. Note: participants cannot add foods that are not in the group of food models provided. This is the "survivor aspect" to the activity: you must make do with what you have.
- Handouts for meal balance, combination foods, and hydration lessons (from Activities 3, 5, and 8)

TEAM DIRECTIONS:

Team #1

Read the following situation to the group. Make sure you allow them to laugh at and embellish the funny parts. Ask the questions that follow the situation. Instruct the group to create menus that are balanced without worrying about serving size.

Have the group create menus using the paper food models provided. As they create their menu, have them put the food models on the poster board for reporting to the group at "Tribal Council." (See below.)

The Situation on Menu Mountain

Mad Man Mark has found himself in a tough situation. He lives on the top of Menu Mountain where there are no stores or restaurants, and Domino's Pizza doesn't even deliver!

Mark didn't plan his week very well and has found himself with only a few foods to make his meals for the day. In order to make it down the mountain to do his shopping, he knows he has to eat balanced meals that include at least three of the bottom five food groups from the Food Guide Pyramid to fuel his body.

Help Mad Man Mark be a "Healthy Survivor" by making his lunch and dinner menus from the odd selection of foods he has in his cabin.

Team #2

Read the following situation to the group. Make sure you allow them to laugh at and embellish the funny parts. Ask the questions that follow the situation. Instruct the group to create a "food equation" from combination foods. Complete one or two examples in the handouts provided in Activity 3. Let the group choose two to four foods to break into food equations. Put the photo of the combination food on the bulletin board with an equals sign (=) next to it. Have a representative from the group place the symbols for the food groups into the rest of the equation separated by plus (+) symbols. The spokesperson for the group will present the food equations to the entire group at "Tribal Council."

The Situation at Combo Corner:

Sly Samantha got carried away in the frozen food section. Instead of buying foods that are easy to tell what food group they come from, she bought a lot of foods that have more than one food group in a serving. These are called combination foods. Sometimes it is hard for Samantha to tell which food groups she is eating so she can decide whether she needs a food from another food group to balance her menu. She wants to know this to be a Healthy Survivor!

As a group, help Sly Samantha do her food equations so she can be a Healthy Survivor!

Team #3

Read the following situation to the group. Make sure you allow them to laugh at and embellish the funny parts. Ask the questions that follow the situation. The team's goal is to identify quick ways to get fluids from drink and food. Use the information in the lesson notes to Activity 8 to remind them which foods provide water and which foods do not provide water or even take water away.

Put a photo of a glass of water on one side of the bulletin board. On the other side put a photo of an empty glass. Have the group sort through the paper food models provided and group them into food and drink that hydrates (or provides water) and foods that do not. This bulletin board is what they will share with the entire group at "tribal council."

The Situation at Hydration Station:

Wilamina is not big on water. She doesn't like the way it tastes, the way it looks, or anything about it. She doesn't drink water.

Wilamina is going on a vacation with her family to Arizona. In the summer it is very very hot in Arizona. It is easy to not get enough fluid and start to feel grumpy, get a headache, and be tired.

When they got to Arizona, Wilamina thought it felt like being in a hair dryer. One afternoon they went for a hike around part of the Grand Canyon. Wilamina felt very hot. Her face was all red. Her head started to pound. She wanted to sit down and take a nap. When her mother suggested she sit in the shade and drink some water, she yelled at her!

What do you think is wrong with Wilamina?

What can she do to feel better?

Since she doesn't like water, what are other things she can do to get fluids?

Wilamina's mother packed some foods in her backpack. Which foods would give Wilamina some fluid and which foods will not help or even make fluid absent?

Tribal Council:

When the individual groups finish, have them come back together as one big group, sitting in their tribes. Ask each tribe to present their situation and how they handled it. After each presentation, ask the group, "Are they Healthy Survivors?" When you do, encourage everyone to cheer.

Remember to provide a reward. A certificate, button, or some sort of token to remind them that they played, and became, "Healthy Survivors."

Appendices

The PEACH Survey

Parent Eating and Nutrition Assessment for Children with Special Health Needs

Agency: _____   Date: _____

Child's Name: _____   Date of Birth: _____

Address: _____   Phone #: _____

Please Circle *YES* or *NO* for each question as it applies to your child.

Does your child have a health problem (do **not** include colds or flu)?　　　YES　　NO (1)
If YES, what is it? _____

Is your child: Small for age?___　　　Too thin?___　　　Too Heavy?___　　　YES　　NO (3)
(if you check any of the above, please circle YES)

Does your child have feeding problems?　　　YES　　NO (3)
If YES, what are they? _____

Is your child's appetite a problem?　　　YES　　NO (1)

Is your child on a special diet?　　　YES　　NO (2)
If YES, what type of diet? _____

Does your child take medicine for a health problem?　　　YES　　NO (1)
(do not include vitamins, iron, or fluoride)
If YES, name the medication. _____

Does your child have food allergies?　　　YES　　NO (1)
If YES, what are they? _____

Does your child use a feeding tube or other special feeding method?　　　YES　　NO (4)
If YES, explain: _____

Circle YES if your child does **not** eat any of these foods:　　　YES　　NO (1)
(*check all that apply*)　　Milk___　　Meats___　　Vegetables___　　Fruits___

continued ▶

Circle YES if your child has problems with: YES   NO (3)
(check all that apply)   Sucking ___   Swallowing___   Chewing___   Gagging ___

Circle YES if your child has problems with: YES   NO (3)
(check all that apply)   Loose stools ___   Hard stools___   Throwing up___   Spitting up___

Does your child eat clay, paint chips, dirt, or any other things that are not food?   YES   NO (2)
If YES, what is it? _____

Does your child refuse to eat, throw food, or do other things that upset your   YES   NO (2)
family mealtime?
If YES, explain: _____

For infants **under** 12 months old who are bottle fed:
Does your child drink less than 3 (8-ounce) bottles of milk per day?   YES   NO (1)

For children **over** 12 months (Check if applies and circle YES)   YES   NO (1)
Is your child **not** using a cup?___   Is your child **not** finger feeding?___

For children **over** 18 months:
Does your child still take most liquids from a bottle?   YES   NO (2)

Circle YES if your child is **not** using a spoon.   YES   NO (2)

Scoring Instructions:

Add the numbers in parentheses next to the questions you have answered "yes." If you answer "yes" four or more times or if your score is four or above, ask your pediatrician or early intervention teacher about a feeding team.

Parent Eating and Nutrition Assessment for Children with Special Health Needs(PEACH).
© 1993 Marci Campbell and Kristine Kelsey. Used with Permission.

FOOD Guide PYRAMID

for Young Children

A Daily Guide for
2- to 6-Year-Olds

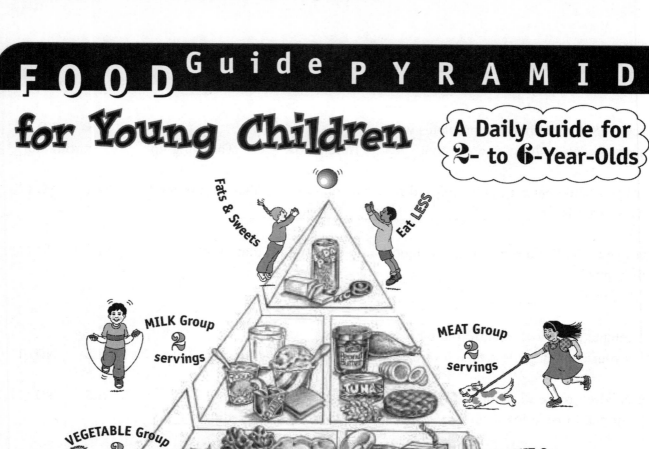

Fats & Sweets
Eat LESS

MILK Group
2 servings

MEAT Group
2 servings

VEGETABLE Group
3 servings

FRUIT Group
2 servings

GRAIN Group 6 servings

U.S. Department of Agriculture
Center for Nutrition Policy and Promotion

January 2000
Program Aid 1652

USDA is an equal opportunity provider and employer.

FOOD IS FUN and learning about food is fun, too. Eating foods from the Food Guide Pyramid and being physically active will help you grow healthy and strong.

WHAT COUNTS AS ONE SERVING?

GRAIN GROUP
1 slice of bread
½ cup of cooked rice or pasta
½ cup of cooked cereal
1 ounce of ready-to-eat cereal

VEGETABLE GROUP
½ cup of chopped raw or cooked vegetables
1 cup of raw leafy vegetables

FRUIT GROUP
1 piece of fruit or melon wedge
¾ cup of juice
½ cup of canned fruit
¼ cup of dried fruit

MILK GROUP
1 cup of milk or yogurt
2 ounces of cheese

MEAT GROUP
2 to 3 ounces of cooked lean meat, poultry, or fish.
½ cup of cooked dry beans, or 1 egg counts as 1 ounce of lean meat. 2 tablespoons of peanut butter count as 1 ounce of meat.

FATS AND SWEETS
Limit calories from these.

Four- to 6-year-olds can eat these serving sizes. Offer 2- to 3-year-olds less, except for milk.
Two- to 6-year-old children need a total of 2 servings from the milk group each day.

EAT a variety of FOODS AND ENJOY!

Diabetes Care Plan (504 Plan)

SAMPLE SECTION 504 DOCUMENTS

The forms on pages 354-62 can be used as a guide to formulating your child's 504 plan at school. Examples are based on the needs of a child with diabetes, but the forms can also be used for children with celiac disease or other conditions requiring dietary modifications at school. The forms are deliberately generic and need to be individualized according to the student's particular situation. You may wish to develop your own format. The forms are copyrighted by Children with Diabetes and can be found at www.childrenwithdiabetes.com. They are used with permission.

continued ▶

504 Dietary Plan

Section 504 of the Rehabilitation Act of 1973 assures "handicapped students" access to school meal service, even if special meals are needed because of their handicap.

"Handicapped student" means any student who has physical or mental impairment which substantially limits one or more major life activities, has a record of such an impairment, or is regarded as having such an impairment.

If special meals are needed and requested, certification from a medical doctor must: (1) verify that special meals are needed because of the handicap, and (2) prescribe the alternate foods and forms needed.

Completion of the following by a student's doctor/dietitian will provide the necessary certification:

Name of student for whom special meals are requested: _____

Meal Plan Prescribed: _____

Form allowed (e.g., fresh, baked, ground, blended, etc.): _____

Meat and Meat Alternates:
Milk and Milk Products:
Bread and Cereal:
Fruits and Vegetables:

Other dietary information and directions: _____

_____

_____

I certify that the above named student is in need of special school meals prepared from the above-indicated foods and forms because of a handicap.

_____   _____

Physician/dietitian Signature   Date

504 Healthcare Plan: Checklist

STUDENT INFORMATION

Name: _____   DOB: _____

School\Teacher: _____   Grade: _____

Parent\Guardian: _____   Address: _____

Home Phone: (M) _____   Work Phone: (M) _____

(F) _____   (F) _____

Other Emergency Contact: _____   Phone: _____

Physician: _____   Phone: _____

Medical Diagnosis: _____   Preferred Hospital: _____

	Date Requested	Date Received
1. Referral received from:		
2. Parent contact		
3. Authorizations for release of information signed by parent/guardian.		
4. Medical/nursing/educational records:		
5. Nursing assessment: Home visit, school site observation		
6. Individualized Health Care Plan complete:		
7. Emergency Action Plan developed:		
8. Request for written orders to physician:		
9. Parent request for special care on file:		
10. Review of procedure with parent/guardian		
11. Staffing/placement meeting:		
12. Staff/in-service training		
13. Transportation plan completed:		
14. Equipment and supplies checklist:		

_____   _____
School Nurse Signature   Date

504 Diabetes Health History

STUDENT INFORMATION   Date Initiated: _____

Name: _____ DOB: _____ Grade: _____

Father/Guardian: _____

　　　　　　Phone (H): _____ (W): _____

Mother/Guardian: _____

　　　　　　Phone (H): _____ (W): _____

Other Emergency Contacts:

Name: _____

　　　　Relationship: _____ Phone: _____

Name: _____

　　　　Relationship: _____ Phone: _____

Physician: _____ Phone: _____

Hospital Preferred: _____

Transport: ❑ Parent ❑ Ambulance ❑ Other _____

Assessment/Daily Management:

Baseline Information

Temp: _____ Pulse: _____ Resp: _____ BP: _____

Height: _____ Weight: _____ Hearing: _____ Glasses/Contact: _____

Allergies: _____

Date Diabetes Diagnosed: _____ Last Hospitalization: _____

Type of Insulin	Dose	Time Given	Reactions

continued ▶

Emergency Snacks/Medication:

Instructions: _____

_____

BS checks at school:

Time: _____ AM _____ PM

Equipment needed: _____

❑ Transported daily? ❑ Stored at School?

Scheduled PE\Exercise Activities:

Time: _____ AM _____ PM

PE Modification: _____

Food Intake:

Breakfast: _____

Lunch: _____

❑ Brings own food ❑ Selects in Cafeteria ❑ Needs Assistance

Snacks: AM _____ PM _____

Brings Daily _____ Storage _____

Other Health Concerns:

_____

_____

_____

Additional Medication(s):

_____

_____

504 School Health Care Action Plan for Diabetes/Hypoglycemia

To assist your child in maintaining optimum health, it is necessary for the school to have current information regarding his/her diagnosis of diabetes or hypoglycemia. Written permission is required from the parent and physician for the nurse to test your child's blood glucose level at school during a crisis or emergency situation.

Please be aware that:

1. The parents or "911" will be notified depending on the state of the crisis.

2. If equipment is needed for blood glucose testing, this must be provided by the family. The procedure for blood glucose testing will be followed according to instructions provided by the manufacturer of the specific meter.

3. The parent should notify the school if routine blood glucose monitoring is necessary during school hours.

Please complete the following form and return to the school nurse as soon as possible. **Physician and Parent/guardian signatures are both required.** Also, continue to keep the school nurse updated on your child's changing health needs.

School: _____ Phone: _____

continued ▶

Diabetes Health Care—Emergency Action Plan

Name: _____ Grade: _____

Adress: _____

Home Phone: _____

Father/Guardian: _____

             Phone (H): _____ (W): _____

Mother/Guardian: _____

             Phone (H): _____ (W): _____

Other Person to contact in case of emergency:

     Name: _____

     Adress: _____

     Phone (H): _____ (W): _____

Hospital Preferred: _____

Physician(s) Name: _____ Phone: _____

Emergency Items to be Left at School:

     Glucose tablets _____   Blood glucose meter _____

     Snacks _____   Insulin _____

     Syringes _____   Other _____

     Other _____   Other _____

In the event of an insulin reaction, the procedure routinely followed at school is: to give some form of sugar such as ½ carton of milk followed by crackers and peanut butter, ½ cup fruit juice, or ½ cup non-diet soda. If the student is unconscious, "911" is called.

I approve the above health care action plan as written. Yes _____ No _____

Please make the following changes to the health care action plan: _____

_____

_____

_____

continued ▶

List other additional information or significant special health concerns of this student:

_____

_____

_____

I give permission for emergency blood glucose testing by school personnel using equipment I have provided. The parent/guardian will be notified or "911" will be called as needed.

❑ Yes   ❑ No

Additional directions regarding blood glucose testing: _____

_____

_____

_____

Written and Submitted by:

_____   _____
School   Date

Reviewed and Signed by:

_____   _____
Parent/Guardian   Date

_____   _____
Student   Date

_____   _____
Physician   Date

To Be Reviewed: _____   *(Healthcare plan should be revised according to child's*
                    Date   *specific needs, at least annually.)*

Blood Glucose and Insulin Procedures

Name of Student

Grade/Teacher

Physician

Physician's Phone Number

Medication	Dose	Time

MEDICATION MUST BE DISPENSED ACCORDING TO SCHOOL MEDICATION POLICY.

Monitoring Blood Glucose and Administering Insulin:

YES	NO	
		Diabetes checklist returned.
		Demonstrates correct use of blood glucose meter.
		States proper time for blood glucose monitoring.
		Demonstrates documentation of blood glucose monitoring.
		Demonstrates knowledge of self-administration of insulin.
		States proper time for administration of insulin.
		Follows appropriate procedure for disposal of supplies.
		Carries treatment for insulin reactions.
		Agrees to seek assistance from school personnel as needed.

continued ▶

If the student does/does not demonstrate meeting the above specified responsibilities, the privilege of monitoring blood glucose and self-administration of insulin will/will not be allowed and will be performed by designated school personnel.

_____   _____
Student's Signature   Date

_____   _____
School Signature   Date

Comments: _____

_____

_____

_____

My child will be responsible for carrying medication and monitoring equipment. My child will perform self-monitoring and will self-administer medication. My child agrees to follow the district's procedures concerning the handling and administration of this medication.

_____   _____
Parent/Guardian   Date

High Fiber Diet

For adults, a high fiber diet is one that has 20-35 grams of dietary fiber or more each day. For children, the grams of fiber for a high fiber diet are calculated by adding age plus 5 grams. For a 6-year-old, this would be 6+5 or 11 grams of fiber per day. The average American diet has 10-15 grams of fiber per day. High fiber diets are helpful for constipation, moving foods along in the intestine, and for certain specific conditions such as inflammatory bowel syndrome.

It can be tricky to consistently eat enough dietary fiber to qualify as a high fiber diet without eating too many calories overall. For people with lower calorie needs, this can become a real challenge. Here are five tips for increasing fiber without adding a lot of calories to your daily menu:

1. **Choose breakfast cereals that are high in fiber.** Cereals such as Fiber One, 100% Bran, and All Bran Extra Fiber all have 13 grams or more in a ½ cup serving. If your child will not eat these cereals alone, combine them with another lower fiber, higher interest cereal.

2. **Add fresh berries to the menu.** Raspberries, blackberries, and marionberries all have significant dietary fiber and are quite good. A blackberry cobbler is a healthy, high fiber dessert for summer time.

3. **Use legumes in menus.** Legumes and beans such as low fat refried beans, kidney beans, black beans, and lentils are all great sources of dietary fiber. They are easy to add to soups and salads, as well as Mexican dishes. Also include corn on the cob and frozen corn to dishes for another high fiber addition.

4. **Increase your use of fresh fruits and vegetables.** Fresh produce has more dietary fiber than canned or frozen vegetables. If possible, include the skins of apples, pears, and peaches to get the most fiber from the fruit.

5. **Use whole wheat bread, pasta, and brown rice.** While the additional fiber varies in whole wheat products, the more you include, the more fiber your child and you will get from everyday entrées such as salads and dinner rolls.

Equally important to adding dietary fiber is to encourage your child to drink enough fluids, including water, each day. Without enough fluid, the added bulk from the fiber in foods may cause more problems than help.

continued ▶

Recipe: Magic Fiber Cookies

Yield: approximately 4 dozen cookies
Preheat oven to: 375 degrees

Ingredients:
  1 c Oat bran
  1 c Rolled oats
  1 c Fiber One cereal
  1 c Kellogg's Bran Flakes
  1 c Margarine (2 sticks)
  ¾ c Sugar
  ¾ c Brown sugar
  2   Eggs
  ½ tsp Vanilla
  2 c All purpose flour
  1 c Seedless raisins
  1 tsp Baking powder
  1 c Chopped walnuts (optional)
  1 tsp Baking soda
  ½ tsp Salt
  ½ c Water at room temperature

Directions:
  1. Wash hands.
  2. Turn on oven to 375 degrees.
  3. Combine oat bran, oats, cereal, raisins, and nuts in a bowl. Set aside.
  4. Cream margarine, sugar, and brown sugar with mixer until fluffy.
  5. Add eggs and vanilla, then cream some more.
  6. Slowly add flour, baking powder, baking soda, and salt to margarine mixture.
  7. Slowly mix in water until everything is smooth (about 1 minute).
  8. Add bran mixture and blend at medium speed.
  9. Drop by teaspoons onto greased cookie sheet.
  10. Bake in a 375-degree oven or until light brown.
  11. Let cool at least one minute before removing from cookie sheet.
  12. Cool to room temperature and eat.

Per Cookie:
  125 Calories
  63 Calories from fat (9 grams fat)
  2 grams dietary fiber

Activity Ideas for Children with Down Syndrome

The age ranges suggested for specific activities are not exact. Many children with Down syndrome may enjoy doing activities at older or younger ages than suggested here.

AGES BIRTH TO THREE

Exercise
- swimming (anything with water)
- crawling
- climbing
- creeping
- carpet belly flops
- scooter
- dancing
- walking
- kicking a ball

Passive Activity
- swinging
- spinning
- slide

Crafts
- drawing with crayon
- listening to music
- Sing-a-long
- Play dough (supervised)
- ripping paper

Sports-oriented
- watching hockey and basketball
- Nerf® basketball, football
- balloon volleyball
- playing catch

Events
- activities where there are other children
- shopping
- the park
- Sunday school
- parties, such as birthday parties

Media
- tapes
- TV
- radio
- CDs

Other
- read along with Mom or Dad
- Kindermusic
- playing the tambourine or drum

AGES 3-5

Exercise
- swimming lessons
- dancing
- gymnastics
- mini trampoline
- trikes and ride-on toys
- Discovery Zone, McDonald's Play Place (or other indoor playground)

Events
- Birthday Parties at Little Gym (like Gymboree)
- same as for Birth - 3

Sports-oriented
- backyard play
- swinging
- sliding
- basketball
- T-ball
- watching monster truck races or whatever sport appeals to child
- golf (child-sized club)

continued ▶

Crafts
- drawing
- play dough
- water colors, paint with water
- finger paints
- stickers, Colorforms

Other
- computer games
- building toys (blocks, Duplo, Tinker Toys)
- Simon Says
- Musical Chairs
- CDs
- tapes
- TV

AGES 5-8

Sports-oriented
- T-ball
- soccer
- basketball
- four square
- dodge ball
- tetherball
- lawn bowling
- bowling
- croquet
- badminton
- fishing
- boating
- playing catch
- street hockey
- miniature golf

Events
- parties
- participating in holiday events
- school plays and presentations
- Scouting, Camp Fire Kids, or 4-H
- attending fairs
- reading circles at library
- community children's events (parades, festivals)
- watching performances (ice skating, hockey, musicals, etc.)
- theme parks
- camping

Exercise
- playground play
- climbing trees and play structures
- riding a bike (training wheels) or trike
- swimming
- hiking
- horseback riding
- dancing or ballet
- yoga
- gymnastics
- Discovery Zone (tube time)
- mini trampoline

Crafts
- board games (Candy Land, Chutes and Ladders)
- puzzles
- art projects
- collecting (coins, trading cards, Beanie Babies)
- singing
- Glitter Glue
- introduce a musical instrument
- coloring, drawing
- play dough
- water colors
- Wikki Sticks

Other
- hopscotch
- sleepovers begin
- religious services and events
- going to the zoo, children's museum, arboretum, other investigative activities
- group games: duck, duck, goose; hide & seek
- flying kite

continued ▶

Media
- using a CD player or cassette
- using a child's karaoke machine
- TV
- VCR
- video and computer games
- watching slides
- listening to stories
- reading or looking at books
- Playstation/Nintendo

Chores
- Helping to load the dishwasher
- helping with laundry (sorting socks, putting clothes away)
- taking out the garbage
- helping in the garden, watering
- walking or feeding pet (supervised)
- tidying room
- dusting
- washing windows (with cleaning spray)

AGES 9-12

Exercise
- playground play
- climbing trees and play structures
- riding a bike (with or without training wheels)
- riding scooter
- swimming
- hiking
- horseback riding
- dancing/ballet
- yoga
- gymnastics
- jogging
- aerobics
- weight lifting
- roller blading or skating
- Tae kwon do
- trampoline
- jumping rope

Sports-oriented
- T-ball/baseball
- soccer
- basketball
- four square
- dodge ball
- tetherball
- bowling
- lawn bowling
- croquet
- badminton
- tennis
- golf
- Special Olympic activities
- fishing
- boating
- camping
- snow skiing (cross country and downhill)
- tubing behind a ski boat

Media
- using a CD player or cassette
- using a child's karaoke machine
- television
- VCR
- video and computer games
- watching slides
- listening to stories
- reading or looking at books
- using the computer
- doing speech homework with a tape recorder (microphone!)

Chores
- vacuuming
- shoveling snow
- raking leaves
- making bed
- assisting with meal preparation
- helping with bathroom or kitchen clean-up
- same as earlier ages, with less supervision

continued ▶

Events

- parties
- participating in holiday events
- school plays and presentations
- scouting, Camp Fire Kids, or 4-H
- attending fairs
- reading circles at library
- community children's events (parades, festivals)
- watching performances (ice skating, hockey, musicals, etc.)
- attending sporting activities
- movies
- DS Club, "friends first" (8-12 year olds)

Other

- sleepovers
- religious services and events
- going to the zoo, children's museum, other investigative activities
- calling friends on the phone
- being the "announcer" with a microphone
- flying a kite
- camping
- spending time with friends
- visiting relatives
- pets

Crafts

- board games and card games
- puzzles
- art projects
- collecting (coins, trading cards, Beanie Babies)
- singing
- playing a musical instrument
- needlecraft
- woodworking (supervised)
- jewelry making
- scrapbooking
- photography
- leather craft
- building models
- water colors, paint by number
- play dough, modeling clay

AGES 13-15

Exercise

- riding bike or a scooter
- limited use of stationary exercise machines
- karate
- swimming
- dancing
- dance class (jazz, tap, ballet)
- hiking
- horseback riding
- yoga
- gymnastics
- aerobics
- weight lifting
- roller blading or skating
- adapted obstacle courses

Sports-oriented

- baseball/softball
- soccer
- football
- basketball
- four square
- dodge ball
- kickball
- tennis
- bowling
- lawn bowling
- fishing
- boating
- snow skiing (cross country and downhill)
- golf
- Special Olympics activities

continued ▶

Events

- parties
- participating in holiday events
- school plays and presentations
- Scouting, Camp Fire Kids, or 4-H
- attending fairs
- reading circles at library
- community children's events (parades, festivals)
- watching performances (ice skating, hockey, musicals, etc.)
- attending sporting activities
- movies
- kite flying
- watching school sporting events
- camping

Media

- using a CD player or cassette
- using a child's karaoke machine
- television
- VCR
- video and computer games
- watching slides
- listening to stories
- reading or looking at books
- using the computer
- using the copy machine

Chores

- mopping floor
- same as at earlier ages, with less supervision

Crafts

- board games and card games
- puzzles
- art projects
- collecting (coins, trading cards, Beanie Babies)
- singing
- playing a musical instrument
- needlecraft
- woodworking (supervised)
- jewelry making
- scrapbooking
- photography
- leather craft
- building models
- Pen Pals
- drawing

Other

- sleepovers
- religious services and events
- going to the zoo, museum, other investigative activities
- calling friends on the phone
- three weeks of summer camp
- creating new cheers for rally
- creating new dances
- spending time with friends
- visiting relatives
- pets

AGES 16+

Exercise

- riding bike or scooter
- limited use of stationary exercise machines
- karate
- swimming
- dancing
- hiking
- horseback riding
- yoga
- gymnastics
- jogging
- aerobics
- weight lifting
- roller blading or skating
- adapted obstacle courses
- fitness walking
- working out at the gym with a friend
- climbing
- roller skating or roller blading
- water aerobics

continued ▶

Sports-oriented
- baseball/softball
- soccer
- football
- basketball
- four square
- dodge ball
- kickball
- tennis
- badminton
- bowling
- lawn bowling
- volleyball
- golf
- ping pong
- Frisbee
- fishing
- boating, paddle boating
- snow skiing (cross country and downhill)
- Special Olympics activities

Media
- using a CD player or cassette
- using a child's karaoke machine
- television
- VCR
- video and computer games
- watching slides
- listening to stories
- reading or looking at books
- using the computer
- getting on the Internet, e-mailing
- copy machine
- photography
- using video camera
- Game Boy

Chores
- Running nearby errands (mailing letters, buying newspaper, returning library books)
- mowing lawn (with supervision)
- same as at earlier ages, with less supervision

Events
- parties
- Broadway musicals and similar
- "conducting" music
- participating in holiday events
- school plays and presentations
- attending fairs
- reading circles at library
- community social club
- watching performances (musicals, ballet, etc.)
- attending sporting activities
- movies
- kite flying
- Road Runners Club
- drama club
- going to movies with friends
- going to restaurants with friends
- day trips (zoo, museum, beach, etc.)
- community children's events (parades, festivals)

Crafts
- board games and card games
- puzzles
- art projects
- collecting (coins, trading cards, recipes)
- singing
- playing a musical instrument
- needlecraft
- woodworking (supervised)
- jewelry making
- scrapbooking
- photography
- leather craft
- building models
- pen pals
- sculpting with cardboard and duct tape
- word searches
- writing stories
- oil painting
- making collages

continued ▶

Other
- sleepovers
- religious services and events
- going to the zoo, museums, other investigative activities
- calling friends on the phone
- spending time with friends
- visiting relatives
- pets
- paid or volunteer jobs in the community
- music lessons
- overnight summer camp
- drama classes
- writing letters, stories, lists
- copying things from books
- shopping

Determining Calorie Needs

As Chapter 13 explains, research shows that the basal metabolic rate of people with Down syndrome is 10-15 percent lower than in people without Down syndrome. That is, people with Down syndrome burn 10-15 percent fewer calories when at rest than other people do. To maintain a healthy weight, people with Down syndrome either need to consume 10-15 percent fewer calories than recommended for people without Down syndrome, or be more active. Below are several methods of estimating how many calories children and adults with Down syndrome should consume.

Adaptations of Childhood RDAs

The simplest method for determining the calorie needs of **children** with Down syndrome, aged 14 and under, is to use a formula based on the recommended daily amount for children without Down syndrome.

Age in Years	(per kg)	Calories (per cm)	(per in)
Girls			
1-3	122	14.3	36.3
4-6	93	14.3	36.3
7-10	80.9	14.3	36.3
11-14	61	14.3	36.3
Boys			
1-3	109	16.1	40.9
4-6	100	16.1	40.9
7-10	90	16.1	40.9
11-14	80	16.1	40.9

Adapted from Toolbox: A Resource for Dietetics Professionals Working with Adults with Developmental Disorders/Mental Retardation in Community-Based Programs. *Published by Dietetics in Developmental and Psychiatric Disorders and Consulting Dietitians in Health Care Facilities Dietetic Practice Groups of the American Dietetic Association, 1998.*

If you do not know your child's metric measurements:
- to convert pounds to kilograms, divide weight in pounds by 2.2 (65# ÷ 2.2 = 29.5 kg).
- to convert inches to centimeters, multiply height in inches by 2.54 (42" x 2.54 = 106.7 cm).

For example, Sally is a typical five-year-old with Down syndrome. She goes to kindergarten in the morning and daycare in the afternoon. She likes to run through the sprinkler, ride her trike, and play games with her sister. She is 42 inches tall and weighs 42 pounds.

Using the above equation, Sally's calorie needs are calculated as follows:

42 pounds ÷ 2.2 = 19 kilograms (kg)
19 kg x 93 cal/kg = 1767 calories per day.
OR
42 inches x 2.54 = 106.7 cm
106.7 cm x 14.3 cal/cm = 1526 calories per day.

As you can see, there is a difference between the two equations. You may want to use calories per centimeter equation because it doesn't take into account any extra weight your child may have. Either equation gives you a reasonable starting point.

In general, using either of these two equations gives a higher calorie estimation than the Harris-Benedict equations described below. There is no real way to be precise in determining calorie needs. What is most important is to be able to make an educated, reliable estimate of your child's calorie needs—and either of these two methods will help you do that.

CONVERTING KILOJOULES TO CALORIES

Converting from KJS (kilojoules) to Calories:
Multiply the number of kjs by 0.239

1 kjs=0.239 calories
320 kjs=76.48 calories

Converting from calories to KJS:
Multiply the number of calories by 4.184

1 calorie=4.184 KJS
75 calories=313.8 KJS

Adjusted Basal Energy Expenditure Using Harris-Benedict Equations

A second way to calculate calorie needs for **children *and* adults** with Down syndrome is to use the Harris-Benedict Equation for Basal Energy Expenditure (BEE). The following equations calculate 90 percent of the BEE for people without Down syndrome to determine the "Down Syndrome Basal Energy Expenditure" or DSBEE.

INFANTS:
[22.1 + (31.05 x kg) + (1.16 x cm)] x .9 = DSBEE
Remember, to convert pounds to kilograms, divide by 2.2.
Multiply DSBEE by Activity Factor (and Injury Factor if appropriate) for total calorie need for 24 hours. (See next page for Activity Factor.)

CHILDREN & ADULTS:
Men (Non-Metric Formula):
[66+ (6.3 x lbs) + (12.7 x in) – (6.8 x age)] x .9 = DSBEE
Multiply DSBEE by Activity Factor (see below) for total calorie need for 24 hours.

Men (Metric Formula):
66.5 + (13.75 x kg) + (5.003 x cm) – (6.775 x age) = DSBEE
Multiply DSBEE by Activity Factor (see below) for total calorie need for 24 hours.

Women (Non-Metric Formula):
[655 + (4.3 x lbs) + (4.3 x in) – (4.7 x age)] x .9 = DSBEE
Multiply DSBEE by Activity Factor (see below) for total calorie need for 24 hours.

Women (Metric Formula):
655.1 + (9.563 x kg) + (1.850 x cm) – (4.676 x age) = DSBEE

Correction for Obesity:
If your child is more than 125 percent of ideal body weight, there is one additional step to take to get the most accurate measure of calories needed. (See below for information on ideal body weight.) You need to obtain a "corrected weight" to use in place of her actual weight in the above equation. (BEE is corrected for those who are obese because fatty tissue is not metabolically active.) Corrected weights are also important to use when a person is very ill and hospitalized. The correction changes the equation a little, but not dramatically.

[(ABW - DBW) x 0.25] + DBW = corrected weight to use in DSBEE equation.

ABW = Actual Body Weight

DBW = Desired Body Weight (see description below)

ACTIVITY FACTORS

There is no research at this time that indicates that people with Down syndrome use calories for activity differently than people without Down syndrome. Therefore, the number of calories used to walk, swim, or jog are calculated in the same way. When using DSBEE to estimate calorie needs, you must multiply the DSBEE by Activity Factors (AF) which are described below:

Definition of Activity Factors:

Sedentary (1.2)—Spends the majority of the day sitting in a chair or lying in bed or on the couch. This AF is probably an appropriate place to start with estimating calories for the average person with Down syndrome. It does not include people who are involved in sports activities every day or who work out in some way each day. However, it is an accurate AF for school (even with P.E.) and most jobs.

Light (1.3)—Spends the majority of the day standing or sitting using their arms. This would be similar to someone who works on an assembly line or in a repetitive type of job staying at one work station most of the day. At home, it includes watching television and making meals. This AF is appropriate for people who have a job that requires some walking around (grocery store bagger, for instance), and is not sitting a lot when at home.

Moderate (1.4)—Spends the majority of the day walking or standing, uses brisk arm movements, and walks at a good clip rather than sauntering. At home, moderate activity would include being active by walking around the neighborhood and helping around the house with chores. This is a very busy person. It is unlikely that a person with Down syndrome will maintain this level of activity all the time while awake.

High (1.5)—Includes many sports, walking uphill, and other activities that involve intermittent, but frequent spurts of energy that bring heart rate up to the target heart rate range. It is unlikely this AF will be used for a person's entire day.

Rule of Thumb for AF:
Because no one is active in the same way each day, I generally use an average of the activity factors when I calculate energy needs. This estimation takes some experience, which is really an "educated guess." For instance, I will generally begin with an AF of 1.25 if people are making an effort to include an exercise program in their weekly routine. Even so, once estimated calorie needs are calculated, it is important to remember that it is an estimate that can be adjusted over time as needed. Use the estimated calorie needs as a guide, or an idea of how many calories your child needs to maintain weight, rather than a precise line for weight gain or weight loss.

Example of using DSBEE with Activity Factors:

Jon is an eighteen-year-old with Down syndrome who is currently in his junior year of high school. Jon is involved in a foodservice internship at school, where he spends about 2 hours a day in the kitchen on his feet. He spends the rest of the school day like every other student, sitting in a chair. Jon is also involved in a variety of Special Olympic sports. He practices with his team once a week and they have a game every two weeks. Jon walks about a mile total on his way to and from the bus stop on school days. On weekends, Jon likes to watch some of his favorite movies and sometimes rides his bike. Jon is 5' 4" (64 inches) tall and weighs 145 pounds.

Jon's energy needs are:
$[66 + (9.6 \times \mathbf{145}) + (12.7 \times \mathbf{64}) - (6.8 \times \mathbf{18})] \times .9 = $ DSBEE
$[2148] \times .9 = 1933$ calories DSBEE

DSBEE x AF = estimated calories needed to maintain current weight.
$1933 \times 1.25 = 2417$ calories per day to maintain current weight.

Using the DSBEE and an Activity Factor (AF) of 1.25, Jon's estimated calorie need to maintain his current weight is about 2400 calories per day.

Taking this one step further, if Jon were to keep a detailed food diary for a week, we would add up all the calories recorded and divide by 7 to determine his average daily intake and whether he is meeting or exceeding his calorie need. It is fine to eat 3000 calories one day and 1800 the next day. In the end, it will all average out and maintain his current weight.

Desired Body Weight for Children with Down Syndrome

Growth charts for children with Down syndrome give us an idea of growth patterns for children with Down syndrome from birth to eighteen years of age. However, parents and clinicians often say that they feel the growth charts for Down syndrome reflect an overweight population and they prefer to use the growth charts designed for all children. Regardless of which growth chart you use, these charts are best used to determine patterns of growth. They are not designed to determine a child's Desired Body Weight (DBW) or the weight that is appropriate for their age and height.

DBW in people without Down syndrome is the expected weight for a person. Generally, children and adults are considered to be an appropriate weight if they are 90-110 percent of their DBW. DBW for children with Down syndrome is a little trickier to determine since there is a propensity for a short, stocky stature.

Here are the steps to calculating what percentage of DBW your child is that does not require you to keep information over a period of time.

1. Using the CDC growth charts for all children, plot the height of the child at the point where the height is at the 50th percentile. Next, determine the age for this point. This is the "height-age" of the child. (CDC growth charts are printed later in this section.)
2. Determine the weight at the 50th percentile for the height-age of the child. This is the expected average weight for a typically developing child at the same height as the child with Down syndrome. This is the DBW for this child.
3. Divide the actual weight of the child by the weight found in step two. Multiply by 100 to determine his percentage of desired body weight. Your child's DBW range is 90-110 percent of this weight.

It is important to remember that this is a reference point. Including this information was difficult for me to do because if your child is overweight, the percentage of ADBW calculated may be quite high. If you already know your child is overweight, this is not a helpful exercise. However, it is very helpful in borderline situations or in situations where the child's weight is appropriate, but she still appears "soft" or "stocky." Use it with care. There's no need to know the ADBW if it is detrimental to your self-confidence as a parent.

Example:

Blake is a thirteen-year-old boy with Down syndrome. He is currently 120 pounds and 5'0" tall. Calculate his DBW range and the current percentage of DBW.

1. Using the CDC growth charts for all children, plot the height of the child at the point where the height is at the 50th percentile. Next, determine the age for this point. Blake's "height-age" is: 12.5 years. (See left chart on the next page.)

2. Determine the weight at the 50th percentile for the height-age of the child. This is the expected average weight for a typically developing child at the same height as the child with Down syndrome. This is the DBW for this child with DS. Blake's DBW is about 95 pounds. (See right chart on the next page.)

3. Divide the actual weight of the child by the weight found in step two. Multiply by 100 to determine the %DBW. Your child's DBW range is 90-110% of this weight. Blake's %DBW is: 120 ÷ 95 = 1.26. 1.26 x 100 = 126% DBW.

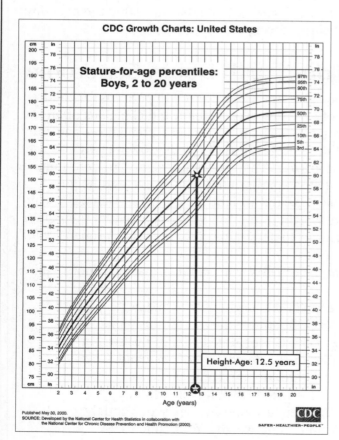

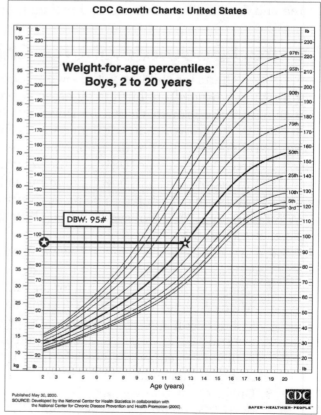

Desired Body Weight (DBW) Range for Adults with Down Syndrome

There is no scientific way to determine DBW for adults with Down syndrome at this time. Differences in metabolism, muscle tone, and body shape make it difficult to use typical measures without making some sort of adaptations. Yet it is often helpful to parents and professionals to have some sort of benchmark that is considered the desired range. For the general population, a "rule-of-thumb" approach is commonly used. Therefore, this is a "rule-of-thumb" approach that is adjusted for adults with Down syndrome.

The "rule-of-thumb" for adults *without* Down syndrome is:

- *Women:* 100 pounds for the first 5 feet in height and 5 pounds for every inch over. The DBW range is 90-110 percent of this number. For example, for a woman who is 5 feet, 5 inches, the DBW would be 90 to 110 percent of 125, or 112.5 to 137.5 pounds (.90 x 125 is 112.5 and 1.1 x 125 is 137.5.)
- *Men:* 106 pounds for the first 5 feet in height and 6 pounds for every inch over. The DBW range is 90-110 percent of this number.

The adjusted rule-of-thumb approach for adults with Down syndrome merely adds 10 percent. This means:

- *Women with DS*: 100 pounds for the first 5 feet in height and 5 pounds for every inch over. Multiply this number by 1.1 to get DBW. The DBW range is 90-110 percent of this number.
- *Men with DS*: 106 pounds for the first 5 feet in height and 6 pounds for every inch over. Multiply this number by 1.1 to get DBW. The DBW range is 90-110 percent of this number.

If the adult with Down syndrome is not 5 feet tall:

- *Women:* subtract 5 pounds from 100 for every inch under 5 feet. Multiply by 1.1 to get DBW. The DBW range is 90-110 percent of this number.
- *Men:* subtract 3 pounds from 100 for every inch under 5 feet. Multiply by 1.1 to get DBW. The DBW range is 90-110 percent of this number.

Height in inches	Adj. DBW		Adj. DBW Range	
	(women)	(men)	(women)	(men)
55 (4'7")	82	94	74-90	85-103
56 (4'8")	88	97	79-97	87-107
57 (4'9")	94	100	85-103	90-110
58 (4'10")	99	103	89-109	93-113
59 (4'11")	105	107	95-116	96-118
60 (5'0")	110	117	99-121	105-129
61 (5'1")	116	123	104-128	111-135
62 (5'2")	121	130	109-133	117-143
63 (5'3")	127	136	114-140	122-150
64 (5'4")	132	143	119-145	129-157
65 (5'5")	138	150	124-152	135-165
66 (5'6")	143	56	129-157	139-172
67 (5'7")	149	163	134-164	147-179

Please remember this is a proposed "rule-of-thumb" approach. To be useful, it requires that you use your eyes and compassionate estimation along with the mathematical formula until a better method of determining desired weights for adults with Down syndrome is devised through research and calculation.

Growth Charts

Growth Charts for Children with Down Syndrome

There are growth charts available specifically for children with Down syndrome. They are available on pages 379-386, or you can download full-color versions at: www.growthcharts.com.

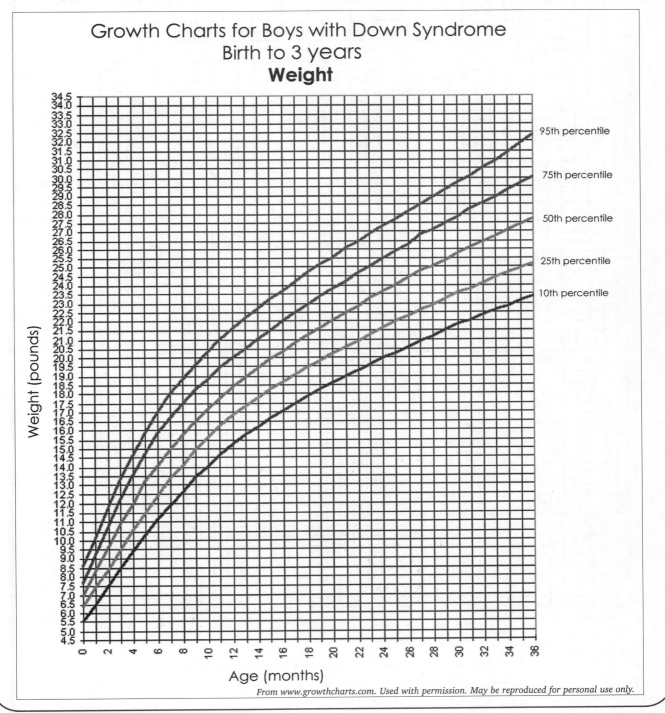

Growth Charts for Boys with Down Syndrome
Birth to 3 years
Weight

From www.growthcharts.com. Used with permission. May be reproduced for personal use only.

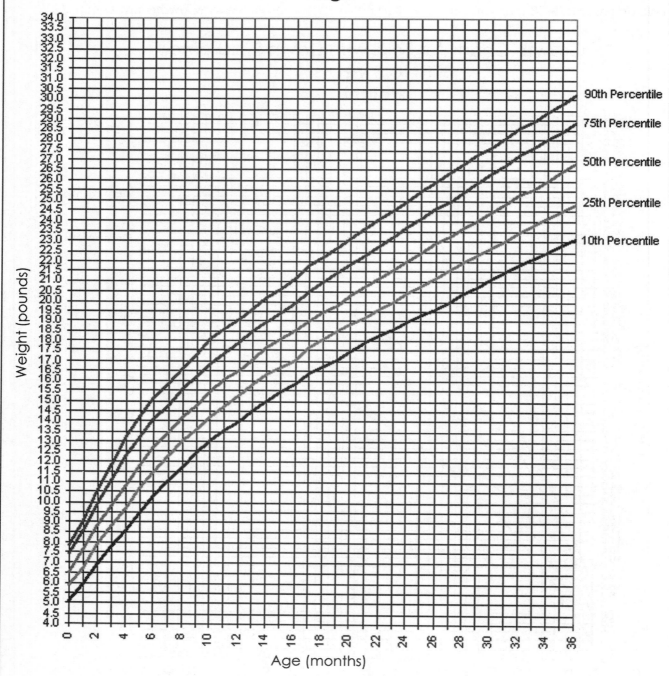

Growth Charts for Girls with Down Syndrome
Birth to 3 years
Weight

From www.growthcharts.com. Used with permission. May be reproduced for personal use only.

Growth Charts for Boys with Down Syndrome
Birth to 3 years
Length

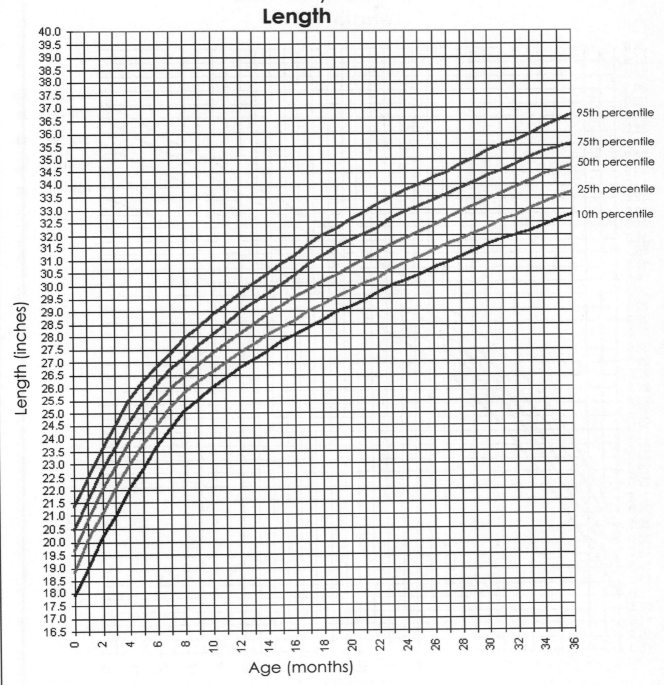

From www.growthcharts.com. Used with permission. May be reproduced for personal use only.

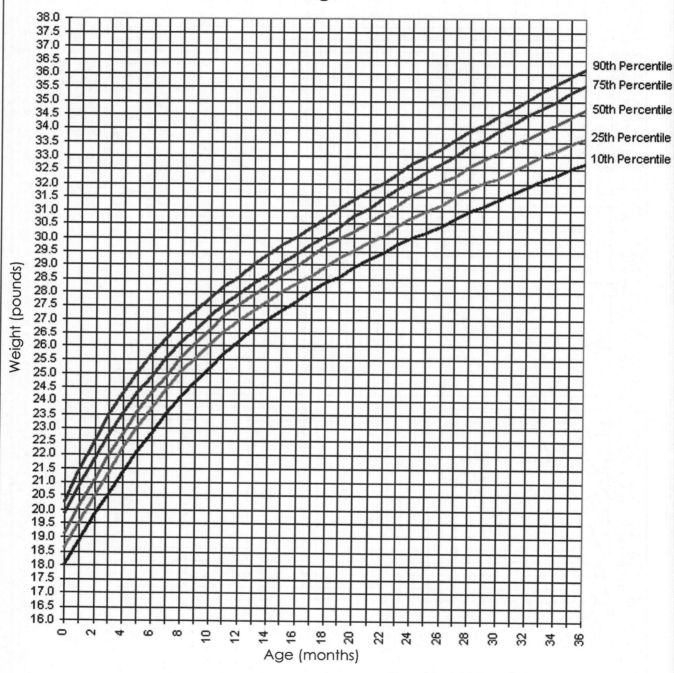

Growth Charts for Girls with Down Syndrome
Birth to 3 years

Length

From www.growthcharts.com. Used with permission. May be reproduced for personal use only.

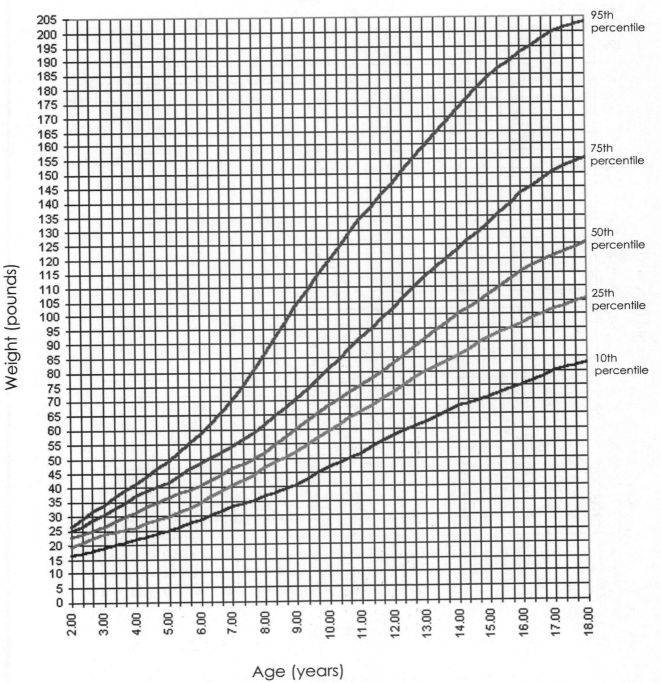

Growth Charts for Boys with Down Syndrome
2-18 years

Weight

From www.growthcharts.com. Used with permission. May be reproduced for personal use only.

Growth Charts for Girls with Down Syndrome
2-18 years
Weight

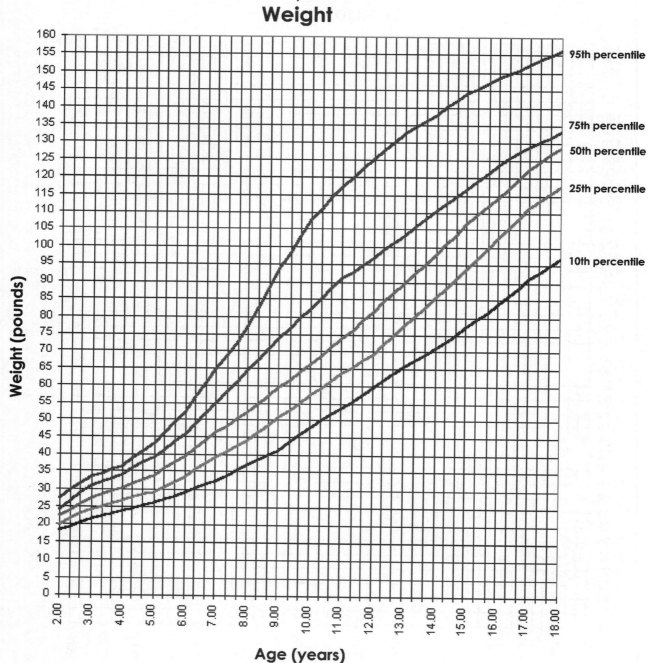

From www.growthcharts.com. Used with permission. May be reproduced for personal use only.

Growth Charts for Boys with Down Syndrome
2-18 Years
Height

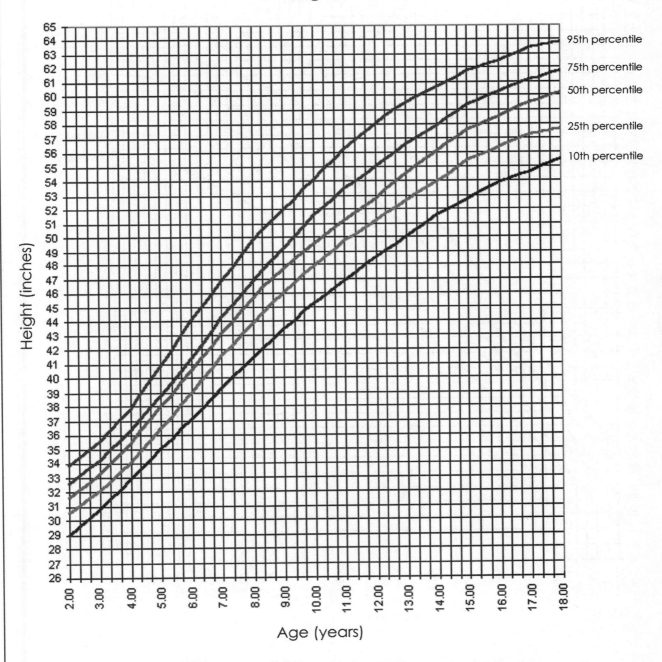

From www.growthcharts.com. Used with permission. May be reproduced for personal use only.

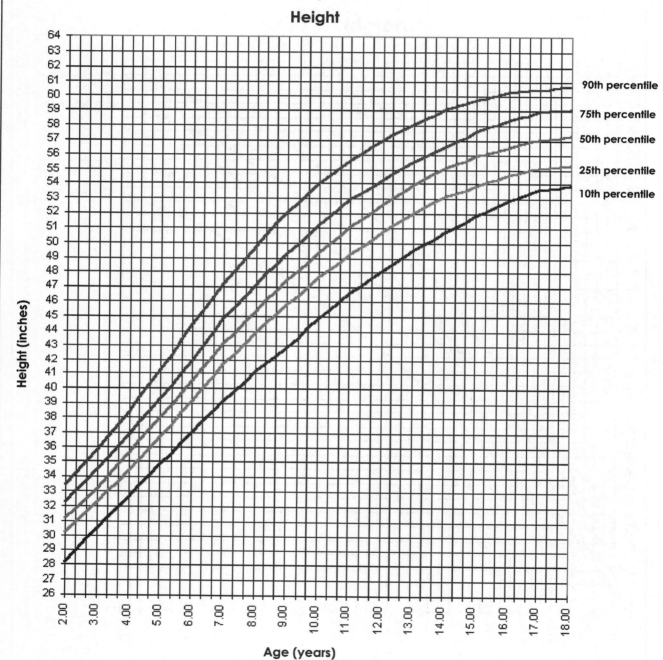

Growth Charts for Girls with Down Syndrome
2-18 years

Height

From www.growthcharts.com. Used with permission. May be reproduced for personal use only.

CDC Growth Charts for Children

The Center for Disease Control (CDC) has updated their growth charts for typically developing children. We have reproduced the height and weight charts on pages 387-394. They can also be downloaded from: www.cdc.gov/growthcharts. This site also includes charts for BMI (Body Mass Index), which are not reproduced here, as this is not a reliable measure for children with Down syndrome.

CDC Growth Charts: United States

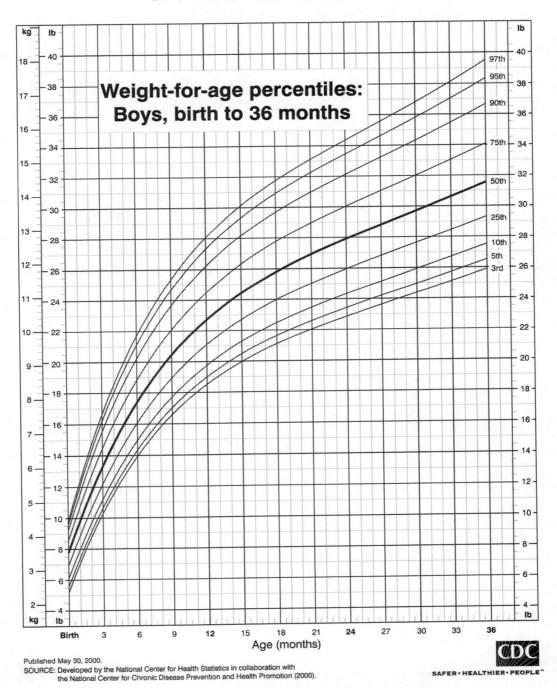

Weight-for-age percentiles:
Boys, birth to 36 months

Published May 30, 2000.
SOURCE: Developed by the National Center for Health Statistics in collaboration with
the National Center for Chronic Disease Prevention and Health Promotion (2000).

SAFER · HEALTHIER · PEOPLE™

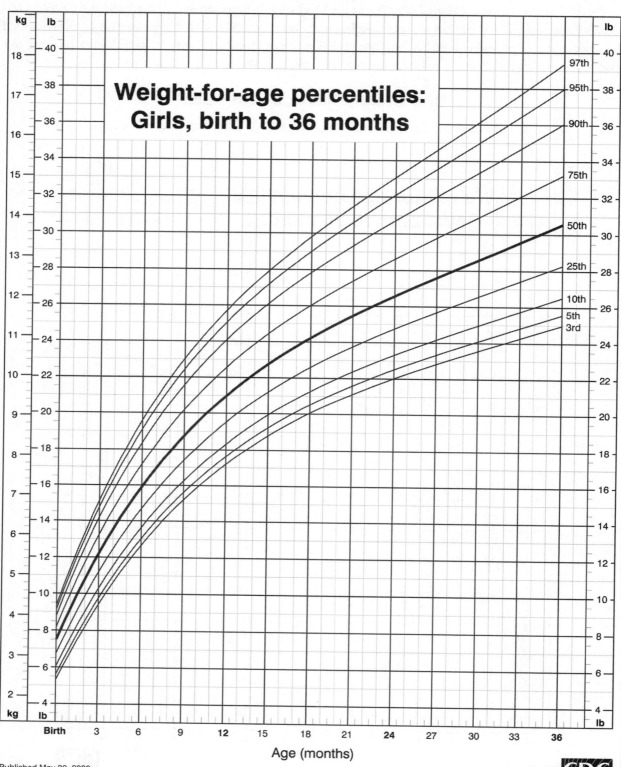

CDC Growth Charts: United States

Weight-for-age percentiles: Girls, birth to 36 months

Age (months)

Published May 30, 2000.
SOURCE: Developed by the National Center for Health Statistics in collaboration with the National Center for Chronic Disease Prevention and Health Promotion (2000).

SAFER · HEALTHIER · PEOPLE™

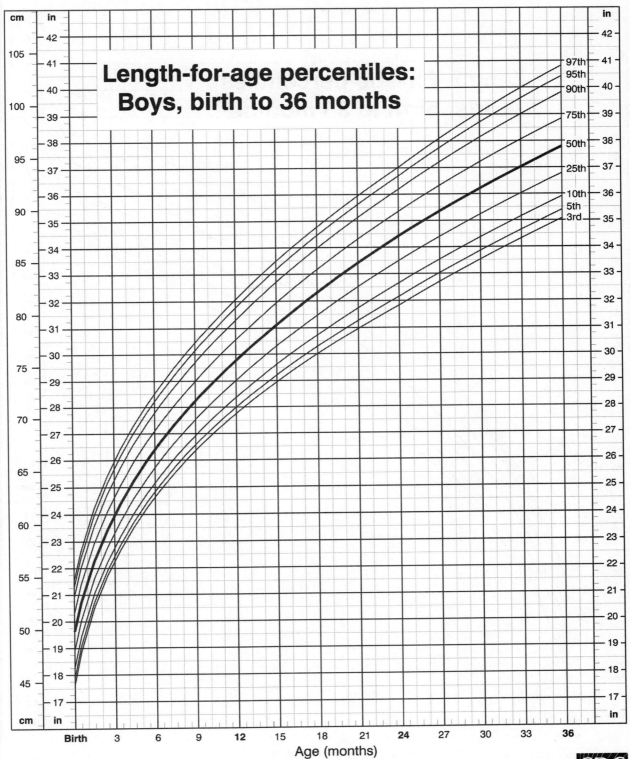

CDC Growth Charts: United States

Length-for-age percentiles: Boys, birth to 36 months

Age (months)

Published May 30, 2000.
SOURCE: Developed by the National Center for Health Statistics in collaboration with
the National Center for Chronic Disease Prevention and Health Promotion (2000).

SAFER · HEALTHIER · PEOPLE™

CDC Growth Charts: United States

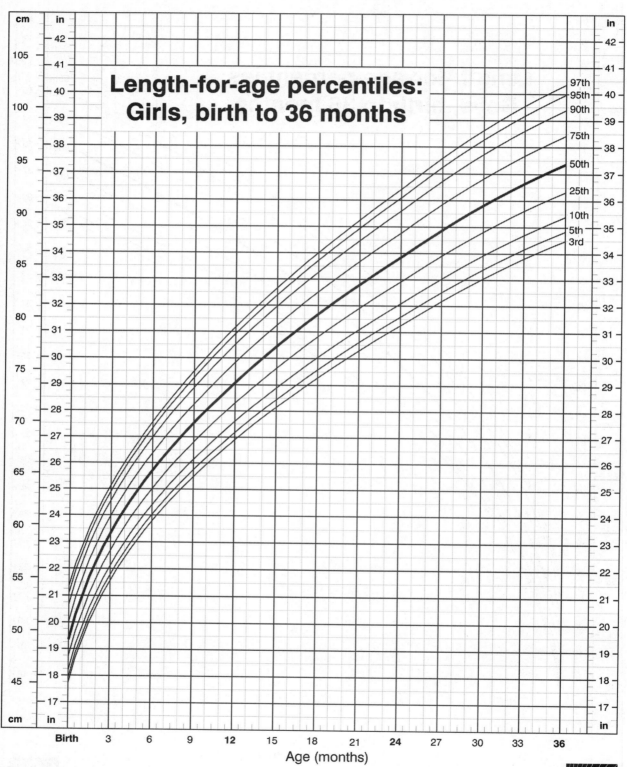

Length-for-age percentiles: Girls, birth to 36 months

Published May 30, 2000.
SOURCE: Developed by the National Center for Health Statistics in collaboration with
the National Center for Chronic Disease Prevention and Health Promotion (2000).

SAFER · HEALTHIER · PEOPLE™

CDC Growth Charts: United States

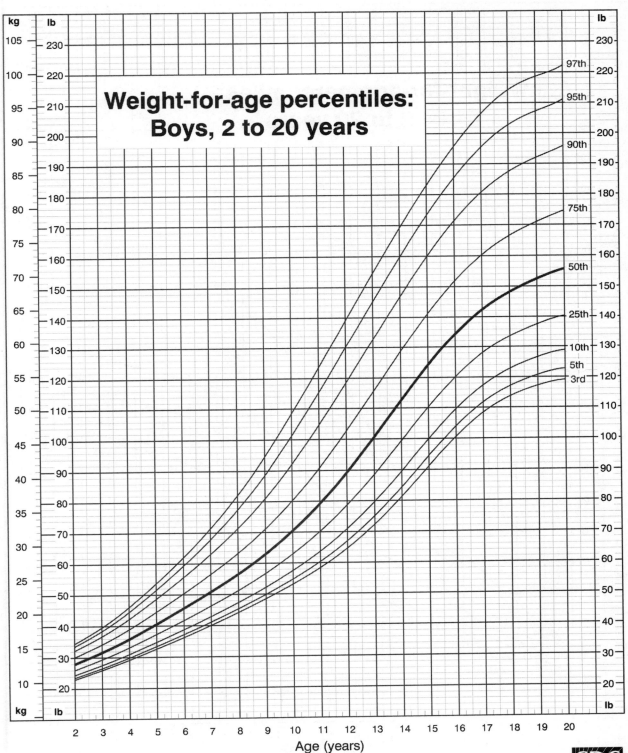

Weight-for-age percentiles: Boys, 2 to 20 years

Published May 30, 2000.
SOURCE: Developed by the National Center for Health Statistics in collaboration with
the National Center for Chronic Disease Prevention and Health Promotion (2000).

SAFER · HEALTHIER · PEOPLE™

CDC Growth Charts: United States

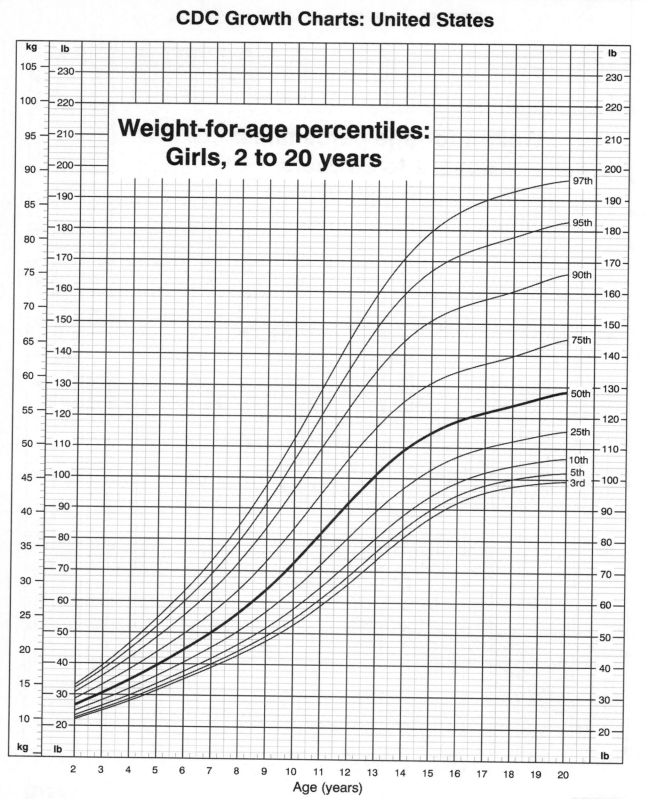

Weight-for-age percentiles: Girls, 2 to 20 years

Age (years)

Published May 30, 2000.
SOURCE: Developed by the National Center for Health Statistics in collaboration with
the National Center for Chronic Disease Prevention and Health Promotion (2000).

SAFER · HEALTHIER · PEOPLE™

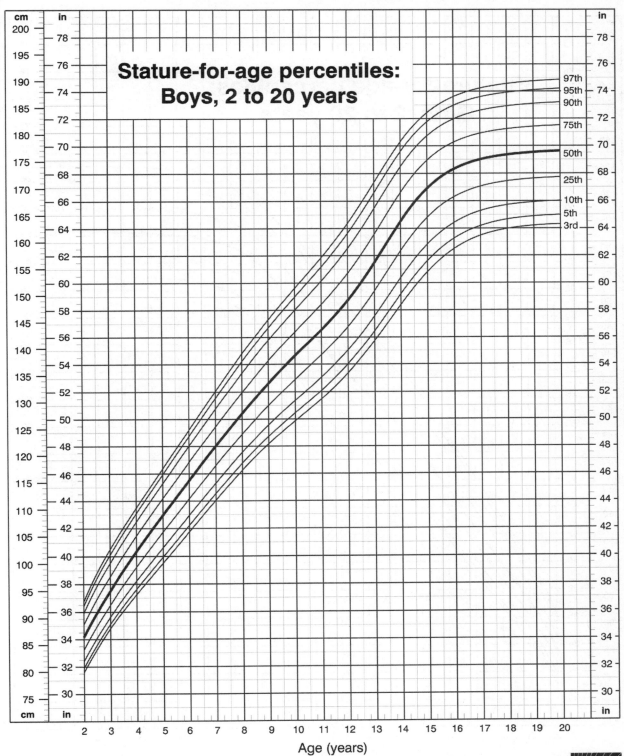

CDC Growth Charts: United States

**Stature-for-age percentiles:
Boys, 2 to 20 years**

Percentile lines labeled: 97th, 95th, 90th, 75th, 50th, 25th, 10th, 5th, 3rd

Left axis: cm (75–200), in (30–78)
Right axis: in (30–78)
X-axis: Age (years) 2 to 20

Published May 30, 2000.
SOURCE: Developed by the National Center for Health Statistics in collaboration with
the National Center for Chronic Disease Prevention and Health Promotion (2000).

SAFER · HEALTHIER · PEOPLE™

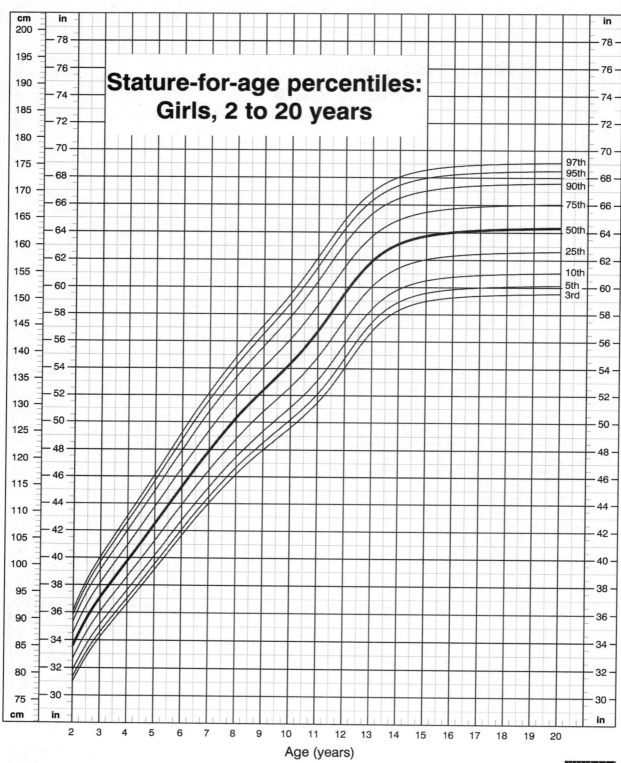

CDC Growth Charts: United States

Stature-for-age percentiles: Girls, 2 to 20 years

Published May 30, 2000.
SOURCE: Developed by the National Center for Health Statistics in collaboration with
the National Center for Chronic Disease Prevention and Health Promotion (2000).

SAFER • HEALTHIER • PEOPLE™

Body Mass Index

Body Mass Index (BMI) is an equation that is used to estimate the amount of body muscle vs. body fat in a person's body. Body Mass Index is widely used in the general population to determine whether a person is underweight, at a healthy weight, overweight, or obese. BMI is also used to assess risk for weight-related disease or injury such as heart disease, stroke, or diabetes. However, BMI has limitations. It is possible to have a BMI in the overweight category yet not be overweight. This is especially true for people who are athletes or who are more muscular than average. In contrast, people with Down syndrome have lower muscle tone and may have a BMI that suggests a higher percentage of body fat than they actually have. The equation used to calculate BMI does not compensate for that lower tone and there is no method of adjusting the equation at this time.

If used as a tool to measure and compare over time, BMI can give you an idea of how your child's body composition may have changed over the course of a year or more. The difference for people with Down syndrome is how BMI is interpreted and used.

Body Mass Index (BMI) is determined as follows:

English Formula:

Weight in pounds ÷ Height in inches ÷ Height in inches x 703 = BMI

Metric Formula:

Weight in kilograms ÷ Height in meters ÷ Height in meters = BMI

For adults:

	Body Mass Index (BMI)
Under weight (increased health risk)	19 and below
"Just right" (not at increased risk)	19-25
Over weight (slightly increased health risk)	25-30
Obese (high risk)	30+

Recipe Template

Makes enough for _____ people.

One serving is _____. (cups, ounces, inches, piece)

It costs $_____ to make this.

It takes ___ hour and _____minutes to make this.

What do I need?
  Ingredients:
-
-
-
-

  Supplies (baking dishes, spatulas, whisk, and so on)
-
-
-
-

How Do I make it?
  Directions:
  Step 1: **Wash Hands.**

  Step 2:

  Step 3:

  etc......

  Step _____: Serve and eat.

  Step _____: Clean up.

How do I store leftovers? ❏ Refrigerator   ❏ Cupboard

When should I throw it away? Su M Tu W Th F Sa

How much do I like it?

What would make it better?

Food Safety

When teaching your child about cooking, it is important to include habits that will promote food safety. This sounds more complicated than it is. There are four primary concepts to food safety:

1. Clean
   - Keep things clean!
   - Wash hands and surfaces often with hot, soapy water.
   - Rub hands for at least 20 seconds when soapy.
   - Use plastic or nonporous cutting boards. Avoid wooden ones.
   - Wash cutting boards in the dishwasher.
   - Use paper towels to wash and dry counters or wash cloth towels often.
   - Clean out the refrigerator regularly. Throw away foods that are more than one week old. (Hint: designate a specific day of the week for clearing out all leftovers and other questionable foods.)

2. Separate
   - Keep meat and poultry separate from other foods.
   - Keep raw meat, fish, and poultry separate from other foods in the shopping cart.
   - Store meat, fish, and poultry separate from other foods in the refrigerator.
   - Use separate cutting boards for meat, fish, and poultry and other foods.

- Wash cutting boards in the dishwasher or in hot soapy water after use.
- Wash plates that had uncooked meat on them before re-using them. Re-using a plate may be convenient, but it's not safe.

3. Cook
   - Cook foods to proper temperatures.
   - Use a meat thermometer to determine the temperature of meats.
   - Cook roasts to a temperature of 145 degrees Fahrenheit.
   - Cook poultry to a temperature of 185 degrees.
   - Cook ground meat (hamburger) to a temperature of 165 degrees.
   - Hint: Buy a meat thermometer with large numbers and mark the "done" temperatures with a permanent marker. Teach your child how to use the meat thermometer: Insert in areas away from the bone so the tip is toward the center of the meat. Or purchase some "pop up" thermometers especially for poultry. Other ways to determine doneness of meat include:
     - ❏ Cook poultry until the meat is white or grayish white and there is no pink meat. There may be some red looking meat near the bone that is pigmented by blood from the marrow.
     - ❏ Cook pork and beef until there is no red meat, but there is juice when you push down on the top of the cut of meat.
   - Cook fish until it is flaky.
   - Cook eggs until yolk and white are firm. Do not eat runny eggs.
   - Bring sauces to a boil (stirring frequently) before serving.
   - Stir and rotate foods cooked in the microwave while they are cooking.

4. Chill
   - Refrigerate foods promptly.
   - Put leftover foods in the refrigerator as soon as the meal is over.
   - Throw away foods left out on the counter longer than two hours.
   - Do not defrost foods on the counter where you prepare foods. Put them in the sink or in a pan and place the pan on the counter.
   - Defrost meats in the refrigerator the night before whenever possible.
   - Divide leftover foods into small servings to refrigerate or freeze. Write the day of the week and date on them when you put them in the refrigerator or freezer.
   - Do not pack your refrigerator too full. Air needs to be able to move around the foods to keep them properly chilled.

References and Suggested Reading

CHAPTER 1

REFERENCES

Campbell, M.K., Kelsey, K.S. "The PEACH Survey: A Nutrition Screening Tool for Use in Early Intervention Programs," *Journal of the American Dietetic Association.* Vol. 94:10, 1994, pp.1156-1158.

Cohen, W.I. (ed). "Health Care Guidelines for Individuals with Down Syndrome: 1999 Revision." *Down Syndrome Quarterly.* 4:3, 1999, pp. 1-16. www.Denison.edu/dsq/health99.shtml

The Community-Based Feeding Team. Washington State Department of Health, Children with Special Health Care Needs Program, 2001.
Available online: depts.washington.edu/cshcnnut/feeding_teams_list.html

Dietetics in Developmental and Psychiatric Disorders and Consulting Dietitians in Health Care Facilities. *Toolbox: A Resource for Dietetics Professionals Working with Adults with Developmental Disorders/Mental Retardation in Community Based Programs.* 1998.

Feucht, S. "Guidelines for the Use of Thickeners in Foods and Liquids," *Nutrition Focus: For Children with Special Health Care Needs.* Vol. 10:6, 1995.

Gisel, E., Lange, L. Niman, C. "Tongue Movements in 4- and 5-Year-Old Down's Syndrome Children During Eating: A Comparison with Normal Children," *The American Journal of Occupational Therapy.* Vol. 38: 10, 1984, pp. 660-670.

Jaffe, M. "Feeding At-Risk Infants and Toddlers," *Topics in Language Disorders.* December, 1989, pp. 13-25.

Kedesdy, J., Budd, K. *Childhood Feeding Disorders.* Baltimore: Brookes Publishing, 1998.

Klein, M.D., Delaney, T.A.. *Feeding and Nutrition for the Child with Special Needs: Handouts for Parents.* San Antonio, TX: Therapy Skill Builders, 1994.

Klein, M.D., Morris, S.E. *Mealtime Participation Guide.* San Antonio, TX: Therapy Skill Builders, 1999.

Lowman, D., Murphy, S. *The Educator's Guide to Feeding Children with Disabilities.* Baltimore: Brookes Publishing, 1999.

Morris, S.E., Klein, M.D. *Pre-Feeding Skills: A Comprehensive Resource for Mealtime Development.* 2nd ed. San Antonio, TX: Therapy Skill Builders, 2000.

Satter, E. *Child of Mine: Feeding with Love and Good Sense*. Boulder, CO: Bull Publishing Company, 2000.

SUGGESTED READING

Lowman, Dianne Koontz and McKeever, Suzanne Murphy. *The Educator's Guide to Feeding Children with Disabilities*. Baltimore: Brookes Publishing, 1999.

If you're having trouble teaching your child to drink from a cup, use a spoon, or positioning her, or she is a "picky eater," you might glean some tricks to try from this book. Designed to support educators working with children who have feeding concerns, this book is a tad clinical, but full of different ideas for a variety of situations.

Satter, Ellyn. *Child of Mine: Feeding with Love and Good Sense*. Rev. Ed. Boulder, CO: Bull Publishing, 2000.

Child of Mine is a one-of-a-kind book for parents of infants and toddlers. Satter does a wonderful job of explaining the importance of how we feed our children as well as what we feed our children. One note of caution: Satter does not pretend to address some of the concerns that children with Down syndrome or related disabilities may encounter. The information she provides will need to be adapted for your own child's developmental progress. Nonetheless, it is a treasure trove of information.

Satter, Ellyn. *How to Get Your Kid to Eat...But Not Too Much: From Birth to Adolescence*. Boulder, CO: Bull Publishing, 1987.

In this book, Satter focuses primarily on the school-age child and the emotional issues that surround eating behavior. She lays out a structure for the responsibilities of parents and children when it comes to feeding which minimizes food-centered battles. If you feel as if your mealtime has become a battlefield, you might find some good advice in this book.

CHAPTER 2

REFERENCES

Aumonier, M.E., Cunningham, C.C. "Breast Feeding in Infants with Down's Syndrome." *Child Care Health Dev*. Vol. 9, 1983, pp. 247-255.

Children's Hospitals and Clinics. *Breastfeeding an Infant with Down Syndrome*. Minneapolis: Children's Hospital and Clinics, 2000. www.childrenshc.org/fp/pdfs/BreastfeedingDown.pdf

Danner, S.C. "Breastfeeding the Neurologically Impaired Infant." NAACOGS. *Clinical Issues in Perinatology Women's Health Nursing*. Vol. 3, 1992, pp. 640-646.

Faille, P., Barone, C., Pettinato, R., Romano, C. "IgG Antibodies to Beta-lactoglobulin and Cow's Milk Protein Intolerance in Down Syndrome." *Down Syndrome Research Practices*. Vol. 5(3), 1998, pp.120-122.

Hattner, J.T. "Pediatric Formula Update 2001." *Nutrition Focus*. Vol. 6 (no. 3), May-June 2001, p. 1.

Horwood, L.J., Darlow, B.A., Mogridge, N. "Breast Milk Feeding and Cognitive Ability at 7-8 years." *Archives of Disease in Childhood, Fetal Neonatal Edition*. Vol. 84, 2001, pp. F23-F27.

Kelleher, D.K., Duggan, C. "Breast Milk and Breastfeeding in the 1990s." *Current Opinions in Pediatrics*. Vol. 11, 1999, pp. 275-280.

La Leche League. *Breastfeeding a Baby with Down Syndrome*. Schaumburg, IL: La Leche League International, 1997.

Nursing Mothers' Association of Australia. *Breastfeeding Your Baby with Down Syndrome*. East Malvern, Victoria: Nursing Mothers' Association of Australia, 1998.

Pinnock, C.B., Graham, N.M., Mylvaganam, A., Douglas, R.M. "Relationship between Milk Intake and Mucus Production in Adult Volunteers Challenged with Rhinovirus-2." *American Review of Respiratory Disease.* Vol. 141(2), Feb. 1990, pp. 352-6.

Reynolds, A. "Breastfeeding and Brain Development." *Pediatric Clinics of North America.* Vol. 48, 2001, pp. 159-171

Ryan, A.S. "The Resurgence of Breastfeeding in the United States." *Pediatrics.* Vol. 99, 1997 (electronic version).

Timko, S.W., Culp, Y.D., Pindell, J.G., Harakal, R. "Breastfeeding the Baby with Down Syndrome." In *Lactation Consultant Series.* Garden City Park, NJ: Avery Publishing Group, 1986.

Uauy, R., Mena, P., Peirano, P. "Mechanisms for Nutrient Effects on Brain Development and Cognition." Nestle Nutrition Workshop Series in Clinical Performance Programme, 2001, pp. 41-70.

SUGGESTED READING

Children's Hospitals and Clinics. *Breastfeeding an Infant with Down Syndrome.* Minneapolis: Children's Hospital and Clinics, 2000. www.childrenshc.org/fp/pdfs/BreastfeedingDown.pdf

La Leche League International. *Breastfeeding a Baby with Down Syndrome.* No. 23a. Schaumburg, IL: LaLeche League International, 1997. (Order from La Leche League International, 1400 North Meacham Road, Schaumburg, IL 60173-4840 or from the web site: www.lalecheleague.org)

Nursing Mothers' Association of Australia. *Breastfeeding Your Baby with Down Syndrome.* East Malvern, Victoria: Nursing Mothers' Association of Australia, 1998.
   Order from: Nursing Mothers' Association of Australia, 1818-1822 Malvern Road, East Malvern, Victoria, 3145, Australia. ACN 005 081 523. Or view on web site at: www.breastfeeding.asn.au/bfinfo/down.html

CHAPTER 3

REFERENCES

Birch, L.L., Fisher, J.A. "Appetite and Eating Behavior in Children." *Pediatric Clinics of North America.* Vol. 42:4, 1995, pp. 931-953.

Birch, L.L., Gunder, L., Grimm-Thomas, K., Laing, D.G. "Infants' Consumption of a New Food Enhances Acceptance of Similar Foods." *Appetite.* Vol. 30:3, 1998, pp. 283-295.

Birch, L.L. "Psychological Influences on the Childhood Diet." *Journal of Nutrition.* Vol. 128:2S, 1998, pp. 407S-410S.

Birch, L.L. "The Role of Experience in Children's Food Acceptance Patterns." *Journal of the American Dietetic Association.* Vol. 87:9 (Supplement), 1987, pp. 36S-40S.

Fletcher, J. "Using Observation to Plan Developmentally Sound Mealtime Environments for Children in Group Settings." 2001, WDSA Conference.

Luke, A., Sutton, M., Schoeller, D.A., Rozien, H.J. "Nutrient Intake and Obesity in Preschool Children with Down Syndrome." *Journal of the American Dietetic Association.* Vol. 96:1272.

Satter, E. *How to Get Your Kid to Eat, But Not Too Much.* Boulder, CO: Bull Publishing, 1987.

Satter, E. *Child of Mine: Feeding with Love and Good Sense.* Boulder, CO: Bull Publishing, 2000.

Satter, E. *Secrets of Feeding a Healthy Family.* Madison, WI: Kelcy Press, 1999.

SUGGESTED READING

Baker, B.L., Brightman, A.J., Blacher, J.B., Heifetz, L.J., Hinshaw, S.P., Murphy, D.M. *Steps to Independence: Teaching Every Day Skills to Children with Special Needs.* 3rd ed. Baltimore: Brookes Publishing, 1997.

Bruni, M. *Fine Motor Skills in Children with Down Syndrome: A Guide for Parents and Professionals (Topics in Down syndrome).* Bethesda, MD: Woodbine House, 1998.

Lowman, D., and Murphy, S. *The Educator's Guide to Feeding Children with Disabilities.* Baltimore: Brookes Publishing, 1999.

Morris, S.E., Klein, M.D., *Pre-Feeding Skills: A Comprehensive Resource for Mealtime Development.* 2nd ed. San Antonio, TX: Therapy Skill Builders, 2000.

CHAPTER 4

REFERENCES

Dorner, K., Gaethke, A.S., Tolksdorf, M., Schumann, K.P., Gustmann, H. "Cholesterol Fractions and Triglycerids in Children and Adults with Down's Syndrome." *Clinica Chimica Acta.* Vol. 142, 1984, pp. 307-11.

Duyff, R.L. *The American Dietetic Association's Complete Food and Nutrition Guide.* Minneapolis: Chronimed Publishing, 1996.

Groff, J.L., and Gropper, S.S. *Advanced Nutrition and Human Metabolism.* 3rd ed. Belmont: Wadsworth Thomson Learning, 1999.

Institute of Medicine. *Dietary Reference Intakes for Calcium, Phosphorus, Magnesium, Vitamin D, and Fluoride.* Washington, DC: National Academy Press, 1997.

Institute of Medicine. *Dietary Reference Intakes for Thiamin, Riboflavin, Niacin, Vitamin B_6, Folate, Vitamin B_{12}, Pantothenic Acid, Biotin, and Choline.* Washington, DC: National Academy Press, 2000.

Institute of Medicine. *Dietary Reference Intakes for Vitamin A, Vitamin K, Arsenic, Boron, Chromium, Copper, Iodine, Iron, Manganese, Molybdenum, Nickel, Silicon, Vanadium, and Zinc. Prepublication Copy.* Washington, DC: National Academy Press, 2001.

Institute of Medicine. *Dietary Reference Intakes for Vitamin C, Vitamin E, Selenium, and Carotenoids.* Washington, DC: National Academy Press, 2000.

Pennington, J.A.T. *Bowes and Church's Food Values of Portions Commonly Used.* Philadelphia: Lippincott, 1998.

Pueschel, S.M., Craig, W.Y., Haddow, J.E. "Lipids in Persons with Down's Syndrome." *Journal of Intellectual Disability Research.* Vol. 36(pt4), 1992, pp. 365-9.

Spence, A.P., and Mason, E.B. *Human Anatomy and Physiology.* 2nd ed. Menlo Park: Benjamin/ Cummings Publishing Company, 1983.

Yia-Hertluala, S., Luoma, J., Nikkari, T. "Down's Syndrome and Atherosclerosis." *Atherosclerosis.* Vol. 76, 1989, pp. 269-72.

SUGGESTED READING

Kalbacken, Joan. *Vitamins and Minerals: A True Book.* Chicago: Children's Press, 1998.
    A high interest/low reading level book about an important topic covered in grades 3-8: Vitamins and Minerals. There is information on the importance of vitamins, their role in the body, and where you

can find them (foods and supplements). The True Book Series is a wonderful set of books that cover high interest topics (not just about health, but history, science, social studies and so on) using easy-to-read language. Other "True books" in this series include: The Digestive System *and* The Food Pyramid.

VanCleave, Janice. *Food and Nutrition for Every Kid: Exciting Ideas, Projects, and Activities for Schools, Science Fairs, and Just Plain Fun.* New York, NY: John Wiley and Sons, 1999.
   In her book VanCleave has gathered a great collection of activities and experiments that explain why foods do what they do in our bodies, as well as in different recipes. Each experiment is broken down into a purpose, list of materials, step-by-step instructions, expected results, and explanations that kids can understand. Every project has been tested and can be performed safely and inexpensively using ordinary household materials.

CHAPTER 5

REFERENCES

Allshouse, M. *Down Syndrome Health Care Conference 2002 Update.* "What's New in Pediatric Surgery: Old Dogs . . . New Tricks." April 12, 2002. Children's Hospital Central California, Fresno, CA.

Groff, J.L., and Gropper, S.S. *Advanced Nutrition and Human Metabolism.* 3rd ed. Belmont: Wadsworth Thomson Learning, 1999.

Habven-Bartz, A. "Dietary Fiber and the Child." *Dietetics in Developmental and Psychiatric Disorders.* Vol. 12:3, 1994, pp.1-2.

Kedesdy, J.H. and Budd, K. *Childhood Feeding Disorders: Biobehavioral Assessment and Intervention.* Baltimore: Brookes Publishing, 1998.

Kessler, D.B. and Dawson, P. *Failure to Thrive and Pediatric Undernutrition: A Transdisciplinary Approach.* Baltimore: Brookes Publishing, 1999.

Leshin, H.L. "Constipation and Down Syndrome." *Down Syndrome Health Issues Web Page,* 1998. www.ds-health.com/constip.htm.

Leshin, H.L. "The Thyroid and Down Syndrome." *Down Syndrome Health Issues Web Page,* 1998. www.ds-health.com/thyroid.htm.

Ogata, B. "Nutrition and Constipation." *Nutrition Focus for Children with Special Health Care Needs.* Vol. 13, 1998, pp. 1-7.

Smith, D. "Recognizing Early Feeding and Nutrition Issues: When to Worry." Nutrition and Feeding Issues for Children with Special Health Care Needs: Strategies for Care in the Community, May 2, 2002. Child Development and Rehabilitation Center Ca Coon Program, Portland, OR.

Spence, A.P., and Mason, E.B. *Human Anatomy and Physiology.* 3rd ed. Redwood City, CA: Benjamin/Cummings Publishing Company, 1987.

SUGGESTED READING

Holub, Joan. *I Have a Weird Brother Who Digested a Fly.* Morton Grove, IL: Albert Whitman and Company, 1999.
   There's a lot of information about digestion described in tandem with a story taken from the rhyme, "There Was an Old Woman Who Swallowed a Fly." The descriptions of the digestive process are fairly simple, but assume a basic understanding of organs. The best section is at the end as the reader is encouraged to consider, "Should I eat a fly?" or what happens if you eat food with your nose plugged.

Swanson, Diane. *Burp! The Most Interesting Book You'll Ever Read about Eating.* Toronto: Kids Can Press, Ltd., 2001.
The title alone is enough to gain a child's interest. The text is dense and difficult to read, so it may be a tough book for your child with Down syndrome to read alone. However, it's a fun book to read together. The text is woven with activities for readers to try to provide hands-on learning with practical outcomes.

Cole, Joanna. *The Magic School Bus: Inside the Human Body.* New York, NY: Scholastic, 1990.
Ms. Frizzle's class has been studying how the human body turns food into energy, when Arnold accidentally swallows the class's miniature school bus. His classmates are treated to a tour of his entire digestive system, as well as his heart, lungs, brain, and other parts of his body. A comic-book style book with many thought bubbles and asides that can be skipped depending on your child's interest level.

CHAPTER 6

REFERENCES

Book, L., Hart, A., Black, J., Feolo, M., Zone, J., Neuhausen S.L. Prevalence and Clinical "Characteristics of Celiac Disease in Downs Syndrome in a US Study." *American Journal of Medical Genetics.* Vol. 98, 2001, pp. 70-74.

Celiac Sprue, A Guide through the Medicine Cabinet. $19, plus $3 shipping and handling. Order from: Stokes Pharmacy, 639 Stokes Rd., Medford, NJ 08055. 800-754-5222. E-mail: pharmacist@stokesrx.com.

George, E.K., Mearin, M.L., Bouquet, J., von Blomberg, B.M., Stapel, S.O., van Elburg, R.M., de Graaf, E.A. "High Frequency of Celiac Disease in Down Syndrome." *Journal of Pediatrics.* Vol. 128, April 1996, pp. 555-557.

Hartsook, Elaine. "Gluten Free Diet Introduction." Portland, OR: Portland/Vancouver Affiliate of Gluten Intolerance Group. (9525 SW 12th Drive, Portland, OR 97219. 503-244-8224/360-695-5568)

Leshin, L. "Celiac Disease and Down Syndrome." *Down Syndrome: Health Issues.* www.davlin.net/users/lleshin/celiac.htm.

Mackey, J., Treem, W.R., Worley, G., Boney, A., Hart, P., Kishnani, P.S. "Frequency of Celiac Disease in Individuals with Down Syndrome in the United States." *Clinical Pediatrics.* Vol. 40, 2001, pp. 249-252.

Pueschel, S.M., Romano, C., Failla, P., Barone, C., Pettinato, R., Castellano, C.A., Plumari, D.L. "A Prevalence Study of Celiac Disease in Persons with Down Syndrome Residing in the United States of America." *Acta Paediatrica.* Vol. 88, 1999, pp. 953-956.

Reeves, G.E., Burns, C., Hall, S.T., Gleeson, M., Lemmert, K., Clancy, R.L. "The Measurement of IgA and IgG Transglutaminase Antibodies in Celiac Disease: A Comparison with Current Diagnostic Methods." *Pathology.* Vol. 32, 2000, pp. 181-185.

Zachor, D.A., Mroczek-Musulman, E., Brown, P. "Prevalence of Celiac Disease in Down Syndrome in the United States." *Journal of Pediatric Gastroenterologic Nutrition.* Vol. 31, 2000, pp. 275-279.

SUGGESTED READING

Bess, Gershon. *A Passover Guide to Cosmetics and Medications.* Published annually. Order from: Kollel - Los Angeles, 7466 Beverly Blvd., #204, Los Angeles 90036. 213-933-7193.

Gluten-Free Living Newsletter. One year (6 issues) is $29, and two years is $49. A sample issue is $5.95. Order from: Gluten-Free Living, P.O. Box 105, Hastings-On-Hudson, NY 10706. 914-969-2018. E-mail: GFLiving@aol.com.

Hagman, Bette. *The Gluten-Free Gourmet* Series of Cookbooks. New York, NY: Owl Books.

Korn, Danna. *Kids with Celiac Disease: A Family Guide to Raising Happy, Healthy, Gluten-Free Children.* Bethesda, MD: Woodbine House, 2001.

Sanderson, Sheri. *Incredible Edible Gluten-Free Food for Kids: 150 Family Tested Recipes.* Bethesda, MD: Woodbine House, 2002.

TCCSSG Gluten-Free Shopping Guide. Published annually, $10. Order from: TCCSSG Shopping Guide, 34638 Beechwood, Farmington Hills, MI 48335. E-mail: tccssg@yahoo.com.

CHAPTER 7

REFERENCES

American Diabetes Association. "Facts and Figures." www.diabetes.org.

Anwar, A.J., Walker, J.D., Frier, B.M. "Type 1 Diabetes Mellitus and Down's Syndrome: Prevalence, Management, and Diabetic Complications." *Diabetes Medicine.* Vol. 15(2), 1998, pp. 160-153.

"Diabetes Advocacy: Keeping Kids Out of School." *Professional Section Quarterly.* Fall, 2000.

Duyff, R.L. *The American Dietetic Association's Complete Food and Nutrition Guide.* Minneapolis: Chronmed Publishing, 1996.

The Expert Committee on the Diagnosis and Classification of Diabetes Mellitus. "Report of the Expert Committee on the Diagnosis and Classification of Diabetes Mellitus." *Diabetes Care.* Vol. 24:S1. American Diabetes Association, 2001.

"The Law, Schools, and Your Child with Diabetes." Diabetes 123 and Children with Diabetes. *Children with Diabetes Website,* 2001. www.childrenwithdiabetes.com/d_0q_600.htm

Leshin, H.L. "Down Syndrome Abstract of the Month: July 1998." *Down Syndrome Health Issues Website.* July, 1998. www.ds-health.com/abst/a9804.htm

Lowe, E, Arsham, G. *Diabetes: A Guide to Living Well.* Minneapolis: Chronmed Publishing, 1992.

Rosenfeld, S.J. "Diabetes in Schools." *EDLAW Briefing Paper.* Vol. 10(2), 2000, pp. 1-7.

Van Goor, J.C., Massa, G.G., Hirasing, R. "Increased Incidence and Prevalence of Diabetes Mellitus in Down's Syndrome." *Archives of Disabled Child.* Vol. 77(2), 1997, p. 186.

Van Dyke, D.C., Mattheis, P., Eberly, S., Williams, J. (eds). *Medical and Surgical Care for Children with Down Syndrome: A Guide for Parents.* Bethesda, MD: Woodbine House, 1995.

SUGGESTED READING

"Checklists Galore." American Diabetes Association Wizdom packet. Available on the Internet at www.diabetes.org/wizdom/basics/checklistspop.html or by writing the American Diabetes Association, ATTN: Customer Service: Wizdom Packet, 1701 North Beauregard Street, Alexandria, VA 22311(800-342-2383). Ask for the Wizdom packet for children with Diabetes. *This set of checklists is a wonderful resource and includes checklists for every type of situation imaginable: Lists for friends and family, exercise, doctor visits, treating hypoglycemia, and treating hyperglycemia.*

Rubin, Alan L., M.D. *Diabetes for Dummies.* Foster City: IDG Books Worldwide, 1999.

Semple, Carol McCormick. *Health Watch: Diabetes, Revised Edition.* Dallas: Enslow Publishers, 2000.

CHAPTER 8

REFERENCES

Anding, R., Campbell, J. "The Safety and Efficacy of Herbal Therapy: What Your Patients Need to Know." *Building Block for Life*. Vol. 24:1, 2000, pp. 1-5.

Ani, C., Grantham-McGregor, S., Muller, D. "Nutritional Supplementation in Down Syndrome: Theoretical Considerations and Current Status." *Developmental Medicine and Child Neurology*. Vol. 42, 2000, pp. 207-213.

Kern, J.K. "Good Research or Bad Research? Understanding the Basics." *Autism-Asperger's Digest*. Sept/Oct 2000, pp. 14-19.

Leichtman, L.G. "Targeted Nutritional Intervention (TNI) in the Treatment of Children and Adults with Down Syndrome: Principles Behind Use, Treatment Protocols, and an Expanded Bibliography." www.lleichtman.org/tni.shtml

Owens, S.C. "Research: Reading Between the Lines." *Autism Asperger's Digest*. Sept/Oct, 2000, pp. 16-17.

Reude, L.J. "The Research Spin Cycle." *Autism-Asperger's Digest*. Sept/Oct 2000, pp. 18-19.

CHAPTER 9

SUGGESTED READING

Bondy, Andy and Frost, Lori. *A Picture's Worth: PECS and Other Visual Communication Strategies in Autism*. Bethesda, MD: Woodbine House, 2002.
    Describes a communication method that is useful for any child, with or without autism, who is having difficulty communicating with speech or sign, or initiating communication with others.

Kumin, Libby. *Communication Skills in Children with Down Syndrome: A Guide for Parents*. Bethesda, MD: Woodbine House, 1994.
    This book covers a number of communication skills a child needs in order to communicate choices, up to about kindergarten age.

CHAPTER 10

REFERENCE

Hertzler, Ann. *Preschoolers' Food Handling Skills*. Blacksburg, VA: Virginia Cooperative Extension, May 1996. www.ext.vt.edu/pubs/preschoolnutr/348-011/348-011.html.

CHAPTER 12

REFERENCES

Conklin, M.T., Nettles, M.F., Martin, J. "Modified Meals: Strategies for Managing Nutrition Services for Children with Special Needs." *School Foodservice and Nutrition*. August, 1998, pp. 46-52.

Rynders, J.E., and Low, M.L. "'Adrift' in the Educational Mainstream: The Need to Structure Communicative Interactions between Students with Down Syndrome and their Nondisabled Peers." *Down Syndrome Quarterly*. Vol. 6:1, 2001, pp. 1-8.

Schmidt, D. "Tools of the Trade: It's All About Access." *School Foodservice and Nutrition*. August, 1998, pp. 78-84.

USDA Food and Consumer Service. *Accommodating Children with Special Dietary Needs in the School Nutrition Programs: Guidance for School Food Service Staff*. May, 1995.

USDA National School Lunch Program Web Page. www.fns.usda.gov/cnd/Lunch/default.htm. Updated August, 2001.

SUGGESTED READING

Evers, Connie Liakos. *How to Teach Nutrition to Kids*. Portland, OR: 24 Carrot Press, 1995.

Although this book is probably best suited for classroom use, it has many topics and ideas that will open up discussions for you and your child about attitudes and choices regarding food and activity. It makes a nice gift for a classroom teacher and provides creative ways to embellish a nutrition unit.

CHAPTER 13

REFERENCES

Fujiura, G.T., Fitzsimons, N., Marks, B., Chicoine, B. "Predictors of BMI among Adults with Down Syndrome: The Social Context of Health Promotion." *Research in Developmental Disabilities*. Vol. 18, 1997, pp. 261-274.

Golden, E., Hatcher, J. "Nutrition Knowledge and Obesity of Adults in Community Residences." *Mental Retardation*. Vol. 35, 1997, pp. 177-184.

Luke, A., Roizen, N.J., Sutton, M., Schoeller, D.A. "Energy Expenditure in Children with Down Syndrome: Correcting Metabolic Rate for Movement." *Journal of Pediatrics*. Vol. 125, 1994, pp. 829-838.

Luke, A., Sutton, M., Schoeller, D.A., Roizen, N.J. "Nutrient Intake and Obesity in Prepubescent Children with Down Syndrome." *Journal of the American Dietetic Association*. Vol. 96, 1996, pp. 1262-1267.

Medlen, J.E. and Peterson, M. "Food, Activity, and Lifestyles: A Survey of Adults with Down Syndrome." *Down Syndrome Quarterly*. Vol. 5, 2000, pp. 6-12.

Rubin, S.S., Rimmer, J.H., Chicoine, B., Braddock, D., McGuire, D.E. "Overweight Prevalence in Persons with Down Syndrome. *Mental Retardation*. Vol. 36, 1998, pp. 175-181.

U.S. Dept. of Health and Human Services, Centers for Disease Control and Prevention, National Center for Health Statistics, Division of Data Services. *The National Health and Nutrition Examination Survey (NHANES) 1999-2001*. 301-458-4636. www.cdc.gov/nchs/about/major/nhanes/nhanes99-01.htm.

U.S. Dept. of Health and Human Services. *Healthy People 2010 (Conference Edition, in Two Volumes)*. Washington, DC: January 2000. (Order from U.S. Government Printing Office, Superintendent of Documents, Washington, DC 20402-9382, Stock Number 017-001-00543-6, ISBN 0-16-050260-8. www.health.gov/healthypeople.)

SUGGESTED READING

Healthy Habits for Life. Portland, OR: Oregon Dairy Council.

A nutrition education program designed for students in middle school. Students use the Food Guide Pyramid and a workbook as the basis for creating a plan to improve nutrition, physical activity and overall health. The workbook is appropriate for people with Down syndrome who are middle school age and older. The energy calculations need to be adapted as listed in the Appendix of this book, but otherwise the information is well presented and practical. The writing may be small or presentation of information a little cluttered for some people with Down syndrome. The program is appropriate with a partner or group. A teacher's guide with 24 student workbooks is $15.00; a teacher's guide with reproducible masters for the student workbooks is $20.00. Additional student workbooks are $0.50. (Available from the Oregon Dairy Council, Nutrition Education Services/Oregon Dairy Council, 10505 SW Barbur Blvd., Portland, OR 97219, 503-229-5033, www.oregondairycouncil.org.)

CHAPTER 14

REFERENCES

Arkansas Department of Education. *Nutrition News*. Vol. 5(1):2, Sept./Oct. 1996.

Council on Physical Education for Children. *Recess in Elementary Schools*. A position paper from the National Association of Sports and Physical Education (NASPE), July 2001.

Coyne, P., Nyberg, C., Vandenburg, M.L. *Developing Leisure Time Skills for Persons with Autism: A Practical Approach for Home, School, and Community*. Arlington, TX: Future Horizons, 1999.

Fernhall, B. "Physical Fitness and Exercise Training of Individuals with Mental Retardation." *Medical Science in Sports and Exercise*. Vol. 25, 1993, pp. 442-450.

Fernhall, B., Pitetti, K.H., Rimmer, J.H., McCubbin, J.A., Rintala, P., Millar, A.L., Kittredge, J., Burkett, L.N. "Cardiorespiratory Capacity of Individuals with Mental Retardation Including Down Syndrome." *Medical Science in Sports and Exercise*. Vol. 28, 1996, pp. 366-371.

Schleien, S.J. and Heyne, L. "Can I Play, Too? Choosing a Community Recreation Program." *Disability Solutions*. Vol. 1:1, 1996, pp.1, 3-5.

SUGGESTED READING

Coyne, P., Nyberg, C., Vandenburg, M.L. *Developing Leisure Time Skills for Persons with Autism: A Practical Approach for Home, School, and Community*. Arlington, TX: Future Horizons, 1999.

Gold, Deborah. "Friendship, Leisure, and Support: The Purposes of 'Circles of Friends' of Young People." *Journal of Leisurability*. Vol. 26:3, Summer 1999. (Available at www.lin.ca/resource/html/Vol26/V26N3A2.htm)

Physical Activity Guidelines for Pre-Adolescent Children. Reston, VA: National Association for Sport and Physical Education, 2001. Publication #304-10175. (800-321-0789.)

Schleien, S.J., Heyne, L. "Can I Play, Too? Choosing a Community Recreation Program." *Disability Solutions*. Vol. 1:1, 1996, pp.1, 3-5. www.disabilitysolutions.org/news.htm

Schleien, S., Green, F., Stone, C. "Making Friends within Inclusive Community Recreation Programs." *Journal of Leisurability*. Vol. 26:3, Summer 1999. (Available at: www.lin.ca/resource/html/Vol26/V26N3A4.htm)

Winders, Patricia C. *Gross Motor Skills for Children with Down Syndrome: A Guide for Parents and Professionals*. Bethesda, MD: Woodbine House, 1997.

FIRST COOKBOOKS

Innovative Cooking Enterprises. *Electric Bread: A Bread Machine Activity Book for Kids*. Anchorage, AK: Innovative Cooking Enterprises, Inc., 1998.

Simply put, I love this book. I ran across it in an exhibit hall at a national conference where they were demonstrating how fun it is to do things with bread. People were creating unique sculptures with colored bread dough and making chocolate or pizza bread. The book covers ways to include bread making in classrooms, as well as the science of bread. And if your child can't resist putting play dough in his mouth, you'll love the idea of using colored bread dough instead. For more information, go to www.electricbread.com.

Magee, Elaine. *Someone's in the Kitchen with Mommy: More than 100 Easy Recipes and Fun Crafts for Parents and Kids*. Lincolnwood, IL: Contemporary Books, 1997.

I really like the premise of this book: to give parents a roadmap for ways they can include their children in the cooking process. Each recipe outlines which activities are best for parents to do, and which are great for children. However, the author has strong opinions regarding brain development and developing a "Nintendo-free zone" that can be daunting for parents of children with Down syndrome and other developmental disabilities, as well as busy parents in general. Yet there are some gems of information regarding activities for kids at varying ages or abilities. Overall, it is a good resource that provides the type of direction busy parents need when teaching cooking skills to children and young adults with, or without, Down syndrome.

Nissenberg, Sandra and Nissenberg, Heather. *I Made it Myself! Mud Cups, Pizza Puffs, and over 100 Other Fun and Healthy Recipes for Kids to Make.* New York, NY: John Wiley & Sons, 1998.

Written by a dietitian for and with her daughter, this cookbook is filled with creative-sounding recipes that are fairly simple to make. Simple food safety measures such as tying back hair and hand washing are covered in the beginning of the book. Throughout the book, the authors weave nutrition education topics through story-telling, knock-knock jokes, word searches, and other child-oriented activities. This book is a nice tool for finding activities to do together.

COOKBOOKS FOR TEACHING COOKING SKILLS (WITH ADAPTATIONS)

Laird, Eileen. *Cooking Made Easy.* Boone, NC: Ellen Laird, 1996. Boone, NC 28607-2117.

Cooking Made Easy *was written for people with developmental disabilities. Laird has organized the recipes logically, estimated the cost, the level of difficulty to prepare, and broken the steps down to one instruction at a time. Those who use the book need to be good readers, however. The recipes lack imagination and some are high in fat content, but it is still a good first cookbook. Order from: Eileen Laird, Cooking Made Easy, P.O. Box 2117, Boone, NC 28607-2117.*

Look 'n Cook Microwave: Easy to Make Illustrated Recipes. Verona, WI: Attainment Company, 1999.

A well-designed notebook with recipes written with words and black and white drawings to illustrate the process. The recipes are simple: preparing condensed canned soup, canned vegetables, Jello, baked potato, and barbequed chicken, all for the microwave. An accompanying set of lesson plans is also available. This program is designed for educational settings: the lesson plans break apart various skills that will be learned with each recipe and the instructions discuss setting up the cooking lab. It is an expensive set, but is one of the few sets available for young people who need pictures to read the recipe. More information at www.attainmentcompany.com.

Ponichtera, Brenda J. *Quick and Healthy: Recipes and Ideas for People Who Say They Don't Have Time to Cook Healthy Meals.* Volumes 1 and 2. The Dalles, OR: ScaleDown, 1991.

Both volumes offer traditional recipes that can be created quickly and very simply. Nutrition information for each recipe and shopping lists to help organize your trip to the store are included. Most recipes are easy enough for new cooks to use successfully.

Raab, Evelyn. *Clueless in the Kitchen: A Cookbook for Teens.* Willowdale, Ontario: Firefly Books, 1998.

A wonderfully practical cookbook filled with recipes for people who long for their mother's home cooking as well as new experiences in the kitchen. The authors describe different cooking skills as though the reader has never attempted cooking before, but with humor all teens and adults can enjoy. Each recipe has a rating for difficulty, category (vegetarian or comfort food, for example), and cost. It is a great cookbook for teens leaving for college, but also a fun-loving book for you to explore cooking with your child with Down syndrome. Caveats: The type is small and language may be difficult.

American Diabetes Association Staff. *Month of Meals Menu Planners.* Series of five books: *Classic Cooking, Ethnic Delights, Meals in Minutes, Old-Time Favorites,* and *Vegetarian Pleasures.* New York, NY: McGraw-Hill, various dates.

The Month of Meals *series of cookbooks is great for visualizing how enticing an appropriate menu can be. Each book has 28 days of menus based on 1500 Calories. Each page is split into thirds, which allows the reader to mix and match seemingly endless combinations of Breakfast, Lunch, and Dinner menus all equivalent to 1500 Calories. The authors carefully define the skeleton meal plan and serving sizes for a variety of calorie levels ranging from 1200-2100 calories a day to guide the reader in menu planning. There are pages of snack suggestions organized by calorie amounts (60, 125, and 170). These books are wonderfully helpful and versatile, but they are not immediately user friendly for people with Down syndrome. They are most appropriately used by parents and support persons for ideas, menu planning guidelines, and recipes to adapt for teens and adults with Down syndrome.*

SECTION 4

SUGGESTED READING FOR KIDS

Carlson, Nancy. *I Like Me!* Lebanon, IN: Pearson Learning, 1988.
A heartwarming book about liking yourself just the way you are.

Creasy, Rosalind. *Blue Potatoes, Orange Tomatoes.* San Francisco: Sierra Book Club, 1997.
A lovely guide for growing a garden full of vegetables. But these aren't just any vegetables—they're blue potatoes, orange tomatoes, purple beans, multicolored radishes, and red popping corn, to name a few. Growing vegetables can increase a child's interest in eating them as well as introduce her to some nice science concepts that will be helpful when growing other plants, too.

Ehlert, Lois. *Eating the Alphabet: Fruits & Vegetables from A to Z.* Orlando, FL: Harcourt, 1989.
A beautifully illustrated alphabet book with a fruit or vegetable for every letter. This book is also available as a "Big Book" for classroom learning.

Frankel, Alona. *Joshua's Book of Manners.* New York, NY: Harper Festival, 2000.
If you have read Once Upon a Potty, *then you already know the characters in this book. Joshua and his mother explain in the same way the different manners Joshua masters as he grows up, including saying "please" and "thank you" and table manners.*

French, Vivian. *Oliver's Fruit Salad.* New York, NY: Orchard Books, 1998.
A delightful story about a boy who is timid when it comes to eating fruit. He enjoys making things with it, picking it, even buying it at the store, but he doesn't eat fruit. That is, until they make a wonderful fruit salad and don't give him a bowl. Everything's better when it's your choice after all.

Haduch, Bill. *Food Rules! The Stuff You Munch, Its Crunch, Its Punch, and Why Your Sometimes Lose Your Lunch.* New York, NY: Puffin Books, 2001.

Kalbacken, Joan. *Food Safety: A True Book.* Danbury, CT: Children's Press, 1998.
Using a large font and simple language, this book covers the details of food-borne illness, how to avoid it, and some of the basic laws that help protect us. There is a good section on rules for the kitchen to prevent contributing to food contamination.

Leedy, Loreen. *The Edible Pyramid: Good Eating Every Day.* Glenview, IL: Scott Foresman, 1994.
Believe it or not, this book was not *written by a dietitian! It is, however, a discussion about the Food Guide Pyramid and the variety of foods that go in each group. While a very nice teaching tool, it is visually cluttered with scattered text and visual concepts on each page. It may be difficult to quickly pull out the important concepts. Otherwise, it is a good story or addition to a lesson on learning about the Food Pyramid.*

O'Brien-Palmer, Michelle. *Healthy Me: Fun Ways to Develop Good Health and Safety Habits: Activities for Children 5-8.* Chicago: Chicago Review Press, 1999.

O'Brien-Palmer, Michelle. *Watch Me Grow: Fun Ways to Learn about Cells, Bones, Muscles, and Joints: Activities for Children 5-9.* Chicago: Chicago Review Press, 1999.
This book and the one above make a great pair for teaching about healthy lifestyles. The author combines activities with songs to help reinforce concepts that can be difficult to teach in a fun and inviting way.

Rockwell, Lizzie. *Good Enough to Eat: A Kid's Guide to Food and Nutrition.* Orlando, FL: HarperCollins, 1999.

Roffey, Maureen. *Mealtime.* New York, NY: Macmillan, 1989. (Not currently available, but may be in your library.)
This is a simple book that opens up discussions about food and other aspects of mealtime: What makes you hungry? What do you eat on a picnic? What goes on the table?

Seuss, Dr. *Green Eggs and Ham.* New York, NY: Random House, 1960.

A timeless story shared by many generations about "That Sam-I-Am" and his finicky eating acquaintance who just wants to be left alone. Now available as a board game and a "Living Book" for the computer, it is a story that can be used in many situations.

Sharmat, Mitchell. *Gregory, the Terrible Eater.* New York, NY: Scholastic Books, 1989.

In this imaginative story, Gregory, a young goat, worries his parents with his interest in eating foods like lettuce, fish, and juice, rather than tires, cans, and other junk from the yard. In the end, Gregory learns that eating a variety of "foods" is the best way to feel good.

VanCleave, Janice. *Food and Nutrition for Every Kid: Exciting Ideas, Projects, and Activities for Schools, Science Fairs, and Just Plain Fun.* New York, NY: John Wiley and Sons, 1999.

The author has gathered a great collection of activities and experiments that explain why foods do what they do in our bodies, as well as in different recipes. Each experiment is broken down in a purpose, list of materials, step-by-step instructions, expected results, and explanations kids can understand. Projects can be performed safely and inexpensively using ordinary household materials.

Resources

La Leche League
1400 North Meacham Rd.
Schaumburg, IL 60173-4840
847-519-7730
Web site: www.lalecheleague.org

To locate someone who can help you with breastfeeding concerns, you can call or visit their web site for a list of La Leche Leagues in your state. They sell a booklet on breastfeeding babies with Down syndrome for a nominal price, and several accounts by parents of children with Down syndrome can be viewed on the web site.

Nursing Mother's Association of Australia
1818-1822 Malvern Rd.
East Malvern, Victoria 3145
Australia
Web site: www.breastfeeding.asn.au/bfinfo

The web site offers many informative articles, including one on breastfeeding a baby with Down syndrome.

SOURCES OF GLUTEN-FREE FOOD

Dietary Specialties, Inc.
P.O. Box 227
Rochester, NY 14601-0227
800-544-0099
Web site: www.dietspec.com

Dietary Specialties, Inc., carries breads, pastas, convenience mixes, crackers, cookies, snacks and other treats, available in wheat-free/gluten-free varieties. Many of their products are carried in local grocery and nutrition stores.

Ener-G Foods
P.O. Box 84487
Seattle, WA 98124
800-331-5222
Web site: www.ener-g.com

Ener-G foods has a variety of gluten-free breads, baking mixes, flours, pastas, and crackers. Many are carried in local grocery and nutrition stores.

The Gluten Free Mall
Web site: www.glutenfreemall.com

The Gluten Free Mall was created by Scott Adams, who is better known in the celiac/gluten-free community for his Celiac Support Page: http://www.celiac.com. The Gluten Free Mall web site is a "one-stop shop" for special dietary food products that allows customers to order from many different companies with one simple, secure transaction.

The Gluten-Free Pantry, Inc.
P.O. Box 840
Glastonbury, CT 06033
Web site: www.glutenfree.com

The Gluten-Free Pantry carries a wide variety of mixes, equipment, and food staples that are gluten-free. From Indian Cuisine to certified Kosher foods, cookbooks to gluten-free pretzels. Web page has some helpful hints for baking bread and some free recipes also.

ORGANIZATIONS

Celiac Disease Foundation
13251 Ventura Blvd., Ste. 1
Studio City, CA 91604-1838
818-990-2354
E-mail: cdf@primenet.com
Web site: www.primenet.com/cdf

Celiac Disease Foundation is a non-profit, public benefit corporation dedicated to providing services and support to persons with celiac disease. Benefits of membership in CDF include: a quarterly newsletter, nationwide mutual support programs, and information about GF foods and the health benefits of a GF diet.

Celiac Sprue Association/United States of America, Inc.
P.O. Box 31700
Omaha, NE 68131-0700
402-558-0600
402-558-1347 (fax)
E-mail: celiacs@csaceliacs.org
Web site: www.csaceliacs.org

The Celiac Sprue Association/United States of America, Inc., is a non-profit corporation with a network of local chapters. Offers a great deal of information about celiac disease and gluten-free living on its website, and publishes a series of low-cost brochures and newsletters. Sponsors an annual conference.

Raising Our Celiac Kids (R.O.C.K.)
Website: www.celiackids.com
E-mail: Danna@celiackids.com

A support group for parents and families of kids with celiac disease, which provides advice on topics such as gluten-free treats for kids, menu ideas, helping children take responsibility for their diets, holiday issues. Visit their website to find the nearest local chapter.

INTERNET INFORMATION SITES

Celiac.com: A Celiac Disease and Gluten-Free Resource
Web site: www.celiac.com

A comprehensive website with information, products, and support for people with celiac disease. Information on this site has been compiled from a variety of sources, including medical journals, books, doctors, scientists, and the *Celiac Listserv News Group*. Includes a comprehensive list of ingredients that are and are not allowed on a celiac diet.

The Gluten Free Page
Web site: www.panix.com/~donwiss
　　This web page has a comprehensive list of gluten-free related web pages that are available. Categories include: sites created by people who have celiac disease, educational resources, cookbooks, associations and organizations, gluten-free vendors, and food science.

DIABETES

American Diabetes Association
1701 North Beauregard St.
Alexandria, VA 22311
800-DIABETES (342-2383)
Web site: www.diabetes.org

Children with Diabetes Web Online
www.childrenwithdiabetes.com

Juvenile Diabetes Research Foundation International
120 Wall St.
New York, NY 10005
800-533-CURE (2873); 212-785-9500
Web site: www.jdrf.org

DOWN SYNDROME

Canadian Down Syndrome Society
811 14th St. NW
Calgary, AL T2N 2A4
Canada
Web site: www.cdss.ca

Disability Solutions
PMB 179
9220 SW Barbur Blvd., #119
Portland, OR 97219
503-244-7662
Website: www.disabilitysolutions.org

Down Syndrome Research Foundation
1409 Sperling Ave.
Burnaby, BC V5B 4J8
Canada
604-444-3773; 888-464-DSRF (toll free in Canada only)
Web site: www.dsrf.org

National Down Syndrome Congress
1370 Center Dr., Suite 102
Atlanta, GA 30338
800-232-NDSC (6372)
Web site: www.ndsccenter.org

National Down Syndrome Society
666 Broadway
New York, NY 10012
800-221-4602
Web site: www.ndss.org

INTERNET INFORMATION SITES
Down Syndrome: Health Issues
Web site: www.ds-health.com
    This comprehensive web site run by a pediatrician with a child with Down syndrome includes articles on a number of health issues and controversies related to individuals with Down syndrome, as well as links to other good sources of information.

Down Syndrome Information Network
Web site: www.down-syndrome.info
    Associated with the Down Syndrome Education Trust in Portsmouth, England, this web site provides access to a number of free and nominally priced publications on specialized aspects of Down syndrome.

FITNESS

American Therapeutic Recreation Association
1414 Prince St.
Suite 204
Alexandria, VA 22314
703-683-9420
Web site: www.atra-tr.org.

American Volkssport Association
1001 Pat Booker Rd.
Suite 101
Universal City, TX 78148
210-659-2112; 210-659-1212 (FAX)
Information Line: 800-830-WALK
Web site: www.ava.org

Fitness Finders, Inc.
133 Teft Rd.
P.O. Box 160
Spring Arbor, MI 49283
800-789-9255; 517-750-4584 (FAX).
    Kits and information on the *Feeling Good Mileage Program* and other walking programs.

IDEAfit.com: The Source for Fitness Professionals and Enthusiasts
www.ideafit.com
    Web site includes articles on topics such as walking, indoor cycling, "Starting Your Child on a Lifelong Fitness Adventure," as well as Fitness Facts, information on locating and working with a personal trainer, etc.

President's Council on Physical Fitness and Sports
Department W
200 Independence Ave., SW
Room 738-H
Washington, DC 20201-0004
202-690-9000; 202-690-5211 (FAX)
    Contact the PCPFS for information about the presidential fitness awards described in Chapter 14. Or, for information on the Presidential Sports Award, visit www.fitness.gov/sports/sports.html. For information on the President's Challenge Awards, visit www.fitness.gov.

Special Olympics, International
1325 G St., NW
Suite 500
Washington, DC 20005
202-628-3630; 202-824-0200 (FAX)
Web site: www.specialolympics.org

TASH
Leisure and Recreation Committee
29 W. Susquehanna Ave.
Suite 210
Baltimore, MD 21204
410-828-8274
Web site: www.tash.org

FOOD SAFETY

Center for Food Safety and Applied Nutrition
Outreach and Information Center
200 C St. SW (HFS-555)
Washington, DC 20204
Web site: www.cfsan.fda.gov

CFSAN is "responsible for promoting and protecting the public's health by ensuring that the nation's food supply is safe, sanitary, wholesome, and honestly labeled." The Center operates the FDA Food Safety Information Hotline, below, and offers publications on almost anything you can think of related to food safety, as well as free materials such as a food safety coloring book and a food safety song for children (all available online).

FDA Food Safety Information Hotline (24 hours)
888-SAFE-FOO(D) or 888-723-3366

Fight Bac Web Site
www.fightbac.org

USDA Meat and Poultry Hotline
800-535-4555

SCHOOL ISSUES

Project Participate
University of Colorado Health Science Center
4200 E. 9th Ave., C221
Denver, CO 80262
303-864-5277; Fax: 303-864-5270
Web site: www.projectparticipate.org

Project Participate provides families, educators, administrators, and therapists with simple strategies to increase the active participation of students with disabilities in school programs. Supported by a U.S. Department of Education grant, Project Participate facilitates team collaboration and promotes the appropriate uses of technology in the classroom.

USDA Child Nutrition Programs Web Page
Web site: www.fns.usda.gov/cnd/Lunch/default.htm

Provides information about the National School Lunch Program, as well as other USDA-sponsored child nutrition programs such as the *School Breakfast Program, Special Milk Program, Summer Foodservice Program, Child and Adult Care Food Program,* or the *Afterschool Snack Program.*

Free Foto.com
Web site: www.freefoto.com/pictures/food_and_drink/index.asp

Free Foto.com is one of the largest collections of free photographs for **_private, non-com-mercial use_** on the Internet. There are a variety of food-related photos, as well as photos in over fifty other categories.

L-Tec Illustrated
6651 Arlington Dr.
W. Bloomfield, MI 48322
Web site: www.l-tec.com

Photos of foods and nutrition concepts available to download from the web site in Acrobat Reader format (for a fee) or on CD-Rom. Some photos do not print with the detail needed for educational materials. Try the sample images on the website first.

Mayer-Johnson Company
P.O. Box 1579
Solana Beach, CA 92075
800-588-4548; 800-550-0084
Web site: www.mayer-johnson.com

Mayer-Johnson Company is the creator of _Picture Communication Symbols (PCS)_, which are widely used in special education settings for augmenting communication and creating visual supports. _Boardmaker_ is a computer program that organizes these symbols in a digital format for creating materials. Many of the symbols used in this book are PCS symbols from Boardmaker libraries (used with permission). Printed masters of PCS symbols and a variety of versions of Boardmaker are available from Mayer-Johnson.

Oregon Dairy Council
10505 SW Barbur Blvd.
Portland, OR 97219
503-229-5033
Web site: www.oregondairycouncil.org

The ODC offers paper food models—punch-out color photos of common foods that are the next best thing to food itself! The back of each food model includes nutrient information. Interesting activity ideas are included in the leader guide. $15.00.

Silver Lining Multi-Media
P.O. Box 2201
Poughkeepsie, NY 12601
845-462-8714
Web site: www.silverliningmultimedia.com

Produces _Picture This,_ an easy-to-use CD with high resolution color photos in 30 categories that can be used for creating flashcards, lotto boards, activity picture schedules, and communication boards. A great tool for early menu writing, food selection, and nutrition education materials. Also available from Woodbine House (800-843-7323; www.woodbinehouse.com).

USDA Photography Center
Room 1544-S
Washington, DC 20250
202-720-6633
Web site: www.usda.gov/oc/photo/opclibra.htm

The USDA has a wonderful photo library with a wide variety of subjects available without royalty or copyright restrictions. On the web site, look under "Crops" for photos of foods grown in the U.S., "Food Safety" for photos to teach about bacteria and food, and "Groceries" for photos of foods in stores, as well as people grocery shopping. Color and black and white prints and transparencies can also be ordered.

Growth Charts for Children with Down Syndrome
Web site: www.growthcharts.com
This web site, operated by the father of a child with Down syndrome, has blank Down syndrome growth charts (height and weight, metric system and non-metric system), as well as typical growth charts from the CDC.

Shape Down
1323 San Anselmo Ave.
San Anselmo, CA 94960
415-453-8886; 415-453-8888 (FAX)
E-mail: shapedown@aol.com
Web site: www.shapedown.com
A weight management program for children and their families. Often available at local hospitals, or contact Shape Down directly.

Weight Watchers
800-651-6000
Web site: www.weightwatchers.com
Some adults with Down syndrome are having success using the Weight Watchers Program. Weight Watchers is a safely designed and implemented weight management program that promotes lifestyle change rather than quick results. The program utilizes record keeping, a point system of counting calories, and both group and individual support. The point system may be difficult to navigate for your child. Weight Watchers now offers a web site for support which may make looking up points for a food easier if your child is computer savvy. For information, look in your local phone book for a Weight Watchers group, call the 800 number above, or visit the web site.

Index